READING GENESIS WELL

Navigating History, Poetry, Science, and Truth in Genesis 1-11

C. JOHN COLLINS

ZONDERVAN

Reading Genesis Well
Copyright © 2018 by C. John Collins

This title is also available as a Zondervan ebook.

Requests for information should be addressed to:
Zondervan, *3900 Sparks Dr. SE, Grand Rapids, Michigan 49546*

ISBN 978-0-310-59857-2

Unless otherwise indicated, Scripture quotations are taken from the *English Standard Version with Apocrypha* (Oxford: Oxford University Press, 2009); ESV® Bible (The Holy Bible, English Standard Version®). Copyright © 2001 by Crossway, a publishing ministry of Good News Publishers. Used by permission. All rights reserved. English translations of the Septuagint also follow the English Standard Version®. Emphasis added is not original to the English Standard Version®.

Image on page 245, "An early concept of the universe," taken from the *UBS Handbook on Genesis* (Reyburn & Fry, 1997), page 27. Used with permission. All rights reserved.

Any Internet addresses (websites, blogs, etc.) and telephone numbers in this book are offered as a resource. They are not intended in any way to be or imply an endorsement by Zondervan, nor does Zondervan vouch for the content of these sites and numbers for the life of this book.

All rights reserved. No part of this publication may be reproduced, stored in a retrieval system, or transmitted in any form or by any means—electronic, mechanical, photocopy, recording, or any other—except for brief quotations in printed reviews, without the prior permission of the publisher.

Cover design: Gore Studio, Inc.
Cover image: Shutterstock
Interior composition: Kait Lamphere

Printed in the United States of America

18 19 20 21 22 23 24 25 26 27 28 /DHV/ 15 14 13 12 11 10 9 8 7 6 5 4 3 2 1

"Anyone struggling to relate Genesis 1–11 to modern knowledge should welcome Collins's work. His literary, rhetorical, and theological analysis breaks the bonds of literalism that bind many scholars and fundamentalists, showing how the text 'gives the faithful the divinely approved way of picturing the events and that there are actual events that the pictures refer to.' His approach, indebted to C. S. Lewis, allows modern readers to appreciate the familiar ancient stories more richly—to read them well!"

Alan Millard
Emeritus Rankin Professor of Hebrew & Ancient Semitic Languages, The University of Liverpool

"In the beginning and throughout the process of reading, there is interpretation. This is true of all books but especially of the Bible. The peoples of the earth have for centuries been reading Genesis according to their own hermeneutical kinds. And God saw that it was *not* always good. I therefore thank God for Jack Collins's masterful guide to reading Scripture's good-faith communication in good faith, with literary sensitivity, an ear to the history of interpretation, and an eye on the present scientific context. *Reading Genesis Well* lives up to its title and then some. The first third treats biblical interpretation in general and is itself worth the price of the book. The rest of the book puts his reading strategy to work. He builds on C. S. Lewis's critical and imaginative approach to reading then offers a contextually sensitive account of just what the author of Genesis is saying and doing in chapters 1–11. It's important for reading the rest of Scripture to get the beginning right, and Collins here provides the resources for doing just that."

Kevin J. Vanhoozer
Research Professor of Systematic Theology, Trinity Evangelical Divinity School

"An intelligent and well-informed discussion about reading the Bible sensibly and sensitively, especially the early chapters of Genesis. Collins brings the delightful common sense of C. S. Lewis to this confused and controversial area, and the result is a book that not only develops a coherent approach to reading but is also entertaining to read. There is an overwhelming amount of literature on the topic of how to read Genesis: It is worth taking time for this one."

Kristen Birkett
Lecturer in Ethics, Philosophy, and Church History, Oak Hill Theological College

"*Reading Genesis Well* is a book aptly titled. Jack Collins once again shows himself to be a careful exegete and wise guide. He skillfully examines the biblical text with an eye attentive to both its ancient Near Eastern setting and its divine revelatory content. His treatment of the relevant biblical, theological, literary, historical, and scientific questions is masterful and judicious."

Paul Copan
Pledger Family Chair of Philosophy and Ethics, Palm Beach Atlantic University, and coauthor of *Creation out of Nothing: A Biblical, Philosophical, and Scientific Exploration*

"Since I first came across Jack Collins's work (some twenty-odd years ago), it stood out for me as a model of honest and respectful interaction between reading the Bible and science. I've always been impressed by his way of combining respect for the Bible's teaching, willingness to let the Word of God speak for itself (without superposing foreign categories on it), insights from modern linguistics, and a thorough concern for dialogue with science."

Lydia Jaeger
Directrice des études, Institut Biblique de Nogent, Nogent-sur-Marne, France

"This book is full of good sense about biblical interpretation. Readers who work through the principles and examples in the early chapters will be prepared for an approach to Genesis that prioritizes the intended message of the sacred text rather than modern disputes. Those who want the Scriptures to set the agenda regarding creation will benefit from this careful appropriation of C. S. Lewis's literary wisdom. Jack Collins has the spiritual sensitivity, exegetical skill, and theological savvy to be a trustworthy guide."

Dan Treier
Knoedler Professor of Theology and PhD Program
Director, Wheaton College Graduate School

"In *Reading Genesis Well*, C. John Collins teaches us how to be good readers of Genesis 1–11. Collins guides conservative readers between the twin errors either of interpreting the text in a woodenly literalistic fashion or of segregating Genesis and science into entirely different realms. Rather, he leads the reader to approach Genesis with linguistic and literary tools provided by C. S. Lewis. The result is an excellent theological reading of the first chapters of Genesis."

Kenneth Keathley
Senior Professor of Theology, Jesse Hendley Endowed Chair of Biblical Theology, and Director of the L. Russ Bush Center for Faith and Culture

"Jack Collins provides the kind of work on Genesis 1–11 we need today: a careful, balanced analysis that will guide readers of good will to greater understanding. Collins cuts through liberal and conservative rhetorical politics to help readers see what is really in this great summative passage."

Paul House
Professor of Divinity, Beeson Divinity School, Samford University

"A trenchant and yet irenic critique of literalistic interpretations of Genesis 1–11, whether on the part of skeptics or of 'Bible-science defenders' . . . an impressive inter-disciplinary investigation that is both informative and thought-provoking."

William Lane Craig
President, Reasonable Faith, and Professor of Philosophy,
Talbot School of Theology and Houston Baptist University

"As a religious Jew, I found Jack Collins's *Reading Genesis Well* to be a highly erudite and fascinating exposition by a religious Christian of the foundational stories of Genesis 1–11. The author is a superior scholar—thoughtful, cautious, measured, and ethically sensitive. I appreciated very much the wealth of information on Christian perceptions of Genesis. It was also encouraging to learn that, both in terms of his methodology of analysis and religious understanding, a considerable fortuitous overlap exists between Christian and Jewish comprehensions. For all the reasons mentioned above, I heartily recommend the book."

Professor Jeremiah Unterman
Herzl Institute and author of *Justice for All:
How the Jewish Bible Revolutionized Ethics*

"We know what Genesis says. But how many of us are confident that we know what it means? In this insightful and imaginative volume, Jack Collins gives us the tools we need to understand these vital opening chapters of the Bible. With C. S. Lewis as a conversation partner, Collins walks us through contested terrain with the settled step of a seasoned trail guide. His writing is precise but not pedantic, learned yet practical. *Reading Genesis Well* delivers even more than it promises, teaching us skills and principles that also apply to the entire Bible."

Rebecca Rine
Assistant Professor of Biblical and Religious Studies, Grove City College

"Every student and scholar of Scripture should read Collins's *Reading Genesis Well*. It is that rare piece of biblical scholarship that manages to be thoroughly conversant in the wide-ranging scholarship relevant to its subject, while managing to be quite readable and intuitive. In the process, it offers a fresh and compelling way of reading the Bible and the opening texts of Genesis with integrity. Collins has found a way through the interpretive thicket that frustrates ordinary Christians and misleads many prominent biblical scholars. Whether you have studied the Bible for decades or just want to read it more carefully, you will benefit from this book."

Jay Wesley Richards
Assistant Research Professor, Catholic University of America

"Just when I think C. John ("Jack") Collins has had his last word on the opening chapters of God's Word, he goes and outdoes himself! In *Reading Genesis Well: Navigating History, Science, Poetry, and Truth*, Collins invites us to sit at the feet of a literary genius—C. S. Lewis—and learn how to read Genesis 1–11 wisely. Drawing insight from the disciplines of linguistics, literary study, and rhetoric, and with help from Lewis, Collins guides us toward a critically rigorous reading strategy that applies not only to Genesis 1–11 but to any and all texts. Become a better reader of Genesis 1–11 by becoming an apprentice of C. S. Lewis—what a novel idea! What a great book! I highly recommend!"

Todd A. Wilson
President, The Center for Pastor Theologians

"What does it mean to be a faithful reader of the Bible? How are we to understand the creation account and the early chapters of Genesis? How does God's revelation in the Word illuminate his created world? How do Christian faith and science relate? These are critical questions facing Christians today. C. John Collins has been at the forefront of giving faithful answers to these questions for years, and with this groundbreaking book, *Reading Genesis Well*, he remains there. Collins gives attention to the text of Scripture and how we are best to read and understand God's revealed, authoritative account of creation. Situating himself in Genesis 1–11, Collins adeptly navigates through this labyrinth by addressing vital issues that impact reading the biblical text well, by focusing on history, poetry, science, and, ultimately, truth. Grounded in the inerrant and authoritative Scriptures, affirming the literal sense along with literary sensitivities, Collins builds on the conventional tools of exegesis by including the literary and linguistic insights of C. S. Lewis. This is a brilliant move to use Lewis as a conversation partner and glean from his literary insights as a gateway to a better understanding of Genesis, along with hermeneutical methods that shed light on reading other texts of Scripture as well. This is a must-read for pastors, biblical scholars, theologians, and scientists. And once you have read the book, teach the material to others. Superbly done!"

Greg Strand
Executive Director of Theology and Credentialing, EFCA,
Adjunct Professor of Pastoral Theology, TEDS

"This new book from the pen of Jack Collins is a treasure, representing the coming together of Collins's multiple interests and competencies in a compelling case for how the early chapters of Genesis should be read. Well written and wide ranging, this book is about much more than just Genesis 1–11 or even the interplay of Bible and science; it is a guide to how to read the Bible as it is meant to be read. Collins asks the right questions and puts his readers on the path of discovering well-founded answers."

V. Philips Long
Professor of Old Testament, Regent College, Vancouver

"This is a book to be read by theologians and scientists alike. Using C. S. Lewis as his guide, Collins brilliantly synthesizes ideas from modern linguistics to show what the much-debated opening chapters of Genesis do say and what they don't. Taking these chapters of Genesis as the introduction to the big story of the Bible, meant to shape the worldview of ancient Israel and their heirs (the church), Collins credibly argues that interpreting these chapters as ancient science is misguided and rooted in the mistaken idea that scientific language is the most accurate and therefore the most truthful kind of discourse. I highly recommend this book to fellow scientists as it has deepened my own understanding of the frontiers of biblical scholarship, increased my appreciation for the complexity of textual interpretation, and invited me to develop a much more nuanced understanding of the features of Genesis 1–11 and their relation to science."

Arend J. Poelarends
Associate Professor of Physics and Astronomy, Wheaton College

For Diane, Joy, and Joseph, with all my love

CONTENTS

Acknowledgments 13
Abbreviations 15

1. Introduction 17
    1.A   The Historical Backcloth: Benjamin Jowett and
           Nineteenth-Century Literalism 18
    1.B   James Barr, Jowett's Heir 23
    1.C   Why Do I Think C. S. Lewis Can Help? 25
    1.D   My Own Background and Stance 29

2. What Is Happening in Literary Communication? 34
    2.A   The Big Idea: How to Approach Any Work of Art 34
    2.B   Linguistics, Rhetoric, Literary Criticism, and Genre 41
           2.B.1   Linguistics 41
           2.B.2   Rhetoric 43
           2.B.3   Literary Criticism 44
           2.B.4   Genre 48

3. Types of Language and Biblical Interpretation 51
    3.A   Speech Act Theory and Biblical Rhetoric 51
    3.B   Lewis's Essay, "The Language of Religion" 61
           3.B.1   Exposition of Lewis's Argument 61
           3.B.2   Extension of Lewis's Analysis 65
    3.C   Metaphor, Thought, and Truth 74
    3.D   Examples of Exegesis 77
    3.E   Is There a Role for Analytical Language? 83
    3.F   Conclusions 86

4. **Good-Faith Communication: What Does It Mean to Speak Truly?** . . 89
   - 4.A How Does Communication Work? 89
   - 4.B What Is "Good-Faith Communication"? 91
   - 4.C What Is the Connection Between a World Picture and a Worldview? 94
   - 4.D Sense, Reference, Rhetoric, and Truth 95

5. **What Do We Have in Genesis 1–11?** *Part 1: Context* 107
   - 5.A Cohesion and Coherence 108
     - 5.A.1 Internal Cohesion 108
     - 5.A.2 Cohesion with Genesis–Deuteronomy. 112
     - 5.A.3 Connected but Separate. 113
   - 5.B Shared World Context 114
     - 5.B.1 Other Nations' Origin Stories 114
     - 5.B.2 Audience Criticism and "Rhetorical Situation" . . . 123
       - 5.B.2.a Date of Genesis. 125
       - 5.B.2.b Implied Audience 125

6. **What Do We Have in Genesis 1–11?** *Part 2: Function* 131
   - 6.A The Pentateuch as "Constitution" 131
   - 6.B Genesis and the Worldview Story. 134
   - 6.C Anachronism and History 138
   - 6.D Literary Style and Language Level 147
   - 6.E Literary Style and Architecture of Genesis 1–11 153

7. **Genesis 1–11: A Rhetorical-Theological Reading.** 158
   - 7.A Creation and the Fall (Gen 1–4) 160
     - 7.A.1 Creation (Gen 1–2) 160
       - 7.A.1.a Genesis 1:1–2:3. 160
       - 7.A.1.b Genesis 2:4–25 168
     - 7.A.2 The Fall and Its Consequences (Gen 3–4) 175
       - 7.A.2.a Genesis 3:1–24 175
       - 7.A.2.b Genesis 4:1–26 179
   - 7.B From Adam to Noah (Gen 5). 181
   - 7.C The Great Flood (Gen 6–9) 185
     - 7.C.1 The Setup (Gen 6:1–4) 187
     - 7.C.2 The Flood Story Proper (Gen 6:5–9:17) 190
     - 7.C.3 The Sequel to the Flood Story (Gen 9:18–29) 192

7.D	All the Families/Clans of the Earth (Gen 10:1–11:9)	194
	7.D.1 The Table of Nations (Gen 10:1–32)	194
	7.D.2 The Tower of Babel (Gen 11:1–9)	198
7.E	From Shem to Abram (Gen 11:10–26)	199

8. What Other Readers Have Seen in Genesis 1–11 201
- 8.A The Big Story 204
- 8.B Creation of Material Ex Nihilo? 208
- 8.C Relation of Genesis 1 and 2 225
- 8.D Human Origins and the Fall 227
- 8.E The Flood Story 233
- 8.F Genesis and Hellenistic Science 239

9. Genesis 1–11: World Picture and Worldview 243
- 9.A What Is the Shape of the World? 245
- 9.B Does the Sun "Rise"? 251
- 9.C Where Does the Rain Come From? 252
- 9.D A Three-Decker Universe? 256
- 9.E Hasn't Explaining Become Explaining Away? 258

10. The Place for Conflict: Divine Action in Genesis 1–11 265
- 10.A How Should We Read God's Action in Creation? 266
  - 10.A.1 Setting out the Biblical Metaphysic 266
  - 10.A.2 Evaluating Objections 276
  - 10.A.3 Divine Action in the Creation Story 277
- 10.B Where the Conflict Really Lies 282

11. Genesis 1–11: A Humane Moral Vision for Israel and the World ... 289
- 11.A Redemptive History as Worldview Story 290
- 11.B "Heirs" of the Story 292
  - 11.B.1 For Israel 293
  - 11.B.2 For Christians 295
- 11.C Conclusion: Reading Genesis 1–11 Well 296

Bibliography 299
Ancient Texts Index 319
Subject Index 329
Author Index 333

ACKNOWLEDGMENTS

As I write these Acknowledgements, the fear of leaving someone out almost paralyzes me. It's inevitable, I suppose: But I apologize beforehand.

This monograph results from a project I carried out as a Senior Research Fellow at the Carl Henry Center of Trinity International University in Deerfield, Illinois, with a generous grant from the Templeton Religion Trust. My contract "requires" that I mention this arrangement, but no requirement is needed, as my gratitude exceeds my ability to express it. At Templeton, I especially thank Michael Murray and John Churchill for encouragement and helpful conversations. At Trinity, the whole University showed enormous hospitality, and faculty members Richard Averbeck, Ingrid Faro, Brad Gundlach, Dana Harris, Tom McCall, Kevin Vanhoozer, Lawson Younger, together with my fellow research fellows John Hilber, Clinton Ohlers, Todd Patterson, and Hans Madueme, provided friendship, Christian love, and intellectual stimulation (even sometimes disagreement!). And the Henry Center administrative staff, Geoffrey Fulkerson and Joel Chopp, did so much to make my stay and my work satisfying—they are an incredible asset.

My colleagues at Covenant Theological Seminary made it possible for me to be away for the entire academic year, 2016–17, and I thank them. I thank them as well for the opportunity to grow as a scholar and as a Christian over a quarter century of service. I mention especially the President, Mark Dalbey, and the Dean, Jay Sklar, as well as Brian Aucker, Jerram Barrs, Hans Bayer, Dan Doriani, Mike Goheen, Robbie Griggs, Mark Ryan, Michael Williams, and Bob Yarbrough (all of whom may recognize some of their fingerprints herein). And nothing much would happen here apart from the work of Jim Pakala and his library team, and Gerry Reimer, the faculty secretary. I think, too, of some of my former students, such as Max Rogland, Mark Stirling, Dru Johnson, Dane Ortlund, Gavin Ortlund, Matt Haynes, AJ Poelarends,

David Illman, Susan Thomas, Cheryl Eaton, and Amy Allan, whose own insights, questions, and pushback have meant much to me. Around the world, other colleagues and friends have contributed to my growth in many ways, among whom are Lydia Jaeger, Esther Meek, Phil Long, John Walton, Steve Moshier, Dan Treier, Tremper Longman III, J. I. Packer, Bruce Winter, Vern Poythress, Deb Haarsma, Jeff Schloss, Jim Stump, Kathryn Applegate, Steve Meyer, Paul Nelson, Mike Keas, Jay Richards, J. P. Moreland, John Lennox, Hugh Ross, Fuz Rana, and Ken Keathley.

I am also grateful to the good people at Zondervan for their interest in and help with this effort. I especially thank Katya Covrett, not only for encouragement, but also for patience (as this project led to delays in another one for Zondervan!), and Nancy Erickson for conscientious, cheerful, and helpful editorial work.

Above all, I thank God for my wife, Diane, and children, Joy and Joseph. They have been after me for years to write my "Forest and Trees Book." This isn't exactly what they had in mind, but that other book will never happen without this one. We have learned together about communication, about our place in God's Big Story, and about mutual love and support. May God give us many more years of learning from and with one another! To whom else could I dedicate this book?

ABBREVIATIONS

AB	Anchor Bible
ANF	*Ante-Nicene Fathers*
AOAT	Alter Orient und Altes Testament
AUSS	*Andrews University Seminary Studies*
BA	*Biblical Archaeologist*
BBR	*Bulletin for Biblical Research*
BCOT	Baker Commentary on the Old Testament
BDAG	Danker, Frederick W., Walter Bauer, William F. Arndt, and F. Wilbur Gingrich. *Greek-English Lexicon of the New Testament and Other Early Christian Literature*. 3rd ed. Chicago: University of Chicago Press, 2000
BDB	Brown, Francis, S. R. Driver, and Charles A. Briggs. *A Hebrew and English Lexicon of the Old Testament*
BECNT	Baker Exegetical Commentary on the New Testament
BibInt	*Biblical Interpretation*
BSac	*Bibliotheca Sacra*
BST	The Bible Speaks Today
BT	*The Bible Translator*
CBQ	*Catholic Biblical Quarterly*
CBSC	Cambridge Bible for Schools and Colleges
CGT	Cambridge Greek Testament
CSB	Christian Standard Bible
CTJ	Calvin Theological Journal
EvQ	*Evangelical Quarterly*
FOTL	Forms of the Old *Testament Literature*
HUCA	*Hebrew Union College Annual*
ICC	International Critical Commentary
IEJ	*Israel Exploration Journal*

JAOS	*Journal of the American Oriental Society*
JBL	*Journal of Biblical Literature*
JESOT	*Journal for the Evangelical Study of the Old Testament*
JETS	*Journal of the Evangelical Theological Society*
JOTT	*Journal of Translation and Textlinguistics*
JSOT	*Journal for the Study of the Old Testament*
JTS	*Journal of Theological Studies*
K&D	Keil, Carl Friedrich, and Franz Delitzsch. *Biblical Commentary on the Old Testament.* Translated by James Martin et al. 25 vols. Edinburgh, 1857–1878. Repr., 10 vols., Peabody, MA: Hendrickson, 1996
LCL	Loeb Classical Library
NCB	New Century Bible
NICOT	New International Commentary on the Old Testament
NIDOTTE	*New International Dictionary of Old Testament Theology and Exegesis.* Edited by Willem A. VanGemeren. 5. Vols. Grand Rapids: Zondervan, 1997
NIGTC	New International Greek Testament Commentary
NPNF[1]	*Nicene and Post-Nicene Fathers*, Series 1
NPNF[2]	*Nicene and Post-Nicene Fathers*, Series 2
OPTAT	*Occasional Papers in Translation and Textlinguistics*
OTG	Old Testament Guides
Praep. ev.	Eusebius, *Praeparatio evangelica*; English translations from *Preparation for the Gospel*, Edwin H. Gifford, trans.; Oxford: Clarendon, 1903
QJS	*Quarterly Journal of Speech*
Rhet.	*Rhetoric*
SBET	*Scottish Bulletin of Evangelical Theology*
SCB	*Science and Christian Belief*
SJT	*Scottish Journal of Theology*
SwJT	*Southwestern Journal of Theology*
TNTC	Tyndale New Testament Commentaries
TOTC	Tyndale Old Testament Commentaries
TJ	*Trinity Journal*
TynBul	*Tyndale Bulletin*
VT	*Vetus Testamentum*
WBC	Word Biblical Commentary
WTJ	*Westminster Theological Journal*
ZAW	*Zeitschrift für die alttestamentliche Wissenschaft*

Chapter 1

INTRODUCTION

Anyone familiar with Judaism and Christianity recognizes that these religions place great value on the book of Genesis, especially on its first eleven chapters. Responses to these chapters range from outright skepticism (as in, "How can anyone intellectually responsible credit these ideas at all?"); to critical appreciation ("the texts are wrong about history and science if we take them literally, but they still teach us valuable moral lessons"); to strong affirmation ("these texts are to be taken literally, which then tells us what true science should look like"). And there are many more options available.

One's view of the biblical texts depends on one's interpretive approach—and generally the interpretive approach is assumed rather than warranted. It is even controversial whether any such warranting is itself warranted or simply "explaining away"!

In this work I aim to develop a reading strategy for Genesis 1–11 that draws its ideas from theories in linguistics, literary study, and rhetoric. These disciplines, which in the usual university curriculum are held separate, nevertheless share a set of common concerns and questions, such as:

- What kind of text is this?
- What authority relationship exists between the author and audience?
- What setting does the text assume by which it is to be received (public reading, song, private reading)?
- How does the author choose words and descriptions to influence the dispositional stance of his audience?
- What does this text intend to do to and for its recipients?
- How does the text's organization support (or hinder) its apparent intended effect?

As I draw on studies from these disciplines, I have a particular orientation: I find C. S. Lewis, a twentieth-century literary scholar and Christian writer, to be an example of someone who displayed an intuitive grasp of these concerns and whose reflections on the reading process, when engaged with these disciplines, can help us to *formulate a critically rigorous reading strategy for Genesis 1–11*.

My way in, however, begins with some history. Much of the twentieth- and twenty-first-century discussion is playing out intellectual developments that came to fruition in nineteenth-century Europe. In particular, ideas came from continental Europe into Britain and North America, and we are still working them through.[1]

1.A THE HISTORICAL BACKCLOTH: BENJAMIN JOWETT AND NINETEENTH-CENTURY LITERALISM

The year is 1860, and a London publishing house has issued a landmark volume with the innocuous title *Essays and Reviews*.[2] Taken together, these essays have made a case for the ready use of "critical" approaches to the Bible and Christian theology in the Church of England and beyond.[3] The historian Josef Altholz, sympathetic to the essayists' program, describes the volume's contents:

> The volume itself was modest in its pretensions and varied in the character and quality of its seven essays. The first, by Frederick Temple, was a warmed-over sermon urging the free study of the Bible. Rowland Williams wrote a provocative essay on Bunsen, denying the predictive character of Old Testament prophecies. Baden Powell flatly denied the possibility of miracles. H. B. Wilson gave the widest possible latitude to subscription to the Thirty-nine Articles and questioned the eternity of damnation. C. W. Goodwin (the only layman among the Essayists) wrote a critique of the attempted "harmonies" between Genesis and geology. Mark Pattison wrote a learned and cold historical study of the evidential theologians of the eighteenth century (perhaps the only

---

1. Roger Beckwith, "*Essays and Reviews* (1860): The Advance of Liberalism," *Churchman* 108:1 (1994), draws on H. G. Reventlow, *The Authority of the Bible and the Rise of the Modern World* (London: SCM, 1984), to argue that the continental ideas derive from the English deists of the seventeenth and eighteenth centuries—though of course the basic outlook is much older, as exemplified by the Epicurean poet Lucretius (first century BC).

2. Frederick Temple, Rowland Williams, Baden Powell, Henry Bristow Wilson, C. W. Goodwin, Mark Pattison, and Benjamin Jowett, *Essays and Reviews* (London: John W. Parker and Son, 1860).

3. To be sure, these critical approaches have a history in continental Europe that stretches much further back. My focus here is on the English-speaking world.

essay of lasting value). The volume was capped by Benjamin Jowett's tremendous though wayward essay "On the Interpretation of Scripture," in which he urged that the Bible be read "like any other book" and made an impassioned plea for freedom of scholarship. Little of all this was original, though it was new to most Englishmen.[4]

As Altholz notes, the responses also varied in their quality.[5] Here, though, I plan not to assess the arguments in *Essays and Reviews* so much as to recognize how some of the authors clearly state the hermeneutical issues—issues that remain with us to this day, whether we are discussing Genesis 1–11 or some other facet of biblical study. (In the same way, I will not analyze the traditionalist responses, except as they present hermeneutical questions.)

The two entries in *Essays and Reviews* that help to focus our attention come from Charles W. Goodwin (1817–78), "On the Mosaic Cosmogony" (pp. 207–53) and Benjamin Jowett (1817–93), "On the Interpretation of Scripture" (pp. 330–433).

Goodwin insisted,

> The Hebrew records, the basis of religious faith, *manifestly countenanced the opinion of the earth's immobility* and certain other views of the universe very incompatible with those propounded by Copernicus.[6]

Of course, this depends on the reading of Bible texts such as Psalm 93:1, "Yes, the world is established; *it shall never be moved*" (see also Pss 96:10; 104:5), which touches the hermeneutical questions that I intend to address. Goodwin makes his own stance clear when he says soon afterward:

> It can scarcely be said that this chapter [Gen 1] is not intended in part to teach and convey at least some physical truth, and *taking its words in their plain sense* it *manifestly* gives a view of the universe adverse to that of modern science.[7]

---

4. Josef Altholz, "The Mind of Victorian Orthodoxy: Anglican Responses to 'Essays and Reviews,' 1860–1864," *Church History* 51:2 (1982): 186–97, quote on p. 186.

5. In Altholz's judgment, the two most prestigious responses were also essay collections: William Thomson, ed., *Aids to Faith: A Series of Theological Essays by Several Writers, Being a Reply to "Essays and Reviews"* (New York: Appleton, 1862); and E. M. Goulburn, H. J. Rose, C. A. Heurtley, W. J. Irons, G. Rorison, A. W. Haddan, and Christopher Wordsworth, *Replies to "Essays and Reviews"* (New York: Appleton, 1862). Bishop Samuel Wilberforce reviewed the work (anonymously) in *The Quarterly Review* 109 (1861): 248–301 and sponsored the *Replies*.

6. Goodwin, "On the Mosaic Cosmogony," 207. Emphasis added here and throughout the chapter.

7. Ibid., 208–9.

Goodwin's syntax is unfortunately convoluted, but his meaning comes through after some reflection. He wants to take the words in their plain sense, and he reads the biblical authors (and especially Genesis) as advocating a physical picture of the world. He is especially clear about this when he objects to any effort to harmonize Genesis with then-current scientific theories: in such efforts "*the plain meaning of the Hebrew text* is unscrupulously tampered with."[8]

Jowett follows a similar course when he describes the task of his ideal interpreter of a biblical passage:

> The office of the interpreter is not to add another [meaning], but *to recover the original one*; the meaning, that is, of the words as they first struck on the ears or flashed before the eyes of those who heard and read them.[9]

On its surface, this sounds entirely uncontroversial. Did not the medievals claim to found their reading on the "simple" or "literal" sense? However, Jowett distances himself from these traditions when he goes on to require:

> The simple words of that book he tries to preserve absolutely pure from the refinements or distinctions of later times.[10]

Jowett's sentiment rejects the use of the theological wrestlings of the early church; but further, it also separates each biblical book from an organic relationship with the rest of the canon. Like Goodwin, Jowett stresses what he calls "the *natural meaning* of particular expressions."[11] Further, "The true use of interpretation is to *get rid of interpretation*, and leave us alone in the company of the author."[12]

Both of these authors have insisted on the primacy of what may be called the "plain" sense of the words. In particular, such plain readings of Genesis find its creation story at odds with the (more credible) story offered by nineteenth-century science, although Goodwin and Jowett reassure us that we might be able to preserve the spiritual value of the Bible nonetheless.

Those holding to traditional forms of Christian belief took one of two tacks in response: either to reject the scientific theorizing altogether (often with replacement theories, which eventually became "Creation Science"), or else to

---

8. Ibid., 211.
9. Jowett, "On the Interpretation of Scripture," 338. Emphasis added here and throughout the chapter.
10. Ibid.
11. Ibid., 352.
12. Ibid., 384.

accept parts of the theorizing and to show the Bible's compatibility with those parts—some form of "concordism." This second tack seems to have been by far the more common approach among the educated in the nineteenth century.[13] In order to support the compatibility argument, traditionalists appealed to what is called "phenomenal language," the idea that the biblical writers spoke in terms of what things look like (e.g., the sun *looks like* it rises). They also aimed to show correspondence between the biblical description and contemporary science—an aim that is problematic, both because it seems inconsistent with the appeal to phenomenal language and because the science (say, the geological ages, or the Nebular Hypothesis) is now considered out of date!

The notion of phenomenal language has recently come into some disrepute, even among traditionalists. It is considered an evasion of the plain meaning of the biblical texts. For example, consider the following from a valuable work on geology released by an evangelical publishing house:

> The ancient world universally believed that the dome-like vault of the sky is a glassy, crystalline solid.... Some commentators attempt to *avoid the force of the statement* by claiming that Scripture is using *phenomenal language*, the language of appearance. But that's our problem. The Israelites would not have seen it that way. The sky didn't just look solid to them; they believed it to be a solid.[14]

It is true that appealing to phenomenal language or poetic description in the course of finding a harmonization between the biblical and scientific accounts has the feel of an arbitrary measure, a kind of apologetic get-out-of-jail-free card. That is, it looks like the principle is to harmonize what one can and then to excuse the rest by invoking some kind of figurative language. Indeed, many treatments in the modern Creation Science movement have the same feel when they propose an alternative "scientific" account for various geological and cosmological features (say, a global flood) and explain other difficulties by supposing that God created some parts of the universe with an appearance of age.

---

13. See, for example, Alexander McCaul (who wrote the response in Thomson, *Aids to Faith*) and Gilbert Rorison (who wrote for *Replies to "Essays and Reviews"*); Charles Hodge, *Systematic Theology* (Grand Rapids: Eerdmans, 1981 [1871]). i:570–74. None of these leading responses called into question the validity of the standard geology of their day or advocated what we might call a "young earth" reading of Genesis. Michael Roberts, "Geology and Genesis unearthed," *Churchman* 112:3 (1998): 225–55, shows that standard geology was widely accepted by the orthodox Anglicans of this era.

14. Davis A. Young and Ralph F. Stearley, *The Bible, Rocks and Time* (Downers Grove, IL: InterVarsity Press, 2008), 206–7.

Some traditionalists, seeing these problems and finding theories of Creation Science unattractive, have resorted to a uniform designation of complementarity between the biblical and scientific accounts—that is, they say that these accounts do not compete with each other, since they do not address the same questions. Such people do not want to go along with Jowett in his theological minimalism, but they do seem to find the Goodwin-esque reading of Genesis to be compelling. Others have redoubled their efforts in Creation Science, seeking to eliminate the seemingly arbitrary employment of inadequate arguments under the conviction that the truth of the Bible requires that we shape our scientific theories accordingly. Still others resort to a kind of fideism or anti-realism when it comes to science in general.

What is one to do in the face of such discussion? The basic question concerns what it means to be a good reader of any material, and especially the material in Genesis. Perhaps Jowett has won the field; how can any reasonable person contend against the following principle?

> A knowledge of the original language is a necessary qualification of the Interpreter of Scripture. . . . To this, however, another qualification should be added, which is, *the logical power to perceive the meaning of words in reference to their context.*[15]

Jowett revealed, however, that beneath his words lies a determined literalism in reading any biblical passage when he lists the numerous "discrepancies" that he finds in Scripture and denounces the "apologetic" cast of those who would resolve them. A case in point is Jesus' "swear not at all" (Matt 5:34, AV), which Jowett finds contradicted by the oath-taking practices of "Christian countries." Any question about "with-respect-to-what" the Dominical dictum was meant to apply is ruled out before even being considered: the precept is "so plain, so universal, so exclusive."[16]

This last comment from Jowett shows that the discussion is wider than science-faith issues (though I am giving that primacy here). Some Christian groups have argued that taking Jesus seriously means embracing pacifism, refusing oaths (even in court), and so on. Do those groups who have justified the use of force and oaths in properly constituted social settings (the majority of Christians) *not* take Jesus seriously—or is it simply that they read his instructions differently?

---

15. Jowett, "On the Interpretation of Scripture," 390–91.
16. Ibid., 364.

1.B JAMES BARR, JOWETT'S HEIR

Jowett and Goodwin have a modern heir to their hermeneutic, James Barr (1924–2006). Barr made his initial splash in biblical studies with his books *The Semantics of Biblical Language* (1961) and *Biblical Words for Time* (1962), trenchant critiques of poor lexicographic methodology in what was then called the Biblical Theology Movement. Together with *Comparative Philology and the Text of the Old Testament* (1968), his books provoked many students to study modern linguistic methods for defining words in Hebrew and Greek.[17] A decade later Barr targeted what he called "fundamentalism," with *Fundamentalism* (1978) and *Beyond Fundamentalism* (1984). He then moved on to argue against the ideas of Brevard Childs (1923–2007) and his school of canonical criticism (which both accepts historical criticism of the biblical books and views the completed canon as the proper context of interpretation).

In 1989 Barr published a pair of articles addressing the issue of "literality"[18] in which he continued to argue that fundamentalists, for all their vaunted devotion to Scripture in its original intention, are very selective in their literalism: "Theological statements of scripture about God, if all taken literally, lead to mutual contradictions, which are usually overcome by abandoning the literal level of interpretation."[19] Further, "Literality should properly require that, just as nothing that is there in words should be ignored, so nothing that is not there in words should be allowed."[20]

Barr denied that the Jowett approach was minimalistic and theologically sterile (see my additional comments in chs. 2 and 8).[21] However, the way Barr carries the Jowett torch and the theological minimalism that it

---

17. In these books Barr himself never expounded a comprehensive method for lexicography, but those influenced by him did. Among these I can include Moisés Silva, *Biblical Words and Their Meaning: An Introduction to Lexical Semantics* (Grand Rapids: Zondervan, 1983), and my own PhD thesis, "Homonymous Verbs in Biblical Hebrew: An Investigation of the Role of Comparative Philology" (University of Liverpool, 1988).

18. James Barr, "Literality," *Faith and Philosophy* 6:4 (1989): 412–28. Barr's work is aimed at fundamentalists more than at anyone else. See also "The Literal, the Allegorical, and Modern Biblical Scholarship," *JSOT* 44 (1989): 3–17, which is aimed especially at Childs, who had argued that modern biblical scholarship follows too much in the tradition of literalism that Jowett exemplifies and thus is theologically impoverished. For this, see Brevard Childs, "The *sensus literalis* of Scripture: An Ancient and Modern Problem," in H. Donner et al., eds., *Beiträge zur Alttestamentlichen Theologie* (Vandenhoeck & Ruprecht, 1977), 80–93.

19. Barr, "Literality," 417.

20. Ibid., 422.

21. See James Barr, "Jowett and the Reading of the Bible 'Like Any Other Book'," *Horizons in Biblical Theology* 4 (1985): 1–44. Paul Noble, "The *sensus literalis*: Jowett, Childs, and Barr," *JTS* 44:1 (1993): 1–23, gives a penetrating critique of Barr's arguments.

produces can be seen in Barr's published lectures on the story of the fall in Genesis 1–3.[22] Barr distances the Genesis narrative from Paul's interpretation in the New Testament. He states, "it is not without importance that the term 'sin' is not used anywhere in the [Genesis] story . . . nor do we find any of the terms usually understood as 'evil,' 'rebellion,' 'transgression,' or 'guilt.'"[23] Barr's sentiment exemplifies his determination to only see what is in the text. His discussion of "surely die" (Gen 2:17) focuses entirely on physical death.[24]

Barr occupied a respected place in biblical studies, and thus he is not the only one who reads this way. Indeed, Jowett's hermeneutic has, in many ways, won the day in how biblical scholars read the Bible.[25] In fact, several scholars who would identify themselves as traditionalist (or even evangelical) follow Barr in their manner of reading and, each in his own way, also in Barr's skeptical conclusions about the Bible.[26] These evangelical scholars, I think, agree with a theme that runs through Barr's work, namely, that anything other than a straightforward literalism is a less-than-fully-honest way of reading the ancient text. Most curiously, many young-earth creationists find Barr's advocacy of literalism (in his book *Fundamentalism*) quite appealing, and they cite it with approval—Barr gives them the chance to claim that they are the honest traditionalists (as over against those who are untroubled about the age of the earth).[27] Now, these young-earth creationists follow Barr selectively. They do not, for example, agree with his take on Genesis 3 or on the valid basis of source criticism in literality and a number of other topics.[28] (Judging whether this strategy is critically sound or not lies outside my current concern.)

---

22. James Barr, *The Garden of Eden and the Hope of Immortality* (Philadelphia: Fortress, 1992). I have given a short review of the book in *Presbyterion* 37:1 (Spring 2011), 59–62.

23. Barr, *Garden of Eden*, 6.

24. Ibid., 8–14.

25. For just one example out of many—but especially relevant to this study—take John Day's, *From Creation to Babel: Studies in Genesis 1–11* (London: Bloomsbury T & T Clark, 2014), with which I interact in chapter 7.

26. For example, Kenton Sparks, *Sacred Word, Broken Word: Biblical Authority and the Dark Side of Scripture* (Grand Rapids: Eerdmans, 2012); Peter Enns, *The Evolution of Adam: What the Bible Does and Doesn't Say about Human Origins* (Grand Rapids: Brazos, 2012); Denis Lamoureux, *Evolution: Scripture and Nature Say Yes!* (Grand Rapids: Zondervan, 2016).

27. See, for example, the essays in Terry Mortenson and Thane Ury, eds., *Coming to Grips with Genesis* (Green Forest, AR: Master, 2008), especially pp. 161, 204.

28. As I note in my book, *Science and Faith: Friends or Foes?* (Wheaton, IL: Crossway, 2003), 364–66, many also appeal to a letter purported to be from Barr to David Watson, a creationist author. (Although some have expressed doubts, I assume the letter to be authentic, and the copy I have comes from Answers in Genesis by way of Steve Jones of Australia.) In that book I offer an analysis of the letter and its use.

1.C WHY DO I THINK C. S. LEWIS CAN HELP?

Everyone engaged in these exchanges about Genesis and science has views of how language and literature work; these views generally lie below the surface, below the level of articulation and defense. The classical disciplines of literary and rhetorical criticism and the modern disciplines of linguistic pragmatics and sociolinguistics (language in use, as I will describe in the next chapter) should come into play here.

But again, how? And can we do this rigorously? I propose to explore the contributions of a creative literary scholar, who had a classical education, to see if some help is available, namely, C. S. Lewis (1898–1963). Lewis has provided us with a raft-load of linguistic and literary ideas that can be developed into tools for careful reading—though he never collected those ideas into a systematic exposition. Highly regarded among religious traditionalists for his apologetics and fantasy stories, Lewis actually trained in philosophy, classics, and English literature (and taught them at Oxford University and later at Cambridge). Though successful primarily as a popular writer, he continues to attract scholarly attention in philosophy, theology, and literature, as recent PhD theses show.[29]

Lewis's ideas in many ways reflect the raw observations that lie at the base of several linguistic disciplines, such as lexical semantics, speech-act theory, and sociolinguistics.[30] These disciplines can be abstruse and sometimes counterintuitive, as well as contradictory between themselves, but Lewis offers a model of someone who intuitively (albeit informally) steers a wise path through the difficulties. Further, insights from these disciplines can help to refine Lewis's informal comments to give us a critically defensible approach to reading.[31] Also, these linguistic disciplines overlap with other disciplines that

---

29. E.g., Steven Lovell, "Philosophical Themes from C. S. Lewis" (Sheffield University, 2003); Michael Ward, "The Son and the Other Stars: Christology and Cosmology in the Imagination of C. S. Lewis" (St Andrews University, 2005); Hsiu-Chin Chou, "The Problem of Faith and the Self: The Interplay between Literary Art, Apologetics and Hermeneutics in C. S. Lewis' Religious Narratives" (Glasgow University, 2008); Jason Lepojärvi, "God Is Love but Love Is Not God: Studies on C. S. Lewis's Theology of Love" (Helsinki University, 2015); Daniel Rafer, "Mythic Structures in the Works of C. S. Lewis" (De Montfort University, 2002).

30. The main sources are Lewis's *A Preface to Paradise Lost* (Oxford: Oxford University Press, 1942); *God in the Dock*, ed. Walter Hooper (Grand Rapids: Eerdmans, 1970); *Christian Reflections*, ed. Walter Hooper (Grand Rapids: Eerdmans, 1967); *Reflections on the Psalms* (London: Geoffrey Bles, 1958); *Studies in Words* (Cambridge: Cambridge University Press, 1967); and *The Discarded Image* (Cambridge: Cambridge University Press, 1964), but offhand remarks appear scattered throughout Lewis' writings.

31. For example, my PhD thesis, "Homonymous Verbs in Biblical Hebrew," applies modern semantics to a vexing issue in Hebrew lexicography. I found that Lewis's *Studies in Words* provides an excellent example of good lexical method applied to reading old texts without worrying about theoretical apparatus.

are often separate, namely, rhetorical criticism and literary criticism. Lewis freely employs them all because human behavior does so—illustrating that what God has joined together in normal human behavior people should not separate for the sake of disciplinary turf. Several scholars in these disciplines have recognized the desirability of bringing their individual disciplinary programs into fruitful interaction, and I plan to have Lewis help me do just that.[32]

This intuitive approach of Lewis will serve us as a virtue, not as a drawback. The various disciplines of linguistics each have competing schools of thought when it comes to theoretical integration of their empirical studies. This is as it should be in any scientific enterprise. At the same time, since these disciplines deal with human behavior, each of us has some ready access to the empirical data—and, with due critical acumen, is entitled to receive, reject, or adapt the practical parts of the theories without yoking ourselves to *every* point made in the theory. Hence, I call my approach "critically intuitive." Walker Percy (1916–1990) put it well: "Language is too important to be left to linguisticians."[33] In the same book Percy recounts "the extraordinary sort of thing language is," to which, in his view, academic linguists had not done proper justice.[34] However, "the extraordinary character of language does not depend for its unveiling upon a piece of research but is there under our noses for all to see."[35] A very Lewisian sentiment.

I will make the case in the next chapter for the use of linguistic pragmatics, which focuses on language as a means of social interaction. This means that I disagree with linguists who hold strictly to the tradition of the premier linguist of the twentieth century, Noam Chomsky (b. 1928), who described language in this way:

> The language faculty is often equated with "communication"—a trait that is shared by all animal species and possibly also by plants. In our view, for the purposes of scientific understanding, language should be understood as a particular computational cognitive system, implemented neurally, that cannot be equated with an excessively expansive notion of "language as communication."[36]

---

32. See, for example, Alois Heuboeck, "Some Aspects of Coherence, Genre and Rhetorical Structure—and Their Integration into a Generic Model of Text," *University of Reading Language Studies Working Papers* 1 (2009): 35–45; Christopher Eisenhart and Barbara Johnstone, "Discourse Analysis and Rhetorical Studies," in Johnstone and Eisenhart, eds., *Rhetoric in Detail: Discourse Analysis of Rhetorical Talk and Text* (Amsterdam: Benjamins, 2008), 3–21.
33. Walker Percy, *The Message in the Bottle* (New York: Farrar, Straus and Giroux, 2000), 10.
34. Ibid., 151.
35. Ibid.
36. Johan J. Bolhuis, Ian Tattersall, Noam Chomsky, Robert C. Berwick, "How Could Language

This tradition has tended to confuse a methodological measure that serves scientific understanding with a practical (perhaps ontological) judgment about the thing under study. Chomskian theories about syntax and its relation to the human mind shed light on many subjects, such as human uniqueness and the problems posed to a purely Darwinian account of the origin of the language capacity, and thus we are all in his debt; but all humans know what they use language for and thus are entitled to assess some of Chomsky's assertions.[37]

Aristotle (384–322 BC), who was as insistent as any Chomskian on the unique role of human language, made these (intuitive) observations (Aristotle, *Politics*, I.1.9ff [1253a], LCL):

> And why man is a political animal in a greater measure than any bee or any gregarious animal is clear. For nature, as we declare, does nothing without purpose; and *man alone of the animals possesses speech*. The mere voice, it is true, can indicate pain and pleasure, and therefore is possessed by the other animals as well (for their nature has been developed so far as to have sensations of what is painful and pleasant and to indicate those sensations to one another), but *speech is designed to indicate the advantageous and the harmful, and therefore also the right and the wrong*; for it is the special property of man in distinction from the other animals that he alone has perception of good and bad and right and wrong and the other moral qualities, and it is partnership in these things that makes a household and a city-state.

In the chapters that follow I will develop a Lewisian, critically intuitive approach to hermeneutics. Although I aim specifically at reading Genesis 1–11, I consider this approach to have benefits more widely in biblical exegesis (though I will not try to develop that here). I will begin in chapter 2 with

---

Have Evolved?" *PLOS Biology* 12:8 (August 2014): e1001934, 1. This represents the position that I was taught in an upper-level linguistics class by a Chomskian, Sol Saporta (1925–2008), at the University of Washington in 1983. See also Marc D. Häuser, Noam Chomsky, W. Tecumseh Fitch, "The Faculty of Language: What Is It, Who Has It, and How Did It Evolve?" *Science* 298 (22 November 2002): 1569–79, which allows a possible (albeit evolutionary) connection between language as computation and language as communication.

37. I am hardly idiosyncratic in demurring from Chomsky on this point. Rajend Mesthrie puts it more forcefully than I might: "Chomskyan linguistics seems better aligned with the fields of robotics and artificial intelligence: the business of computer scientists, robot designers, automatic translation experts, and so on . . . When the automatons wish to turn human, they will need to learn about individual and communal language identities, relations of status, gender, and age between humans, and the rules of social interaction." See Mesthrie, "Introduction: The Sociolinguistic Enterprise," in Mesthrie, ed., *The Cambridge Handbook of Sociolinguistics* (Cambridge: Cambridge University Press, 2011), 1–14, quote on pp. 1–2.

some simple observations from Lewis that point us to questions whose best answers lie in the areas of linguistic studies commonly called pragmatics. I will also argue that these areas can be brought into fruitful engagement with what are often treated as separate departments of study: rhetorical and literary criticism.

In chapter 3 I will build on one of Lewis's unpublished essays dealing with the ways a language can be used for different kinds of communicative purposes. In chapter 4 I will discuss how communication takes place against a backdrop of a shared experience of the world. From here I can describe the relationship between rhetoric and truth.

Chapters 5–6 will then treat various aspects of reading Genesis 1–11: the different kinds of context (ch. 5) and the function (ch. 6) of these chapters. From there we should be able to see what these passages aimed to do and to distinguish that from what they did not aim to do. We should also be able to judge just what kind of cosmic picture is inherent in the texts and what role that picture has in their communication. I will put these ideas to work in chapter 7, where I will offer a rhetorical-theological reading of Genesis 1–11. Because I argue, from a sociolinguistic perspective, that we should greatly respect what audiences from organically connected cultures have seen in these chapters, I examine what readers from such audiences have said on selected topics (ch. 8). Many Bible passages have been taken as describing an outdated picture of the world and of God's action in it; I will examine some of these passages in chapters 9–10 in light of the tools I develop in the preceding chapters. My concluding chapter deals with responsible appropriation for the ancient context and the modern believer.

This outline shows that I am not writing a general study on the overall theme of creation in the Hebrew Bible. The standard study on the subject, by Jon Levenson, contains many exegetical judgments, and to evaluate every one of them would take a longer book than he wrote.[38] I prefer to say more than he does on certain texts and will do so with more self-awareness of reading strategy and the rhetoric employed by the biblical writers. I will leave interaction with what he says on other texts to the many commentaries on those texts. Besides, Levenson has offered his reasons for *not* regarding the social use of certain texts as a guide for exegesis in search of an original meaning that predates the canonical—his pursuit asks different questions than mine.[39]

---

38. Jon D. Levenson, *Creation and the Persistence of Evil: The Jewish Drama of Divine Omnipotence* (Princeton: Princeton University Press, 1988).

39. Jon D. Levenson, "The Bible: Unexamined Commitments of Criticism," *First Things* 30 (Feb 1993): 24–33.

It should also be clear that I am not suggesting that the linguistic-rhetorical-literary approach I am developing here displaces conventional tools of exegesis, such as lexicography, syntax, and history. Many of these other tools are themselves intuitive and well grounded in ordinary practice. Rather, I see my approach as allowing these conventional tools to function properly, and that is what I intend as I get into actual exposition.

Jowett and company, like many literalists today, assume that "what I see" is the same as "what is there." Contemporary philosophy of science has shown how indefensible this notion is in general, but it is especially hasty when reading an ancient text from a foreign culture. A recurring issue and a basic insight from this is to deny that "what I see" is necessarily the same as "what is there." Lewis warned his students against how easily they could fall into this trap:

> We turn to the helps only when the hard passages are manifestly hard. But there are treacherous passages which will not send us to the notes. They look easy and aren't.[40]

Although Lewis wrote these words for students, seasoned scholars run the risk of committing the same mistake. Hence, "This author clearly says X" should more fully be "I read this author to say X, and here is why you should too." Responsible readers, then, will aim to justify their readings. Hence, if I do not see what another person sees, that may mean I am blind (whether by lack of skill or by ideology); or it may mean I make different literary and linguistic judgments; or it may mean I am pursuing different questions. We must take these case by case. At the same time, these differing compartments are not airtight: a methodology might lead us to attend to some details more than to others, provide tools for making judgments, and set the kinds of questions that are worth asking. I certainly think that the linguistic-rhetorical-literary methodology that I develop here works in all three departments.

1.D MY OWN BACKGROUND AND STANCE

A word about my own background and personal orientation is in order here. While some people can come to many studies with utter neutrality about what they will do with their findings, this rarely happens when these studies

---

40. Lewis, *Discarded Image*, vii. See also *Studies in Words*, 1ff.

deal with basic ideas of what it means to be human—so it is only right to be straightforward about such things. My initial education, undergraduate and graduate, was in science and engineering at MIT (the Massachusetts Institute of Technology in Cambridge, Massachusetts). After a few years' work in engineering, I attended a seminary and then earned my PhD in Hebrew and Comparative Semitic Linguistics at the University of Liverpool in England.

In the early stages of my academic work I focused on lexical semantics in Hebrew as well as in Greek; then I became fascinated with verbs and syntax. This led me to text grammar, which then led to larger questions about how acts of communication work. There is an irony lurking here: I owe a great deal to the work of James Barr, whose work in lexical semantics introduced me to what linguistic rigor should look like. However, linguistic rigor includes these other dimensions of study as well, dimensions to which, as I judge, Barr did not give their proper due. It was Barr who let that genie out of the bottle.

Two figures stand out among many in my intellectual development: Alvin Drake of MIT (1935–2005) taught me probability and employed me as a graduate teaching assistant, and Alan Millard of Liverpool University (b. 1937) supervised my PhD. Both of these mentors insisted on careful critical thinking, not only in their academic fields but also in the whole of life. I hope they will not feel their efforts were wasted in my case.

Further, like C. S. Lewis I am a religious traditionalist. I much prefer that label to fundamentalist, a term that once had a definite meaning, namely, as someone who agrees with *The Fundamentals*, a series of ninety Protestant traditionalist essays published from 1910 to 1915. Lewis's 1958 denial of being a fundamentalist shows how the term had changed in less than fifty years:

> I have been suspected of being what is called a fundamentalist. That is because I never regard any narrative as unhistorical simply on the ground that it includes the miraculous. Some people find the miraculous so hard to believe that they cannot imagine any reason for my acceptance of it other than *a prior belief that every sentence of the Old Testament has historical or scientific truth*.[41]

By that definition I am not a fundamentalist either—nor, as matter of fact, are most traditionalists. Lewis was clear, here and elsewhere, that his issue of whether to read passages as historical truth was a literary judgment

---

41. Lewis, *Reflections on the Psalms*, 109. Compare also his 1959 address to a group of ministry candidates, "Modern Theology and Biblical Criticism," in Lewis, *Christian Reflections*, 152–66: "We are not fundamentalists" (163), implying that "we" accept some kinds of criticism, especially textual.

about the particular texts. In principle, traditionalists agree with this procedure, even when they might make different literary judgments.

A third "Al," the philosopher Alvin Plantinga (b. 1932), has incisively analyzed the current usage of the term fundamentalist:

> We must first look into the use of this term "fundamentalist." On the most common contemporary academic use of the term, it is a term of abuse or disapprobation, rather like "son of a bitch," more exactly "sonovabitch," or perhaps still more exactly (at least according to those authorities who look to the Old West as normative on matters of pronunciation) "sumbitch." When the term is used in this way, no definition of it is ordinarily given. (If you called someone a sumbitch, would you feel obliged first to define the term?) Still, there is a bit more to the meaning of "fundamentalist" (in this widely current use): it isn't simply a term of abuse. In addition to its emotive force, it does have some cognitive content, and ordinarily denotes relatively conservative theological views. That makes it more like "stupid sumbitch" (or maybe "fascist sumbitch"?) than "sumbitch" simpliciter. It isn't exactly like that term either, however, because its cognitive content can expand and contract on demand; its content seems to depend on who is using it. In the mouths of certain liberal theologians, for example, it tends to denote any who accept traditional Christianity, including Augustine, Aquinas, Luther, Calvin, and Barth; in the mouths of devout secularists like Richard Dawkins or Daniel Dennett, it tends to denote anyone who believes there is such a person as God. The explanation is that the term has a certain indexical element: its cognitive content is given by the phrase "considerably to the right, theologically speaking, of me and my enlightened friends." The full meaning of the term, therefore (in this use), can be given by something like "stupid sumbitch whose theological opinions are considerably to the right of mine."[42]

Let me explain how I conceive this work in relation to an apologetic program—as anyone who invokes C. S. Lewis must surely address. The discipline of apologetics is oriented toward defending an intellectual position. In normal usage of the word, that intellectual position is religious traditionalism (here, either Jewish or Christian). I am not aiming at apologetics as such; instead I aim to find an interpretive program for biblical material, especially that of

---

42. Alvin Plantinga, *Warranted Christian Belief* (Oxford: Oxford University Press, 2000), 245.

Genesis 1–11. As Mark Brett noted, "Clearly, one can grasp an author's point without being persuaded by it."[43]

I thus have a twofold goal. The first is to provide guidance to those who want to consider how these Bible passages relate to the findings of the sciences. The second is to establish patterns of good theological reading, patterns applicable for other texts. Those who focus on one of these more than the other should understand that to me the two are intertwined, each playing a role in what it means to be a responsible audience.

At the same time, two things are true. First, the interpretive program has a bearing on apologetics, since it clarifies what it is that someone seeks to defend or to criticize. I have already in this chapter shown how I judge that both defenders and critics have failed interpretively.

The second truth is that the apologetic enterprise has a bearing on our interpretation. Many of the critical approaches, for example, suffer from a want of imagination: they *assume* a way of reading and do not entertain whether one *must* read that way.[44] At the same time, an apologetic motivation in interpretation can lead a person to defend a weak position—again because of a failure in imagination, which becomes a failure to consider other possibilities. Hence, I will argue for the *critical* use of a *disciplined imagination*.

Apologetics, honestly and rigorously engaged, serves faithful believers by enabling them to commend their beliefs to the world outside their faith community. It also serves them in their own appropriation of the Scriptures. As Austin Farrer (Lewis's Oxford colleague and friend, and a clergyman who ministered to Lewis in his final illness) put it,

> For though argument does not create conviction, the lack of it destroys belief. What seems to be proved may not be embraced; but what no one shows the ability to defend is quickly abandoned. Rational argument does not create belief, but it maintains a climate in which belief may flourish.[45]

Although I make comments along the way about the ways I find certain kinds of source criticism unhelpful, I do not intend to comment on that subject

---

43. Mark G. Brett, "Motives and Intentions in Genesis 1," *JTS* 42:1 (1991): 1–16, quote on p. 12 n25.
44. A ready example comes from Kenton Sparks, "Genesis 1–11 as Ancient Historiography," in *Genesis: History Fiction, or Neither? Three Views on the Bible's Earliest Chapters*, ed. Charles Halton (Grand Rapids: Zondervan, 2015), 110–39. There is no consideration of whether one may offer a different reading of Genesis, and his is treated as if it were self-evident.
45. Austin Farrer, "The Christian Apologist," in *Light on C. S. Lewis*, ed. Joceyln Gibb (London: Geoffrey Bles, 1965), 23–43, quote on p. 26.

in general.⁴⁶ At the same time, as Barr has rightly observed, "*biblical source criticism*, the operation which in the Pentateuch detected sources like, J, E, D and P, the very critical method that fundamentalists so detest, *is also the result of 'taking the Bible literally.'*"⁴⁷ Perhaps if the literalism that Barr presupposes can be properly subjected to review, the advocates of source criticism might have to be more modest.

About my use of secondary sources: Since I am using Lewis as a gateway to a greater awareness of rhetoric, discourse analysis, and sociolinguistics, I count it my chief responsibility to draw on resources from these disciplines. But since I am contending for a way of reading biblical passages and am also arguing that this way of reading has not received full attention in recent biblical scholarship, I offer what I take to be reasonable amounts of documentation on that score. I do not claim completeness, nor do I claim to have written a critical commentary on the passages I address. I hope, however, that my readers will judge that I have given reasons for the positions I take.

Since I am arguing that the rhetorical and linguistic insights are best seen as intuitions and everyday experiences under critical examination, I also draw on Christian writers (especially John Stott) who exhibit some of these intuitions at work—even when their performance is uneven. The reason I do this goes beyond my general enjoyment of opinions well thought out and well stated: I want my readers to appreciate that there is nothing ad hoc or esoteric about the kinds of insights I am putting to work.

Also for this purpose, I will occasionally commend my methodology by showing its potential fruitfulness for a wider range of theological and exegetical topics than those associated with the science-and-faith discussion.

---

46. When various kinds of criticism are essentially applied naturalism, they run afoul of the trenchant critique that C. S. Lewis offered in his "Modern Theology and Biblical Criticism," in *Christian Reflections*, ed. Walter Hooper (Grand Rapids: Eerdmans, 1967), 152–66.

47. Barr, *Fundamentalism*, 46.

Chapter 2

WHAT IS HAPPENING IN LITERARY COMMUNICATION?

2.A THE BIG IDEA: HOW TO APPROACH ANY WORK OF ART

One of C. S. Lewis's earliest published books—which does not receive much attention—was *The Personal Heresy: A Controversy*, an exchange between him and E. M. W. Tillyard (1889–1962), a prominent Cambridge scholar of sixteenth- and seventeenth-century English literature.[1] In short (and to oversimplify), they debated whether we read poetry to see *into the soul of* the author (Tillyard's position) or to see *by means of* the author the thing the poem is about (Lewis' position). Or, as Lewis summarized it, does the poem make the poet a spectacle, or does it provide a pair of spectacles for seeing some aspect of the world?[2]

The seeds of many of Lewis's literary ideas are manifest in this work. He put some of them into practice when he gave a set of guest lectures at the University College of North Wales in 1941, which were then published as *A Preface to Paradise Lost*.[3] It is here where Lewis makes a number of critical points about how to read poetry, which have more general application to reading most things (especially from the ancient world).

Lewis opens with a famous sentence:

> The first qualification for judging any piece of workmanship from a corkscrew to a cathedral is to know what it is—what it was intended to do and how it is meant to be used.[4]

---

1. C. S. Lewis, *The Personal Heresy: A Controversy* (Oxford: Oxford University Press, 1939).
2. Lewis, Essay 1 in *The Personal Heresy*, 11–12.
3. C. S. Lewis, *A Preface to Paradise Lost* (Oxford: Oxford University Press, 1942).
4. Ibid., 1.

Straightaway Lewis has drawn our attention to three aspects of a work of literary craftsmanship:

- *What it is* (issues of "genre," style, and register): What is the relation of literary form and the content?
- *What it was intended to do*: What effect does the work aim to produce in its users?
- *How it is meant to be used*: What kind of users are envisioned by the work, what knowledge and beliefs do they share with the author, and what kind of social setting is the normal locus of use?

In this chapter I will show that if we follow Lewis's advice, we will venture into areas studied by linguists and rhetoricians and literary theorists. But first let me pull out a few more points from the book.

Lewis continues in this vein (similar to his entries in *The Personal Heresy*):

> Every poem can be considered in two ways—as what the poet has to say, and as a *thing* which he *makes*. From the one point of view it is an expression of opinions and emotions; from the other, it is an organization of words which exists to produce a particular kind of patterned experience in the readers.[5]

He focuses on the second part, what it does for the audience. Indeed, in the course of discussing the presence of stock expressions in classical epic, he notes that one scholar explained that the poet used these as an aid to his own oral composition and performance. Lewis counters:

> But all art is made to *face* the audience. Nothing can be left exposed, however useful to the performer, which is not delightful or at least tolerable to *them*. . . . We must therefore consider what these repetitions do for the hearers, not what they do for the poet. And we may observe that this is the only *aesthetic* or critical question. . . . Good poetry means not the poetry men like composing, but the poetry men like to listen to or to read.[6]

For now I will draw on one more passage. Lewis adds this about the poet's means of achieving his or her ends, namely, the use of "rhetoric":

---

5. Ibid., 2 (emphasis original).
6. Ibid., 19 (emphasis original).

> I do not think (and no great civilization has ever thought) that the art of the rhetorician is necessarily vile. It is in itself noble, though of course, like most arts, it can be wickedly used. . . . Both these arts [rhetoric and poetry], in my opinion, definitely aim at doing something to an audience. . . . The proper use [of rhetoric] is lawful and necessary because, as Aristotle points out, intellect of itself "moves nothing": the transition from thinking to doing, in nearly all men at nearly all moments, needs to be assisted by appropriate states of feeling. . . .
>
> Poetry certainly aims at making the reader's mind what it was not before.[7]

Before we turn to the disciplines Lewis points us toward, we must ensure that we see his basic claims. First, Lewis respected the primacy of what is called "authorial intention," a claim that requires some clarification. Certainly, it is clear from our own experience that we intend things with our speech and writing; most people at most times have a sense of what the true interpretation of their words would be and would dislike it if someone twisted those words (especially uncharitably). Even those who write dissertations denying the relevance of intention *intend* for their theses to be taken seriously and interpreted correctly.[8] Nevertheless, our ascertaining of authorial intention comes from the text itself and from the situation in which it is to be used rather than from a psychoanalysis of the author from afar.

Scholars have made a case against what may be called "the intentional fallacy." Some, because of that very title, take this as a decisive refutation of the idea that authors' intentions may mean anything to literary interpretation; but this does not follow. First, the designation "fallacy" is misleading, as the classic exposition of the fallacy (an article by the American literary critics William Wimsatt and Monroe Beardsley) argues a point of literary criticism and not of logic.[9] However, the primary point is that, once produced, "The poem belongs to the public," and what the author *wanted* to do, if that

---

7. Ibid., 51–53. Lewis probably had in mind Aristotle, *Nicomachean Ethics*, 6.2.5 [1139-*ab*]. See also 2.3.2 [1104-*b*] on education as preparing a person with the right set of likes and dislikes.

8. The thesis of Bernard Minton, "What Not to Do with Words: Uses of Speech Act Theory in Biblical Hermeneutics" (PhD thesis, University of Sheffield, 2014), here comes to mind. Minton insists throughout, without a clear argument (almost taking his position as needing no demonstration), that the speech act distinction of illocution (intended effect) and perlocution (actual effect) is invalid because the notion of intention is wrong. I will examine these topics in what follows with (I hope) sufficient nuance to avoid the common pitfalls (some of which Minton rightly identifies).

9. William Wimsatt and Monroe Beardsley, "The Intentional Fallacy," published first in *Sewanee Review* 54 (1946): 468–88, and then in their book *The Verbal Icon: Studies in the Meaning of Poetry* (Lexington, KY: University of Kentucky Press, 1954).

is separate from what the work of art actually *is*, is neither desirable nor accessible.[10] That position hardly constitutes an argument against the role of intention that I present here; in fact, I aim to account for Wimsatt and Beardsley's valid points in the way I frame my discussion.

Consider how Lewis treats Milton's poem, drawing on the debates and literary conventions of Milton's own time. Lewis makes an important distinction:

> But the words "really meant" are ambiguous. "What Milton really meant by the poem" may mean (*a*) his total thought about all the subjects mentioned in it; (*b*) the poem he meant (i.e. intended) to write, the instrument for producing a certain experience in the readers which he intended to make.[11]

Failure to make this distinction comes up frequently in discussion of biblical materials, especially on topics such as cosmic picture, and we will return to it later. What matters for the interpreter is Lewis's item (b)—indeed, many of the attempts to recreate item (a) for a biblical author suffer from serious problems. Further, by observing this distinction we can also be careful not to confuse proper concern for authorial intention with an unwarranted treatment of texts as if they were contributions to the authors' autobiographies.

Things can get complicated for the Bible, however. For example, it is always possible that material from several authors (or communities of authors) have been joined together editorially. This is commonly held to be the case for Genesis. Further, those who held power in the ancient community, who determined how a text was to be used, might have employed a text in a way different from what the author had in mind. This may be the case, say, with certain psalms: Whatever might have been their poets' original purpose, they have been incorporated into a songbook for use in public worship.[12]

Usually the putative sources do not exist, except as inferences in scholars' reconstructions. In such cases (and others like them) we can still meaningfully speak of intention if we refer to the final form of the text and the normal

---

10. This bears some resemblance to Mark Brett's distinction between "motives" (what moved the author to write) and "communicative intentions" (what the author is trying to say), in "Motives and Intentions in Genesis 1."

11. Lewis, *A Preface to Paradise Lost*, 89.

12. This point about the Psalms as a songbook may also be disputed by those who think that the songbook function of the Psalter has been superseded by a canonical arrangement. Nevertheless, advocates of this position will agree that this arrangement needs only a loose connection with the original intentions of the authors, who probably thought they were writing songs. I have given reasons briefly for preferring the songbook classification in "Psalms 111–112: Big Story, Little Story," *Religions* 7(9) (2016): 115, and will do so more fully in a forthcoming commentary on the Psalms.

(normative) use of the biblical book in ancient Israel—the evidence for which may in some cases be limited to after the exile.

The question of intention for these texts in Genesis brings up a matter that I will keep coming back to in this work, especially in chapter 8 (What Other Readers Have Seen in Genesis 1–11); for now, I will make a few preliminary observations. Most biblical writers wrote in the context of what we now know as the canon, the authorized writings to guide the people of Israel (and afterwards the church). In such a setting it seems, upon reflection, unreasonable to find one author correcting or undermining another, since there are no grounds for believing that the collectors of the sacred writings would have accepted such subterfuge. Hence disagreement among canonical texts is an unlikely direction to look in ascertaining the book's intention. Also, the ways in which later authors, especially canonical ones, reflected on one particular text should take pride of place in our discerning of intention; at the very least we should be reticent to set these at odds with each other. As Lewis argued elsewhere,

> The idea that any man or writer should be opaque to those who lived in the same culture, spoke the same language, shared the same habitual imagery and unconscious assumptions, and yet be transparent to those who have none of these advantages, is in my opinion preposterous.[13]

While Lewis meant this to apply specifically to the early followers of Jesus who gave us the New Testament, it also applies to the Bible more generally; but we must exercise caution here. It is theoretically possible that (apart from "inspiration," which is not my subject) someone *could* misunderstand an earlier author—so we are here talking about burden of proof. We must also be careful when reading, say, a later author who cites an earlier one: the citation *might* be an indication of the writer's interpretation, but it might also be an example of his use (even sometimes playfully or ironically). And, since the biblical authors believed (rightly or wrongly) that their God had in some fashion breathed out the Scriptures and that he was sovereign over his words, there is always the possibility that they felt authorized to go beyond, or add something that was not in, the earlier writings. (How frequent or infrequent this is does not concern me now.)[14]

---

13. Lewis, "Modern Theology and Biblical Criticism," in *Christian Reflections*, ed. Walter Hooper (Grand Rapids: Eerdmans, 1967), 152–66, quote on p. 158. This, by the way, offers a clear alternative to the notions of Benjamin Jowett as discussed in chapter 1 above.

14. Lewis attempts to deal with this topic in his chapter 12, "Second meanings in the Psalms," in *Reflections on the Psalms* (London: Geoffrey Bles, 1958). Again, for the present purposes it matters not how we would handle these issues, but we ought to acknowledge the challenges.

Further, once the founding documents (in this case, the canon) are in place, it is always possible (some even say likely) that the Israelite, and then Christian, social systems' practices might veer from the canonical ideal—as prophets, reformers, and other repristinators typically allege. It is unlikely, though, that canonical materials are in themselves critiques of other canonical materials: at least, we should require a high burden of proof for arguments that such critiques are present.

These public-usage considerations will affect the way I approach Genesis 1–11. I aim to respect the canonical location of a text and the tradition of interpretation, and to do justice to the actual social situation of Israel and the early Christians.

We sometimes hear that the ancient world did not share our interest in authorial intent. On the face of it, that is hard to believe, since we know that humans generally, ancient and modern, intend. But perhaps the point means that they did not accord the same regard to a sacred text? The evidence we have, however, shows that the ancients were at least capable of attending to an author's intentions. For example, the apostle Paul can point out his own intention in a previous set of instructions, expecting that this intention would have been manifest to a sympathetic reader with his wits about him; but just in case, he gets more explicit (1 Cor 5:9–11, discussed further in ch. 3).

What is more, Herodotus records an instance in which the people of Athens try to discern what a particular oracle meant in terms that evoke what modern exegetes do (*Hist.*, 7.141–143).[15] The Pythian oracle at Delphi that included the famous passage about the "wall made of wood" that would help Athens against the Persians under Xerxes (480 BC) occasioned a great deal of discussion over its proper interpretation. People in Athens debated whether the wooden walls were a thorn hedge protecting the Acropolis or if they were perhaps the navy. A problem for this latter interpretation arose from the words in the oracle (*Hist.*, 7.141.4):

> O Salamis Divine, the children of women you will yet destroy
>   While Demeter is scattered or while she is gathered.

Many took this as foretelling a naval defeat around Salamis for the Athenians. However, a certain Themistocles offered this reasoning (*Hist.*, 7.143.1–2):

---

15. English taken from Robert Strassler, ed., *The Landmark Herodotus: The Histories* (New York: Anchor, 2007), 554–56.

He said that if the real import of these verses to the Athenians was that the inhabitants were to end their lives around Salamis, then he did not think it would have used such mild language, but would have said something like "O Salamis Cruel" rather than "O Salamis Divine." But if, in fact, one understood the oracle properly, this part of it was directed by the god not to the Athenians but to their enemies. And so the god had advised them to prepare for a sea battle, and their fleet was what he meant by the wooden wall.

We can easily recognize that Themistocles was trying to ascertain the god's intention based on the choice of words.[16]

The second of Lewis's claims is that we should attend not to the poet but to whatever he or she wrote about. It is conceivable that poets write in order to unburden—or even expose—themselves. Certainly, this happens in the contemporary Western world, but I would be surprised if it was common in the ancient environment.

I have spoken with a few contemporary poets and found that they do prefer to be taken in Lewis's fashion, providing a set of spectacles—but these may be unrepresentative. Let us look at two examples of popular poet-songwriters from the late twentieth and early twenty-first century, who write for popular consumption. The first of these is James Taylor (born 1948 in Boston), who wrote "Fire and Rain" (released 1970). This poem has numerous references to Taylor's own experiences and is unintelligible without specific knowledge of the poet's life: for example, is the "Suzanne" he refers to a real person, and what happened to her?

The second poet is Bruce Cockburn (born 1945 in Ottawa), who wrote "Little Seahorse" (released 1975) as a meditation on the coming birth of his first child. Knowing the occasion for the poem matters in the sense that one can then enter the imagery in which the developing embryo is likened to a seahorse "swimming in a primal sea." The song expresses a mixture of wonder and anticipation, together with fear for how the dangerous world might "sweep you away." This poem would be a failure, however, if we heard it simply as a bit of Cockburnian autobiography. Rather, it provides a vehicle to guide any expecting parent, especially a father, in reflecting on the mysterious process by which a child forms in the womb, and it offers assurance of love

---

16. Herodotus also records the actions of Mardonius (485 BC), who manipulated the oracles for his own advantage at the Persian court: "If some oracles portended failure for the barbarian, he did not mention them" (*Hist.*, 7.6.4)—that is, his report overrode the actual intentions of the oracle, intentions that were ascertainable. (This account comports with the ancient Near Eastern scruples against modifying an oracle once it has been given.)

and connection to a child yet in the womb. That is, the poet has given his audience a pair of spectacles. I do not know how much or little Cockburn's own inner life embodied these fine sentiments—nor would it affect the way the song functions.

For the materials that we encounter in the Bible, as probably also with Milton, we ought generally to expect what Lewis has described. These writings were used in public, whether we are thinking of the Pentateuch (read aloud in sacred gatherings; e.g., Deut 31:11–13) or Psalms. We do not expect to find the kind of poetry we might expect in the contemporary world with "the solitary, private, and armchair associations which the word 'poetry' has for a modern."[17]

2.B LINGUISTICS, RHETORIC, LITERARY CRITICISM, AND GENRE

What then are these other disciplines that I have alluded to, and how does Lewis's discussion bring us to them?

2.B.1 LINGUISTICS

As linguistics developed in the twentieth century, it included the subfields of phonology (the sounds of a language); morphology (the way words are formed); semantics (how meaning is conveyed by words); and syntax (how sentences are formed). After 1960, pragmatics (how people use language to accomplish effects) was added. This latter subfield has an array of subsets of its own, including discourse analysis (how we make sense of texts); text grammar (how the parts of the text work together to produce a coherent whole); speech act theory (analyzing the text as an action performed by a speaker or writer); conversation analysis (how we understand the ways speakers interact); and relevance theory (how audiences select the appropriate parts of context and background).[18] It has considerable overlap

---

17. Lewis, *A Preface to Paradise Lost*, 18.
18. A helpful survey appears in Dan Sperber and Deirdre Wilson, "Pragmatics," in *The Oxford Handbook of Contemporary Philosophy*, ed. Frank Jackson and Michael Smith (Oxford: Oxford University Press, 2007), online edition. See also Joan Cutting, *Pragmatics and Discourse: A Resource Book for Students* (London: Routledge, 2002); George Yule, *The Study of Language* (Cambridge: Cambridge University Press, 2006); Gillian Brown and George Yule, *Discourse Analysis* (Cambridge: Cambridge University Press, 1983); Robin Wooffitt, *Conversation Analysis and Discourse Analysis: A Comparative and Critical Introduction* (London: Sage, 2005); Barbara Johnstone, *Discourse Analysis* (Oxford: Blackwell, 2008); Stephen Levinson, *Pragmatics* (Cambridge: Cambridge University Press, 1983); and Deborah Schiffrin, Deborah Tannen, and Heidi E. Hamilton, eds., *The Handbook of Discourse Analysis* (Oxford: Blackwell, 2001). For an early effort, see Teun A. van Dijk, *Text and Context* (London: Longman, 1977). Robert Longacre, of both the Summer Institute of Linguistics and University of Texas at Arlington, developed

with sociolinguistics (how language use functions to preserve or subvert a social system)[19] as well as with psycholinguistics (how biological, cognitive, and psychological factors enable people to acquire and use language).[20] One challenge for the non-specialist—especially in pragmatics—is that no one regulates the terminology, which means that it can vary and thus one cannot be sure which definition a scholar is using unless he or she states it plainly.[21] Further, within each of these subfields there are theoretical disputes; as Lynell Zogbo (a Bible translation specialist in Africa) put it, "there is no one 'school' of discourse, neither is there a defined model."[22] In keeping with my critically intuitive approach, I do not need to adjudicate these disputes or the nomenclature; I will instead recognize the orientation that these fields offer and appropriate it.

These linguistic approaches invite us to explore a variety of social factors. For example:

- What is the presumed relationship between the author and the audience?
- Who are the presumed audience, and what is their social standing and knowledge of the world?
- How does the text interact with what the audience members already know?
- What are the social situations in which the text is normally used?

---

a brand of discourse analysis (alternatively called textlinguistics) aimed at identifying features of a text that make for cohesion as well as grammatical conventions for signaling such things as prominence versus background. Those that Longacre has influenced have further examined how the text operates on the world of the audience to produce its intended effects. See Shin Ja Hwang and William Merrifield, eds. *Language in Context: Essays for Robert E. Longacre* (Dallas: SIL International, 1992). Also see Bruce Hollenbach and Jim Watters (both associated with Summer Institute of Linguistics), "Study Guide on Pragmatics and Discourse," *Notes on Translation* 12:1 (1998): 13–35.

19. See Rajend Mesthrie, ed., *The Cambridge Handbook of Sociolinguistics* (Cambridge: Cambridge University Press, 2011).

20. Compare Geert Brône and Jeroen Vandaele, eds., *Cognitive Poetics: Goals, Gains, and Gaps* (Berlin: de Gruyter, 2009); Peter Stockwell, *Cognitive Poetics: An Introduction* (London: Routledge, 2002); Dan Slobin, *Psycholinguistics* (Glenview, IL: Scott, Foresman and Company, 1974).

21. For example, some suggest that discourse analysis is the American name for what Europeans call textlinguistics, while others say they are separate fields. Further, discourse analysis can range from a very syntactical orientation (a sophisticated version of sentence diagramming) within the sentence and between sentences to a sociolinguistic consideration of how people wield power in social settings. For an example of the former as applied to biblical studies, see Calinda Hallberg, "Storyline and Theme in a Biblical Narrative: 1 Samuel 3," *OPTAT* 3:1 (1989): 1–35; and for the latter, see Ernst Wendland, *Language, Society, and Bible Translation: With Special Reference to the Style and Structure of Segments of Direct Speech in the Scriptures* (Cape Town: Bible Society of South Africa, 1985).

22. Lynell Marchese Zogbo, "Advances in Discourse Study and Their Application to the Field of Translation," in *UBS Monograph: Issues in Translation*, ed. P. C. Stine (United Bible Societies, 1988), 1–29, quote on p. 2.

Lewis also showed himself adept at appreciating how people can choose and manipulate their words in order to wield social power (as contemporary discourse analysis and sociolinguistics carefully examine). In *Studies in Words*, Lewis describes the phenomenon he calls "tactical definitions": "attempts to appropriate for one side, and to deny to the other, a potent word."[23] Lewis's example is the way English critics treated the word *wit*; but the sociolinguistic awareness will come in handy when we deal with potentially potent words such as literal, poetical, critical, fundamentalist, and science.

> A certain type of writer begins "The essence of poetry is" or "All vulgarity may be defined as," and then produces a definition which no one ever thought of since the world began, which conforms to no one's actual usage, and which he himself will probably have forgotten by the end of the month. The phenomenon ceases to be puzzling only when we realise that it is a tactical definition. The pretty word has to be narrowed *ad hoc* so as to exclude something he dislikes. The ugly word has to be extended *ad hoc*, or more probably *ad hunc*, so as to bespatter some enemy.[24]

2.B.2 RHETORIC

Classical Western scholarship did not neglect the question of how texts convey "meanings": the topics that linguistic pragmatics treats were conventionally grouped under the discipline of rhetoric.[25] The English noun *rhetoric* joins words like *semantics* and *politics* as those unfortunate derivatives of Greek adjectives ending in *-ikos* that, in popular usage, are taken as indicating obscuration of what ought to be clear and good—but they actually designate potentially noble activities (as Lewis saw clearly).

Historians typically trace the study of rhetoric to Aristotle's treatise, *The "Art" of Rhetoric*, and to the tradition of study that he started.[26] Aristotle concerned himself with the use of argument in public settings, which came in three general categories (*Rhet.*, 1.3.3–6): the "deliberative" (the assembly must decide on a course of action), the "forensic" (the assembly must decide on guilt or innocence), and the "epideictic" (the assembly must praise or blame some

---

23. Lewis, *Studies in Words*, 17–19.
24. Ibid., 19.
25. Many rhetoricians recognize this. See, for example, Paul Newell Campbell, "A Rhetorical View of Locutionary, Illocutionary, and Perlocutionary Acts," *QJournSp* 59 (1973): 284–96; James Benjamin, "Performatives as a Rhetorical Construct," *Philosophy and Rhetoric* 9:2 (1976): 84–95; Walter Beale, "Rhetorical Performative Discourse: A New Theory of Epideictic," *Philosophy and Rhetoric* 11:4 (1978): 221–46.
26. James Herrick, *The History and Theory of Rhetoric* (Boston: Allyn and Bacon, 2001), provides an overview of rhetoric and a survey of its origins and early history. See especially chs. 1–2.

set of actions). This is quite a narrow range of settings, and many prefer to think of the subject more broadly, as the art of persuading people in the arena of beliefs, practices, and dispositions. Indeed, Jeffrey Walker has argued that at an earlier stage of Greek society, rhetoric and poetics were joined together. Here is how Walker envisioned this earlier stage:

> The category of the *epideiktikon*, in contrast, was more amorphous and inclusive, though it was generally identified with discourse delivered outside judicial and legislative forums, such as speeches performed at festivals and ceremonial or symposiastic occasions, and it was typically conceived as the discourse of praise and blame.[27]

I do not know whether the historical side of Walker's thesis will prevail. Nevertheless, it does helpfully encourage us to use the word *rhetoric* in this more general application; it might provide some models for the way in which at least some of the biblical narratives functioned.

At this point I must distinguish the study of rhetoric in general from what is often called "rhetorical criticism" in biblical studies. Most of the effort in biblical studies has been focused on the concern for what in textlinguistics is called "cohesion" (see ch. 5 below) or what others call "literary coherence."[28] New Testament studies also sometimes shows an interest in applying Aristotle's three categories to classify texts. The larger question, of how does this text function to shape the beliefs, practices, and dispositions of the target communities, to enable what Lewis called "the transition from thinking to doing," does not get enough attention, but this will be my concern here.

2.B.3 Literary Criticism

Lewis also practiced literary criticism. In Lewis's hands the discipline of literary criticism studies not only whether a particular literary item is good or bad and what contributes to its goodness or badness, but also the proper interpretation of the literary item. It is for this latter part that I am laying Lewis under contribution. In his day, as in ours, the role of a particular author's intention in interpretation was under dispute; and, as we have seen, Lewis weighed in on respecting authorial intention. As he playfully put it,

---

27. See Jeffrey Walker, *Rhetoric and Poetics in Antiquity* (Oxford: Oxford University Press, 2000), chapters 1–3. There is ancient evidence for grouping poetry into the epideictic category. The classic study is by Theodore Burgess, "Epideictic Literature," *University of Chicago Studies in Classical Philology* 3 (1902): 95–261.

28. As acknowledged by David Howard, "Rhetorical Criticism in Old Testament Studies," *BBR* 4 (1994): 87–104.

There are, I know, those who prefer not to go beyond the impression, however accidental, which an old work makes on a mind that brings to it a purely modern sensibility and modern conceptions; just as there are travellers who carry their resolute Englishry with them all over the Continent, mix only with other English tourists, enjoy all they see for its 'quaintness', and have no wish to realise what those ways of life, those churches, those vineyards, mean to the natives. They have their reward. I have no quarrel with people who approach the past in that spirit. I hope they will pick none with me. But I was writing for the other sort.[29]

We should remember Lewis's playful tone here: no doubt there are other motivations than those he mentions for disregarding, or even countering, the intentions of an author (to the extent we can discern them). Nevertheless, we can say at the very least that interest in intentions is a valid one.

A number of scholars—among whom Meir Sternberg and Robert Alter are in the top rank—have developed and applied to the Bible what we might call conservative methods of literary criticism that honor authorial intention.[30] These methods stem from the observation that the biblical narratives are stories and hence involve characters, events (plot), and scenes. To call them stories is not to downplay whatever historical claims they might make, since if the literary kind is one that tells history, then one must address these; instead, labeling them as stories directs our attention to the narrator's ways of portraying characters' good and bad traits and of displaying or hiding the narrator's own point of view. V. Philips Long offers a helpful survey of these approaches in his published PhD thesis, *The Reign and Rejection of King Saul*.[31] Some of the features we find in the Old Testament narratives include the following:

- The narrator is *reliable* and *omniscient*: He serves as the voice and perspective of God.[32]
- The narration is *scenic*: The emphasis is on direct action and interaction of the characters rather than on descriptive detail of the environs.

---

29. C. S. Lewis, *The Discarded Image* (Cambridge: Cambridge University Press, 1964).

30. A classic example can be found in Meir Sternberg, *The Poetics of Biblical Narrative: Ideological Literature and the Drama of Reading* (Bloomington, IN: Indiana University Press, 1985); see further Robert Alter, *The Art of Biblical Narrative* (New York: Basic Books, 1981); and Jean-Louis Ska, *Our Fathers Have Told Us: Introduction to the Analysis of Hebrew Narratives* (Rome: Pontifical Biblical Institute, 1990).

31. V. Philips Long, *The Reign and Rejection of King Saul* (Atlanta: Scholars Press, 1989); see especially Long's section on "Selected Features of Hebrew Narrative Style," 21–41.

32. Traditionally the narrators are called "prophets"—that is, divinely approved spokespersons.

- The narratives are *sparsely written*: They focus on what is essential for the narrative.
- The author will use *Leitwortstil*: He will repeat a key word or word root to draw attention to thematic issues.
- The author employs *wordplay*, such as words or roots used with different meanings or words that sound alike; these are generally used for ironic contrasts.
- The author signals *heightened speech* using poetic diction: Elevated diction of a speech is evidence of its significance;[33] often oracular, it may even be divine speech.
- The author uses *repetition*, such as similar kinds of events and scenes in different circumstances.
- The author employs *analogy* and *contrast*, where the characters and scenes are like and unlike one another.

The result of these features is that, generally speaking, the author communicates his point of view by indirect and laconic means. The emphasis will be on *showing* (displaying the heart by action and speech) versus *telling* (explicitly stating what kind of person the character is).[34]

Further, Gordon Wenham has argued that faithful readers of the Hebrew stories are expected to engage actively, evaluating the actions of the characters for their adherence to the moral norms of the Mosaic covenant; that is, the act of reporting a set of deeds, even of a hero, does not imply endorsement of them.[35]

Hence, if we want to be good readers of biblical narratives, we will pay attention to, for example, how people speak: We will look for the relation between what they say and what they do, between what the narrator has reported and what the character reports, and between what someone says (or is told) he will say and what he does say. The biblical narrators show themselves fully aware that humans are sinful and that even the best have mixed motives and imperfect morality. Very few important biblical characters come away with a purely positive portrayal since the authors rarely intend to make heroes out of their characters.

---

33. This will often include poetic devices such as parallelism, chiasmus, artistic word order, and vocabulary choice.

34. This feature is not distinctive of the biblical narrators. In C. M. Bowra's study, *Heroic Poetry* (New York: Macmillan, 1952), we read that the narrative of heroic poetry celebrates great doings "not overtly by praise but indirectly by making them speak for themselves . . . This degree of independence and objectivity is due to the pleasure which most men take in a well-told tale and their dislike of having it spoiled by moralizing or instruction." See p. 4 for quotation.

35. Gordon Wenham, *Story as Torah: Reading Old Testament Narratives Ethically* (Grand Rapids: Baker, 2004).

Methods of literary interpretation have been refined in the time since Lewis, but these refinements do not overturn his basic literary judgment. In fact, Lewis employed roughly the same hermeneutic. For example, in the course of discussing those critics who reasoned (mistakenly, in Lewis's opinion) that since Milton portrayed Satan with such care in his *Paradise Lost*, then Milton must actually have identified with (and perhaps approved of) Satan's "sense of injured merit" that he expresses in one of his speeches, Lewis comments that Milton "did not foresee that his work would one day meet the disarming simplicity of critics who take for gospel things said by the father of falsehood in public speeches to his troops."[36] That is, Lewis attended to *showing* over *telling*—he also recognized that the narrator might not necessarily endorse what the characters say or do; the onus is on the audience to discern.

Now, one committed to the Jowett-esque style of limiting oneself to the actual words of the text might complain that the way of reading narrative that Long and Wenham advocate is artificial, or even worse *etic* rather than *emic*, an imposition from a foreign culture's way of reading in place of a natural reading from within the Hebrew culture. The complaint is worth addressing, but how shall we do so when we lack an ancient Hebrew manual for narratology? I suggest that we employ the rubrics used in philosophy of science for assessing the value of a theory. To be good, a theory must satisfy four criteria:

1. It covers all the data, without "fudging" (saving the phenomena).
2. Other things being equal, the theory that covers the data with the fewest possible complicating assumptions is preferable (Ockham's razor).
3. The theory is coherent both internally and with other things we have a right to believe.
4. The theory is fruitful, opening up fresh avenues of understanding.[37]

It is true that some modern scholars offer what they call a close reading, which seems too modern in its orientation (by systematic suspicion of *all* characters), but that does not nullify the careful argumentation of scholars like Long, Wenham, and Sternberg. Further, we will find that the fourth criterion, of fruitfulness, helps us. That is, with these tools we can explain how a later audience—such as Jesus or Paul—got the readings they did, as we

---

36. Lewis, *A Preface to Paradise Lost*, 98.
37. The first two of these are classical, and Lewis expounded them in his *Discarded Image* (Cambridge: Cambridge University Press, 1964), 14–15. Criterion 3 and 4 are adapted from Ian Barbour, *Religion in an Age of Science* (New York: HarperCollins, 1990), 34–35. Further, Michael Keas has refined these in his "Systematizing the Theoretical Virtues," *Synthese* (2017), doi:10.1007/s11229–017–1355–6.

will see in chapters 7 and 8 below. Indeed, it is possible that Jesus and Paul offered emic readings!

2.B.4 GENRE

Finally, Lewis contributed on another front. Scholars in literary, linguistic, and rhetorical studies have all discussed the kinds of texts one can encounter in a given language community. Terms to describe the different kinds of texts, along various dimensions of differences, include genre, register, and style.

For scholars in biblical studies, *genre* can be a catchall term for the literary form. However, scholars use the word inconsistently, and more factors than literary form are usually in play. For example, one commentary might say that the Psalms fit in the genre poetry and also in the genre hymnody. In the same context we might find a discussion whether the genre of a particular psalm is lament or thanksgiving. Some scholars indicate that Genesis as a whole fits into the genre of narrative and that a particular pericope within Genesis has the genre of genealogy.

This kind of usage is confusing. It stems from a failure to appreciate that the literary form is one dimension by which we classify texts but not the only one (or even the most salient one). In 1984 the rhetorician Carolyn Miller argued that "a rhetorically sound definition of genre must be centered not on the substance or the form of discourse but on the action it is used to accomplish."[38] She has here focused on the rhetorical, pragmatic, and social concerns. This is helpful, as a technical term ought to have only a small number of possible meanings. Since Miller also endorses Northrup Frye's dictum, "The study of genres has to be founded on the study of conventions," we might use her approach to think of a genre as, *A social and communicative act, with its associated linguistic, rhetorical, and literary conventions and expectations.* But we must admit that this rhetorical orientation for genre is not widely shared in biblical studies, and we may have to be content with using other terminology that makes explicit the various dimensions of a text in order to reduce confusion.[39]

---

38. Carolyn Miller, "Genre as Social Action," *QJS* 70 (1984): 151–67. See further Miller's update and reaffirmations, "Rhetorical Community: The Cultural Basis of Genre," in *Genre and the New Rhetoric*, ed. Aviva Freedman and Peter Medway (London: Taylor & Francis, 1994), 67–78, and "Genre as Social Action (1984), Revisited 30 Years Later (2014)," *Letras & Letras* 31:3 (2015): 56–72. See also Amy Devitt, "Integrating Rhetorical and Literary Theories of Genre," *College English* 62:6 (2000): 696–718; and Anis S. Bawarshi and Mary Jo Reiff, "Rhetorical Genre Studies," in *Genre: An Introduction to History, Theory, Research, and Pedagogy*, ed. Bawarshi and Reiff (West Lafayette, IN: Parlor Press, 2010), 78–104.

39. For example, Vern Poythress, in "Dealing with the Genre of Genesis and Its Opening Chapters," *WTJ* 78 (2016): 217–30, discusses genres "embedded within larger pieces of discourse that have their own

One of these additional dimensions that distinguish texts is *register*. This too is hard to define, although a language community recognizes it. It refers to the level of the language that is best suited to the subject matter and social function of the text. More technically,

> A register is a publicly recognized cluster of linguistic features (e.g., pronunciation, specific words, syntactic constructions, morphology, intonation patterns, sometimes also gestures) associated with particular cultural practices and types of people who engage in them (e.g., radio announcers, waiters, medical doctors, school teachers, street vendors, flight attendants).[40]

Not surprisingly, register and genre can be readily conflated. To the extent that there is a difference, "Registers impose constraints at the linguistic level of vocabulary and syntax, whereas genre constraints operate at the level of discourse structure."[41] Again, we have no guarantee that anyone in exegetical studies will use the terms with such distinctions in mind.

A further dimension of textual difference is *style*, another term with varied definitions.[42] Traditionally style has been used for what makes a particular author or speaker distinct from others and thus the focus has been on the author's choices. But we may fruitfully recognize that some authors, especially those working in an established tradition (such as we typically see in ancient literature), follow and adapt the conventions that they have been given; radical originality is not always a virtue in such settings, and rhetorical invention has limits. The author makes his style suit the literary form, social setting, and register, which are given by his culture.[43]

As Lewis notes, the mind of the ancient world inclined to the sentiment, "What is the point of having a poet, inspired by the Muse, if he tells the stories just as you or I would have told them?"[44] He goes on to celebrate

---

genre." See p. 223 for quotation. Poythress has given one reasonable way of dealing with the problem I am discussing here, but I am offering an alternative, which I hope lowers the potential confusion.

40. Alessandro Duranti, "Linguistic Anthropology," in *The Cambridge Handbook of Sociolinguistics*, ed. Rajend Mesthrie (Cambridge: Cambridge University Press, 2011), 28–46, quote on p. 42.

41. Anna Trosburg, "Text Typology: Register, Genre and Text Type," in *Text Typology and Translation*, ed. Trosburg (Amsterdam: Benjamins, 1997), 3–23.

42. For a newer discussion, see Brian Ray, *Style: An Introduction to History, Theory, Research, and Pedagogy* (West Lafayette, IN: Parlor, 2014).

43. As Arnold Zwicky and Ann Zwicky note, "The distinction between style and register is not always an easy one to draw"; see their essay, "Register as a Dimension of Linguistic Variation," in *Sublanguage: Studies of Language in Restricted Semantic Domains*, ed. Richard Kittredge and John Lehrberger (Berlin: de Gruyter, 1982), 213–18.

44. Lewis, *A Preface to Paradise Lost*, 20.

language that is constrained by the audiences' expectations, as appropriate to the social setting and use of a classic epic (and perhaps of a text like Genesis, as we shall see):

> Epic diction, Christmas fare, and the liturgy, are all examples of ritual—that is, of something set deliberately apart from daily usage, but wholly familiar within its own sphere. . . . It is a pattern imposed on the mere flux of our feelings by reason and will, which renders pleasures less fugitive and griefs more endurable, which hands over to the power of wise custom the task (to which the individual and his moods are so inadequate) of being festive or sober, gay or reverent, when we choose to be, and not at the bidding of chance.[45]

The sum of all this is that we recognize with Chaim Rabin, "Texts are of different kinds (*Textsorten*), largely corresponding to social conventions dictating different varieties of one and the same language to be employed in circumscribed social situations"—and this will apply to literary forms, registers, and styles.[46]

In summary, Lewis is my guide in employing rhetoric, linguistic pragmatics, sociolinguistics, and literary criticism as aspects of a particular kind of human behavior—namely, the goal of shaping the likes and dislikes of the members of a community. Since terminology can get cumbersome, I will use "rhetoric" as my general word for what I am pursuing. With these orienting notions, we move on to appropriate one of Lewis's contributions to a rhetorical-pragmatic-sociolinguistic matter.

---

45. Ibid., 20–21.
46. Chaim Rabin, "Discourse Analysis and the Dating of Deuteronomy," in *Interpreting the Hebrew Bible: Essays in Honour of E. I. J. Rosenthal*, ed. J. A. Emerton and Stefan C. Reif (Cambridge: Cambridge University Press, 1982), 171–177, quote on p. 173. While Rabin defines register, the overall idea applies more widely.

Chapter 3

TYPES OF LANGUAGE AND BIBLICAL INTERPRETATION

What do we mean when we speak about the meaning of a sentence or text? Can we discern the meaning simply from the form of words that an author has used, or is there more to it than that? Linguists and rhetoricians have been busy with this subject; to their discussions I will add some insights from an unfinished and under-appreciated essay by C. S. Lewis.

3.A SPEECH ACT THEORY AND BIBLICAL RHETORIC

In chapter 2 I mentioned the field of linguistic pragmatics, which is the study of how people use language to accomplish effects. The particular subfield of pragmatics called speech act theory has recognized that in every utterance (or text) we can identify three aspects:

Locution: the actual form of words spoken;
Illocution: the intended effect of those words (on beliefs, actions, attitudes);
Perlocution: the actual effect of the words.[1]

For example, a father might ask his children during the evening, "Do you know what time it is?" The form and words of the question provides what we call the **locution**, and if the locution made up the entire communication, the proper reply would be "yes" or "no." Most people know quite well that this

---

1. Joan Cutting, *Pragmatics and Discourse: A Resource Book for Students* (London: Routledge, 2002), 15–23, provides a helpful survey of speech act theory, including a frank awareness of its limitations (which are primarily simplistic applications of the theories).

kind of reply would be, in most cases, uncooperative; according to context, the desired reply would be something along the lines of, "It is eight o'clock" or "My goodness, we should go watch the baseball game!" or even, "Yes, Dad, I'm almost finished with my homework and I'll be getting to bed soon." The **illocution**, then, would be the goal of eliciting the desired reply and its associated actions (look at the clock, put on the television show, close the book, etc.) and attitudes. The response Dad received is the **perlocution**; and the communication event is successful if the actual and desired responses match to an adequate extent.

Although the exact terms locution, illocution, and perlocution may seem to be an innovation, there is nothing mysterious about the distinction. Educated people have known for ages about rhetorical questions. In such a case the locution (the form of the question) is a way of eliciting a behavioral response from an audience. Probably most questions in the Bible are of this sort: "For if you love those who love you, what reward do you have? Do not even the tax collectors do the same?" (Matt 5:46) is not a request for information but a device to shape the disciples' way of leaning into their world, to define their community identity with a certain set of likes and dislikes. By the same token, our default guess about God's questions (e.g., in Gen 3:9, 11; 4:9—see ch. 7 below) is that they too are rhetorical—which means that the questions intend to offer the hearers an opportunity to do something, more than they express actual ignorance.

We have also long known about other tropes or rhetorical figures, such as (apparent) *paradox* ("the last will be first, and the first last," Matt 20:16; "washed their robes and made them white in the blood of the Lamb," Rev 7:14); *metonymy* ("the house of David"); *personification* ("When the waters saw you, they were afraid," Ps 77:16); *hyperbole* ("specks" and "logs," Matt 7:3–5); *adynaton* ("it is easier for a camel to go through the eye of a needle than for a rich person to enter the kingdom of God," Matt 19:24); and *sarcasm* ("Present that to your governor!" Mal 1:8).[2] Each trope has its own effect, which an audience is expected to discern.

We can also find a sarcastic insult in the Bible, and failure to appreciate it led to amusing results. The prophet Ezekiel must pass on to the inhabitants of Jerusalem in his day this saying from God (Ezek 16:3):

> Your origin and your birth are of the land of the Canaanites; your father was an Amorite and your mother a Hittite.

---

2. Classifying and defining the rhetorical tropes has a long tradition in Greco-Roman culture, but such tropes are not limited to these cultures, as the biblical examples show. For an entertaining and enlightening catalog of tropes, see Mark Forsyth, *The Elements of Eloquence: Secrets of the Perfect Turn of Phrase* (New York: Berkley Publishing, 2013).

In context, the prophet is telling a racy parable about Jerusalem as a faithless bride to Yahweh. He likens them to a castaway baby girl, left to die of exposure: "no eye pitied you," but the Lord passed by and rescued her and raised her, eventually taking her as a bride (vv. 4–7).

The declaration of heritage, then, serves the imagery of an exposed and unwanted child and fits into the category of insult or verbal abuse.[3] Cooperation in such case would involve the people accepting God's portrayal of them as pathetically helpless as well as repenting of the ingratitude with which they have responded to his initiatives. That is, the text offers no kind of assertion about the actual genealogy of either Israel as a whole or Jerusalem in particular. The premier Semiticist G. R. Driver, however, missed the sarcasm and took the text as implying an ethnically mixed ancestry for the Hebrews, which thus encouraged him to posit that the Hebrew language was a mixture of various strands (including the non-Semitic Hittite). A Cambridge University PhD student, Leslie McFall, whose thesis was a critical review of various theories of the Hebrew verbal system, was obliged to treat Driver's argument with due seriousness; in his analysis of Driver's rationale (which he rejects, rightly as I judge), he gives no evidence of perceiving that Ezekiel has used a sarcastic insult, which supplies no information about supposed Hebrew traditions of their origins.[4] The key point: *literalism about the locution produced no useful results.*

Another likely example of sarcasm that some have missed, with odd results, comes from Titus 1:12, a passage ostensibly from Paul to his disciple Titus:

> One of the Cretans, a prophet of their own, said, "Cretans are always liars, evil beasts, lazy gluttons."

The quotation has been attributed to Epimenides, a philosopher and poet from Crete (seventh–sixth century BC), in a context in which the people of Crete speak unreliably about a religious matter.[5] Some have reasoned that calling the gentile Epimenides a "prophet" means that the term *prophet* in the New

---

3. In linguistic pragmatics, this would fall under the rubric of impoliteness. See Jonathan Culpeper, "Towards an Anatomy of Impoliteness," *Journal of Pragmatics* 25 (1996): 349–67. See also Giuseppe Lentini, "The Pragmatics of Verbal Abuse in Homer," in *The Rhetoric of Abuse in Greek Literature*, ed. H. Tell (Issue 11 [2013] of the open access journal *Classics@* (Center for Hellenic Studies, Harvard). Culpeper notes that this area of study is "much neglected" (p. 366). While his sentiment might be true of scholarly study in linguistics, most people have an intuitive grasp of how such "impoliteness" (with sarcasm) works.

4. G. R. Driver, *Problems of the Hebrew Verbal System* (Edinburgh: T&T Clark, 1936), 151; Leslie McFall, *The Enigma of the Hebrew Verbal System* (Sheffield: Almond Press, 1982), 136–37.

5. See John Chrysostom, *Homilies on Titus*, Homily 3, attributing the snippet in Acts 17:28 to the same source.

Testament involves lesser authority than the same term in the Old.[6] Others suggest the sentiment, throwing "ethnic slurs at Cretans," is one in a list of moral defects of the New Testament.[7] However, the surface self-contradiction of the statement, with a Cretan declaring Cretans to be liars, clues us in to the sarcastic humor. Thus, calling Epimenides a prophet is to be taken as irony employing an *arguendo* concession: "the fellow *they* call a prophet." As E. K. Simpson wrote,

> The title of *prophet* clung to Epimenides throughout Greek literature; it is endorsed by Plato. The commentators take the term quite seriously; but we cannot help surmising that Paul wrote 'a prophet of their own' with a twinkle in his eye. For he has them on the horns of a dilemma. . . .[8]

Some mildly sardonic playfulness to relieve the stresses Titus faced in ministering in a difficult environment seems harmless enough; these other, more literalistic, interpretations seem to have missed the point of the text. Certainly, the text offers no information on the lexical range of the word *prophet* (still less in other contexts), nor does it provide an index to anyone's ethnic attitudes. The rest of the letter assumes a firm expectation that members of the church in Crete can and will attain to exemplary Christian character.

Let me add one final example to help us appreciate that our rhetorical discussion is well-established and intuitive. Consider what happens in Isaiah 38:1–6:

> In those days Hezekiah became sick and was at the point of death. And Isaiah the prophet the son of Amoz came to him, and said to him, "Thus says the LORD: Set your house in order, for you shall die, you shall not recover." Then Hezekiah turned his face to the wall and prayed to the LORD, and said, "Please, O LORD, remember how I have walked before you in faithfulness and with a whole heart, and have done what is good in your sight." And Hezekiah wept bitterly.

---

6. So, Wayne Grudem, *The Gift of Prophecy in the New Testament and Today* (Wheaton, IL: Crossway, 2000), 39.

7. Kenton Sparks, *Sacred Word, Broken Word: Biblical Authority and the Dark Side of Scripture* (Grand Rapids: Eerdmans, 2012), 71.

8. E. K. Simpson, *The Pastoral Epistles: The Greek Text with Introduction and Commentary* (London: Tyndale Press, 1954), 100 (emphasis original). See also John Stott, *The Message of 1 Timothy and Titus* (Downers Grove, IL: InterVarsity Press, 1996), 181.

Then the word of the Lord came to Isaiah: "Go and say to Hezekiah, 'Thus says the Lord, the God of David your father: I have heard your prayer; I have seen your tears. Behold, I will add fifteen years to your life. I will deliver you and this city out of the hand of the king of Assyria, and will defend this city.'"

The locution (v. 1) is a straightforward command built on a simple prediction about the future. The perlocution, however, is not compliance but prayer (vv. 2–3). From the divine approval (vv. 4–6), we may infer the illocution, namely, that God actually intended for Hezekiah to appeal for a different outcome. (Actually, Hezekiah's appeal is itself indirect, mentioning his faithfulness as an implied ground for God to reconsider.) Most people are familiar with such gambits: the threat or promise, in the form of a bare prediction, has an unstated, "condition unless something relevant changes," and the goal of issuing the bare prediction is to elicit the response. The Scottish Old Testament scholar Patrick Fairbairn (1805–1874) helpfully employed such reasoning to his understanding of biblical prophecy, arguing for criteria by which we can discern whether specific promises or threats are inherently conditional or unconditional, regardless of whether explicit conditions are laid out.[9] This finds confirmation in the way that Jeremiah's persecutors recall an unfulfilled threat from more than a century earlier: Judah had perceived the illocution and averted the fulfillment by their repentance (Jer 26:17–19, drawing on Mic 3:12).

We might likewise apply these ideas to the seeming problem that arises from the apostle Paul having "resolved in the Spirit to pass through Macedonia and Achaia and go to Jerusalem" (Acts 19:21).[10] While along the way, various Christian disciples "through the Spirit were telling Paul *not* to go on to Jerusalem" (Acts 21:4), and, in response to a prophet's warning about impending imprisonment, "we and the people there urged him *not* to go up to Jerusalem" (Acts 21:12). One might wonder whether the sources of Acts disagree with one another; or, more darkly, whether these narratives

---

9. Patrick Fairbairn, *Prophecy Viewed in Its Distinctive Nature, Its Special Functions, and Proper Interpretation* (Edinburgh: T&T Clark, 1865), 58–82 (republished in 1964 by Banner of Truth as *The Interpretation of Prophecy*). Fairbairn shows a good instinctive grasp of many other rhetorical features of the biblical prophets (such as poetic elevation, foreshortening, idealization) in his discussion of "The Prophetic Style and Diction" (83–181) and repays sympathetic reading. His detailed exegetical section (Part II), however, is quite dated.

10. The Greek construction makes it clear that the trip to Jerusalem was the focus of Paul's resolve: ἔθετο ὁ Παῦλος ἐν τῷ πνεύματι διελθὼν τὴν Μακεδονίαν καὶ Ἀχαΐαν πορεύεσθαι εἰς Ἱεροσόλυμα places the passing through Macedonia (the participle διελθών) as the enabling action to Jerusalem (with the infinitive πορεύεσθαι, complementing the verb ἔθετο).

portray the Spirit as fickle or even deceptive. Or, perhaps the human parties were mistaken about what the Spirit was telling them. Conversation analysis—an aspect of linguistic pragmatics—comes to our aid. All of these other suggestions, depending on the locution alone, raise more questions than they answer. We do better to recall that in ordinary interactions we issue challenges in the locutionary form of a prediction. "Jumping that high will hurt you badly when you land" can often serve as a test of the jumper's resolve or even a spur for the jumper to prove the speaker wrong.[11] Here, the effect is to ensure that Paul has counted the cost of his plan to go to Jerusalem and to have him display his willingness to bear even the utmost cost to fulfill his calling (as Paul himself insists in Acts 20:24; 21:13). That this was the illocution becomes clear when we see how the disciples, upon seeing Paul's response (the perlocution), acquiesce (Acts 21:14).[12] Indeed, Paul apparently portrays his arrival at Rome as the fulfillment of Agabus's warning: just as Paul would be "bound" and "delivered into the hands of the Gentiles" (21:11), so he came to Rome in "bonds," having been delivered into the hands of the Romans (28:17).

I suspect that this approach, of ascertaining the illocution by observing responses to the perlocution, would help us in our consideration of the Pentateuch passages about exterminating the Canaanites (e.g., Deut 7:1–5; 20:16–18), which sound utterly uncompromising: "save alive nothing that breathes" (Deut 20:16). In the carrying out, however, the people of Israel *do* spare some of these inhabitants, such as the family of Rahab (Josh 6:22–25) and the Gibeonite coalition (Josh 9:17–21). These people are incorporated into Israel: according to tradition, Rahab became the mother of Boaz, the hero in Ruth (Matt 1:5), while to cut wood and draw water for the sanctuary (Josh 9:27) is a privileged task. That is, the perlocution, of sparing certain persons who respond positively to the Lord, receives commendation; the sparing of others, however, receives condemnation (Judg 2:12). The difference apparently lies in the reason for sparing.[13] Now, this does not settle the question of whether it was right in the first place to invade Canaan, but since

---

11. Compare Joshua's warning to the assembled people, "You are not able to serve the LORD" (Josh 24:19), which has the air of an athletic coach or drill sergeant declaring, "You are not able to run that 5K course."

12. Perhaps another factor is how Acts evokes the model of Socrates, who preferred to obey God rather than man (see Acts 5:29 and Plato, *Apology*, 29*d*—a resemblance noted by Eusebius in his *Praep. ev.*, 662-*c*). Charles Talbert, *Reading Acts: A Literary and Theological Commentary on the Acts of the Apostles* (New York: Crossroad, 1997), suggests some Socratic parallels with the presentation of Paul in Athens (pp. 158–60) as well as "Socrates' resistance of his followers' pleas to avoid his death—Plato, *Phaedo*, 116E–117A" (p. 191).

13. A recent study that takes this line (though without the linguistic apparatus) is William Ford, "What about the Gibeonites?" *TynBul* 66:2 (2015): 197–216.

I am not writing an apologetic, I leave that aside. Attention to the rhetorical side of things, however, allows us more clearly to see what we will either defend or denounce.

Users of rhetoric have also long known the power of *understatement*. If you were in Rome in 49 BC and someone told you, "Julius Caesar has led his army across the Rubicon," you would both accept the information and react with dread or joy, and perhaps you would either take up arms or flee (depending on your loyalties and social position). You would be thought cold or even defective if you stopped with receiving the information.

To be sure, it has not always been easy to identify tropes, and it always involves a judgment call. For example, researchers from the Department of Communication Science at the Free University of Amsterdam undertook to make hyperbole detection a rigorous procedure; they called their result "the Hyperbole Identification Procedure"—and even gave it an acronym, HIP. The actual principle is almost self-evident, inherent in the definition: "our operational definition of hyperbole as '*an expression that is more extreme than justified given its ontological referent.*'"[14]

Alan Millard, familiar with historiographical conventions from the ancient Near East, suggests that hyperbole is well-attested, and there is no reason to resist finding it in the Bible:

> To speak of Solomon's wealth as so great that silver had no value, "as common in Jerusalem as stones" (1 Kgs 10:27), is oriental hyperbole of exactly the same sort as the assertions by indigent Mesopotamian kings who wrote to the Pharaoh, "Gold is like dust in your land, one simply scoops it up" (El Amarna Letters 16, 19, 20, 29). The writers were describing unusual riches in phrases that convey the thought clearly enough, without demanding a literal interpretation.[15]

The Christian pastor John Stott (1921–2011) serves as an example of someone using good sense in the way he intuitively discerns some of the rhetorical tropes in the Bible. In his popular commentary on the Sermon on the Mount,[16] he identified a paradox in the form of the Beatitudes: "Happy

---

14. Christian Burgers, Britta Brugman, Kiki Renardel de Lavalette, and Gerard Steen, "HIP: A Method for Linguistic Hyperbole Identification in Discourse," *Metaphor and Symbol* 31:3 (2016): 163–78, quote on p. 166 (emphasis original).

15. A. R. Millard, "Story, History, and Theology," in *Faith, Tradition, and History: Old Testament Historiography in its Near Eastern Context*, ed. A. R. Millard, James K. Hoffmeier, and David W. Baker (Winona Lake, IN: Eisenbrauns, 1994), 37–64, quote on p. 49.

16. John R. W. Stott, *Christian Counter-culture: The Message of the Sermon on the Mount* (Downers Grove, IL: InterVarsity Press, 1978).

(blessed) are the unhappy" (on Matt 5:4). Its function is to draw attention to the way Jesus "contradicted all human judgments."[17] He also recognized, without using the terms, that the instruction "do not let your left hand know what your right hand is doing" (Matt 6:3) is either hyperbole or adynaton: "Of course it is not possible to obey this command of Jesus in precise literalness."[18] As a final example, he rightly recognizes the paradox presented by "the gate is narrow and the way is hard that leads to life" (Matt 7:14), in comparison with "my yoke is easy and my burden is light" (Matt 11:30):

> And in a sense this is "hard." Yet in another sense, as Chrysostom pointed out centuries ago, Christ's hard and narrow way is also to be welcomed as his "easy yoke" and "light burden."[19]

Responsibility lies with the discerning audience to ascertain which of the senses is in focus in the separate passages; that is, the passages do not address speculative or theoretical questions but instead address different aspects of what it means to follow Jesus—sometimes the disciple is mostly aware of the hard and uncompromising claim Jesus makes and at other times of the tender care that Jesus promises.

In his commentary on the Letters of John, Stott notices the relationship between the author and his audience: "So John can call those to whom he writes both his 'little children,' which indicates his authority as well as his age, and his 'brethren,' on an equal footing with them."[20] That is an intuitive and effective appreciation of the rhetorical situation.

The classicist-turned-biblical-scholar F. F. Bruce (1910–1990) likewise shows an intuitive awareness of how this works. In the course of explaining his take on a well-known interpretive challenge in the letters of John (1 John 3:6, "No one who abides in him keeps on sinning; no one who keeps on sinning has either seen him or known him"), he offers the following:

> In saying that no one who "abides" in him sins, John is not asserting that it is impossible for a believer to commit an occasional act of sin. He has already pointed to the provision made for such an emergency by means of confession (1.9) and Christ's activity as His people's Advocate (2.1 f.), and has warned his readers against unfounded claims to be

---

17. Stott, *Christian Counter-Culture*, 40.
18. Ibid., 130.
19. Ibid., 194.
20. John R. W. Stott, *The Epistles of John*, Tyndale New Testament Commentaries (Grand Rapids: Eerdmans, 1964), 33. Stott also discusses "The Author's Self-Conscious Authority" (pp. 34–35).

sinless within or without (1.8, 10).... When a boy goes to a new school, he may inadvertently do something out of keeping with the school's tradition or good name, to be told immediately, "That isn't done here." A literalist might reply, "But obviously it *is* done; this boy has just done it"—but he would be deliberately missing the point of the rebuke.[21]

Bruce, the classicist, was addressing what he would likely have called the rhetorical relationship between the words and their intended effect; a linguist would call it the relationship between the locution and illocution. He invokes a principle of assumed consistency in referring to what the letter writer had already said. He also notes how a simple declarative sentence, which has the appearance of a description, can actually function as providing an identity for a community (here a British boys' school of the early twentieth century),[22] a set of ideals and aspirations to govern the community's behavior. The literalist reply is actually non-cooperation. Bruce has used interpretive moves familiar to us from everyday experience.

Stott also shows an intuitive awareness of how situational context functions: the words and sentences of a discourse (including a sacred one) mean what they do in reference to the situation the words address. Stott explains why John would say "But you have been anointed [lit., you have an anointing, Gk. *chrisma*] by the Holy One, and you all have knowledge [Gk. *gnōsis*]" (1 John 2:20):

> It is probable that they [namely, the opponents] used the word *chrisma* as a technical term for initiation into a special *gnōsis*. If so, it is in direct contradiction to their exclusive claim that John says *all* his readers have the same *gnōsis* because they have all received the same *chrisma*.[23]

Neither Stott nor Bruce is fully consistent in his application of these ideas. I suggest that is because it was intuitive for them more than it was critical. In aiming at an overall critically intuitive approach, I am seeking just the rigor and consistency that I find occasionally wanting in their overall work.

I am not minimizing the value of contemporary linguistics by saying that we have long known these things. Linguistic studies put the intuitions on a sound intellectual footing and refine the intuitions. However, these intuitions

---

21. F. F. Bruce, *The Epistles of John* (Grand Rapids: Eerdmans, 1970), 90.
22. Bruce presents the boys' school experience in a much more positive light than Lewis ever did. Fortunately, we need not judge either of them in order to get the point.
23. Stott, *Epistles of John*, 107.

about rhetoric were available to Jowett and those who follow his methods and therefore provide common ground for evaluation.

A key to communication, then, is to ascertain the relationship between the locution and the illocution, and to do this well requires both a social and cultural awareness (such as children learn in a household or school) and a cooperation between speaker and hearer. In this cooperation the speaker must provide enough clues to his intentions, and the audience should be willing to go beyond the mere form of words, and to do so with enough sympathy with the speaker to perceive what he or she wants—*compliance* with the speaker's intentions, of course, is another matter.

We find places where Bible writers bring the need for this kind of cooperation to the surface, and sometimes the author even draws attention to it. Consider, for example, 2 Timothy 2:4–7:

> No soldier gets entangled in civilian pursuits, since his aim is to please the one who enlisted him. An athlete is not crowned unless he competes according to the rules. It is the hard-working farmer who ought to have the first share of the crops. Think over what I say, for the Lord will give you understanding in everything.

"Think over what I say" in order to go from the locution to the illocution; by way, first, of analogy (How is my situation like that of the soldier, athlete, and farmer here?) and then of action (What does he want me to aspire for and to do?).

One more item from linguistics and rhetoric will finish laying the groundwork for this chapter. Lexical semantics describes the meaning of a word in terms of its *reference* and *sense*. The *reference* is the thing the word is about (a tree, a man, a deity), while the *sense* is the dictionary definition of the word. The referent can be part of what is acknowledged to be the real world (e.g., England or God) but can also be part of a fictional world (e.g., Aragorn or Narnia).[24]

Some authors describe sense in terms of information the speaker or author is supplying about the referent. It gives us more insight into communication, however, to describe sense in terms of rhetoric or illocution—that is, by using a particular sense a speaker aims to shape the stance that the audience takes toward the referent. For example, a particular referent might be a middle-aged male teacher of biblical studies with traditionalist beliefs. A speaker

---

24. Lewis shows his practical grasp of this principle in lexical semantics when he writes of "the word's meaning" (=sense) and "the speaker's meaning" (=referent) in *Studies in Words*, 14–17.

might refer to him as "a person," "a man," "that man," or "the fundamentalist professor"—and each of these differing designations, with their differing senses, represents a differing illocutionary goal. In careful discourse, these differing senses are less concerned with what the speaker thinks and more with how he wants his audience to think about the referent.[25] For example, as Stott helpfully notes, Paul applies terms in Romans 1:7 ("to all those in Rome who are *loved by God* and *called* to be *saints*") to a mixed congregation of Jewish and gentile believers with a rhetorical motivation:

> Since "beloved," "called" and "saints" were all Old Testament epithets for Israel, it seems probable that Paul deliberately uses them here to indicate that all believers in Christ, Gentiles as well as Jews, now belong to the covenant people of God.[26]

Sometimes, of course, the means of referring is conventional, and the conventionality is part of the communicative intention. In such cases of conventional reference, the rhetorical force is invisible—that is, the audience is invited to attend to the referent without any strong affirmation of the means of referring. For example, competent English speakers recognize that "the four corners of the earth" is conventional and waste no time wondering whether the earth really has four corners.

Now we can appreciate the remarks that I cited in chapter 1, from Charles Goodwin, Benjamin Jowett, and James Barr, which stressed the primacy of what they called "the plain sense," "natural meaning," or "literal interpretation" of biblical passages. From a linguistic point of view, they were equating their desired approach with a literalistic take on the locution. Our discussion here paves the way for assessing whether this equation is adequate. I suggest that it is not, and that the equation (ironically) stands in the way of receiving the pragmatically plain sense of the biblical text.

3.B LEWIS'S ESSAY, "THE LANGUAGE OF RELIGION"

3.B.1 EXPOSITION OF LEWIS'S ARGUMENT

I have mentioned the task of ascertaining the relationship between the locution and the illocution and some of what that involves. But we must also

---

25. For this reason it is a mistake to argue, as the linguist Greg Thomson does, that "sense" is dispensable in translation, so long as we convey the referent. See Thomson, "What Sort of Meaning is Preserved in Translation? Part Two: Sense," *Notes on Translation* 3:1 (1989): 26–49. His orientation is highly cognitive, and thus he misses how the sense is actually a pragmatic-rhetorical issue.

26. John R. W. Stott, *The Message of Romans* (Grand Rapids: InterVarsity Press, 1994), 55–56.

take into account what kind of language use we find in the locution. Is it low or high? Is it technical or lay? Is it conversational or pedantic—that is, what is the register and style? What relationship between speaker and audience seems to lie behind it? What degree of detail does the speaker expect the audience to apply, and what background knowledge does he or she intend for them to invoke? An essay that Lewis never finished, "The Language of Religion," can help us.[27] The essay expands some of the material Lewis had contributed to *The Personal Heresy*.[28]

Lewis invites us to consider the following three sentences:

1. It was very cold.
2. There were thirteen degrees of frost.
3. Ah, bitter chill it was!
   The owl, for all his feathers, was a-cold;
   the hare limped trembling through the frozen grass,
   and silent was the flock in wooly fold:
   numb'd were the Beadsman's fingers. [29]

Each of these sentences describes a winter night, but they do so in different ways. The first sentence is what we can call "ordinary language"—it is how English speakers talk in regular, day-to-day speech. The second sentence is what we can call "scientific," because it is what people need when they are concerned with measurements that can be tested with an instrument; it allows them to predict various effects of the cold on the animals and plants. The third sentence is "poetic": it conveys more of what it would be like to experience that cold night.

---

27. C. S. Lewis, "The Language of Religion," in *Christian Reflections*, ed. Walter Hooper (Grand Rapids: Eerdmans, 1967), 129–41. Hooper found the previously unpublished manuscript among Lewis's papers and was unable to date it. Two pages have gone missing from the original, though the argument survives. Possibly this was a draft for a book on the nature, function, and origin of language that Lewis had planned to write with J. R. R. Tolkien. See Humphrey Carpenter, *Tolkien: A Biography* (Boston: Houghton Mifflin, 1977), 199. Lewis's analysis, though truncated, is more helpful than an essay with similar concerns: Paul Fueter, "The Therapeutic Language of the Bible," *International Review of Mission* 75 (1986): 211–21 (also published in *BT* 37: 3 [1986]: 309–19). Fueter puts the "digital" (informational, scientific) into too stark a contrast with the "analogical" (poetic, experiential), to the advantage of the analogical (without enough consideration of what purposes each kind serves).

28. C. S. Lewis, *The Personal Heresy* (Oxford: Oxford University Press, 1939).

29. In the second sentence, thirteen degrees of frost means thirteen degrees (°Fahrenheit for Lewis) below freezing, or 19°F (about −7.2°C). For a sense of its scientific feel for Lewis, see, for example, Andrew White Tuer's 1887 book, *The First Year of a Silken Reign (1837–8)* (London: Field & Tuer, 1887): "On the 12th the thermometer registered thirteen degrees of frost" (p. 83). The third excerpt above comes from John Keats' poem, "The Eve of St Agnes" (1819; St Agnes's Eve is January 20).

Lewis illustrates that the scientific and the poetic languages are specialized uses of the ordinary language:

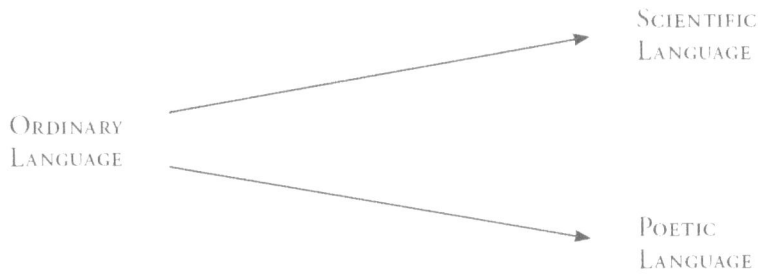

What are the features of these kinds of language? The distinguishing feature of ordinary language is that its level of detail is adequate for the communication at hand—that is, we are happy to use round numbers and so on. Further, it is *phenomenological*—that is, we speak in terms of what things look like, without making much of a claim about the inner workings of the referents. We may say of the sun that it rises, or of a rain storm that the windows of heaven are opened, or of our children's shoes that they are getting too small for their feet. When Strider leads the Hobbits toward Weathertop, Tolkien notes, "The hills drew nearer."[30] It does not follow that we necessarily believe that this is literally how the events work; we rightly get irritated with someone who interprets our words this closely.

Scientific language aims at a high level of detail with as little ambiguity as possible and seeks to explain the inner workings of what it describes. It is not enough to say that a cut healed; it is important to detail what the cells do and which ones do what, by what means, and how fast. We may therefore call it *analytical*, because it is interested in distinctions.

Poetic language aims to allow the reader to imagine what it was like to see what it describes—even if what it describes is not real and even if we have no experience of the referent. As Lewis put it,

> This is the most remarkable of the powers of Poetic language: to convey to us the quality of experiences which we have not had, or perhaps can never have, to use factors within our experience so that they become pointers to something outside our experience.[31]

---

30. J. R. R. Tolkien, *The Fellowship of the Ring: Being the First Part of the Lord of the Rings* (Boston: Houghton Mifflin, 1965), chapter 11. The Modern Hebrew version (Tel Aviv: Zmora, Bitan, Modan, 1976) makes the phenomenal expression even stronger, הגבעות התקרבו והלכו *haggebaʿot hitqarebu wehaleku*, "the hills were drawing themselves near."

31. Lewis, "The Language of Religion," 133.

To achieve this, poetic language tends to be more *imagistic* than ordinary language. Often its level of detail is higher than ordinary and sometimes even than scientific (as in the three sample sentences above), but those details are there to convey the quality of the experience. These literary and linguistic features serve the communicative purposes of the poetic text: to celebrate what it describes, to mourn over it, to enjoy the description, to enable the audience to see and feel things differently, and so on.

We may fill out our chart thus:

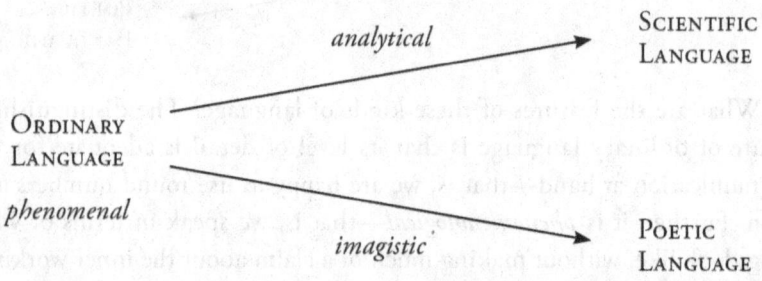

We must avoid some common misconceptions. For example, we ought not suppose that the scientific language is more literal in the sense that it lacks metaphor. Indeed, all our talk about anything beyond immediate sense experience is metaphorical,[32] and philosophers of science are well aware of the role of "models" (a kind of metaphor) in scientific theories.[33]

Further, we ought not imagine that poetic language is in itself any less referential than ordinary or scientific. That is, a poem can be about something in the external world just as much as a scientific description can be. Many wrongly assume that because poetry involves emotion it therefore expresses emotion for its own sake and thus is limited in what it can say about the real world. The truth, however, is as Lewis put it: "Poetic language often expresses emotion not for its own sake but in order to inform us about the object which aroused the emotion."[34] Any of these language types can express and arouse emotion, so that cannot be the distinctive province of the poetic. For example, Lewis asks us to imagine the non-poetical sentence, "Fifty Russian divisions landed in the South of England this morning," which would certainly have

---

32. Compare C. S. Lewis, "Bluspels and Flalanspheres: A Semantic Nightmare," in *Selected Literary Essays* (Cambridge: Cambridge University Press, 1969), 251–65. "When we pass beyond pointing to individual sensible objects, when we begin to think of causes, relations, of mental states or acts, we become incurably metaphorical" (p. 263).

33. For brief remarks on the place of models in science, see Ian Barbour, *Religion in an Age of Science* (San Francisco: HarperSanFrancisco, 1990), 41–45; C. John Collins, *Science and Faith: Friends or Foes?* (Wheaton, IL: Crossway, 2003), 43, 47.

34. Lewis, "The Language of Religion," 131.

an effect. As he laconically observed, "Momentous matter, if believed, will arouse emotion whatever the language."[35]

The case is similar with ordinary language: The mere fact that in an ordinary description we have not specified all the details of the inner workings of the events (such as the relative movements of the earth and sun when we speak of a sunrise) hardly means that we have not spoken about a real event. In the next chapter I will take up the question of in what way a particular kind of language involves a commitment on the speaker's part to some conception of these inner workings.

The distinctions between these language uses stem from the communicative purposes to which we put the language. It would thus be foolish to ask which of these uses is best—we must ask in return, best for what? For a man to express affection to his children, ordinary language is probably the best; to tell his wife how much he loves her, he would do well to wax poetic. If, on the other hand, a physician is diagnosing an ailment and needs to communicate to a pharmacist how much of which medication a patient should take, then he or she will find the scientific description best.

Consider another example. One evening, shortly after a bathroom in my house was remodeled, my wife remarked that the bathroom walls change color depending on whether the light source is sunlight or the new light fixture. Since both she and I have advanced scientific educations, I began to chide her for such an inaccurate way of putting it: Surely, she should talk about the differing proportions of light frequencies in the two sources. She answered with, "And I am looking forward to the sun rising tomorrow." The implication was clear: I should have recognized that she was fully capable of being scientific and that she was being phenomenological. The fact that I was chiding meant that I was not cooperating with her intent. I was not listening: the defect was in *me*, not in *her*.

3.B.2 Extension of Lewis's Analysis

It is no fault of Lewis's article that it does not consider sociolinguistic factors. Lewis did not address how these different language levels can serve differing social and rhetorical purposes, but we can enrich our appropriation of Lewis's ideas by adding these factors in.

Consider what happens if we use a poetic statement: We are probably implying that the subject matter deserves the extra effort it takes to work through the imagery. This is likely the case in Proverbs 5:15–20, where the

---

35. Ibid., 136.

father urges his son, "Drink water from your own cistern." It is only as we keep reading and meet the imagery halfway that we can discern that the water source here (cistern, well, springs, streams) is a figure for the young man's wife, particularly viewed from the perspective of sensual enjoyment. Then it becomes clear how the question in verse 16 ("Should your springs be scattered abroad?") is functioning: If the wife is the water source, no sensible man would want her to share herself sexually with other men. Once we see that, the whole passage becomes a poetical form of "do as you would be done by"—a man should show the same faithfulness to his wife as he expects her to show to him. The difference, however, between the ordinary language summary I have given and the poetical presentation in Proverbs is the effort it takes to grasp the imagery and, in turn, to be grasped by it.[36]

Using scientific language, with its claim to precision, can function as an exercise in wielding authority—the numbers settle all disputes.[37] This has been so in all ages, although in earlier times the name for what we call science was philosophy. The modern era, however, has provided more tension in the social situation: Once the natural sciences developed, the empirical work that had described motion, chemistry, and physiology began to be applied to more central matters, often with reductionist assumptions. As Lewis put it, prior to some time in the nineteenth century:

> Science was not the business of Man because Man had not yet become the business of science. It dealt chiefly with the inanimate; and it threw off few technological by-products. When Watt makes his engine, when Darwin starts monkeying with the ancestry of Man, and Freud with his soul, and the economists with all that is his, then indeed the lion will have got out of the cage.[38]

The social situation now is that we have writers borrowing prestige from the natural sciences to speak with seeming authority on those topics that matter the most to human life. An obvious response to that is to set the Bible

---

36. Some Bible translations have sought to explicate what they take to be the import of the passage and thus deprive the reader of the exercise. Ironically, they generally miss the point of the imagery: The TEV, for example, renders "springs scattered abroad" as the man's seed producing illegitimate children; while the NLT takes it as the man's promiscuity.

37. Compare the remark of Donald McCloskey about a particular piece of writing on economics: "To evoke a sense of scientific power, to claim precision without necessarily using it." See McCloskey, "How to Do a Rhetorical Analysis, and Why," in *Economic Methodology*, ed. Roger Backhouse (London: Routledge, 1994), 319–42, quote on p. 319.

38. C. S. Lewis, *"De descriptione temporum,"* in *Selected Literary Essays*, ed. Walter Hooper (Cambridge: Cambridge University Press, 1969), 1–14, quote on p. 7.

over against the sciences with a higher authority—or even to invest the Bible with scientific authority. I do not find that response to be wise. I reply to it in two ways: (1) It is better to let the Bible do the things that it does in the way that it does them; (2) It is worth our while to examine critically the cultural assumptions behind these various moves and the logic behind their use. My focus here is on the first point, and as for the second, the apologetic task, I refer the reader to the apologetic tools that Lewis provided.[39]

In addition, the style of modern scientific writing creates an atmosphere of distance from the object of study. Rather than say "I used 5 ml of this fluid," the writer would say, "5 ml of this fluid was used," and the person who did the work fades from the picture.[40] This is the glory of the sciences, their universality—namely, that a Christian, a Hindu, and an atheist should all find the same results so long as they all do the same things. We do not care who designed the airplane we fly in, so long as they followed the universal rules of science and engineering. But it is also a danger: the universality depends on abstracting away everything that makes for particular cases, that is, for real experiences. In fact, not everything is suited to numerical description. Lewis cites from a poem by Robert Conquest:

> Observation of real events includes the observer, "heart" and all;
> (The common measurable features are obtained by omitting this part.)[41]

Scientific language, in its proper sphere—say the deductions of a Sherlock Holmes—cannot be beat. Outside its proper sphere—say the inferences of a Father Brown—it is not so reliable.

A further sociolinguistic feature that we can add to Lewis's treatment and a further aspect of the interaction between locution, illocution, and perlocution is the way statements function in the social system. Adherents of an ideology are frequently told by their critics, "If you were logically consistent, you would do X. The fact that you refuse to do X shows that your system is not worthy of your adherence." Now, the critic may have identified an irreparable inconsistency fatal to the system, but he may also have failed to grasp how people within the system actually use these various statements. We have to take them case by case.

---

39. Say, in Walter Hooper's collections of his essays in *God in the Dock* (Grand Rapids: Eerdmans, 1970) and *Christian Reflections* (Grand Rapids: Eerdmans, 1967).

40. See Joseph Williams, *Style: Toward Clarity and Grace* (Chicago: University of Chicago Press, 1995), 36–42.

41. Robert Conquest, "Excerpts from a Report to the Galactic Council," 1954 (cited from Lewis, "The Language of Religion," 134).

It is easy to see how this works in the case of conventional folk wisdom. People who focus entirely on locutions will wind up pronouncing that the English proverbs "too many cooks spoil the broth" and "many hands make light work" are contradictory or at least incompatible. But folk wisdom (not to mention the wisdom in Proverbs) does not work that way. Rather, the adept person uses good judgment to discern which rule applies best in the given situation. Inculcating a bent toward such discernment is a key part of the illocution of having an array of such sayings.

Other theological conclusions, which separate Christians from one another, regard whether the faithful who wish to be fully consistent should be pacifist, take a civil oath, or resort to a physician; and we are often told that only the literalist reading of Genesis is the fully consistent biblical position.[42] Typically, one side appeals to the plain reading of biblical texts, with what I count as at best a superficial regard for how the text functioned in ancient Israel, Second Temple Judaism, or the early church.

All three of Lewis's types of language have a further similarity: their speakers expect the audience to fill things in, that is, to bring to bear knowledge of the world and values they share in common. For example, ordinary language is rarely (if ever) unqualified. If I say that I *never* take a sick day from work, a reasonable person will realize that I mean *ordinarily* and that there may be exceptions. If I instruct my children, "*Always* tell the truth," I do not mean that they should give up any Jews they are hiding when tormenters come to the door—and I expect them to appreciate that. That is, we normally speak with respect to something. In terms used in conventional logic, failure to recognize the unstated qualifications of statements made *simpliciter* (without qualification) is the *secundum quid* fallacy.[43] The linguist might say that perceiving these qualifications and knowing how to apply them is part of the illocution.

Strictly speaking, it is possible that some of these ordinary statements with unstated qualifications are actually instances of hyperbole—a hyperbole that is recognizable by its conventionality. We will simply note, then, that there is a fuzzy line between an unstated qualification and a hyperbole without having to decide which is which.

Consider a biblical example of unstated qualifications, when Paul recounts what he wrote previously and how he fears he was misunderstood (1 Cor 5:9–11):

---

42. From the critical side, see James Barr, *Fundamentalism* (Philadelphia: Westminster, 1978), 40; and from the fundamentalist side, see the essays in Terry Mortenson and Thane Ury, eds., *Coming to Grips with Genesis* (Green Forest, AR: Master, 2008).

43. For exposition, see, H. W. B. Joseph, *An Introduction to Logic* (Oxford: Clarendon, 1916), 589.

> I wrote to you in my letter not to associate with sexually immoral people—not at all meaning the sexually immoral of this world, or the greedy and swindlers, or idolaters, since then you would need to go out of the world. But now I am writing to you not to associate with anyone who bears the name of brother if he is guilty of sexual immorality or greed, or is an idolater, reviler, drunkard, or swindler—not even to eat with such a one.

It would appear from the wording here that Paul's initial instruction was, "Do not associate with immoral people," and that he expected his Corinthian readers to fill in the blanks by discerning that he was speaking *with respect to* "anyone who bears the name of brother." Paul argues that his expectation was reasonable: "For what have I to do with judging outsiders?" (v. 12). We may infer that at least some of the readers failed to discern what Paul was intending or perhaps labelled the instruction absurdly restrictive by focusing on a literalistic interpretation of the locution. Since we do not have the earlier letter we can refrain from deciding whether Paul's instructions were ambiguous or unclear (or even whether Paul is upbraiding his audience or else admitting his infelicity). At any rate, Paul exemplifies something most humans can readily recognize as something they have done at one time or another. In the canonical letter he goes on to clarify what he represented as a readily accessible illocution (v. 11).

Also consider the narrator's statement in Acts 2:5, "Now there were dwelling in Jerusalem Jews, devout men from every nation under heaven." *Every* nation? John Stott applied a common-sense qualification to his reading of this text:

> That we must not press Luke's "every nation under heaven" literally to include, for example, American Indians, Australian aboriginals and New Zealand Maoris, is plain from what follows. He was speaking, as the biblical writers normally did, from his own horizon not ours, and was referring to the Graeco-Roman world situated round the Mediterranean basin, indeed to every nation in which there were Jews.[44]

Stott was a thoughtful writer who rarely wasted words, which makes one wonder what kind of literalism he had encountered that called forth this seemingly unnecessary clarification. Many of the "all" and "every" statements

---

44. John R. W. Stott, *The Message of Acts*, BST (Downers Grove, IL: InterVarsity Press, 1990), 63.

we find in the biblical writers are of this sort, as in Romans 1:8, where the Roman Christians' faith is proclaimed "in all the world."[45]

Lewis employs this principle himself in the course of explaining "Why I am not a Pacifist," an essay that began as a talk he gave to a pacifist society in Oxford in 1940.[46] He argues that "The whole Christian case for Pacifism rests, therefore, on certain Dominical utterances, such as 'Resist not evil: but whosoever shall smite thee on thy right cheek, turn to him the other also' [Matt 5:39]."[47] Does not the Pacifist position arise from a straightforward reading of such texts? Lewis replies,

> I think the text means what it says, but with an understood reservation in favour of those obviously exceptional cases which every hearer would naturally assume to be exceptions without being told. . . . Indeed, as the audience were private people in a disarmed nation, it seems unlikely that they would have ever supposed Our Lord to be referring to war.[48]

Lewis suggests his audience is in danger of committing the fallacy of failing to account for *secundum quid*.[49]

Even scientific language employs unspoken and implicit terms. For example, as Lewis and many others pointed out, when we articulate laws of nature we usually leave unstated the obvious qualification, "provided nothing interferes" (often called *ceteris paribus*, "other things being equal" qualifications). Thus, a full statement of the behavior of billiard balls would be "when billiard balls are moving on a billiard table, each ball will decelerate due to friction and drag (always provided no one interferes)." Observation of billiard balls will never tell you how likely it is that someone might intervene, and the normal statement of the law leaves this out entirely (and properly so).[50]

---

45. Compare Gen 41:57, where the famine was in "all the earth," referring to the eastern end of the Mediterranean; Rom 5:18 that states justification of life "for all men," which surely means "all those represented by the respective figures." It is a commonplace in New Testament studies that expressions such as "all Israel" (Rom 11:26) do not mean "every Israelite without exception" (reflecting Old Testament and rabbinic use of "all Israel.")

46. Lewis, "Why I Am Not a Pacifist," in *The Weight of Glory and Other Addresses*, ed. Walter Hooper (New York: Simon & Schuster, 1996), 53–71.

47. Lewis, "Why I Am Not a Pacifist," 67.

48. Ibid., 68.

49. See also Stott, *Christian Counter-Culture*, 96, regarding the "exception clause" found in Matthew's texts about divorce (5:32; 19:9) but missing from the texts in Mark and Luke that touch on the subject (Mark 10:11–12; Luke 16:18): "It seems far more likely that its absence from Mark and Luke is due not to their ignorance of it but to *their acceptance of it as something taken for granted*" (emphasis added).

50. Lewis pointed out more than once that this comes into play in discussion of miracles. See also Stephen Bilynskyj, "God, Nature, and the Concept of Miracle" (PhD diss., University of Notre Dame, 1982), 48; Lydia Jaeger, *What the Heavens Declare: Science in the Light of Creation* (Eugene, OR: Cascade,

Consider another biblical example where discerning with-respect-to-whatness is essential to good reading, 1 John 4:20. There the writer insists, "He who does not love his brother whom he has seen cannot love God whom he has not seen." John Stott wisely takes the ordinary language statement, "he cannot love God," and explains it more precisely: "This 'cannot' [Gk. οὐ δύναται] expresses not so much the man's incapacity to love God, as the proof that he does not."[51] In this light, we might paraphrase, "he cannot legitimately say that he loves God." This certainly fits the overall argument of 1 John and also coheres with the recognizable use of ordinary language. It might even be the case that part of the rhetorical (or illocutionary) intention is to provoke a closer analysis of a statement that seems a little off on its surface.[52]

Thus, most authors, regardless of their language type, leave it to their audiences to work out the with-respect-to-whatness of their statements; often this requires a disciplined imagination. The biblical authors are no different. In this light, we can assess the validity of the simple assertion that when Paul says that death entered the world by way of Adam's sin (Rom 5:12–14), he disagrees with the Wisdom of Solomon, which had said that death entered the world through the devil's envy (Wis 2:23–24).[53] Now, it takes a combination of literalism and zero-sum-game thinking (which itself needs warrant) to find these two statements to be disagreeing—and it is more likely that each stresses different aspects of the events for their particular communicative goals.[54] The same considerations would apply to 2 Samuel 24:1 (where the Lord's anger incited David to number the people) and 1 Chronicles 21:1 (where Satan incited David): These only contradict each other if the options are mutually exclusive, which in conventional theology they are not. Those who claim contradictions in places like this are failing to use their imaginations and thus failing at the linguistic and literary task of cooperation.

If we can show that these filled-in blanks and with-respect-to-what considerations are inherent in the particular communicative act we are examining,

---

2012), 53–57; Alvin Plantinga, *Where the Conflict Really Lies: Science, Religion, and Naturalism* (Oxford: Oxford University Press, 2011), 78.

51. John R. W. Stott, *The Epistles of John*, 171, drawing on C. H. Dodd, *The Johannine Epistles*, Moffatt New Testament Commentary (London: Hodder & Stoughton, 1946), 124.

52. Some manuscripts read, "how can he love God?" (exchanging Gk. πῶς for οὐ). This would be a rhetorical question, whose illocution would be quite close to what Stott sees in the more widely accepted Greek reading: "How can he (legitimately claim to) love God?"

53. Peter Enns, *The Evolution of Adam: What the Bible Does and Doesn't Say about Human Origins* (Grand Rapids: Brazos, 2012), 99, finds exactly this contrast, "not through Adam's disobedience." Further expression of Enns's determined literalism comes when he suggests in his next sentence that "Equating the serpent with the devil is itself an interpretive move, since in Genesis the serpent is simply a cunning creature." We will come back to how to read the serpent in Genesis 3 in chapter 7 below.

54. The fact that the Greek of Wis 2:24 and Rom 5:12 is quite similar heightens our sense of complementarity. See further discussion in chapter 8 below.

then—as with inferences based on the laconic showing style—we should accept them as part of the legitimate illocutions of this act. Such an explanation will clarify for us what it means to say that something is actually "in" the text and part of its "plain reading"; it also shows that the literalistic, locution-focused approach that Benjamin Jowett (and James Barr after him) advocated is deeply inadequate.

When Lewis wrote in the mid-twentieth century (and to an educated English-speaking world), he had to oppose two tendencies regarding the use of language. One was the idea that poetry was a separate *kind* of language, whose primary function was to express and arouse emotion, and thus was minimally referential.[55] The other was the claim that religious language was also a special compartment of language: Any talk about God is either non-referential (since God was taken to be a fiction) or else it had primarily to do with the experience of persons and communities (of trust or love) but had little actual content.[56] Lewis's discussion shows that poetry is not a special kind of language primarily about emotion. It is about the possible experience of the referent (whether a referent in the real world or in an imaginary one) on the part of the audience. Note that religious statements can use any of the three kinds of language, and any of these three can refer (though they do so with different goals and conventions). Thus, when Christians affirm that Jesus rose from the dead, they are (at least in their own minds) saying something that is as much akin to "I parked my car in the faculty car park" as it is to "I feel assured of God's love"—in liturgy it partakes of both, and includes a commitment of the worshipper to the community that professes this.[57]

I have one final point to make in this section. The language type is not the same as the literary form; it aligns more with the style and register axes. That is, a piece of writing that has the literary form of a prose narrative can use ordinary, scientific, or poetic language types; knowing the literary form does not settle all the most important interpretive questions. This can be

---

55. For critical discussion of this idea, see Mary Louise Pratt, *Toward a Speech Act Theory of Literary Discourse* (Bloomington: Indiana University Press, 1977), Introduction (pp. xi–xix) and "The 'Poetic Language' Fallacy" (pp. 3–37).

56. Compare Lewis's reference to the Romantic poet Samuel Taylor Coleridge (1772–1834) in *Screwtape Letters* (London: Geoffrey Bles, 1942), letter iv: "One of their poets, Coleridge, has recorded that he did not pray 'with moving lips and bended knees' but merely 'composed his spirit to love' and indulged 'a sense of supplication.'" (The poem is Coleridge's "The Pains of Sleep" from 1803.) The philosophical and theological discussions are extensive. For a start, see Langdon Gilkey, "Cosmology, Ontology, and the Travail of Biblical Language," *Concordia Theological Monthly* 33:3 (1962): 143–54; Jerry Gill, "J. L. Austin and the Religious Use of Language," *Sophia* 8 (1969): 29–37; Arthur Holmes, "Three Levels of Meaning in God-Language," *JETS* 16:2 (1973): 83–94.

57. See Anthony Thiselton, *Language, Liturgy, and Meaning* (Bramcote, Notts: Grove Books, 1986); Jean Ladrière, "The Performativity of Liturgical Language," in *Liturgical Experience of Faith*, ed. Herman Schmidt and David Power (New York: Herder & Herder, 1973), 50–62.

confusing, since the name of one of the language types, poetic, overlaps with the name of one of the literary forms, poem.

Indeed, some songs and hymns have the literary form of a poem (in English, rhythm and rhyme) but are primarily ordinary language—which may lead the *literati* to judge them to be failures as poetry. C. S. Lewis was converted after he had begun his Oxford teaching career, which probably explains his literary judgment of the hymns he found sung at church: "fifth-rate poems set to sixth-rate music."[58] Rather than search a hymnal for the perfect example, I will take one from the popular song, "My Life Would Suck Without You" (songwriters: Claude Kelly, Lukasz Gottwald, Martin Sandberg, sung by Kelly Clarkson in 2009); the song invites its audience to imagine a scene, with two young lovers in a stormy relationship. The woman uses a quasi-scientific word, "dysfunctional," to describe their time together; combined with the title word "suck," this clearly signals the language of ordinary conversation. (Confirmation of this impression comes from the words pseudo-psychological words "issues" and "messed up.") Perhaps this is less a defect and more an artifact of the presentation, by which we are asked to imagine a pair of young people who talk in this (dull) fashion. The song is properly a poem, not simply for its literary form but also for its imagined scene; but it is not very high on the scale of poetic language.

Another example comes from the Christian songwriter John Mark McMillan, "How He Loves" (2002), which compares God's address to humankind to "a sloppy wet kiss."[59] This simile attempts to create an image, but the adjective "sloppy" defeats any effort to move to a poetic level of language. The rest of the song, with its adverb "violently" and the expression "maintain these regrets," is also fairly ordinary (and bland) language.

Both of these songs are still in the literary form of "poetry," but identifying the literary form does not capture everything we need in order to receive the poems.

In what sense do literary form, style, and language level (aspects of the locution) guide us in cooperating with the author—that is, in the illocution? Does, for example, something in the literary form of a narrative of itself purport to be a straightforward account of the "facts?" Of course it does not. A dry style, for example, giving the appearance of straight recounting, can convey irony or even mockery. Or suppose we encounter a narrative that begins, "Once upon a time, there was an American president, with the

---

58. C. S. Lewis, "Answers to Questions on Christianity," in *God in the Dock*, ed. Walter Hooper (Grand Rapids: Eerdmans, 1970), 48–62, quote on p. 62.

59. When the David Crowder Band recorded a cover version (2009), they secured permission to change "sloppy wet kiss" to "unforeseen kiss," which moves at least that line in a more evocative direction.

unusual name of Ronald Reagan." The literary form, a fairy tale, meets the referent (a real person and event) to produce a clash. The result is simple: to answer the question about illocution will require a judgment call, on a case by case basis, taking into account the form, the language level, and the relation of sense to the referent.

3.C METAPHOR, THOUGHT, AND TRUTH

I noted above that language uses commonly involve imagery; and this holds not only in poetical language but also in science. But it is also true that imagery is particularly characteristic of poetical language. In many cases, as in Keats's poem, "The Eve of St Agnes" (see §3.B.1 above), the images are concrete pictures to be held in the mind in order to envision the whole scene better, and thus to grasp more fully the details of the occasion.

Another kind of imagery is *simile*, in which one thing is likened to another: "the kingdom of heaven is *like* a treasure" (Matt 13:44). An intelligent listener will discern ways in which the likeness pertains and those in which it does not.

Like unto simile is the *metaphor*, where one thing is said to *be* another: "Go and tell that fox [Herod]." Syntactically we may think of the metaphor as a simile without the explicit "like." Whether or not this is a valid psychological description of what happens is not my concern. What interests me is the relation of such images to truthfulness and their role in thinking clearly. Some have suggested that the images are dispensable; we could translate them into simple (and scientific) prose if we need to, and the translation might even be preferable.[60] Perhaps this is why many easily dismiss metaphors as *merely* metaphor—a dismissal that embeds some highly problematic assumptions about how language and thought work.

Walker Percy helpfully frames the issue:

> Why is the metaphor *Flesh is grass*, which is not only wrong (flesh is not grass) but inappropriate (flesh is not even like grass), better and truer than the sentence *Flesh is mortal*, which is quite accurate and logical?

---

60. For a ready example, see C. K. Ogden and I. A. Richards, *The Meaning of Meaning* (New York: Harcourt, Brace & World, 1946), 4: "It is impossible to handle a scientific matter in such metaphorical terms [as those used in a text on semantics they discuss], and the training of philologists has not, as a rule, been such as to increase their command of analytic and abstract language. The logician would be far better equipped in this respect were it not that his command of language tends to conceal from him what he is talking about and renders him prone to accept purely linguistic constructions, which serve well enough for his special purposes, as ultimates."

That particular feature of metaphor . . . has most troubled philosophers: that it is "wrong"—it asserts of one thing that it is something else—and further, that its beauty often seems proportionate to its wrongness or outlandishness.[61]

C. S. Lewis shows the role of metaphor in clear thinking in his 1939 essay, "Bluspels and Flalansferes."[62] Metaphors, Lewis argues, are part of thought: "When we pass beyond pointing to individual sensible objects, when we begin to think of causes, relations, of mental states or acts, we become incurably metaphorical."[63]

Lewis contends that there are two classes of metaphors, those we invent to teach by ("the Master's metaphor") and those from which we learn ("the Pupil's metaphor"). The Master's metaphor is a device that does not very much affect the thought of its maker. The Pupil's metaphor, however, "is the unique expression of a meaning that we cannot have on any other terms."[64] Lewis notes that "in practice very few metaphors can be purely magistral; only that which to some degree enlightens ourselves is likely to enlighten others."[65]

We might restate Lewis's categories of metaphor as, on the one hand, those that assist comprehension but are not indispensable to it. On the other hand, we have those that are essential to comprehension, so essential, in fact, that with the metaphor we open up fresh avenues of understanding.

Lewis lists what it takes for metaphors to function well:

What truth we can attain in such a situation depends rigidly on three conditions. First, that the imagery should be originally well chosen; secondly, that we should apprehend the exact imagery; and thirdly that we should know that the metaphor is a metaphor. (That metaphors misread as statements of fact are the source of monstrous errors need hardly be pointed out.)[66]

Let us consider an example from the Bible. Psalm 31:2 asks God to be a "rock of refuge for me, a strong fortress to save me." These images use two words of similar meaning for "rock" (v. 2, צוּר [*tsur*]; v. 3, סֶלַע [*sela'*]) and a

---

61. Walker Percy, *The Message in the Bottle* (New York: Farrar, Straus and Giroux, 2000), 5, 65–66.
62. Lewis, "Bluspels and Flalansferes: A Semantic Nightmare," in *Selected Literary Essays*, ed. Walter Hooper (Cambridge: Cambridge University Press, 1969), 251–65 (first published in Lewis, *Rehabilitations*, 1939).
63. Ibid., 263.
64. Ibid., 255.
65. Ibid., 257.
66. Ibid., 254.

common word for a fortress (vv. 2–3, מְצוּדָה [*metsudah*]) and for "refuge" (vv. 2, 4, מָעוֹז [*ma'oz*]). A large rock in the environment of ancient Israel would be a place of safety, say from a flash flood (such as described in 18:16)—and the flood can be an image for troubles in general (perhaps 61:5) or, more specifically, for pursuing enemies (as in 27:5).[67]

In Lewis's terms we might call this a Master's metaphor, although we should be mindful that it is probably not purely magistral. We can paraphrase it, but the rhetorical power of the metaphor comes from the images that lie ready to hand for the ancient singing congregation. That is, even in the Master's metaphors, the image is bound up in the communication event, since communication involves more than simply conveying information. The familiar "The LORD is my shepherd" (Ps 23:1) is similar. As Tremper Longman put it, "It would take a page of prose to communicate what the psalmist has stated in a clause, and it would do so with less impact."[68] Perhaps for the faithful, all metaphors in the Bible have this character.

A special kind of metaphor is what some have called *homology*.[69] These are images that we recognize from our own experience, but, once we have grasped them, they in turn cause us to revise the way we carry out the activity. An example would be God as father; as Proverbs 3:12 has it, "for the LORD reproves him whom he loves, as a father the son in whom he delights." There is no reason to suppose that the compilers of Proverbs had a too-rosy view of what actual human fathers are like; they could no doubt be every bit as distant, abusive, short-tempered, or just plain inconsistent in Israel as they can in the modern West. But most people have an intuition of what a father *ought* to be and can use that for thinking about God. The image has a varied texture. Another instance is Psalm 103:13, "As a father shows compassion to his children, so the LORD shows compassion to those who fear him." Those who meet the image halfway, allowing imagination and intuition to prevent experience from making them cynical, may find that their own practice of fathering is changed to be more like what they perceive God's to be, infusing tender compassion into moral education. I will employ this concept later in expounding the rhetoric of Genesis 1.

The biblical material, then, is highly pictorial; this is not a weakness, it is a strength. It does not prevent the Bible writers from speaking truly;

---

67. See further Alec Basson, "'You Are My Rock and Fortress': Refuge Metaphors in Psalm 31. A Perspective from Cognitive Metaphor Theory," *Acta Theologica* 25:2 (2005): 1–17.

68. Tremper Longman III, *How to Read the Psalms* (Downers Grove, IL: InterVarsity Press, 1988), 117.

69. See, for example, Gilbert Rorison, "The Creative Week," in *Replies to "Essays and Reviews,"* ed. E. M. Goulburn, et al. (New York: Appleton, 1862), 242–98, quote on p. 291.

it actually enables them to achieve their rhetorical goals.[70] In the following chapters I will explore the ways that Genesis in particular employs its imagistic descriptions.

3.D EXAMPLES OF EXEGESIS

Let me illustrate what I derive from Lewis's discussion by considering a few Bible passages and the theological constructs we might infer from them. It is common to distinguish between *religion* and *theology*—*religion* is a person's faith as he or she lives it out, and *theology* is his or her reflection on and systematization of religion. Religion normally uses ordinary and poetic language, or a combination of them—because these language levels normally correspond to the kind of relational and experiential intimacy suited to a lived-out faith. Theology—particularly systematic theology in the Christian scholastic tradition—has typically used scientific language because that is the level of language that theologians have deemed suitable for the effort to define, prescribe, defend, and exclude.

In following this common distinction I do not mean to agree with the opposition between religion and theology that we often encounter. I have no doubt that without good theology religion is shallow and before long goes bad. At the same time, theology is not an end in itself: it both depends upon and serves the religion of the people of God. Further, in following this distinction I am declaring no allegiance to those who assert the inability of analytical language to tell us truth about God, as I will show below. My main goal in allowing the distinction is to read the Bible better, on its own terms.

Scientific or technical language is rare in the Bible. It may appear in Leviticus, for example, in the lists of what animals are clean and unclean (permissible or impermissible to eat).[71] Notice the scientific language in Leviticus 13 describing the different kinds of skin diseases. Note that we should under-

---

70. In keeping with my critically intuitive approach, I have not thought a full critical examination of recent developments in the philosophy of metaphor to be necessary. These developments seem to me to be generally quite in line with what Lewis had argued. A fair survey appears in Eric Nels Ortlund, *Theophany and Chaoskampf: The Interpretation of Theophanic Imagery in the Baal Epic, Isaiah, and the Twelve* (Piscataway, NJ: Gorgias, 2010), 1–94; Benjamin Foreman, "'Who Teaches Us More Than the Beasts of the Earth?' Animal Metaphors and the People of Israel in the Book of Jeremiah" (PhD thesis, University of Aberdeen, 2009), 1–36.

71. However, there may be a better way to read the lists of animals. Jonathan Burnside, "At Wisdom's Table: How Narrative Shapes the Biblical Food Laws and Their Social Function," *JBL* 135:2 (2016): 223–45, suggests that the lists function as paradigms from which an intelligent lay person can generalize quickly. By his reckoning, then, "the food laws are only rules of thumb," tolerating the possibility of some acceptable foods being deemed unclean in order to eliminate the possibility of unclean foods being deemed permissible (p. 243).

stand the scientific language in relation to the culture of the speaker, not in relation to the way we think today in our culture. The terms in Leviticus are geared to the level of medical care of the time rather than to what we think of as medical practice today.

The terminology of holiness in Leviticus can be technical and can vary from a wider sense to a narrower one. The wider sense appears in texts that speak of Israel as God's "holy nation" (e.g., Exod 19:6; Lev 20:26). The people are consecrated to God, owing him their gratitude and obedience. In a narrower sense, the term can designate people who actually practice their consecration (see Lev 11:44–45, "be holy"). Still more narrowly, the term can designate a person or object specially consecrated for a specific purpose (Exod 29:31, "a holy place"; Lev 21:6–8, where the priests are "holy"; Num 6:8, where a Nazirite is "holy" during the period of his vow). These usages are technical, and they denote the ritual status of a person or thing, which indicates their eligibility for certain activities within the ceremonial system. At the same time as these usages are careful and technical, they are also in their own way phenomenal in that they describe persons and things by how they appear to the human eye and do not comment on the inner condition of the heart.

This kind of designation, by the way, explains why a New Testament author can call all Christians "saints" or "holy ones" (Rom 12:13; Eph 1:1) and can also urge their audiences to "be holy" in conduct (1 Pet 1:15, 16; cf. Eph 1:4; 5:27; 1 Cor 7:34; 1 Thess 3;13) and refer to exemplary persons as "holy" (1 Pet 3:5).

Leviticus 4 also has a category of sins done unintentionally (in the Septuagint, ἀκουσίως). The passage never explains the category nor does it give criteria by which one can decide whether it applies. This is different from the analytical Aristotle whose *Nicomachean Ethics* has a detailed discussion of the difference between the intentional (ἑκούσιον) and unintentional (ἀκούσιον) act.[72]

Now consider New Testament descriptions of faith and apostasy. In Luke's version of the parable of the sower and the soils (Luke 8:4–15 // Matt 13:1–9, 18–23; Mark 4:1–9, 13–20), there are two categories of people who initially respond as they should to hearing the word. There are those who, in verse 13, "receive it with joy" (μετὰ χαρᾶς δέχονται τὸν λόγον) and "believe for a while" (πρὸς καιρὸν πιστεύουσιν),[73] only to fall away under testing. Then there are those who, in verse 15, "hold it fast" and "bear fruit." The parable presents the cases phenomenologically, that is, until the test distinguishes

---

72. Aristotle, *Eth. nic.*, 3.1.1 (1109-*b*–1110-*a*). Unless otherwise noted, Greco-Roman texts are cited from the LCL editions.

73. Matthew 13:21 (cf. Mark 4:17), "endures for a while" (πρόσκαιρός ἐστιν).

those who fall away from those who persevere, there is no difference that is obvious to the human onlooker. To "receive the word with joy" and "believe" are proper and highly commendable responses after all.[74] We are not offered any criteria by which we can distinguish these before the decisive event. That is, the biblical words πίστις, "faith," and πιστεύω, "believe," are not technical (or scientific) terms.[75]

We would lose the point of the parable if we were to suppose that the faith of those who fall away was never real faith to begin with and that the test simply revealed what was there already. We should instead imagine that, according to the Gospel writers, Jesus wanted his hearers to accept that there is a real experience in the temporary believers and the word faith may legitimately be applied to it. The illocutionary force is less about confirming whether the hearers have real faith and more about encouraging them to stand fast under testing.[76]

Similarly, Hebrews 6:4–6 describes a kind of person who falls away after being a member of the church:

> For it is impossible, in the case of those who have once been enlightened, who have tasted the heavenly gift, and have shared in the Holy Spirit, and have tasted the goodness of the word of God and the powers of the age to come, and then have fallen away, to restore them again to repentance, since they are crucifying once again the Son of God to their own harm and holding him up to contempt.

Again, we find in the text no criteria by which a human observer could have told, prior to the apostasy, the difference between such a person and one who perseveres. Indeed, in this author's portrayal, such a person has received the benefits that come from being in the church's worship, where God is especially present with his people—for which the person is all the more culpable. No doubt our author would have shared with his audience the belief that God knows the difference, and they might even have attributed

---

74. For "receive the word with joy," compare 1 Thess 1:6. For the argument that this term refers to a positive response to the public ministry of the word, see C. John Collins, "Coherence in James 1:19–27," *JOTT* 10 (1998): 80–88, pp. 81–82 n9.

75. Once again, at an informal level, careful and thoughtful readers have recognized this. For example, John Stott, *The Message of Acts*, BST (Downers Grove, IL: InterVarsity Press, 1990): "There is no need to suppose that [Simon] was only pretending to believe. New Testament language does not always distinguish between believing and professing to believe" (p. 149).

76. The idea that the test revealed what was already there all along—or not there—actually assumes a kind of static anthropology, that is, the idea that people do not change. Perhaps that assumption itself needs evaluating.

human perseverance to the help of the Holy Spirit—but this is not under consideration in this context, because the author wants his readers to stand firm in the face of temptations that are threatening to intensify (12:4).

I do not doubt that, properly understood, the New Testament writers are concerned to offer assurance of God's steadfast love to the faithful (see Rom 8:28–39). At the same time, the writers themselves do not bring this notion to bear in these particular places. So, we make a mistake if we use an idea, expounded in some texts, in order to undercut the communicative force of other texts.

We may argue that there are places in Paul's writings that approach the language of systematic theology, but they are not many and not nearly as technical as the scholastic tradition. This absence of technicality is so pronounced that Vern Poythress enshrines it in two of his maxims for theology:

- No term in the Bible is equal to a technical term of systematic theology.
- Technical terms in systematic theology can almost always be defined in more than one way.[77]

Let us take another example. The question of how to harmonize Paul and James on justification is readily recognized, and some even count harmonization impossible. Consider the problem:

James 2:24: You see that a person is justified by works and not by faith alone.
Romans 3:28: For we hold that one is justified by faith apart from works of the law.

Can we put these together? Some think that the two passages are literally contradictory and thus illustrate the presence of different theological ideas in the Bible.[78] One path is to examine the differences between the two sentences in the Greek; another is to say that the faith that justifies leads to obedience, though that obedience is not the meritorious ground of justification. These may be good paths, but I suggest that we make a better start by recognizing that Paul did not write the book of James, and thus that his standard usage need not be the same as that of James.

---

77. Vern Poythress, *Symphonic Theology* (Grand Rapids: Zondervan, 1987), 74–79.
78. For one example out of many, see James Barr, "Literality," *Faith & Philosophy* 6:4 (1989): 412–28, especially pp. 417–18.

Then we move on to ponder what the Greek verb "justify" (δικαιόω) means and how each author employs the verb. The verb has a range of meanings, including "to declare righteous" (as in a court) and "to show that one is righteous" (that is, "to vindicate publicly"). Paul is using the first of these senses, portraying a person before the judgment seat of God; James is using the other, since he is arguing that Abraham's faith, which was counted to him as righteousness (Jas 2:23, drawing on Gen 15:6), was completed through his supreme obedience (Jas 2:22, drawing on Gen 22:12). Thus, Abraham was "shown to be righteous."[79] We can then consider what sense "faith" has in each argumentative context. In Paul it is a disposition of trust, while in James 2:18–26 it refers to verbal profession, as we can see in verse 19 (compare v. 26, where it is like the "body.") We find, then, that the two authors use their words differently. Since Paul and James are using words differently and speaking on different topics, we need not do anything to harmonize them; we may instead call them already harmoniously complementary.[80]

If we should be careful not to read Paul as if he were writing as a systematician and not to read James as if Paul wrote it, still less should we read something like the Psalms or Proverbs as if either Paul or a scholastic wrote them. Consider Psalm 51:11 in the light of the standard theological discussion of the Christian believer's security:

> Cast me not away from your presence,
>   and take not your Holy Spirit from me.

Theological discussions have revolved around the question of whether the Holy Spirit can be taken from someone in the Old Testament—with a bearing on specifically Christian approaches to whether one can lose the Holy Spirit's indwelling by unfaithfulness.[81] Thus, some take this text to imply that the Holy Spirit can indeed be taken from someone, at least in the

---

79. Actually, the Pauline writings themselves use different parts of the semantic range of this verb. For example, in 1 Tim 3:16 Jesus ἐδικαιώθη ἐν πνεύματι ("was vindicated by the Spirit" / "vindicated in spirit"). It would be a mistake to identify the occurrence of the verb δικαιόω with a contribution to the doctrine of justification, but this is just what Richard Gaffin does in his *Resurrection and Redemption* (Phillipsburg, NJ: Presbyterian and Reformed, 1987), 121. See also N. T. Wright, *The Resurrection of the Son of God* (Philadelphia: Fortress, 2003), 270–71. Gaffin writes that Jesus' resurrection is his justification (in the sense in which it is then applied to the one who is in him), but it is far better to see it as his being shown to be righteous (cf., BDAG, 249b and Rom 3:4 with the same sense).

80. From this it should be clear that I am not opposing harmonization in general.

81. An alternative is to suggest the rendering, "the [human] spirit of your holiness," which would then fall into line with the other uses of the word "spirit" in the psalm. See, for example, W. Creighton Marlowe, "'Spirit of Your Holiness' in Psalm 51:13," *TJ* 19:1 (1998): 29–49. However, the same Hebrew construction appears in Isa 63:10–11, where "his Holy Spirit" is surely the right reading (see also Wis 9:17 and Rom 1:4 for the same syntax in Greek). A traditional Jewish commentator such as Amos

Old Testament. Others have suggested that the Holy Spirit is understood here as empowering David for his kingly duties and that this is a prayer that God not take the kingship and the divine anointing for kingship from David as he did from Saul (1 Sam 16:13–14).[82] To make sense of the expression, however, we should first observe that the Old Testament rarely discusses the divine Spirit's role in cleansing the inner life; Ezekiel 36:27 is the only (other) clear reference on the subject. The Hebrew Bible does not enter into technical questions of the Spirit's permanent indwelling. Further, the fact that Psalm 51 is a psalm for the whole congregation argues against the idea that it is David's personal prayer about his kingship; rather, each member of the congregation is identifying with the "I" of the psalm. The tenor of this psalm, then, is that if strict justice were God's only consideration, he would have the right to bring dire judgment on those who sin (which includes all of his own people), and therefore the only possible appeal is to his mercy. Were the song to engage in technical theologizing (and thus cease to be poetry), it would run something like,

> I know that by my misdeeds I deserve for you to remove all signs of your love toward me, your Holy Spirit included; please show me mercy rather than give me what I deserve.

The function of the psalm, as a song that a congregation sings, is to shape the hearts of those who sing it so that they feel this at the deepest level lest they ever presume upon God's grace. As Derek Kidner puts it, "This verse is not concerned with the bare doctrine of perseverance but with the practice of it."[83]

An example from Acts will illustrate the interaction of ordinary language, which describes things by their appearance, and the understated literary technique that pervades the Bible—a technique that invites the reader to an active role as interpreter. In Acts 1:10, after a cloud took Jesus from his disciples' sight, "two men stood by them in white robes." Luke calls them "men," and the Greek is normally unambiguous (ἄνδρες). Nevertheless, they are clearly *angels*, not *men*: the same term appears in Luke 24:4 ("two men in dazzling apparel") and in Acts 10:30 ("a man stood before me in bright clothing"). In Acts 10:3 the narrator had told us that Cornelius's visitor was in fact an angel. Certainly, the bright or dazzling clothing was the prompt for the attentive

---

Hakham, *Sefer Tehillim*, Da'at Miqra' (Jerusalem: Mossad Harav Kook, 1979), 300, sees a reference to the disposition of God as corresponding to the disposition of man in v. 12.

82. For example, Franz Delitzsch, *Psalms*, K&D (Edinburgh: T&T Clark, 1871 [1867]), 2:139–40.

83. Derek Kidner, *Psalms 1–72*, TOTC (Downers Grove, IL: InterVarsity Press, 1973), 192.

audience to realize that these were anything but mere men: as John Stott remarked, with his characteristic sanity, "Luke calls them 'men' because that is how they appeared, but their shining dress and authoritative tone indicate that they were angels."[84]

There is a further question of whether the Bible conveys a picture of the universe—a geocentric picture of a flat disk resting on pillars, with water beneath and a solid canopy above, a picture that we can no longer accept. I will save this topic for chapter 9.

Is there then no place for systematic theology and for analytic or metaphysical (and non-biblical) language in Christian thinking? Yes, there is, and that takes us to the next section.

3.E IS THERE A ROLE FOR ANALYTICAL LANGUAGE?

It is a simple observation to say that the Bible rarely speaks in scientific, philosophical, or analytical language. At the same time, there is a response that does not follow from this: that philosophical and analytical questions are unimportant, or even impertinent (which is how some people read Col 2:8; 1 Cor 1:18–31). This is a mistake, first because philosophers and their questions are not normally what the biblical writers are addressing. Second, biblical writers would remind us that not all forms of philosophy are barriers to biblical faith: witness the way that Wisdom of Solomon and Acts 17:22–31 find points of contact with lines of Greek philosophy in order to commend biblical faith. Indeed, some New Testament terms are co-opted from Hellenistic philosophy (such as "providence," "invisible" applied to God, and "hold together" applied to the cosmos).[85] And the third reason this conclusion is a mistake is that it is simply false to suppose that using non-philosophical language is the same as having no philosophical implications.

I have argued here that the phenomenal usage is a feature of ordinary language, that the imagistic usage is a feature of poetic language, and that such language usages are what we regularly find in the Bible. We would err if we were to suppose that this kind of language renders it impossible to answer analytical questions, but the trick is to discern just how to follow the implications properly. Such discernment is a skill developed through instruction, experience, and correction (that is, through discipleship).

---

84. John R. W. Stott, *The Message of Acts*, BST (Downers Grove, IL: InterVarsity Press, 1990), 49.
85. See, for example, C. John Collins, "Colossians 1,17 'Hold Together': A Co-Opted Term," *Biblica* 95:1 (2014): 64–87; idem., "1 Corinthians 8:6 and Romans 11:36: A Pauline Confession with a Hellenistic Setting," *Presbyterion* 43:2 (Fall, 2017): 55–68.

The goal of biblical interpretation is to learn how to cooperate with the authors' intent. I judge that the biblical material speaks largely in terms of historical matters and of a worldview and asserts that these are true. I will show why that is the best way to read Genesis 1–11 as we proceed. This means that we do best if we focus on these matters and then see how a cooperative audience might respond to them. We will also come back to this when we consider (in ch. 10) the presentations of God's actions in Genesis 1–11.

At times, though, we can go further; indeed, we should.[86] An example of good practice comes from Jay Wesley Richards' book *The Untamed God*.[87] He subtitles it *A Philosophical Exploration of Divine Perfection, Simplicity, and Immutability*—and it is indeed a work in philosophical theology, arguing that a position called "essentialism" provides us with the tools to talk meaningfully about the triune God. But Richards also makes "biblical normativity" a key criterion for theological accuracy; he acknowledges that

> Historical theological treatments of God's perfection, sovereignty and aseity often outstrip explicit biblical testimony. But they are often an appropriate extension of biblical ideas.[88]

The virtue of Richards's approach is that he distinguishes between the biblical statements themselves and the extrapolations we may draw from them. He does not allow the extrapolations to displace or correct the Bible itself.

> Certainly for the traditional Christian, the specific way in which God has revealed himself must constrain the content of the PP [*principle of perfection*] and the SAC [*sovereignty-aseity conviction*]. Nevertheless, if extrabiblical extrapolations of these themes have no legitimate role to play in Christian theology, then their ubiquity in the history of Christian theology would make that history theologically suspect.[89]

Richards recognizes that this kind of language is necessary for articulating and defending the "true" Christian faith. Consider the controversy in the fourth century over the deity of Christ:

---

86. Compare also Kenneth Seeskin, *Thinking about the Torah* (Philadelphia/Lincoln: JPS/University of Nebraska, 2016), 11, who speaks of a text's "trajectory," which may go beyond what the original author had envisioned but is still a natural extension of it.

87. Jay Wesley Richards, *The Untamed God: A Philosophical Exploration of Divine Perfection, Simplicity and Immutability* (Downers Grove, IL: InterVarsity Press, 2003).

88. Richards, *The Untamed God*, 36.

89. Ibid., 39.

The need to preserve Jesus' full deity against this Arian heresy required precision, an ample motivation for adopting philosophical terms. . . . The Nicene Fathers introduced these terms [*homoousios, hypostasis,* and *ousia* as applied to the Trinity] over the objections of the Arians, who claimed that the terms were unbiblical. The Nicene Fathers, who prevailed in the controversy, contended that the terms, although drawn from philosophy, provided certain ontological distinctions necessary to draw out biblical claims and preserve the implications of the faith. Ironically, if the Nicene Fathers were correct [as Richards thinks they were], then the Biblicist Arians were less faithful to Scripture than the Fathers who introduced extrabiblical terminology.[90]

Note again that Richards recognizes that the type of language is geared to its communicative purpose. Richards writes with respect for the ways that scholastic Christians have described God, but he shows respect as well for the critique presented by more biblically oriented theologians, especially that the scholastic approach abstracts God from the way he has revealed himself in the acts of redemptive history and leaves us with a remote—even cold—deity. Although Richards develops a sturdy set of philosophical tools for talking about God, he is fully aware that "such esoterica rarely enter the minds of pious believers"—but that hardly invalidates his project, which has the object of strengthening our confidence in the coherence of God-talk and of providing safeguards against improper literalism (as in "openness of God" theology) or unwarranted extrapolations (as in making God remote or unfeeling).[91] The value of all this for piety is that it helps the faithful to see the story of redemption more clearly and to know and love the God who acts in this story.

Along similar lines, the Reformed theological tradition has used the expression "covenant of grace" for the overall plan of God to save human beings after the primal disobedience of Adam and Eve. When such theologians are self-aware, they are clear that this term is a theological abstraction; the individual covenants in the Bible are said to be expressions of the one covenant of grace (see, for example, *Westminster Confession of Faith,* 7.3). Now, this may or may not be a legitimate abstraction, and it might also

---

90. Ibid., 43. The process of introducing vocabulary not found in the Bible itself for the sake of christological precision began much earlier than the fourth century. Compare Ignatius's (*Trallians* 9:1 longer text, ca. AD 107) expression ἀνέλαβε σῶμα ("he took a body"); Irenaeus's (*Haer.* 1:10:1, ca. AD 180) phrases τὸν σαρκωθέντα ("who became incarnate"), τὴν ἐκ παρθένου γέννησιν ("the birth from a virgin"), and ἔνσαρκον ("incarnate"), none of which occurs in the New Testament. See further the Greek texts laid out in Philip Schaff, *The Creeds of Christendom* (Grand Rapids: Baker, 1998), 2:11–14.

91. Richards, *The Untamed God,* 250.

be confusing to use as a technical theological term a word that appears in the Bible with a different sense. Those questions are not my concern here. Rather, I am saying that the theologians are acting appropriately in making the abstraction to express what they see as a unity that underlies the varying covenantal contexts of the Bible. However, these theologians can go wrong with their abstractions: within the Reformed tradition some began portraying the covenant individualistically, "the treaty between the triune God and the elect sinner."[92] One may try to warrant this way of putting it by arguing that it captures the importance of personal faith, but it so obscures the biblical notion of membership in a community of people united to God by covenant that it has at this point probably diverged too far from the biblical portrayal to be useful any more.

This helps us to see one of the criteria for evaluating theological constructs: They are not to be a replacement for the Bible story nor a downgrading of the form in which that story comes to us; rather, they should provide us with the background beliefs that will enable us to read the biblical material more faithfully in order to cooperate with it more fully. My discussion of divine action (see ch. 10 below) will put these principles into practice.

3.F CONCLUSIONS

Biblical language has a variety of functions, and the information conveyed in a particular text is relevant to the author's communicative purpose. It is a mistake, though, to suppose that the function of the text is limited to that of conveying information. It goes beyond that, to shaping a view of God and the world, his people's place in the world, and their role in the unfolding story of God's work in the world.

I resist implying that the terms *scholastic* or *philosophical* are of themselves negative adjectives. Rather, such concerns can serve a useful purpose provided we recognize the difference between these kinds of language and what we typically find in the Bible. In the same way, I do not make the terms *devotional* or *warm* the criterion of biblical faithfulness, since traditional Christian thinking demands a piety harnessed to clear and critical thinking. As C. S. Lewis sagely observed,

> I believe that many who find that "nothing happens" when they sit down, or kneel down, to a book of devotion, would find that the heart

---

92. Friedrich Lampe (1782), cited in Heinrich Heppe, *Reformed Dogmatics* (Grand Rapids: Baker, 1978), 382–83.

sings unbidden while they are working their way through a tough bit of theology with a pipe in their teeth and a pencil in their hand.[93]

The advice that Lewis gave in his *Letters to Malcolm* regarding analogical language about God can be applied more widely. He wrote (letter x):

> We are constantly represented as exciting the Divine wrath or pity—even as "grieving" God. I know this language is analogical. But when we say that, we must not smuggle in the idea that we can throw the analogy away and, as it were, get in behind it to a purely literal truth. All we can really substitute for the analogical expression is some theological abstraction. And the abstraction's value is almost entirely negative. It warns us against drawing absurd consequences from the analogical expression by prosaic extrapolations. . . .
>
> I suggest two rules for exegetics. (1) Never take the images literally. (2) When the *purport* of the images—what they say to our fear and hope and will and affections—seems to conflict with the theological abstractions, trust the purport of the images every time. For our abstract thinking is itself a tissue of analogies: a continual modelling of spiritual reality in legal or chemical or mechanical terms. Are these likely to be more adequate than the sensuous, organic, and personal images of scripture—light and darkness, river and well, seed and harvest, master and servant, hen and chickens, father and child? The footprints of the Divine are more visible in that rich soil than across rocks or slag-heaps. Hence what they now call "de-mythologising" Christianity can easily be "re-mythologising" it—and substituting a poorer mythology for a richer.[94]

An example of applying Lewis's rules for exegetics would be in how we read God's questions (Gen 3:9; 4:9) and his remembering (8:1; 9:15–16). Does the text really represent God as lacking or forgetting information? Since God is a being great enough to have done what Genesis 1 records, the expositional tradition that has appealed to the abstraction of God's omniscience and thus finds rhetorical questions and anthropomorphic language in these texts, handles the exegetical task quite well.

---

93. C. S. Lewis, "On the Reading of Old Books," in *God in the Dock*, ed. Walter Hooper (Grand Rapids: Eerdmans, 1970), 200–207, quote on p. 205. Originally, this was Lewis's preface to Sister Penelope's translation of Athanasius, *On the Incarnation of the Word of God* (London: Geoffrey Bles, 1944).

94. C. S. Lewis, *Prayer: Letters to Malcolm* (London: Collins, 1966), 54–59 (emphasis original).

88 • *Reading Genesis Well*

The "abstraction" here is philosophical and systematic theology expressed in analytical language; and it serves a purpose. But that purpose is never to blunt the force of the biblical text itself. Rather, a well-executed abstraction provides us with the tools we need in order to exercise what I have called a disciplined imagination—without which we cannot expect to become cooperative readers.

Chapter 4

GOOD-FAITH COMMUNICATION: WHAT DOES IT MEAN TO SPEAK TRULY?

I take it as a given that Bible authors wrote in order to communicate and that these authors' main aims in communicating had to do with shaping the worldview of the people of God and thus equipping the faithful to play their part in the unfolding story of God's work in the world. They would have said that they were aiming to tell the truth about the story—and that is what the faithful have always thought the authors achieved. But in order to talk about truth and falsehood we have to be able to discern what sorts of things the authors are actually affirming—and to do this we must exercise care to be sure we hear what they are saying and that we do *not* hear what they are *not* saying, on their own terms.

4.A HOW DOES COMMUNICATION WORK?

In order to see what it means to be careful, consider what happens in an act of communication.[1] First, we have an author (or speaker) and an audience, and the author conveys a text (written or spoken) to the audience. How does a text convey meaning? The author and his audience share a notion of the world—their knowledge, beliefs, values, experiences, language, and literary

---

1. These ideas are developed from my *The God of Miracles* (Wheaton, IL: Crossway, 2000), chapter 4 and *Genesis 1–4: A Linguistic, Literary, and Theological Commentary* (Phillipsburg, NJ: P&R, 2006), chapter 10. See also Kerry Robichaux, "Text-Knowledge Relationships," in *Language in Context: Essays for Robert E. Longacre*, ed. Hwang and Merrifield (Dallas: SIL International, 1992), 363–89 (drawing on his 1986 dissertation under Longacre's direction), which investigates the way in which a text interacts with the users' perception of the world.

conventions. A text operates on this shared notion of the world in order to produce some effect, such as adding new things for the audience to know or to believe, correcting the things that they thought they knew, reminding the audience of what they believe or have experienced so that they will act upon it, evoking some aspect of their shared world picture so that they will celebrate or mourn it, or re-orienting their worldview. We may diagram it in this way:

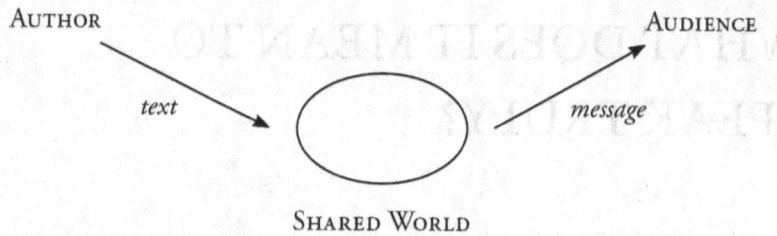

The text corresponds to the locution (as I discussed in ch. 3), while the intended interaction of text and shared world constitutes the illocution. We have not really apprehended the act of communication until we have considered this interaction.

To see this in action, consider how English proverbs function. If I say, "You can lead a horse to water but you can't make him drink," I assume you know what a horse is and that you share the popular view that one cannot compel a horse to drink from its trough. Since the proverb is true of all kinds of animals—dogs, cats, snakes, grasshoppers—this popular view of horses is part of what makes the proverb work. I also assume that you recognize the conventions for applying proverbs: namely, I am not speaking about how ranchers should care for horses, but I am making an analogy, usually to the effect that one can offer advice but cannot force the advisee to accept it. The proverb is a much more colorful—and thus more memorable—way of expressing this idea. I can imagine saying it when I have counseled a student about improving his marriage, but as he walks out of my office I am not sure he will take my counsel. I can also imagine saying it to a friend who has tried to help someone else see the right course of action but to no avail; I want to help my friend stop torturing himself over the "failure." These attitudes are the message of this particular act of communication.

One of the challenges we face when we are interpreting any ancient text—where both the author and the original audience have been dead for a long time—is that often we must *infer* the features of that shared world that are most applicable to our text when the text does not state them explicitly or reflect upon them. This happens, for example, when the text speaks of physical components of that world, such as animals and landscape—hence researchers have supplied critical discussions in natural history or historical geography to discern the assumed referents of various Bible words and phrases. It happens as well, and perhaps more elusively, when the text presupposes a basic structure of social relationships between persons.

How can we test whether these features we infer, especially the ideological ones, actually were a part of the assumed shared world? The most important test, of course, is the degree to which it helps us to make sense of the biblical texts we are studying. Besides that, we should look for any texts that might make the ideas more explicit. If the idea seems to be widely spread, underlying a variety of different passages, that makes it even more compelling. Perhaps we might add the livability test as well: that is, we expect that our proposed inferred feature can actually be lived by real people.

4.B WHAT IS "GOOD-FAITH COMMUNICATION"?

This leads us to our question: Under what circumstances may we say that an author asserts that part of his world picture is (in some sense) *true*? To begin, I take it for granted that the Bible authors have made what we can call a "good-faith act of communication," meaning any act of communication will allude to some parts of the world picture shared between author and audience. If the validity of the speaker's point depends on the truth value of the thing alluded to, then we may say that a good-faith act of communication implies that the speaker is also affirming the alluded part. Otherwise, the speaker is communicating by deceptive means and thus is not acting in good faith.

Some examples can clarify this. In several Gospel pericopes (e.g., Luke 20:27–40; Matt 19:1–12) the Jewish opponents question Jesus on the basis of what Moses wrote in the Pentateuch. Thus, the Mosaic origin of the Pentateuch is part of their world picture. Jesus replies with something else that he attributes to Moses to show that his opponents have misread Moses. In other words, he shares that part of their world picture that has Moses as the primary source of the Pentateuch, and his reply requires that to be true (in some meaningful way) for its validity. So, even though the origin of the Pentateuch is not the topic of discussion, and even though the level of language is not very formal, we can still say that Jesus affirms this position by implication (unless we want to say that he is conceding it for the sake of the argument). Note that the question of whether *we* accept that position is another matter altogether; I am focusing on what sorts of things we may properly say that our authors and the characters in their narratives that they admire affirm.

Consider another example: 1 Timothy 4:7 describes Paul telling Timothy to avoid "irreverent and old wives' myths" (as we might render Gk. τοὺς βεβήλους καὶ γραώδεις μύθους; "irreverent, silly myths" [ESV]). When the author uses the adjective γραώδεις ("typical of old women"), he is apparently using a standard trope found in other Greek writers, referring to stories not worth the attention of serious people—much as I have heard people speak in English of "old wives' tales."[2] Now it may—or may not—have been the case that these other Greek authors had a low view of women's intellectual abilities, that they thought older women have no capacity for serious discourse, and that this opinion lay behind their use of the trope. But does the use of that expression in 1 Timothy commit the biblical author to such a view? Apparently not. We can tell that our author did not hold that view (see 1 Tim 5:9–10; Titus 2:3; 2 Tim 1:5),[3] and his point does not depend in any way on whether as a matter of statistics old wives actually tell such tales. Perhaps if we pressed our author, he would say that these tales appeal to a certain kind of older woman who is not sweetened by divine grace and that comparable older men have their own kind of silliness, but this is no matter. We can identify the kind of tale he had in mind well enough. The ordinary language found in 1 Timothy allows us to identify the tales and hence enables the author to communicate. This particular good-faith communication does not of itself invoke any derogatory view of older women as such.

The concept of good-faith communication can also help us in thinking about the use of analytical language (as in ch. 3). The analysis that leads to our abstractions can help to clarify the ideas that a text explicitly talks about, the ideas that are legitimate extensions of what the text talks about, and the ideas that underlie the text as part of its world picture. All of these come into play in formulating, for example, a biblical understanding of the Trinity or of the incarnation—and good-faith communication will play a part in my treatment of divine action (ch. 10 below).

This analytical process can also help in considering ethical questions on which the biblical writers are silent. There is little or nothing in the Bible that is actually about the topic of, for example, elective abortion; and yet

---

2. For example, Plato (428–347 BC) in his *Theaetetus*, 176B, dismisses a false motivation for virtue as "old wives' chatter, as the saying is" (ὁ λεγόμενος γραῶν ὕθλος). The historian Strabo (ca. 64 BC–AD 19) in his *Geography*, 1.2.3, decries a man who makes Homer's poetical art out to be "old wives' fables" (γραώδη μυθολογίαν).

3. We must admit, though, that the NASB rendering, "worldly fables fit only for old women," makes Paul sound like he *did* subscribe to such a view, but I doubt that this is the best rendering.

traditional Christians have generally agreed that most cases of deliberate abortion are morally wrong. How can such Christians have any biblical right to this conclusion? The standard texts include Psalm 51:5 ("I was brought forth in iniquity, and in sin did my mother conceive me"); 139:13–16 ("you knitted me together in my mother's womb . . . my frame was not hidden from you when I was being made in secret . . . your eyes saw my unformed substance"); Jeremiah 1:5 ("before I formed you in the womb I knew you, and before you were born I consecrated you"); Luke 1:44 ("the baby in my womb leaped for joy"). Now it is clear that none of these passages deals with abortion as such, and none of them is specifically aimed at asserting that the unborn child be viewed as a human person who is thus to be protected by the sixth commandment.

At the same time, it should be equally clear that each of these texts, to be good-faith communications, requires that the child developing in the womb is a "person." In Psalm 51:5 the worshiper traces his or her sinfulness back to the very beginning of his or her existence, even preceding birth. In Psalm 139:13–16 the worshiper celebrates God's intimate care for and involvement with him or her, even before the mother knew she was pregnant. Jeremiah 1:5 comes in the context of God calling Jeremiah to the prophetic task; even before Jeremiah, or anyone else, had plans for the man's life, God had this particular plan and was overseeing Jeremiah's development with this plan in mind. (This helps to fortify Jeremiah for the tremendous difficulties he will face, see Jer 1:16–19.) And in Luke 1:44, the not-yet-born John the Baptist exercises his prophetic role, which the angel had foretold (1:15, "he will be filled with the Holy Spirit, even from his mother's womb.")

We can say, therefore, that the biblical materials taken as a whole do indeed endorse the human personhood of the child in the womb. However, the generally non-technical language of the biblical writers, which does not get into details, say, of the difference between an embryo and a fetus, does not settle any question about when this human personhood comes into being. The process of empirical investigation and critical thinking can therefore supplement the biblically based ethical reasoning. That process shows, for example, that there is no obvious addition of any information after conception. Together these lead to the conclusion that the unborn are humans and thus persons to be protected at all stages of their development.

Not every good-faith act of communication requires that the speaker endorse what he alludes to. Suppose, for example, that I refer to things that Sam and Frodo did, and at the same time I do not clarify whether I believe that *The Lord of the Rings* is historical. I am not breaking faith with anyone, unless of course I had led my audience to believe that the account was historical when I knew it was not. A person competent in a culture has the know-how to discern the generic clues: my children, before they were five, could tell the difference between the *Chronicles of Narnia* and the book of Acts, and I did not have to make explicit a stance toward the actuality or otherwise of the events. I suspect that this explains why Jude 14 does not need to explicate its stance toward whether the traditions that we know as the book of Enoch are canonical—he shares a stance with his audience and leaves them to see that.[4]

Biblical authors at times refer to pagan myths. Whether or not the author himself believed the myth to be true has no impact on whether he made his point in good faith: It is enough to suppose that he is using the ideas in a different setting from their original or evoking the emotional overtones of the mythic names for the purpose of asserting the LORD's superiority over them all.[5] A talented writer like C. S. Lewis could readily use deities such as Aphrodite/Venus or Eros as personifications without asking anyone to believe in them.

4.C WHAT IS THE CONNECTION BETWEEN A WORLD PICTURE AND A WORLDVIEW?

I have hinted at what I think is a helpful distinction, namely, between world *picture* and world*view*. The world picture is just what the name implies: what one imagines to be the shape of the world and the things in it, such as how large the earth is, what shape it has, where the land leaves off and the sea begins, what is under the ground and over the sky, the behavior of horses at watering troughs, and so on. The worldview, as I have used the term, is one's basic dispositional stance toward the world, such as whether it came from God or exists on its own, whether there is a universal moral code, and so on. The worldview is intended to be normative and to transcend culture and time period, while the world picture need not do so.

The biblical authors and their audiences will generally share a great deal of their world picture. They commonly operate using this shared picture in order to shape the worldview of their audiences. Part of our concern will be, especially in cases where we do not share the same picture due to new knowledge, the extent to which a good-faith communication is tied to the specific

---

4. Peter Enns, *Inspiration and Incarnation* (Grand Rapids: Baker Academic, 2005), 145–46, simply notes the reference in Jude and assumes that this reflects a high regard for the book—without taking account of any of these linguistic-pragmatic features.

5. See J. N. Oswalt, "The Myth of the Dragon and Old Testament Faith," *EvQ* 49:3 (1977): 163–72. Oswalt also shows that some alleged allusions are not allusions at all.

world picture. At least as it appears at first glance, the connection can be loose indeed. For example, I, a modern who accepts contemporary cosmology as part of my world picture, can share a worldview with some medieval (or Reformer such as John Calvin for that matter)[6] whose world picture perhaps involved a stationary earth with an orbiting sun. As I will explain in chapter 6, this is because the changing cosmological theory has not changed the underlying story. We therefore must treat each particular instance on its own.

4.D SENSE, REFERENCE, RHETORIC, AND TRUTH

What makes an act of communication "true"? How do rhetoric and poetical features affect our answer—can we even apply a word like true to items with poetic and rhetorical devices? What do we mean by the word "true"? Is something like "trustworthy" a better rubric?

We must always be careful about framing a priori abstract definitions that fail to match our experience. Rather, we can reasonably try to articulate and analyze our intuitions and to make them more rigorous.[7]

Let us consider some examples. Suppose I tell someone that it is 500 km from St. Louis to Chicago, and I add that one travels north to get there. Have I told the truth? Most people would not answer until they knew what purpose I had in mind for conveying this information. Was I aiming to explain why an afternoon visit by car is not feasible? Perhaps I had in mind to give a sense of why the winters differ in these places. In these cases, most people would say that I told the truth well enough for my conversational purpose. If, however, I was supposed to give directions for travel together with a timetable, then I had failed to supply an adequate representation of the world. In the same way, the standard schematic of the London Underground is the right tool for someone who wants to get from the School of Oriental and African Studies to the Waterloo railway station, and for such a person (as I once was) we can say that the schematic tells the truth. But an engineer may require a geographic map of the system; the schematic is *too* schematized.

Robert Burns famously declared that his "Luve" was "like a red, red rose // That's newly sprung in June." Did he tell the truth? Most people would say that it depends on what his subject was really like, that is, on whether the

---

6. See Calvin's *Genesis*, Calvin Translation Society (Grand Rapids: Baker, 1979), 61: "We indeed are not ignorant, that the circuit of the heavens is finite, and that the earth, like a little globe, *is placed in the center*" (emphasis added).

7. In addition to the intuitions and linguistic sources mentioned here, this discussion has also profited from Kevin Vanhoozer's contributions to the book edited by James Merrick and Stephen Garrett, *Five Views on Biblical Inerrancy* (Grand Rapids: Zondervan, 2013).

simile really fits. We would guess that, in the case of romantic poetry, a rose is a better image than an onion—at least the onions Burns and his readers would have known.[8] Further, the overall content of Burns' poem fends off any over-interpretation, such as wondering what aspect of the Luve corresponds to the thorns that one finds on rose bushes.

Try another example. Many years ago I was invited to address a theology conference, specifically to provide a perspective on a controversial topic, a perspective quite different from that of the organizers and most of the attenders. My children were under ten years old at the time, very aware of the controversy, and sure that their father could supply potent arguments to overcome any disagreement. I gave my talks, fielded questions, and even spoke with small groups of people after the sessions. When my children asked me to tell them about the conference, I said:

There were *thousands* of them, and they just kept coming, and I kept swinging. Every time I knocked one down, five would rush in to take his place. But I stood my ground, and when it was over, there they were, lying in heaps, and I was still on my feet.

My children had no difficulty imagining the scene—a dozen or more earnest people asking what they thought were knock-down questions, whom I felt I had answered well. They enjoyed my portrayal of the scene as a combat, with me a sort of Horatio at the bridge, and of course they viewed me as heroic, which is what I wanted. Did I tell them the truth? I answer, "yes": unless, perhaps, my self-portrayal as a valiant warrior was morally questionable. What I said and the way I said it was suited to the communication going on; and there was a real referent for them to imagine, which they did successfully.

In other words, to be "true" there must be a real referent (even if it is an abstraction such as goodness or conflict), and the speaker's way of representing the referent should be appropriate both for the referent and for the communication event. Further, a communication event invites the audience to cooperate, and we assume that the audience has some access to the kind of cooperation suited to the event, and that if they do so, they will not be misled.

The word "literal" has come to bedevil such analyses, particularly as it relates to assessing truthfulness. Often when a person claims to be literal he

---

8. As Lewis observed concerning the medieval *Romance of the Rose*, "If roses did not smell sweet Guillaume de Lorris could never have used a rose to symbolize his heroine's love. An onion would not do instead." See *"De audiendis poetis,"* in *Studies in Medieval and Renaissance Literature*, ed. Walter Hooper (Cambridge: Cambridge University Press, 1966), 1–17, quote on p. 17.

is really advocating a kind of literal*ism*, which assumes a straightforward relationship between how the speaker or author conceives things to be, how he represents things in his text, and what he is actually affirming and asking his audience to accept. We may call these three aspects of communication *conception*, *characterization*, and *commitment*. From a linguistic point of view, literalism focuses on the locution in the narrowest way, without attending to how it serves the illocution.[9]

A way to test this discussion comes from Norman Maclean's account of the disastrous Mann Gulch Fire of 1949, *Young Men and Fire*. Of the sixteen men fighting that fire, thirteen died. The foreman, Wagner Dodge, survived (only to die a few years later of Hodgkin's Disease) and testified to the investigators. Some years later Maclean, who had fought forest fires in his native Montana before becoming a professor of English in Chicago, researched the events for a more up-to-date and scientific take on them. The result:

> Therefore, when Dodge spoke of a solid "wall of flame" behind him, 250 to 300 feet deep, he was *speaking figuratively as a poet, as most of us do*. What was behind him were hundreds of thousands of little fires multiplying so fast that only a computer could keep up with them.[10]

Of course, normal people, even when speaking carefully, describe things in terms of what they see (phenomenally), as did Dodge. For the sake of his testimony, his description was surely true (as Maclean recognized)—because the commitment that Dodge was seeking from his audience was to the *picture* of the fire and not to its *physics*. The mathematical study that Maclean participated in, however, was concerned with other communicative and behavioral ends (such as how to avoid such catastrophic loss of life in the future).

Let us explore a few more examples. In the first *Star Wars* film, *Episode 4: A New Hope*, Luke is on board the Millennium Falcon, learning the ways of the Force. He cannot block the shots from the remote droid until Obi-Wan makes him put on a helmet with an eye cover, explaining, "Your eyes can deceive you. Don't trust them."[11] Similarly, in *The Two Towers* (part of *The Lord of the Rings*), as Gandalf restores King Théoden of Rohan to health,

---

9. In biblical studies, the approach to a "literal" or "plain" meaning found in Jowett and Barr (described in ch. 1) fits this depiction.

10. Norman Maclean, *Young Men and Fire* (Chicago: University of Chicago Press, 1992), 260 (emphasis added). Maclean is better known for his collection of novellae, *A River Runs through It* (Chicago: University of Chicago, 1976).

11. In the DVD, this occurs in chapter 27: at about 59:17 of the original theatrical release (1977), and 1:01:50 of the remastered edition (2008).

he says: "Your fingers would remember their old strength better, if they grasped a sword-hilt."[12]

Now, a modern neuroscientist could object: the eyes do not deceive, and the fingers do not remember; instead, it is the processing of the signals that takes place in the brain. So perhaps Obi-Wan and Gandalf simply betray some aberrant science?

But our neuroscientist, by insisting on scientific terminology, is actually hindering communication. We can easily identify the experiences that Obi-Wan and Gandalf are talking about, and their words portray just what it feels like—even when we accept the neuroscientist's explanation. Actually, the more popular way of describing these activities is easier for us to picture precisely because that is what it feels like. We do not have to resort to saying that Gandalf and Obi-Wan referred successfully but incorrectly, since neither wise person was intending to speak scientifically. Neither one invited his audience to embrace a theory of neural processing.

In the same way, someone might object to the term "centrifugal force" to explain what happens if one twirls a string with a stone tied to its end, because he insists that the real force (as Newtonian mechanics describes it) is centri*petal*—that is, a force imposed on the stone to make it travel toward the center, making it circle. But the common expression, centrifugal force, allows the audience to identify the referent and to imagine the experience—in fact, it does so far better than the more Newtonian term! (I leave aside the status of the Newtonian description as a model.)

People who watch broadcasts of American football will hear announcers from time to time speak of "the football gods": these gods will allow a team to mount an otherwise unbelievable comeback, scoring the game-winning points just as time expires. Or the gods may thwart such an effort, leaving nothing but disappointment. Someone unfamiliar with American culture might wonder what to do with the locution. Does it represent a genuine belief in these gods? But anyone inside the culture is well aware that this is a conventional way of describing imponderable or uncontrollable factors in outcomes (whether of caprice or of merit); most of the broadcasters, if they have any religion at all, are nominally Christian. The expression "Hail Mary pass"—a desperation measure with little chance of succeeding—became especially common after Roger Staubach (a very devout Roman Catholic) played quarterback for the Dallas Cowboys (1971–79). It is a popular phrase, even for sports commentators with no actual belief in Marian assistance.

---

12. J. R. R. Tolkien, *The Two Towers* (Boston: Houghton-Mifflin, 1965), 121 (book III, ch. VI).

These expressions are, nevertheless, truthful. They provide once-interesting means of referring to the inscrutable, which are now clichés, and audiences know how to understand them (with awe or dismay, not with religious affirmation).

At the same time, the referent imposes limits on artistic license. In *Star Wars Episode 6: Return of the Jedi*, Luke has learned that Darth Vader is really his father, and he reproaches Obi-Wan's ghost for telling him that Vader had *killed* his father. Obi-Wan explains, "Your father was seduced by the dark side of the force. He ceased to be Anakin Skywalker and became Darth Vader. When that happened, the good man who was your father was destroyed. So, what I told you was true, from a certain point of view." Luke's incredulous reply: "A certain point of view?"[13] Even the highly accomplished Alec Guinness, who portrayed Obi-wan, could not manage a facial expression of conviction in that scene. I expect he agreed with Luke's incredulity; I certainly do.

Complicating factors do in fact arise that make it difficult to declare something simply, or partly, true or false. For example, the speaker or author might not have ensured that the audience can ascertain the information (as can happen with irony). Or, the audience might not have received the communication correctly—perhaps because they do not have access to the key aspects of the original shared world that enable understanding or because they have failed to exercise the appropriate goodwill (whether through laziness, antipathy, impatience, or even excusable ignorance). So, we will have to be suitably modest.

The cases we are discussing in this study involve narratives, which have characters, events, and settings to which the narrators refer. Thus, the question of truth has to do with whether such characters, events, and settings existed and whether the way the text refers to them is appropriate. Or perhaps the tale is intentionally and recognizably fictional but illustrative of genuinely existing concepts such as badness or obedience. The terms true and false are not normally applied to things such as commands and laws, but in these cases we do usually exercise some level of discernment. For example, does the text give us a simple command, or does it have implied exceptions and qualifications, or is it sarcastic? Is the person giving the command worthy of my respect, or, more strongly, my ready compliance? As C. S. Lewis observed,

> When the poets call the directions or "rulings" of Jahweh "true" they are expressing the assurance that these, and not those others, are the "real"

---

13. In the DVD, this occurs in chapter 15: at about 45:20–23 of the original theatrical release (1980), and 46:07–30 of the remastered edition (2008).

or "valid" or unassailable ones; that they are based on the very nature of things and the very nature of God.[14]

Hence questions of truth and falsehood do come into play here as well. And, if we think rhetorically, that is not a surprise. Commands are communicative acts in which the illocution is made more explicit.

A further example is the case of the rhetorical concession *arguendo*, that is, a concession that allows premises to be provisionally accepted for the sake of the argument without agreeing that the premises are actually valid. For example, suppose I am speaking with a child whose parents told him that babies are delivered by a stork, and suppose that I do not agree that this is the best way to defer explaining reproduction to children. Suppose further that, in my value system, I should not interfere with other people's parenting strategies. Can I still speak truthfully with such a child? Certainly. I can say, "How old were you when your sister arrived?" I might even say, if he told me his parents' story about the stork, "How old were you when the stork brought your sister?"

That is to say, we find cases in which *not denying* something need not be the same as *affirming*, just as *not mentioning* something need not equate to *denying* it. Speakers generally expect their audiences to exercise discernment and even to revise their initial impressions based on this discernment.

Let us apply these thoughts to some biblical texts. In Mark 4:31 (see also Matt 13:31–32) a mustard seed is called "the smallest of all the seeds on earth" (μικρότερον ὂν πάντων τῶν σπερμάτων τῶν ἐπὶ τῆς γῆς). The locution sounds absolute and unqualified. As it happens, the mustard seed is not the smallest; the orchid is said to hold that title.[15] We might wonder whether the word γῆ should be "land" instead of "earth"; and we might also think of taking the form μικρότερον as "rather small," but let us concede, *arguendo*, the traditional translation for the moment. Our discussion so far has shown that people normally speak hyperbolically or with respect to something, and certainly the sayings of Jesus are all in either ordinary or poetic language. In fact, it is likely that the mustard seed's tiny size is a conventional image for something as small as conceivable.[16] Thus we may conclude that the mustard seed is the smallest of all the seeds *that are relevant to this conversation*; this is reasonable, since these gospel texts speak of seeds being "sown" (Gk. σπείρω),

---

14. C. S. Lewis, *Reflections on the Psalms* (London: Geoffrey Bles, 1958), 60–61.
15. United Bible Societies, *Fauna and Flora of the Bible* (London: United Bible Societies, 1980), 145.
16. In the Talmud see Berakot 31-a: "The daughters of Israel were stringent with themselves; to the extent that even if they see a drop of blood *corresponding to the size of a mustard seed* she sits seven clean days for it" (ET from Epstein, *Soncino Talmud*).

and thus Jesus was talking about crops.[17] We can go further if we factor in the way the text interacts with the audience's preexisting knowledge of the world. The plant to which Jesus referred is probably either the black mustard (*Brassica nigra*) or the white mustard (*Sinapis alba*).[18] Either way, it is what we would call a tall weed (approximately 2–3 meters high) and, while birds could find refuge in the shade of a field of mustard plants, the expression "the birds of the heavens can make nests in its shade" (variants in Matt 13:32; Luke 13:19) evokes Old Testament texts about powerful empires (Ezek 31:6; Dan 4:12, 21) and the destiny of God's people (Ezek 17:23). With these notions in their cognitive background, the disciples and early Christians would not have confused the parable's details as a lesson in botany; their attention would have gone elsewhere. As Musselman concludes:

> It is helpful to consider the mustard story within the context of the other parables of the Kingdom in Matthew 13. One of the recurring themes is that something small, or easily overlooked (the treasure in the field, the leaven in the meal, the tares in the wheat), can become large or important.[19]

Indeed, the echoes suggest that the kingdom will eventually supersede the pretensions of human empires with a reign of universal benevolence.[20] That is, the meaning of the saying is the interaction of the locution with the shared knowledge of the world.

In the same way, a grain of wheat must fall to the ground and "die" in order to bear fruit (John 12:24). For the purposes of the analogy that Jesus made (one must "hate" one's life in this world), this is a suitable description and probably conventional (1 Cor 15:36). In fact, the convention makes good sense: The seed is dropped, perhaps gets covered with soil, and to all appearances is dead. After all, the hating of one's life is also a figure of speech. To take either of these as remarks in the realm of natural history is a failure to cooperate with the text due to a failure to appreciate the conventional nature of the locution. We have not been asked to accept a particular theory of plant science.

---

17. Orchids grow in Israel, apparently predominately wild. As Lytton John Musselman, *A Dictionary of Biblical Plants* (Cambridge: Cambridge University Press, 2012), puts it, "When any crop member of the mustard family (the Brassicaceae) is compared to the common crops, such as lentils, wheat, barley, chickpea, and broad bean, the mustard is discernibly the smallest" (p. 95).

18. See Musselman, *Dictionary of Biblical Plants*, 94–96; F. Nigel Hepper, *Illustrated Encyclopedia of Bible Plants* (Grand Rapids: Baker Academic, 1992), 133; Michael Zohary, *Plants of the Bible* (Cambridge: Cambridge University Press, 1982), 93; UBS, *Fauna and Flora*, 145–46. Hepper is undecided, though general opinion tends toward the black mustard.

19. Musselman, *Dictionary of Biblical Plants*, 96.

20. For exegesis of the passage in Mark, see Hans F. Bayer, *Das Evangelium des Markus* (Giessen: SCM R. Brockhaus, 2008), 207–8.

I suspect that concession *arguendo* explains the New Testament references to Leviticus 18:5. In the original context the passage says, "You shall therefore keep my statutes and my rules; if a person does them, he shall live by them: I am the LORD." Some have read this as implying that the Pentateuch provides a system by which a person is justified by law keeping, and thus they read the New Testament references as supporting that very reading (see Rom 10:5; Gal 3:12). However, there are plenty of texts in the Old Testament that connect doing and living (Deut 4:1; 8:1; Ezek 20:11, 13, 21; Neh 9:29). These passages are clear that the doing is the right response to God's grace that provides both covenant and moral instruction to man; they never present obedience as the way of gaining that grace. In fact, Jesus says the same thing (John 15:10): "If you keep my commandments, you will abide in my love." In conventional theological terms, this comes under the rubric of perseverance.

The clue comes in Luke 10:25, 28:

> ²⁵"Teacher, what shall I do to inherit eternal life?" . . . ²⁸And he said to him, "You have answered correctly; do this, and you will live."

The question allows us to see the assumptions behind *some* first-century Jews' usage of our text: literally the Greek reads, "What having done, shall I inherit eternal life," that is, "*by having done what* shall I inherit eternal life?" The man apparently assumes a reading of Leviticus 18:5, namely, that the doing qualifies him for eternal life; and Jesus answers him on the basis of this assumption with intensive demands, which the man cannot fulfill (vv. 26–27). Luke makes it clear what the man wanted in all this: to "justify himself" (θέλων δικαιῶσαι ἑαυτόν, v. 29).²¹ By using a concession *arguendo* Jesus can move on to what he counted as the deeper issue.

Another example comes from the way that some biblical critics found the two accounts of Jael's slaying of Sisera to be at odds with each other. In Judges 4:17–24 we have a prose narrative of how Sisera, fleeing a defeat, took refuge in Jael's tent. As he slept she drove a tent peg through his temple and killed him. The next chapter features a poem by the judge Deborah, celebrating the great victory. In Judges 5:26–27 we read:

> She sent her hand to the tent peg
>   and her right hand to the workmen's mallet;

---

21. As I noted in ch. 3, we ought not assume that a gospel writer is using words in the same way as Paul did. However, if we take the conventional association of Luke with Paul (Col 4:14; Phlm 24; 2 Tim 4:11; Acts 16:10), we may readily suppose he expected his readers to catch the Pauline echoes.

> she struck Sisera;
>> she crushed his head;
>> she shattered and pierced his temple.
> Between her feet
>> he sank, he fell, he lay still;
> between her feet
>> he sank, he fell;
> where he sank,
>> there he fell—dead.

In a standard critical commentary, George Foot Moore supposed that we have two originally different accounts in the Judges. In the poem, "As [Sisera] was hastily draining the bowl, Jael seized some heavy object that lay close at hand and felled him to the earth with a blow."[22] Moore even tells readers *not* to interpret the poem in light of the accompanying prose account.

Without a doubt, that reading represents a striking failure in literary sense on Moore's part. The prose narrative has its own artistry, especially in its sparse and understated description. The poem has a different purpose, namely, to celebrate. Its very nature is to invite its audience to picture the events *as if* they were as portrayed here—as if, in this case, the mighty Sisera had engaged a woman in combat and been defeated—perhaps as an image of Israel's defeat of Sisera's stronger forces. The reference to "between her feet" may subtly and gently evoke a gender difference. The poem goes on to envision Sisera's mother peering out the window, wondering why he is so long in returning from the battle. The poet portrays the princesses suggesting that there is so much Israelite spoil to be taken that the armies are occupied; they even include Israelite girls in the spoil, to be used sexually (v. 30, "a womb or two for every man"). An Israelite audience would find this repulsive, and exult in Sisera's defeat and ignominious death—which fulfills the poem's purpose. The poetic portrayal does not compete with the prosaic one.

But surely we can find some examples that do not lend themselves so readily to this kind of treatment—examples where "explaining" is clearly "explaining away" and sleight of hand? I will take some of these up in chapter 9

---

22. George F. Moore, *Judges*, ICC (Edinburgh: T&T Clark, 1895), 163; see also G. A. Cooke, *The Book of Judges*, CBSC (Cambridge: Cambridge University Press, 1913), 66. Michael David Coogan found it unprofitable to relate the two accounts, as "poets are not historians." See Coogan, "A Structural and Literary Analysis of the Song of Deborah," *CBQ* 40 (1978): 143–66, quote on p.144. Coogan also refers to C. M. Bowra's helpful study, *Heroic Poetry* (London: Macmillan, 1952). Further, by "history" Coogan seems to mean something like what I have called "antiquarian history" (see ch. 6 below), and thus the opposition is not as stark on the referential level as he implies.

below in discussing whether the material in Genesis (and the Bible as a whole) offers an actual world picture. Here I will add an example that *may* be taken as resting upon a faulty bit of natural history.

In Job 20:16 Zophar describes one feature of the inevitable judgment God will send on the wicked:

> He will suck the poison of cobras;
> the tongue of a viper will kill him.

And in Psalm 140:3 we find this description of violent persons:

> They make their tongue sharp as a serpent's,
> and under their lips is the venom of asps.

Some have suggested that passages like these reflect an ancient belief that the snake's venom is somehow connected to its tongue, perhaps as the place where it is stored or even as the means by which it might be delivered by a sting.[23] Josephus might also have held such a view, since he portrayed God as having "put venom beneath [the serpent's] tongue" in punishment for beguiling the first human pair (*Ant.*, 1, 50 [1.1.4]).

We may wish to grant, in light of Josephus, that some people did think this way about snakes and venom. It is clear, however, from the biblical materials, that Israelites understood that a venomous snake delivers its goods by *biting* (see, for example, Num 21:6–9; Amos 5:19; 9:3; Jer 8:17) so that whatever the tongue does, it is not of itself the danger. This being the case, it makes sense to represent the venom as "under the lips" (Ps 140:3). We could dismiss the text in Job from consideration by recalling that it is, after all, in a poetic passage (as the speeches generally are in that book); we might also recognize that it occurs in a speech of Zophar, whose overall views the author of Job does not endorse (see 42:7). We could easily imagine that the ancients had some kind of convention in depicting how a snake injects its venom.

Suppose, however, we were to insist that the text does reflect actual notions of serpentine anatomy, which we do not share. Does that render the text false? Certainly not. The text has the goal of referring to a danger, and the exact location where a snake stores its venom is irrelevant. In fact, it would be silly beyond measure for a scientific Westerner to disregard a warning from someone like Josephus if it came in this form: "Mind where you put your

---

23. On the basis of these two texts, United Bible Societies, *Fauna and Flora of the Bible*, 72, states: "The serpent's weapon of attack is its poison fang, but in biblical times it was believed to be the tongue."

hands! That snake has some nasty venom under its tongue!" The ability of the warning to refer faithfully does not in any way depend on anatomical views.

But, as a matter of fact, the idea that the texts involve any real assertions about animal biology beyond the danger of serpents' venom—which, as everyone knew, is delivered through the teeth—strains credulity. Rather, the authors used experiences that the audiences were all too familiar with and depicted them vividly.

The episode of Reuben and the mandrakes (Gen 30:14–18) may make a similar allusion to popular views during this ancient period. Reuben, the son of Jacob by Leah, collected some mandrakes and gave them to his mother. The rival-wife Rachel requested some of them. Many suppose that people in that culture imagined that mandrakes might aid in fertility, which explains Rachel's request.[24] It is indeed possible that Rachel and Leah so thought; but the most that the author asks of us is to acknowledge that the popular thought existed—he does not require us to affirm the thought. Further, the storyteller rejects any kind of *magical* view of the plant (if by "magical" we mean, "able to override not only physical properties but even the divine will"), since Leah trades to Rachel some of the mandrakes in exchange for spending the night with Jacob. It is Leah, not Rachel, who conceives here—the mandrakes play no role in that. The account actually asks the audience to recognize the usual role that sexual relations play in conception, and that this role is, like everything else, subject to God's confirmation.

Hence, at least for the most part, the biblical materials are not even in the category of, for example, a medieval person who subscribes to the Greek idea of the four humors as fundamental to health. Were such a person to tell us, "Do not drink this potion, it will do bad things to your humors," we would wisely observe the admonition. We might assess the degree to which our medieval informant was making a physiological affirmation about humors, depending on where he fit in the social scale: a scholar would be making such an affirmation, a peasant probably would not. A poet would use accepted ideas in order to create an atmosphere. But in any case, we would not drink the potion, which is the point that matters—and we would not need to commit even to the scholar's affirmation in order to cooperate.

This discussion shows a crucial feature of communication: We cannot always say how an author *conceived* of his referents; what we can say is how he *portrayed* them. Further, the portrayal may represent actual conceptions of the referents, either the author's or that shared between him and his audience; or it

---

24. Ibid., 138–39.

may represent conventional depictions that the audience is familiar with and recognizes as not making scientific claims. These portrayals represent communicative goals (or illocutions), which may sometimes include imparting or reaffirming physical information, but, in normal human usage, focus on other things such as attitudes and actions.

C. S. Lewis gives us an autobiographical example of how conventionality works, particularly of how it does not imply a theory. He tells us about how, as a child, he "evolved the theory that a candle-stick was so-called 'because it made the candle *stick* up.'" But, he tells, us, "that wasn't why I called it a candlestick. I called it a candlestick because everyone else did."[25] The communicative goal in using the standard name for something is clear, namely, ready identification of the referent.

We can extend the lexical idea of "sense" to include this portrayal, with its associated illocutions; and the author invites his audience to imagine the referent *as if* this were a suitable designation for this context. Proper cooperation involves imagining and discerning the extent to which the author is making "scientific" affirmations about his referent.

This aspect of communicating by way of portrayals happens even in the sciences. Imagine that I am teaching adolescents about electron energy levels in the atom. I may have to use a Bohr-Rutherford planetary model of the atom as an aid to visualization. I may want to tell them that actual physicists think things are more complicated than that, but I do not have to. The model is an adequate *portrayal* for the kind of communication I am carrying out, even when it does not represent my *conception*.

---

25. Lewis, *Studies in Words*, 11 (emphasis original).

Chapter 5

WHAT DO WE HAVE IN GENESIS 1–11?
Part 1: Context

In the previous chapters I have laid out the orientation by which I intend to examine Genesis 1–11. Now I can turn to applying the pragmatic and sociolinguistic perspective to reading this material. In this chapter I will take up the matter of context and use textlinguistic and rhetorical principles to consider how the context of Genesis 1–11 serves to guide its interpretation. In the next chapter I consider the function of these eleven chapters of Genesis in the communities of ancient Israel and their religious heirs. Then we can offer a rhetorical-theological reading of Genesis 1–11 (ch. 7) and afterwards (ch. 8) look at how other writers, especially canonical ones, have used Genesis 1–11 and what that tells us about how to read these passages well.

In chapter 1 I quoted Benjamin Jowett to the effect that a good interpreter needs "the logical power to perceive the meaning of words in reference to their context." The areas of linguistic pragmatics that I have been describing offer us a way to think more fully and carefully about context than it appears Jowett did.

There are at least two levels of context. The first is the *literary context*, that is, how the text fits together within itself and how it fits within the larger body of text of which it is part. The second is the *context of the shared world* between the author and the audience (such as I have discussed in ch. 4). The aim of this context is to know how the details of the text should produce a message for the audience. Further, this shared world has subtopics: (a) Do the kindred stories that we find among other peoples show us what kinds of literary and referential concerns a narrative like Genesis 1–11 might have?;

(b) What sorts of lifestyle and social setting of the audience might the text presuppose and speak to?

5.A COHESION AND COHERENCE

Discourse linguists use the terms "cohesion" and "coherence" to talk about how a text holds together to do its job of communicating.[1] *Cohesion* has to do with the way features of the text display its overall unity and flow: repeated words or synonyms, grammatical links (such as "next" or "therefore"), use of pronouns once the noun has been introduced, and so on. *Coherence* has to do with the unified subject matter of the text and sometimes with the audience's ability to discern that unity, to make a mental representation of it. Cohesion plays a role in discerning coherence but so do other factors such as background knowledge and social setting. Both notions are concerned with context—cohesion looks especially at the literary context and coherence looks at the larger referential context.

In this chapter and those following, I will examine how Genesis 1–11 functions in its context, focusing especially on literary and cultural context here, then on its social context (ch. 6) and at how other qualified and competent readers, in and around the canon, have understood and used the material (ch. 8).

5.A.1 Internal Cohesion

Let us first tackle the internal cohesion. Do we find textual indicators that the parts of Genesis 1–11 function together to make a unified whole? After all, scholars commonly assign the different pericopes in Genesis 1–11 to separate sources.[2] For example, we often read that Genesis 1–2 present two different creation accounts (1:1–2:3 and 2:4–25), which may even be difficult to reconcile with each other.[3]

If we can establish that the current form of Genesis invites us to read Genesis 1–11 as a coherent whole, then we can say that any reading that fails

---

1. See, for example, Joan Cutting, *Pragmatics and Discourse: A Resource Book for Students* (London: Routledge, 2002), 2; Robert A. Dooley and Stephen H. Levinsohn, *Analyzing Discourse: A Manual of Basic Concepts* (Dallas: SIL International, 2000), chs. 5–6. Literary scholars who are not discourse linguists will not follow this somewhat artificial distinction between the two words. Rather, they may simply use coherence for both concepts.

2. For a recent survey of the field as it applies to Genesis 1–11, see Jan Christian Getz, "The Formation of the Primeval History," in *The Book of Genesis: Composition, Reception, and Interpretation*, ed. Craig A. Evans, Joel N. Lohr, and David L. Petersen (Leiden: Brill, 2012), 107–35.

3. For two relevant examples, see Peter Enns, *The Evolution of Adam: What the Bible Does and Doesn't Say about Human Origins* (Grand Rapids: Brazos, 2012), 140; and Daniel Harlow, "Creation According to Genesis: Literary Genre, Cultural Context, Theological Truth," *Christian Scholars Review* 37.2 (2008): 163–98.

to incorporate such coherence is inadequate—and that this is so regardless of what we think about the prehistory of the individual pericopes.

Consider, then, the cohesive factors for all of Genesis 1–11. Well-known links include those between Adam and Noah, presenting Noah as a "new Adam" (compare Gen 9:1 with 1:28).[4] Further, there are clear links between Genesis 1 and 5, such as 1:26–27 and 5:1–5 (the life of Adam) and between Genesis 4 and 5, such as 4:25–26 and 5:3–11 (Seth and Enosh). There may be a link between the genealogy descended from Cain (4:17–22) and that from Seth (5:6–32), especially in the names Enoch, Methushael / Methuselah, and Lamech (compare 4:18 with 5:18, 21, 25), although this is uncertain.[5]

The flood story, Genesis 6–9, is widely held to be a showcase example of how analyzing the Pentateuch into its component sources has succeeded. It is quite common to see the story in the present text in Genesis as primarily a combination of materials from the Yahwist (J) and the Priestly source (P).[6] In 1978 Gordon Wenham published an article arguing for "The coherence of the flood narrative," based on his study of the chapters from the perspective of literary structure; and in 1987–88 John Emerton replied with a rejection of the arguments made by Wenham (and by several others).[7] Besides patterns of referring to the deity, Emerton finds what he counts to be duplications and even contradictions in the current form of the flood story. Now, Emerton's argument depends on a fairly simple notion of what constitutes a contradiction and of whether a repetition might serve some literary and communicative end. He also considers the burden of proof to lie upon those who see coherence (or cohesion). However, for my purposes here, I do not need to adjudicate that discussion. Rather, I note that Robert Longacre, a linguist who has developed a textlinguistic approach to Hebrew narratives, wrote a pair of articles on the flood story from his textlinguistic perspective (1976 and 1985), which contributes to the

---

4. See, e.g., William Dumbrell, *Covenant and Creation: A Theology of the Old Testament Covenants* (Carlisle: Paternoster, 1997), 27; Tremper Longman III, *How to Read Genesis* (Downers Grove, IL: InterVarsity Press, 2005), 117–18; Bruce Waltke and Cathy J. Fredericks, *Genesis* (Grand Rapids: Zondervan, 2001), 127–28.

5. See my *Genesis 1–4: A Linguistic, Literary, and Theological Commentary* (Phillipsburg, NJ: P&R, 2006), 201, where I suggest that maybe the contrast between the two families is prominent. Perhaps this indicates that the decline we see in Cain's family was not an inevitable outcome of being human; rather, it flowed from the moral orientation of the members, which in turn is influenced by the orientation of the head member of the list. We might also suspect that the author saw the orientation of Cain's line as becoming dominant and perhaps drawing Seth's descendants away from God so that "the wickedness of man was great in the earth" (6:5).

6. Richard Elliott Friedman, *The Bible with Sources Revealed: A New View into the Five Books of Moses* (New York: HarperCollins, 2003), 42–47, lays out the analysis.

7. Gordon J. Wenham, "The Coherence of the Flood Narrative," *VT* 28 (1978): 336–48; John A. Emerton, "An Examination of Some Attempts to Defend the Unity of the Flood Narrative in Genesis: Parts 1 and 2," *VT* 37 (1987): 401–420 and for Part 2, *VT* 38 (1988): 1–21. Emerton addresses arguments put forth by Cassuto, Nielsen, Andersen, and Radday in addition to those of Wenham.

discussion, but which Emerton did not invoke.[8] Longacre's study accounts for the features of the whole narrative reasonably well, and he contends:

> We do not find that the fragments which we can assemble into a putative source prove to be a coherent piece of discourse structure while the whole in which the "source" is incorporated can be shown to have a remarkably unified and cohesive structure. . . . The discourse analyst is left, therefore with an attitude of agnosticism towards the sources: undoubtedly, for whoever wrote the story, sources existed, but just as probably those sources are completely irrecoverable.[9]

The flood story in the present text of Genesis has a logical flow, and the tensions (for example, between the numbers of animals Noah brought aboard) can be handled from a rhetorical perspective (for example, the initial command followed by a clarification).[10] Perhaps some of the other tensions can be relieved by reference to the other nations' stories that are the backcloth to the biblical telling. For example, the sending of the raven (Gen 8:7) is held to belong to the Priestly source, while in the Yahwist source Noah sends out the dove (8:8).[11] In the Gilgamesh Epic the Noah figure releases a dove, then a swallow, and then a raven.[12] The account in Genesis follows a logic that is obvious to anyone familiar with the birds. The raven, a hardy and intelligent scavenger, could fly to and fro, finding plenty of carrion to keep itself busy; there was no need to return to the ark. The dove, on the other hand, could not survive on its own until it found vegetable matter to eat; when the third dove did not return, that indicated that the lowlands were clear enough for the ark's passengers to disembark.[13] In sum, whatever prehistory there might have been behind the Genesis flood story, the product has an internal cohesion and coherence, as well as cohesion with the rest of Genesis 1–11.[14]

---

8. Robert Longacre, "The Discourse Structure of the Flood Narrative," in *Society of Biblical Literature 1976 Seminar Papers*, ed. G. MacRae (Missoula, MT: Scholars Press, 1976), 235–62. See also Robert Longacre, "Interpreting Biblical Stories," in *Discourse and Literature*, ed. Teun A. van Dijk (Amsterdam/Philadelphia: John Benjamins, 1985), 169–85.
9. Longacre, "Interpreting Biblical Stories," 170.
10. Longacre, "Discourse Structure," 259.
11. Friedman, *The Bible with Sources Revealed*, 45.
12. Gilgamesh, XI.iii.146–153. For English translation see Alexander Heidel, *The Gilgamesh Epic and Old Testament Parallels* (Chicago: University of Chicago Press, 1949), 86; Stephanie Dalley, *Myths from Mesopotamia* (Oxford: Oxford University Press, 2000), 114.
13. See the comparative discussion in Heidel, *Gilgamesh Epic*, 251–53. See also George Cansdale, *Animals of Bible Lands* (Exeter: Paternoster, 1970), 173, 182–83; United Bible Societies, *Fauna and Flora of the Bible* (London: United Bible Societies, 1980), 67–68.
14. I do not hold Longacre's discussion to be above critique. In ch. 7 on exposition I will show why I take Genesis 6:1–4 as part of the whole flood story (*pace* Longacre).

Genesis 10–11 are also cohesive with the flood story since these chapters record the sequel to the great flood with the descent of various peoples from the family of Noah (see 10:1), as linked by the genealogies (see 11:10, picking up the line of Shem), with 11:10–19 paralleling 10:21–25 (through Peleg) and 11:20–26 bringing the line down to Abram, Nahor, and Haran (who, with their descendants, will feature in the rest of Genesis).

Within Genesis 1–4 there are also clear linkages. First, Genesis 2–4 is commonly assigned to the J source, with a few redactions; their overall unity is not controversial.[15] Second, I agree with those who take Genesis 2:4–25 as elaborating the sixth day of Genesis 1 (see further ch. 7 below). Third, the common assertion that the P creation story (Gen 1) is free of anthropomorphisms is mistaken;[16] this story actually depends on an anthropomorphism, namely, the portrayal of God as one who goes through his work week and enjoys his Sabbath rest (a point I will develop later).[17] Genesis 2 contributes its own anthropomorphism to this pattern, depicting God as if he were a potter "forming" the first man (2:7), and a worker who "builds" the first woman (2:22, ESV margin).

Finally, several verbal links indicate that whatever separate origins the individual pericopes might have had, they have been edited in such a way as to exhibit cohesion. For example, in 1:28 we read, "And God *blessed* them. And God said to them, 'Be fruitful and *multiply*....'" In Genesis 3 the "blessing" (ברך, *brk*) has turned to "curse" (ארר, *'rr*), the proper antonym. And whereas the blessing was for them to *multiply* by having children, after their disobedience God says to the woman that he will "surely *multiply* your pain in childbearing"—the arena of blessing has turned into one of pain and danger. The genealogical chapter 5 also refers to God's curse on the ground: "And [Lamech] called his name Noah, saying, 'Out of the ground that the LORD has cursed [ארר, *'rr*] this one shall bring us relief from our work and from the painful toil [עצבון, *'itsabon*] of our hands'" (5:29, echoing 3:16–17).

Further, three enigmatic first-person plurals, by which God addresses "us," appear throughout Genesis 1–11: 1:26; 3:22; and 11:7. Many suppose that these (or at least the first) are God addressing his angelic council, although I judge the best explanation to be a "plural of self-address."[18] The

---

15. See Friedman, *The Bible with Sources Revealed*, 35–40, and my discussion in *Genesis 1–4*, 227–28.

16. Asserted in, e.g., Friedman, *Bible with Sources Revealed*, 12; S. R. Driver, *The Book of Genesis*, Westminster Commentary (London: Methuen, 1904), xxv.

17. Argued in, e.g., in C. John Collins, *Science and Faith: Friends or Foes?* (Wheaton, IL: Crossway, 2003) and *Genesis 1–4*, 77.

18. For relevant discussion, see Collins, *Genesis 1–4*, 59–61. More recently, Lyle Eslinger, "The Enigmatic Plurals like 'One of Us' (Genesis i 26, iii 22, and xi 7) in Hyperchronic Perspective,"

specific conclusion here does not matter for my purpose. The point is that this is a distinctive feature of this stretch of material from supposedly separate sources.

5.A.2 COHESION WITH GENESIS–DEUTERONOMY

The present text of Genesis 1–11 is now part of the whole structure of Genesis. The organizing function of the *toledot* (תולדות, "generations") in Genesis is well-known: see Genesis 2:4; 5:1; 6:9; 10:1, 32; 11:10, 27; 25:12, 19; 36:1, 9; 37:2. According to the *toledot*, Genesis 1 (really 1:1–2:3) stands as a kind of preamble to the whole book, while Genesis 2–4 (2:4–4:26) is the next section, and so on.[19]

I have argued above that Genesis 1–11 (1:1–11:26) has its own cohesion, and we can see that it stretches over several sections marked by *toledot*. At the same time, as Moberly has noted, there is no real grammatical break from Genesis 11 to Genesis 12.[20] The story as a whole progresses smoothly.

Now consider how Genesis 1:28 records God's blessing on the human couple, urging them to "be fruitful and multiply." These themes run throughout Genesis and beyond. In Genesis 9:1 Noah is a kind of new Adam: "And God *blessed* Noah and his sons and said to them, "*Be fruitful* and *multiply* and fill the earth." In Genesis 12:2–3 the LORD will *bless* Abram and make him a channel of blessing for his own descendants and for the rest of the world. These promises are repeated to Abraham's heirs: to Ishmael (17:20), Isaac (26:3–4), and Jacob (28:3; 48:3–4). The book of Exodus opens by telling us, "But the people of Israel *were fruitful* and increased greatly; they *multiplied* and grew exceedingly strong, so that the land was filled with them" (Exod 1:7). Deuteronomy promises that the people of Israel, when they are faithful, will continue to enjoy this blessing (30:16, cf. 7:13):

> If you obey the commandments of the LORD your God that I command you today, by loving the LORD your God, by walking in his ways, and by keeping his commandments and his statutes and his rules, then you shall live and *multiply*, and the LORD your God will *bless* you in the land that you are entering to take possession of it.[21]

VT 56.2 (2006): 171–84, argues that these plurals reflect a heightened focus on the divine-human difference. I am not convinced and retain what I find to be a simpler, and more exegetically based, explanation.

19. See discussion in Collins, *Genesis 1–4*, 229.
20. R. W. L. Moberly, *The Theology of the Book of Genesis*, Old Testament Theology (Cambridge: Cambridge University Press, 2009), 121.
21. See also Leviticus 26:9 and in the prophets, Jeremiah 3:16; 23:3; Ezekiel 36:11.

All of this allows us to read Genesis as focusing on the ways God has made new starts after Adam and Eve—with Noah and then with Abram and his offspring. That is to say: Noah, Abram, and Israel are "new Adams," which shows how fully Genesis 1–11 is integrated into the whole Pentateuch.

In the context of the Pentateuch, then, the purpose of Genesis is to identify the people of Israel, who followed Moses, as the heirs of God's promises to Abram (Abraham). In Genesis 12 God called Abram so that his family would be the vehicle of blessing to "all the families of the earth" (v. 3)—and, since Genesis 10 recounts the various "families" (or "clans," Heb. מִשְׁפָּחוֹת, *mishpehot*) of the earth, this means to all gentile peoples everywhere. Thus Genesis 1–11 serves to clarify that the God who called Abram is in fact the one true God, the Maker of heaven and earth, for whom all humankind yearns.

God's calling of Abram, therefore, is not simply for his own benefit but also for the rest of the world.[22] One of the chief themes of Old Testament messianic hope is the expectation that under the leadership of the Messiah, the people of God will succeed in bringing God's light to the gentile world. The shape of this biblical story assumes that all human beings have a common origin, a common predicament, and a common need to know God and have God's image restored in them. This assumption comes from including Genesis 1–11 in the story with some version of the conventional reading of the fall of the whole human family.[23]

5.A.3 Connected but Separate

I therefore see Genesis 1–11 as well integrated into the whole of Genesis and the Pentateuch. At the same time, it will serve us well to appreciate that there is a sense in which these chapters stand somewhat separately, as a kind of preface.

---

22. Here I agree with Christopher J. H. Wright, *The Mission of God: Unlocking the Bible's Grand Narrative* (Downers Grove, IL: InterVarsity Press, 2006), 194–221, against Moberly, *Theology of the Book of Genesis*, 141–61. Wright's position does better justice than Moberly's to (1) the likely sense of the passive or reflexive verb in Gen 12:3 ("all the families of the earth shall be blessed / shall find blessing for themselves," rather than "shall bless themselves"); (2) the context of Gen 12:1–3 in Genesis, with its evocation of 1:28 and the other "blessing" texts addressed to Abraham's descendants; (3) the biblical themes of blessing coming to the gentiles by way of Abraham's family; (4) the way that Ps 72:17 echoes Gen 22:18. On points (2) and (4), see further T. D. Alexander, "Further Observations on the Term 'Seed' in Genesis," *TynBul* 48:2 (1997): 363–67; C. John Collins, "Galatians 3:16: What Kind of Exegete was Paul?" *TynBul* 54:1 (2003): 75–86. As for the sense of "*in* you," Moberly makes no place for covenant inclusion, but this seems to me to be the best explanation of the Hebrew term. People are "in" someone when they are members of the people that the someone represents. This general perspective plays no part in the argument of Enns, *Evolution of Adam*.

23. Joseph Blenkinsopp, *Creation, Un-creation, Re-creation* (London: T&T Clark, 2011), 1–6, argues both that Gen 1–11 shows signs of having been "an originally independent text" from the rest of Genesis and that the conventional theme of the fall does not figure much in the Old Testament as a whole. These views lead to a way of reading that runs counter to the one here.

I have mentioned Moberly's observation that there is no real *grammatical* break from Genesis 1–11 to Genesis 12 (strictly speaking, at 11:27). But there is a clear *literary* break: The timeline, which has been barreling rapidly down the ages, slows down as we begin the story of Abram and his descendants—the ratio of narration time to elapsed time changes dramatically, and this is true regardless of what length of time we think is covered in Genesis 1–11. Further, if we accept that Genesis 1–11 provides important parallels with Mesopotamian materials (see the next section), then we have confirmation of this literary intuition.

Finally, Jan Fokkelman observed that the Primeval History consists of two sections (1:1–4:26 and 6:1–11:9), each followed by a "long genealogical register."[24] Further, these genealogies are quite similar in their structure and cover ten generations each—features that they do not share with other genealogies in Genesis (see ch. 7 below for more discussion).

In this light we may read Genesis 1–11 as a kind of preface that provides the universal setting for which the particularizing call of Abram is the solution. That is, Israel is one of the families of the earth, called for the sake of all the other families to address a universal need.

5.B SHARED WORLD CONTEXT

5.B.1 OTHER NATIONS' ORIGIN STORIES

An attentive reader intuitively sees a transition between Genesis 1–11 and the rest of Genesis, as we have just seen. Stories from other cultures in the ancient Near East confirm our intuition.[25] Although there are important materials from all the cultures of the ancient Near East, those most directly pertinent to Genesis 1–11 come from Mesopotamia. Specialists on the ancient Near East find the most promising parallels with Genesis 1–11 to include the Sumerian King List (c. eighteenth century BC), the Atrahasis Epic (c. eighteenth century BC), and the Eridu Genesis / Sumerian Flood Tale

---

24. Jan Fokkelman, *Reading Biblical Narrative: An Introductory Guide* (Louisville: Westminster John Knox, 1999), 156. Fokkelman himself counts Gen 10 as part of the final genealogy. This would mean, however, that 11:1–9 interrupts the flow. The discussion in chapter 7 below will show why it is better to take 10:1–11:9 as an entire unit.

25. Archaeological activity since the middle of the nineteenth century has certainly multiplied the availability of these ancient sources. However, Peter Enns is mistaken when he asserts, "These discoveries *for the first time*—and irrevocably—placed Israelite religion in a larger context" (*Evolution of Adam*, 35, emphasis added). Jewish writers from the Second Temple period, and early Christian writers as well, already knew of these issues. For specific discussion of the flood story, see my article, "Noah, Deucalion, and the New Testament," *Biblica* 93:3 (2012): 403–26. What these discoveries have changed is access to earlier versions of these stories in their ancient tongues rather than in Greek translation.

(c. sixteenth century BC).²⁶ (Another story, Enuma Elish, or the Babylonian Epic of Creation, once seemed a promising source for comparisons as well, and some biblical scholars still turn to it; Assyriologists, however, seem less willing to endorse as strong a comparison as they formerly did.²⁷) I do not deny, of course, that other ideologies, such as Egyptian and Canaanite,²⁸ also supply relevant background to the biblical account—but the Mesopotamian sources especially correspond to the basic narrative structure of Genesis

---

26. See, for example, David T. Tsumura, "Genesis and Ancient Near Eastern Stories of Creation and Flood: An Introduction," in *I Studied Inscriptions from before the Flood: Ancient Near Eastern, Literary, and Linguistic Approaches to Genesis 1–11*, ed. Richard S. Hess and David T. Tsumura (Winona Lake, IN: Eisenbrauns, 1994), 27–57, especially pp. 44–57; Richard Averbeck, "The Sumerian Historiographic Tradition and its Implications for Genesis 1–11," in *Faith, Tradition, and History: Old Testament Historiography in its Near Eastern Context*, ed. A. R. Millard, James K. Hoffmeier and David W. Baker (Winona Lake, IN: Eisenbrauns, 1994), 79–102; Kenneth A. Kitchen, *On the Reliability of the Old Testament* (Grand Rapids: Eerdmans, 2003), 423–25; and Anne Drafkorn Kilmer, "The Mesopotamian Counterparts of the Biblical *Nephilim*," in *Perspectives on Language and Text*, ed. Edgar W. Conrad (Winona Lake, IN: Eisenbrauns, 1987), 39–43. Richard S. Hess, "The Genealogies of Genesis 1–11 and Comparative Literature," *Biblica* 70 (1989): 241–54 (reprinted in Hess and Tsumura, *I Studied Inscriptions*, 58–72), adds some helpful cautions about the differences between the biblical genealogies and the king lists. Tikva Frymer-Kensky, "The Atrahasis Epic and Its Significance for Our Understanding of Genesis 1–9," *BA* 40.4 (1977): 147–55, supports the parallel between the biblical flood story and Atrahasis over Gilgamesh; at the same time, with her helpful observations about the contrast between the biblical and Mesopotamian accounts, I do not find all of her specific exegetical points on Genesis to be compelling.

27. For the Babylonian Creation Epic (or Enuma Elish) as a viable comparison being problematic, see W. G. Lambert, "A New Look at the Babylonian Background of Genesis," *JTS* 16:2 (1965): 287–300. He contends on p. 291: "The first major conclusion is that the Epic of Creation is not a norm of Babylonian or Sumerian cosmology. It is a sectarian and aberrant combination of mythological threads woven into an unparalleled compositum. In my opinion it is not earlier than 1100 BC." See also Alan R. Millard, "A New Babylonian 'Genesis' story," *TynBul* 18 (1967): 3–18 and Kitchen, *On the Reliability of the Old Testament*, 425. A further argument that the notion of *Chaoskampf* (such as that found in Enuma Elish) is absent from Genesis 1 comes from Gordon H. Johnston, "Genesis 1 and Ancient Egyptian Creation Myths," *BSac* 165.658 (2008): 178–94. Johnston contends that the Egyptian stories are a promising backcloth for Genesis. Alan Millard goes so far as to deny that *Chaoskampf* is the right term for what we find even in Enuma Elish, let alone in Genesis. See Millard, "From Woe to Weal: Completing a Pattern in the Bible and the Ancient Near East," in *Let Us Go Up to Zion: Essays in Honour of H.G.M. Williamson*, ed. I. Provan and M. Boda (Leiden: Brill, 2012), 193–201. Similarly, John H. Walton, "Creation in Genesis 1:1–2:3 and the Ancient Near East: Order Out of Disorder After *Chaoskampf*," *CTJ* 43.1 (2008): 48–63, rejects both *Chaoskampf* and "theomachy" but goes on to argue that Genesis 1 is a "temple cosmology," as in his popular *The Lost World of Genesis One: Ancient Cosmology and the Origins Debate* (Downers Grove, IL: InterVarsity Press, 2009) and in his academic work, *Genesis 1 as Ancient Cosmology* (Winona Lake, IN: Eisenbrauns, 2011). Bruce Waltke, on the other hand (see Waltke and Fredericks, *Genesis*, 23), still finds what he considers important parallels in Enuma Elish, as does Enns, *Evolution of Adam*, e.g., 38–43—but they do not address the reasons for reducing the importance of Enuma Elish for comparisons.

28. Strictly speaking, we have virtually no Canaanite material besides the reports in the Old Testament itself. The Ugaritic language and people are not properly Canaanite. On this topic see A. R. Millard, "The Canaanites," in *Peoples of Old Testament Times*, ed. D. J. Wiseman (Oxford: Oxford University Press, 1973), 36. It is best to distinguish Ugaritic language and Canaanite literature. Certainly they overlapped considerably, but it is better to use the specific name Ugaritic and not to prejudice the matter at any given point. A. F. Rainey, "A Canaanite at Ugarit," *IEJ* 13 (1963): 43–45, cites evidence from Ugarit that shows that Canaanites were regarded as foreigners: "Perhaps we should henceforth refrain from calling the people of Ugarit Canaanites since they did not consider themselves as such" (p. 45). See also John Huenergard, *An Introduction to Ugaritic* (Peabody: Hendrickson, 2012), 10, for agreement.

(and biblical literature traces Israel's origins back to Mesopotamia, Gen 11:27–12:3).[29]

Kenneth Kitchen lays out the connections among these sources:[30]

Sumerian King List	Atrahasis Epic	Eridu Genesis	Genesis 1–11
1. Creation assumed; kingship came down from heaven	1. Creation assumed, gods create humans to do their work	1. Creation; cities are instituted	1. Creation (Gen 1–2)
2. Series of eight kings in five cities	2. Noisy humans alienate deities	2. [Alienation]	2. Alienation (Gen 3), genealogies (Gen 4–5)
3. The flood	3. The flood; ark	3. The flood; ark	3. The flood; ark (Gen 6–9)
4. Kingship again; dynasties follow, leading to— 5. "Modern times"	4. New start (5. "Modern times," implied)	4. New start (5. "Modern times," implied)	4. New start; then genealogies, down to— 5. "Modern times"

There is much to say about the connections and about the ways in which Genesis 1–11 is both similar and dissimilar to these other sources, but space forbids. The point of interest for now is that this overarching pattern from Mesopotamia provides a literary and ideological context into which Genesis 1–11 speaks; and it does so as a whole.

And what do these connections tell us about the function of Genesis 1–11? The Mesopotamian sources provide what Assyriologist William Hallo calls "prehistory"—the period of human existence before there are any secure written records—and "protohistory"—the earliest stages for which there are records.[31] Further, it appears that the Mesopotamians aimed to accomplish their purpose by founding their stories on what they thought were *actual persons and events*, albeit told with a great deal of imagery and symbolism.

---

29. Some have suggested that Canaanite (or Ugaritic) stories of conflict lie behind the Genesis 1 creation story. For the problems in this proposal, see David Tsumura, *The Earth and the Waters in Genesis 1 and 2: A Linguistic Investigation* (Sheffield: Sheffield Academic Press, 1989), 50–51.

30. This table is based on Collins, *Did Adam and Eve Really Exist?* (Wheaton, IL: Crossway, 2011), 141, which in turn derives from Kitchen, *On the Reliability of the Old Testament*, 424, Table 34.

31. William W. Hallo, "Part 1: Mesopotamia and the Asiatic Near East," in *The Ancient Near East: A History*, William W. Hallo and William K. Simpson (Fort Worth, TX: Harcourt Brace College Publishers, 1998), 3–181, quote on p. 25.

Consider, for example, the Sumerian King List.³² The list includes a group of kings who reigned "after the kingship descended from heaven" and "before the flood swept over." The kingship resided in a succession of Sumerian sites; and the reigns last from 18,660 years at the lowest to 43,200 years at the longest. After the flood, the kingship descended from heaven again, and the lengths of reign trend downward. They range in the hundreds of years until we get through quite a few kings to Gilgamesh, who reigned 126 years. After that, with Gilgamesh's son reigning thirty years, the numbers are mostly in the realm of the believable-at-face-value.³³

Students of ancient Mesopotamia face many questions about this list, not the least of which are whether some of these reigns might have overlapped (they certainly seem to, though no one knows whether the compiler of the list was aware of this), and what to make of the enormous numbers with their downward trend. We may propose various ways of handling these issues, but we can say that the list seems to present actual persons and their reigns. For example, Enmebaragesi, who preceded Gilgamesh and reigned 900 years, and Gilgamesh himself, who reigned for 126 years, are regarded by Assyriologists as actual persons. After Gilgamesh, many more names have other epigraphic evidence for their historicity. Millard's judgment about the reign lengths seems sound: "dismissing them as worthless is no solution" to the puzzle.³⁴

Hence for these relevant background materials, the audiences took them to refer to persons and events. We may disagree, and that is our prerogative. At the same time, our (and presumably the Babylonians') inability to take these numbers and the sequences literally does not entitle us to call the list unhistorical.³⁵ It is better to say that it has an historical basis, and that this basis is presented with various rhetorical purposes in mind that go beyond the simple conveyance of information—even if we do not know all the devices to achieve those rhetorical purposes. The communicative conventions (which we must infer) require that we be careful in discerning what the historical referents are.

---

32. The Sumerian text is available online, with English translation, from Oxford's Electronic Text Corpus of Sumerian Literature at http://etcsl.orinst.ox.ac.uk/cgi-bin/etcsl.cgi?text=t.2.1.1&charenc=j#.

33. John Walton has suggested a way in which the numbers for reigns and life-spans can be brought together. See Walton, "The Antediluvian Section of the Sumerian King List and Genesis 5," *BA* 44:9 (1981): 207–8. For another suggestion, see Dwight Young, "The Influence of Babylonian Algebra on Longevity Among the Antediluvians," *ZAW* 102 (1990): 321–35.

34. A. R. Millard, "King Lists," in *Dictionary of the Ancient Near East*, ed. Piotr Bienkowski and A. R. Millard (Philadelphia: University of Pennsylvania Press, 2000), 169a–170a, quote on p. 169b.

35. Contrast Daniel Harlow, "After Adam: Reading Genesis in an Age of Evolutionary Science," *Perspectives on Science and Christian Faith* 62.3 (2010): 179–95, especially pp. 185–87, who notices symbolic and pictorial elements in both Genesis and the Mesopotamian stories and oddly pronounces them both unhistorical.

And what might be some of those rhetorical purposes? The story of Atrahasis shows the way.[36] The story opens at the time "when the gods instead of man did the work, bore the loads"; because the work was too hard, "the great Anunnaki," the (senior) gods, made the Igigi, a group of "junior" gods, to do the work (such as digging canals).[37] When the Igigi objected to the work and went on strike, the gods decided not to destroy them for rebellion but instead to decree the formation of humankind who would then do the hard work. The gods slew one of their number and mixed his blood and flesh with clay and their spittle to make humankind in seven couples (without setting a limit on their life spans). Unfortunately, humankind was a noisy lot whose population grew and spread, which disturbed the gods' rest and tranquility. The gods sent plague and famine to control the population and finally resorted to a great flood. Certain of the gods secretly spared Atrahasis, who made a special boat and saved animals and some people (the text is damaged, so the details are uncertain). Stephanie Dalley suggests this for the ending of the story:

> Scholars now agree that damaged text near the end of the Epic refers to the gods' decision to institute death as a normal end to human life; the restoration is supported by a newly discovered piece of Sumerian text. This late decision rectified the mistake the gods made in the initial creation of man.[38]

Further, the Sumerian King List, by using exorbitant lengths of the reigns of its early kings, places the origins of Sumerian civilization back in the dim mists of antiquity. The kingship itself "descended from heaven," which implies that the Sumerian kingship is not only an ancient institution but also a divine gift, a special arrangement—and thus the text supports the Sumerian social system and thereby places anything that undermines it as rebellion against the gods (which is always dangerous for a human to toy around with).[39]

The people who heard and believed these tales would derive from them a stance toward their lives in the world: that is, they would see and feel that their purpose was for each person to take his or her place in stratified

---

36. English cited from Stephanie Dalley, *Myths from Mesopotamia*, 1–38.
37. Ibid., 9.
38. Ibid., 8.
39. See W. G. Lambert and A. R. Millard, *Atra-hasis: The Babylonian Story of the Flood* (Winona Lake, IN: Eisenbrauns, 1999 [1969]), 18: "From Sumerian literature to Berossus it is everywhere assumed that the human race was at first and naturally barbarous. Civilization was a gift of the gods, and that is the way to understand kingship coming down from heaven [as in the Sumerian King List]. The gods gave it as an institution for regulating society." See also Thorkild Jacobsen, "The Eridu Genesis," *JBL* 100:2 (1981), 513–29.

Mesopotamian society, to do the work their superiors told them to do, to accept death as inevitable, and to refrain from aspiring to any other arrangement. That is, the Mesopotamian status quo is the way things ought to be.[40]

The Egyptologist Kenneth Kitchen calls this "propaganda";[41] we might use the less judgmental expression "worldview formation." The Mesopotamian stories include divine action, symbolism, and imaginative elements; the purpose of these stories is to lay the foundation for a worldview without being taken in a literalistic fashion. The Atrahasis story, then, forms part of the front end of its culture's worldview story by providing especially "prehistory."

The notion of a worldview and a worldview story is something I develop further in chapter 6 below. There I argue that Genesis offers an alternative front end to the worldview story, and that it intends to offer the "true" story, not simply of Israel, but of the world (for whose sake Israel is said to exist). In such a framework, we will not be surprised if, for example, the Mesopotamian stories offer the basic outline of events and topics that such a front-end narrative should include—with the way in which it tells the story providing correctives both to the nature of particular events and to how the manner of presentation induces the audience to lean into their world. As Alan Millard put it, "If there was borrowing [by the Hebrews from the Mesopotamians] then it can have extended only as far as the 'historical' framework, and not included intention or interpretation."[42]

It is crucial to be clear on what I am and am not saying in using such comparisons. First, some will conclude that since Genesis 1–11 has some connection to other origins stories (especially those from Mesopotamia), we may consider Genesis to be just another one of these. Thus, a skeptic will say that I have made Genesis just as worthless as the others, and a certain kind of creationist will say that I have shown why the comparisons are invalid (by showing their unacceptable consequences).

As to the skeptic, I have argued that Genesis accepts a basic structure of events and then narrates them in what its author considered the right way, in order to correct the audience's perceptions of those events. Whether there are actual events and persons for the texts to refer to and what is the "right way" to refer to them, is a discussion for historians and apologists.

And to the creationist objector, I reply that the key question is whether these concepts from the rest of the ancient world are part of the relevant

---

40. For a description of Mesopotamian social structure, see Thorkild Jacobsen, "Mesopotamia," in *The Intellectual Adventure of Ancient Man*, ed. H. and H. A. Frankfort, John Wilson, Thorkild Jacobsen, and William Irwin (Chicago: University of Chicago, 1977), 125–219.
41. Kitchen, *On the Reliability of the Old Testament*, 300.
42. Millard, "A New Babylonian 'Genesis' Story," 17.

context for Genesis. When it comes to whether we *should* compare the material we find in the Bible to the materials we find from the surrounding cultures, it seems almost obvious that we should. The Bible writers spoke into a specific context and regularly warned their audiences against the blandishments of the competing worldviews. Whether it be an Old Testament prophet inveighing against idolatry and syncretism or a New Testament apostle reminding people about Greco-Roman depravity, these warnings are common to the literature. Surely a sane interpreter will do what he or she can to discover what these dangers were. For example, how did idol worship and temple building function in the ancient Near East? Were they different in Egypt, the western Levant, and Mesopotamia? Or, many researchers on 1 John have resorted to Irenaeus's descriptions of the heretic Cerinthus as the likely occasion for the letter (1 John 2:18–19). We may decide that this is a helpful identification, or unhelpful—but the idea of such a resort was certainly worth a try. We always have the danger that some will misuse the comparisons; but surely the right stance is to bend every effort to make a good and wise use of this extra material.

Further to these objections, important people loyal to Genesis as Scripture have been aware of the potential comparisons, and have argued from comparisons with the other nations' stories (in Greek translation) *in support of* the Genesis story. Certainly, the Jewish writer Josephus (AD 37–ca. 100) did so (e.g., *Ant.*, 1, 93–95 [1.3.6]), as did the Christian historian Eusebius of Caesarea (ca. AD 260–340) throughout his *Preparation for the Gospel* (*Praep. ev.* ca. AD 313). In other words, the modern effort is not new; the contribution of modern studies is access to the other nations' stories in older forms and in the ancient languages.

Let us bring the literary voice of C. S. Lewis into the conversation. In several places he addressed the question of a story being in some sense derived from an antecedent. Lewis considered some ideas common in "anthropological interpretations" of his day, such as the suggestion about a particular medieval story, "that Gawain's property of growing stronger as the sun ascended is causally linked, through many intermediate stages, with a story about a sun-god." Lewis replied,

> It is an equally gross error to suppose that the ritual or myth from which some ingredient in a romance or poem originated necessarily throws any light on its meaning and function in that romance or poem.[43]

---

43. C. S. Lewis, "*De audiendis poetis*," in *Studies in Medieval and Renaissance Literature*, ed. Walter Hooper (Cambridge: Cambridge University Press, 1966), 1–17, quote on p. 9. See also Lewis, "The Anthropological Approach," in *Selected Literary Essays*, ed. Walter Hooper (Cambridge: Cambridge University Press, 1969), 301–11.

That is, the mechanics by which the narrative originated matters less than what function the narrative plays in the coherent literary work in which it appears—unless, of course, we can show that between the author and the audience the originating process was part of their shared world.[44]

Specifically, for Genesis, Lewis addressed the possibility that its creation story is in some way "derived from earlier Semitic stories which were Pagan and mythical"—a view that had become widely spread by his time and which was held to discredit Genesis.[45] Lewis shows his literary and philosophical good sense by first insisting, "We must of course be quite clear what 'derived from' means. Stories do not reproduce their species like mice."[46] He observed that it is *persons* who do the retelling and revising of stories, for various ends:

> Thus at every step in what is called—a little misleadingly—the "evolution" of a story, a man, all he is and all his attitudes, are involved. And no good work is done anywhere without aid from the Father of Lights. When a series of such re-tellings turns a creation story which at first had almost no religious or metaphysical significance into a story which achieves the idea of true Creation and of a transcendent Creator (as *Genesis* does), then nothing will make me believe that some of the re-tellers, or some one of them, has not been guided by God.[47]

Hence, although Lewis found much that he deemed poetical, or even mythical, in the Genesis creation story, he nevertheless attached to it some kind of referent. For example:

---

44. As an example, Michaela Bauks offers a fascinating study of tree imagery in the ancient Near East in "Sacred Trees in the Garden of Eden and Their Ancient Near Eastern Precursors," *Journal of Ancient Judaism* 3 (2012): 267–301. She concludes (p. 301) that the "trees are ambivalent, because they are the source of contestation and of progress at the same time. They transform human self-understanding, serving as a reminder of their subjection to the divine. The various mythologems—including trees, the garden of God, snake, cherub—reflect the complexity of this ambivalence." Her study can help show why trees would be an evocative symbol for an ancient, beyond their obvious relevance as a source of nourishment (surely the first thing that an Israelite would think of). But the key question is always, what role do they play in the story itself? Bauks is mistaken when she dismisses readings of Gen 2–3 as "narration of the fall of mankind," which does not account properly for "its original ancient Near Eastern context" and ascribes this to an "Augustinian heritage" (p. 270). See further the discussions in chapters 7 and 8 below.

45. In Lewis's day the chief point of comparison was the story Enuma Elish. The Christian Assyriologist Alexander Heidel (1907–1955) wrote to support the comparison and to refute the skeptical implications. See *The Babylonian Genesis* (Chicago: University of Chicago Press, 1951). For an account of just such theorizing about the original meaning behind the creation story, see Mark G. Brett, "Motives and Intentions in Genesis 1," *JTS* 42:1 (1991): 1–16. Brett does not categorically reject such theorizing.

46. C. S. Lewis, *Reflections on the Psalms* (London: Geoffrey Bles, 1958), 110 (ch. 11).

47. Ibid., 110–11.

We read in *Genesis* (2,7) that God formed man of the dust and breathed life into him. For all the first writer knew of it, this passage might merely illustrate the survival, even in a truly creational story, of the Pagan inability to conceive true Creation, the savage, pictorial tendency to imagine God making things "out of" something as the potter or the carpenter does. Nevertheless, whether by lucky accident or (as I think) by God's guidance, it embodies a profound principle. For in any view man is in one sense made "out of" something else. He is an animal; but an animal called to be, or raised to be, or (if you like) doomed to be, something more than an animal. On the ordinary biological view (what difficulties I have about evolution are not religious) one of the primates is changed so that he becomes man; but he remains still a primate and an animal.[48]

The second point for clarification has to do with whether I am suggesting that Genesis has any actual texts in mind (such as those I have mentioned). Now, there is evidence that, for example, Atrahasis was available in the west early enough to be known to an educated Egyptian such as Moses is portrayed to have been, and thus at any time that Genesis might have existed.[49] But the ability to read such texts would not have been widely spread, since reading and writing cuneiform requires specialized training—thus the necessary training, which Moses might have had, would not have extended to the rest of Israel. Rather, it makes better sense to suppose that versions of these other stories were part of the oral environment in which the ordinary Israelites lived: Israel traced its origins to Mesopotamia, after all. Hence, even though we might accept reasons for thinking that the current text of, say, Enuma Elish, was less pertinent to Genesis, that does not mean that some of its motifs (such as watery beginnings) are irrelevant. Indeed, at least one prominent Assyriologist, S. N. Kramer, argued that the Babylonian epic derived from an earlier Sumerian tale, which might well have put the motifs into the air.[50]

Another premier Assyriologist, Thorkild Jacobsen, noted succinctly both the similarities and the differences between Genesis and the Mesopotamian tales:

---

48. Ibid., *115.*
49. See W. G. Lambert, "A New Look at the Babylonian Background of Genesis," *JTS* 16 (1965): 289–300, especially pp. 299–300; Millard, "A New Babylonian 'Genesis' Story," 5.
50. S. N. Kramer, "Review of Alexander Heidel, *The Babylonian Genesis: The Story of Creation*," *JAOS* 63:1 (1943): 69–73.

If we accept—as I think we very clearly must—a degree of dependency of the biblical narrative on the older Mesopotamian materials, we must also note how decisively these materials have been transformed in the biblical account, altering radically their original meaning and import.[51]

Now, Jacobsen's word "dependency" might be problematic, although he made it clear that he does not mean that Genesis simply took over uncritically the Mesopotamian stories. If we change it to "responsiveness," we will capture what I think we have a right to say.

Here is the point to take away from this discussion: We have gained a great deal when we notice that Genesis really *does* have parallels with the stories that come from other ancient Near Eastern cultures. One of these gains is to realize that "history" is an appropriate category for such a tale; another is to recognize that no one expected the stories to be read in a thoroughly literalistic fashion.

I noted that William Hallo calls these Mesopotamian stories "prehistory" and "protohistory." To use the terms of my earlier discussion of "genre" (ch. 2), we must be clear that "prehistory" and "protohistory" are not literary forms; they instead perform a social function, namely, to tell the story of the distant past as part of the worldview story that gives the community its distinctive identity and values. In the case of Mesopotamia, the literary forms used include narrative poems and king lists—in Israel we have (as I discuss in ch. 6) an overall narrative that incorporates varying styles and sub-forms.

5.B.2 Audience Criticism and "Rhetorical Situation"

But can we say more specifically what Genesis 1–11 was supposed to *do* in the life of ancient Israel? To answer this we must consider who the audience was likely to be and what their needs would have been. Most traditionalist Christians would stress that the Genesis material should perform a similar function for the Christian audience as well.

Understanding the audience will help us to appreciate what the rhetorician Lloyd Bitzer calls the "rhetorical situation":

> Rhetorical situation may be defined as a complex of persons, events, objects, and relations presenting an actual or potential exigence which can be completely or partially removed if discourse, introduced into the situation, can so constrain human decision or action as to bring

---

51. Thorkild Jacobsen, "The Eridu Genesis," *JBL* 100:2 (1981): 513–29, quote on p. 529.

about the significant modification of the exigence.... Any *exigence* is an imperfection marked by an urgency; it is a defect, an obstacle, something waiting to be done, a thing which is other than it should be.[52]

We assume that our text is what Bitzer calls a "fitting response" to the situation, addressed to "those persons who are capable of being influenced by discourse and of being mediators of change."[53]

This introduces what we might call "audience criticism," that is, an assessment of who the audience might have been and how the text addressed them. First, we must make some qualifications. When we speak of the audience, particularly in a narrative, we have several levels that must be distinguished. There are the characters within the story (for example, Abraham or Moses). Then we have the audience of the literary presentation of these characters and their events with an author's (or editors') selection and viewpoint. This is what we have access to. But of these literary audiences, we have what we may call the implied audience, those whom the reader is to imagine reading the story. Then we have the real or empirical audience; and of those, we might also construct an ideal audience, namely, those who are best equipped, both in knowledge and disposition, to cooperate with the text. Along the same lines we may speak of an implied author and a real author (which may be an editor or team of editors).

In fiction, for example, J. R. R. Tolkien had as his implied author someone who found the *Red Book of Westmarch*, while the implied audience are those who live in a world where hobbits were "more numerous formerly than they are today."[54] The real author, of course, was an Oxford don, writing in the middle of the twentieth century; the real audience was, first, that don's family and closest friends, and second, the modern world after World War II. The ideal audience would be people who share some of Tolkien's love for ancient stories, especially of European peoples, and who have a sympathetic grasp of his Catholic faith.

As an example from the Bible, we have the prefaces to Luke and Acts, which present us with an implied author who has some level of cultural polish and who has taken pains to research carefully the persons and events he writes about—someone we are invited to trust as a reporter. The implied audience is the "most excellent Theophilus," a person of higher social standing (Luke 1:3).

---

52. Lloyd Bitzer, "The Rhetorical Situation," *Philosophy and Rhetoric* 1:1 (1968), 1–14, quote on p. 6.
53. Bitzer, "The Rhetorical Situation," 8.
54. J. R. R. Tolkien, *The Fellowship of the Ring: Being the First Part of the Lord of the Rings* (Boston: Houghton Mifflin, 1965), 10.

The real author may be the same person as the implied, which is the traditional view of Christians, associating him with Luke, the companion of Paul and "beloved physician" (Col 4:14). The real audience might well have included Theophilus but probably was intended all along to include Christians in general, especially among the gentiles. An ideal reader would be someone familiar with the variety of first-century Greco-Roman cultural practices.

Let us apply these considerations to Genesis 1–11.

5.B.2.a Date of Genesis

Most peoples, ancient and modern alike, have a story of where the world came from in order to explain why things today are the way that they are. The book of Genesis was intended for ancient Israel; Jews have traditionally understood it to have come from Moses, to have been addressed to the people of Israel as they prepared to take the promised land. Many people today think that the book received its final form a bit later, perhaps in the time of David and Solomon;[55] but that will not change what we do with the book here.

Note that the postexilic books describe Ezra's activity of teaching the law of Moses, or Torah (Neh 8:1–8), and many suppose that he had a large role in bringing the Torah to its final form, that is, the form with which we are familiar. This may be so, but probably should not be taken to imply that it did not exist in the previous era: after all, an earlier postexilic generation had appealed to the Torah (Ezra 3:2), and Ezra is said to have been a skilled student of the Torah (Ezra 7:6, 10), which implies that it had some form before he studied it. Further, much of the Torah reflects a preexilic life-setting—for example, the Canaanite form of idolatry that it denounces is widely thought to have been eliminated from Israel by the exile.

The date of the final edition, however, does not determine for us the implied audience, although of course it speaks to the empirical first audience.

5.B.2.b Implied Audience

We can use the literary notion of the implied author and audience to help us appreciate the communication event that is taking place here in Genesis.

---

55. See Gordon Wenham, *Story as Torah: Reading Old Testament Narrative Ethically* (Grand Rapids: Baker Academic, 2000), 41–42, for a fair treatment: "The Mosaic era certainly accounts for many of the key features in Genesis" (41). And while what he calls "critical orthodoxy" prefers a date in the fifth-century postexilic era, he shows some of the problems with that view. "None of these observations are problems for a date in the united monarchy period" (42). On the other hand, Iain Provan, *Discovering Genesis* (Grand Rapids: Eerdmans, 2016), contends that Genesis reached its "final form" in the Persian period. The exact sense of "final form" is ambiguous, and thus there might be ways I could accept this position. But overall, the concerns of the people addressed fit far better in the preexilic era than in the postexilic.

The canon presents the Pentateuch as the work of Moses and thus invites us to think of him as presenting the constitution for Israel (as we will see more fully in ch. 6 below). Moses spoke as a prophet, with the divinely warranted task of specifying the right beliefs and practices and correcting the wrong ones.

Under this presentation (or fancy, depending on one's perspective), the implied first audience would be the Israelites who crossed the Jordan River under Joshua's leadership, and each subsequent audience should imagine themselves as the heirs of this first one. The members of the implied audience knew that their God had crushed the gods of Egypt (embodied in the Pharaoh), and Genesis 1–11 explains why he could do so: The God of Israel is far more than just a tribal god; he is the One True God who made heaven and earth.

This implied audience, and every Israelite audience after them, holds to the view that they are descended from Isaac and Rebekah. This means that for passages such as Genesis 22 (the binding of Isaac) and 24 (acquiring a wife for Isaac), we should not overplay the factor of suspense in reading them. The audience already knows how things turn out: Isaac must survive, and Rebekah must join Isaac. Besides, any suspense as to the events will be gone once the passage has been read—so we should look elsewhere for the passages' meaning (such as, to reinforce the providential origins and protection of Israel).

In the Pentateuch, Israel will have a calling in the world—to be the vehicle of God's blessing to all nations (Gen 12:2–3). That is, Israel's God has something to say to the whole world, since he created the whole show and since all humankind comes from a common source.

The people are going to live in the promised land where they will be farmers, using the same skills that other people have learned. They need to be reassured that this is *God's* world, that the land is God's land, and that God has the right to instruct human beings how to live and how to use his stuff.

Their external circumstances may change over time, but the Pentateuch still sets out the constitution for the people, and the creation story still establishes the ideal toward which the members should aim. The laws are there to preserve social civility so that the members are safe and free to pursue the flourishing of their social and private lives.[56]

Some of these changes will include the introduction of kingship, and particularly the Davidic dynasty. I see this new feature not as replacing the

---

[56]. This perspective on the laws is a major contribution of Gordon Wenham, *Story as Torah*, and Christopher Wright, *Old Testament Ethics for the People of God* (Downers Grove, IL: InterVarsity Press, 2004).

Sinai covenant of the Pentateuch but as specifying how the people are to live it out—just as the Sinai covenant did not replace the Abrahamic covenants but specified their manner of realization.[57] The ultimate heir of David will have the task of bringing the light of the true God to all the gentiles, finally leading the people in carrying out the Abrahamic calling.[58]

The economic situation of the vast majority of Israelites during the pre-exilic era would have been oriented around subsistence agriculture. By the time of the exile, an artisan class had developed (2 Kgs 24:14), as well as merchants and aristocrats, though most of the people were still tied to the soil.[59] No doubt fishermen plied their trade as well, though they do not get much mention (see Ezek 47:10). As Lewis colorfully described their situation,

> Those [ancient Israelites] were peasants or farmers. When even a king covets a piece of his neighbour's property, the piece is a vineyard; he is more like a wicked squire than a wicked king.[60]

Indeed, such people would have been well familiar with animals of all sorts, from the perspective not of natural history but of the utilitarian needs of subsistence farmers. If they were so familiar with the animals they encountered, there is virtually no likelihood that they would ever have considered the animal taxonomies of Genesis 1 (aquatic and aerial: vv. 20–21; land: vv. 24–25) scientific.[61] The taxonomies are not even functional for an agriculturalist, since they do not distinguish animals enough by their characteristics.[62] Is a dog, for example, livestock or a beast of the earth? What about the wolf, from which the dog is held to have been domesticated (perhaps with jackal as well)? Although dogs were commonly semi-feral scavengers for the ancient

---

57. I discuss the relations of successive covenants in a forthcoming essay, "The New Covenant and Redemptive History."
58. Much more needs to be said on this. For my approach, see *Science & Faith: Friends or Foes?* (Wheaton, IL: Crossway, 2003), 154–57.
59. See S. Bendor, *The Social Structure of Ancient Israel: The Institution of the Family (*beit 'ab*) From the Settlement to the End of the Monarchy* (Jerusalem: Simor, 1996), especially pt. III, ch. 1.
60. Lewis, *Reflections on the Psalms*, ch. 8 on "Nature."
61. Denis Lamoureux, "No Historical Adam: Evolutionary Creation View," in *Four Views on the Historical Adam*, ed. Matthew Barrett and Ardel Caneday (Grand Rapids: Zondervan, 2013), 37–65, especially pp. 55–57, mistakenly takes the taxonomy as "ancient biology."
62. In fact, it would be a mistake to read English taxonomy into the Hebrew Bible. For example, the Hebrew term rendered "birds" in Gen 1:20 and Lev 11:13 is not as limited as the English word; it refers to "flying thing" (see ESV footnotes) and thus can include bats and large insects. Likewise, to "chew the cud" (Lev 11:3) need not correspond to the modern notion of "ruminant"; it can include the rabbits and hares, which practice what is now called "pseudo-rumination" or "refection," in which the animal re-chews certain of its droppings. See George Cansdale, *Animals of Bible Lands* (Exeter: Paternoster, 1970), 131–32. Denis Lamoureux, *Evolution: Scripture and Nature Say Yes!* (Grand Rapids: Zondervan, 2016), 103, makes just this mistake.

Israelite (Exod 22:31; 1 Kgs 14:11), there is evidence of their use as work animals as well—not only in Egypt and Mesopotamia but also in Israel (Isa 56:10–11; Job 30:1; see also Tob 5:16; 11:4).[63]

These Israelite farmers would also already have known that plants and animals reproduce according to their kinds. That is, they knew how to get more sheep: you breed them from your sheep and not from camels. They knew that if they wanted to grow barley, they must plant barley seeds and not oats. (In Matt 13:24–30, a parable spoken by a peasant to other peasants, a farmer sensibly recognizes that someone has sown another kind of seed.) That is, the communicative concern of the texts about the different kinds likely has less to do with the *imparting of information* (the information was already there) and more with the *inculcating of a stance* toward the referents: This is Yahweh's stuff, and he has the right to tell us how to use it. Genesis hardly overthrows ordinary, or common-sense, knowledge of the world; quite the opposite, it endorses it.

The audiences would also have known without much argument that humans are different from other animals—indeed, as herdsmen they already exercised a kind of dominion over some of the beasts. As I will argue in chapter 7, the literary features of the narrative of Genesis 1–11 invite the reader to infer what the "image of God" is, especially since that distinguishes the description of humankind's making from that of the other animals. Anything that sets humans apart from the other animals is a candidate for the components of the image.

Since water in the sky plays a key role in our section of Genesis—the dividing of waters in the creation story and the rain water in the flood story—we will need to explore what the ideal audience might have known about the phenomena. However, in order to keep the material all in one place, I will hold the exploration off until the proper place in chapter 9.

Further, Israel already had a seven-day week (Exod 16:23, 26), consisting of six days of work and a Sabbath day of rest. They also knew the seasons (Gen. 1:14) as liturgical "appointed times" (Heb. מוֹעֵד, *mo'ed*, see Exod 13:10), which would have supplied their rubric for understanding the purpose of the sun, moon, and stars—namely, to enable humans properly to worship their Maker. In fact, there may be a subtle irony here: rather than being deities whom humans must serve, these entities—whatever their ontology—exist to serve humans, helping them to direct their adoration to the Maker of all.

---

63. See Oded Borowski, *Every Living Thing: Daily Use of Animals in Ancient Israel* (Walnut Creek: AltaMira, 1998), 133–40; see further Geoffrey David Miller, "Attitudes Toward Dogs in Ancient Israel: A Reassessment," *JSOT* 32:4 (2008): 487–500.

The audience would also have been familiar with marriage as a basic human institution, observed by all kinds of peoples (although not always monogamous). No doubt they were also aware that it takes a man and a woman to make a baby—which means that the function of Genesis 2 is not about explaining the biological fact but about establishing the pattern as divinely ordained (a pattern that Israel is to make their own ideal). They likely already knew that being naked is commonly associated with being humiliated or ashamed (see 1 Sam 19:24; Isa 20:2–4; Hos 2:3; 2 Sam 10:4–5; 1 Sam 20:30; Mic 1:11; Deut 25:11, מבושים [*mebushim*], "private parts, items for shame").

Further, the audience had experience of various kinds of sacrifices (such as those employed by Cain and Abel, and Noah). They knew of the technological achievements of superior cultures; perhaps they even knew that some cultures held the less technologically developed peoples in disdain. Hero stories were widely spread, as were tales of a great and catastrophic flood. They knew that other human clans were scattered through the world and that it was possible to contract fertile marriages with at least some of them. Perhaps they also knew of Mesopotamians' usage of fired bricks for building. They carried tales of the Mesopotamian origins of their ancestors, which no doubt created special interest in that region. They also held that their more recent ancestors had endured harsh servitude in Egypt and that their God had marvelously delivered them from slavery.

The point is that providing this information would not be a likely function of this set of stories (except insofar as the Pentateuch challenges "dangerous" misrepresentations of the information); rather, the stories set the audience's knowledge into a proper context.

With these reflections we can appreciate something of the "exigence" that Genesis addresses, to use Bitzer's term cited above. In fact, Bitzer's student Allen Michael Scult gave reasons, first, for seeing the Pentateuch as an "argument," namely, a "process by which people reason their way from one set of problematical ideas to the choice of another." Second, he contends that "the exigence which organizes and gives direction to the argument in the Pentateuch is the pagan world-view of the Mesopotamians and the Egyptians which that argument must combat."[64] As I will show in the following chapter, things are probably more complicated than Scult has put it—but his clear statement does help to advance our approach to Genesis as having a rhetorical (or pastoral) motivation.

---

64. Allen Michael Scult, "The Rhetoric of the Pentateuch: An Analysis of the Argument for the Hebrew Concept of God" (PhD diss., University of Wisconsin, 1975), 22, 24.

In the social setting described here, many scientific questions would go unaddressed, being irrelevant to telling the story. It would be a mistake, however, to suppose that not addressing them means committing to some (primitive or errant) view of them. What C. S. Lewis said of ordinary people in the Middle Ages would apply here: "There were ditchers and alewives who . . . did not know that the earth was spherical; not because they thought it was flat but because they did not think about it at all."[65] We might even be able to say the same as well about how to read writings from the nearby cultures.[66]

---

65. Lewis, *Discarded Image*, 20.
66. Cf. Wayne Horowitz, *Mesopotamian Cosmic Geography* (Winona Lake, IN: Eisenbrauns, 1998), xiii-xiv. Hence the simple citation of pictures and quotations from the other cultures proves nothing. We still must exegete *them*. Even a philosophical work such as Plato's *Phaedo*, which includes a "myth" describing the earth's shape, leaves room for doubt exactly how scientific it aims to be. As David Sedly, *Creationism and its Critics in Antiquity* (Berkeley: University of California Press, 2007), remarks, "Whether or not Plato takes seriously the fantastic geography contained in the myth, he succeeds in conveying his point" (p. 94).

Chapter 6

WHAT DO WE HAVE IN GENESIS 1–11?
Part 2: Function

As Lewis stated, to understand a text we must know how it is meant to be used. In this chapter I will examine how Genesis 1–11 was to function in the ancient Israelite community and what literary features it has that support that function.

6.A THE PENTATEUCH AS "CONSTITUTION"

Jews and Christians have always taken Genesis 1–11 as the front end of the story of Abraham, which begins in Genesis 12. Abraham is the forefather of the Jewish people and the father of faith for Christians (Rom 4:12). These readers have also attributed the material to Moses and see it as Scripture—and thus canonical and authoritative—by virtue of its origin from Moses, a man with a prophetic role. According to this understanding, it was to be read regularly for the gathered assembly of God's people.

We can see the presentation of the Mosaic origin, for example, in Moses's special role as intermediary between Israel and the Lord (Exod 19:1–9); in the numerous references to how God "spoke to" or "called to" Moses in Exodus through Numbers (as in Lev 1:1, etc.); in the passages that speak of Moses writing down the law and committing it to the care of Joshua and the priests (Deut 31:1–13, 24–26; Josh 1:7–8); and in the postexilic appeals to the law's authority (as in Ezra 3:2; 7:6; Neh 8:1, 14; 9:14). Further, the entire Pentateuch shows a narrative unity: Exodus requires Genesis if we are to make sense of it; Exodus, Leviticus, and Numbers are all part of the same tale;¹ and Deuteronomy has as its setting the scene at the end of Numbers. I am not at this point discussing whether or not this view is credible, only considering that it was part of the communication act that took place when the Israelite assembly read from the law (at least by the Second Temple era).

Moses, in the biblical presentation, is not just a wise lawgiver—just as the other prophets are not simply preachers or theologians or philosophers, wrestling with the problems arising from God's promises and Israel's history. Rather, the idea is that these are persons uniquely and divinely called to speak on God's behalf. The inclusion of the call story of Moses (Exod 3–4) serves to present this special role, and thus the authority of the writings connected to him, as do the call stories of Isaiah, Jeremiah, and Ezekiel. These stories are not paradigmatic for the general run of the faithful, but they establish why the faithful will treasure what these messengers have to say.

From this perspective we can assess a trait common among biblical scholars, namely, that of describing the Pentateuch as Israel's effort at *self-definition*. An example comes from Gerhard von Rad's comments on the call of Abram in Genesis:

> In this call and this road which was taken, *Israel saw* not only an event in her earliest history, but also a basic characteristic of her whole existence before God. Taken from the community of nations (cf. Num. 23:9) and never truly rooted in Canaan, but even there a stranger (cf. Lev. 25:23; Ps. 39:12), *Israel saw herself being led* on a special road whose plan and goal lay completely in Yahweh's hand.²

But nothing could be further from the truth than attributing the Pentateuch to the community's effort to understand themselves—at least if the prophets are to be believed. Rather, the Pentateuch presents itself as providing the authoritative story that specifies how Israel *ought* to see herself and which she too often refused. That is, we must distinguish *the constitutional function*

---

1. Seeing this, Hendrik Koorevaar argues for treating Exodus–Numbers as a single book. See "The Torah as One, Three or Five Books: An Introduction to the Macro-Structural Problem of the Pentateuch," *Hiphil* 3 (2006): http://www.see-j.net/hiphil; "The Books of Exodus, Leviticus and Numbers, and the Macro-Structural Problem of the Pentateuch," in *The Books of Leviticus and Numbers*, ed. Thomas Römer, Bibliotheca Ephemeridum Theologicarum Lovaniensium 215 (Leuven: Peeters, 2008), 423–53. Since the five-book arrangement appears to be old enough to have influenced the five books of the Psalms, I do not wish to revise it. See also Roger T. Beckwith, "The Early History of the Psalter," *TynBul* 46:1 (1995): 1–27, especially p. 6. Nevertheless, the observation itself helps with numerous difficulties that researchers have had, especially with Numbers, which has been caricatured as the "junk room of the priestly code" for its apparently catchall collection of laws and narratives. Gordon Wenham, *Numbers*, OTG (Sheffield: Sheffield Academic Press, 1997), 40, mentions and rejects this caricature.

2. Gerhard von Rad, *Genesis* (Philadelphia: Westminster, 1956), 154 (emphasis added).

of the Pentateuch from *the history of Israel's religion*—the *normative* from the *empirical*.

The Pentateuch presents itself as normative rather than empirical. Josiah instituted reforms in response to the public reading of the Torah (2 Kgs 23:1–25). The postexilic community supplies a good example of how this worked: In the midst of adapting the ancient laws for their new circumstances (Neh 12:44 speaks of portions for priests and Levites, while the law only speaks of them for priests; see Lev 7:33), they also confessed their failures to observe the Torah (Neh 9:16, 26, 33–35) and changed their practices to conform to it (Neh 8:14–18; 13:1–3). This normative function, then, shows why rhetoric suits the Pentateuch in its effort to shape a people's way of life.

The Pentateuch presents itself, then, as the *constitution of Israel as a church-state nexus*.[3] But if it is a constitution, it is a most odd one, since it has laws in the context of a narrative that tells Israel where it came from, how God got them to where they are, and what purpose God has in mind for them as a people (blessing of the nations).[4] Once we acknowledge that, then we see that our hermeneutics should derive from this social function, this shaping of an identity, this forming of a worldview based on a big story—in the corporate whole and also in the particular members of the people.[5] That is, our hermeneutic should begin with how this literature functions in a social

---

3. See F. R. Hoare, *Eight Decisive Books of Antiquity* (London: Sheed & Ward, 1952), 77: "The Mosaic Code is one, covering indifferently what we now separate as religious and secular matters, moral and positive law, public and private law, or civil and criminal law . . . In the Hebrew nation there was to be no distinction between Church and state, so that it was entirely appropriate that civil, criminal, administrative and canon law should be incorporated in a single code." Josephus is the earliest writer to call this form of polity a "theocracy" (θεοκρατία); see his *Ag. Ap.*, 2,165 [2.17]. Josephus uses *theocracy* for the form of government found in the Pentateuch, "ascribing the authority and power to God." In using the Greek term πολιτεία for the "constitution" (*Ant.*, 1, 10 [Preface §3]), Josephus clearly brought the Mosaic form of government into conversation with Greek philosophers' discussions of "polities" (e.g., Aristotle, *Politics*, 2.9.9 [1274-b, 26]). According to Herodotus (*Hist.*, 3.80–82), it was a group of Persians that began discussing the relative merits of diverse forms of government such as democracy, oligarchy, and monarchy. Plato's *Republic*, Book 8, and Aristotle's *Politics* continue the discussion, although Plato and Aristotle narrow the arena to the governing of a city state.

4. I am saying more than the obvious point that once we get to Exodus the Pentateuch interweaves narratives and laws—as thoughtfully discussed in Joel R. Humann, "The Ceremony of the Red Heifer: Its Purpose and Function in Narrative Context" (PhD thesis, Durham University, 2011). Rather, the laws come in the context of reported speech; the speeches are themselves events in the overarching narrative (usually introduced by a *wayyiqtol* verb). And although most of Deuteronomy is hortatory speech, it too is introduced in the narrative (1:1–5) and then closes with several narrative episodes (chs. 31–34).

5. For this reason a source analysis that finds competing agendas offers little insight into how the text works. For an example of such analysis, see Kenton Sparks, "Genesis 1–11 as Ancient Historiography," in *Genesis: History Fiction, or Neither? Three Views on the Bible's Earliest Chapters*, ed. Charles Halton (Grand Rapids: Zondervan, 2015), 110–39. My own critique can be added to that of Gordon Wenham, who responds to Sparks (pp. 150–54).

system, asking questions about social and linguistic conventions for carrying out these functions.[6]

In the previous chapter I argued that if we can ascertain the social and linguistic conventions of neighboring cultures, that might help provide us with some guidance in how Genesis aims to do its job. Certainly we must be careful to be sure that we have found genuinely comparable materials; and we have to be sure we have found enough of these materials to make a meaningful induction. And most important, we have to allow that, though the *functions* of these comparable materials may be similar, the actual *content* and even *form* may be distinct. And therefore, if we find that other peoples are not concerned with some topic, it does not follow that an Israelite, speaking for God, must also be unconcerned (more on this anon).

6.B GENESIS AND THE WORLDVIEW STORY

In chapter 5 I explained how Genesis 1–11 offers to Israel, and thus to Christians, pre-history and proto-history: the account of things before there are any written records and of things at the earliest stages of written records. I suggested that the relevant and comparable Mesopotamian stories would have shaped the stance of their own audiences toward their lives in the world—their worldview—and that they did so by referring to what their audiences took to be real events, with a great amount of pictorial and symbolic elements in the description.

Now it is time to apply this to Genesis 1–11 as the front end of the biblical worldview story. But first we will explore the notion of worldview and story.

I belong to a specific Christian body, with its own theological tradition (one of the "rooms," to use C. S. Lewis's analogy in his preface to *Mere Christianity*). I aim here, however, to offer a "catholic" perspective, which fits traditional mere Christianity. I begin with an observation from Lewis:

> Christianity, going on from [the Hebrew Bible], makes world history in its entirety a single, transcendentally significant, story with a well-defined plot pivoted on Creation, Fall, Redemption, and Judgement.[7]

---

6. These considerations show why the list of "narrative genres in the Old Testament" found in G. W. Coats, *Genesis, with an Introduction to Narrative*, FOTL (Grand Rapids: Eerdmans, 1983), 5–10 (i.e., saga, tale, novella, legend, history, report, fable, etiology, myth) does not really help us to understand Genesis 1–11 as Scripture. These are narrowly focused on presumed literary forms, without saying anything helpful about their rhetoric or social function.

7. C. S. Lewis, *The Discarded Image: An Introduction to Medieval and Renaissance Literature* (Cambridge: Cambridge University Press, 1964), 174 (and several other places).

I consider this to be a fair summary of such early Christian thinkers as Irenaeus (late second century) and Athanasius (early fourth century) but will save that discussion for another occasion. This narrative underlies the Nicene Creed, if we allow that the fall is included in the phrase "for our salvation"—otherwise what do we need saving from? Several New Testament passages seem to allude to early creeds (such as 1 Cor 15:3–8; 1 Tim 3:16),[8] and this overall narrative makes sense of these passages. Christians certainly affirm that Jesus died for sins and rose from the dead as actual events—but these events are not alone; they are epoch-making steps in the larger story (as Paul has it in Rom 1:1–6).[9]

This outlook helps us because agreement on this basic shape of the story, or of a story that does the same job, can serve as a diagnostic criterion for common Christianity. That is, what supports that story is inside this common Christianity, while what counteracts the story is outside. Further, this way of describing things enables us to see whether scientific theories really are at odds with the faith by asking whether they would have us change the shape of the story. Thus, though a medieval theologian might have conceived of the earth as stationary, while I do not, we have not necessarily told a different story.

This story-orientation offers another advantage: In the latter twentieth century, students of worldview came to appreciate that a community inculcates its worldview into its members by means of its big story, which answers key questions, such as:

Where did we come from?
What does the good life look like?
What has gone wrong?
What has been done about it (by gods, or nature, or man, or some combination)?
Where are we now in the whole process?
Where is the whole thing headed?[10]

---

8. See further Philip and David Schaff, *The Creeds of Christendom* (New York: Harper & Row, 1931), 2:3–8.

9. Paul uses the word "gospel" in Rom 1:1 in a common Greek sense of "an announcement of a great event," referring to the resurrection of Jesus as his installation into his Davidic kingship. For the argument, see C. John Collins, "Echoes of Aristotle in Romans 2:14–15: Or, Maybe Abimelech Was Not So Bad After All," *Journal of Markets and Morality* 13:1 (Spring 2010): 123–73, especially p. 137.

10. For something similar, see N. T. Wright, *The New Testament and the People of God* (Minneapolis: Fortress, 1992), 122–26. Wright indicates that he is drawing on the work of Brian Walsh and J. Richard Middleton, but replacing the "I" in their questions with "we" to reflect a more communal approach, he adds the *what time is it* question in his *Jesus and the Victory of God* (Minneapolis: Fortress, 1996), 443 n1. David Frankfurter, "Narratives that Do Things," in *Religion: Narrative Religion*, ed. Sarah Iles Johnson (Farmington Hills, MI: Macmillan Reference USA, 2017), 95–106, makes some helpful observations

Such a big story situates the community's members in their places in the world; it also calls them to indwell the story and to participate in its outworking, to play their part in it as it unfolds.[11] Perhaps another way to put it is that the big story redirects the question, "Who am *I*?" to the larger questions, "Who are *we*? Where are we? How are we? Why are we? When are we?"

The worldview, then, describes the way the community members lean into life—how they relate to the divine, to others, and to the world around them—and it comes to the community by way of a story. If the worldview story is well told, it captures the imaginations of those who own it, thereby driving them on and holding their loyalty. At the same time, tellers of such stories are quite sure that the story they tell is in some sense true, that is, that it refers to real events and the proper interpretation of those events.

Some have suggested that the phenomenon of a worldview story is a feature primarily of premodern and prescientific peoples,[12] but they are mistaken. Modern western culture does just the same. For example, the prominent evolutionary biologist George Gaylord Simpson (1902–1984) drew this conclusion from his study of evolution: "Man is the result of a purposeless and natural process that did not have him in mind."[13] This is in fact a story, albeit a bleak one, that claims to put people's lives in perspective. Actually, if it is the true story of the world, it sounds like a heightened version of what Macbeth described in Shakespeare's play once he discovered that Lady Macbeth had committed suicide: "Life's . . . a tale told by an idiot, full of sound and fury, signifying nothing."[14]

The biblical story, as Christians have traditionally understood it, therefore functions as a big story. Its components (agreeing with Lewis's summary) include:

- a good creation,
- marred by human fall into rebellion,
- where God is active to redeem humankind and all they affect,
- which God will bring into final judgment and complete fruition.

---

about such identity-shaping stories that define a community, though there are places I would adjust his discussion before applying it to either Israel or the church.

11. See also Craig Bartholomew and Michael Goheen, "Story and Biblical Theology," in *Out of Egypt: Biblical Theology and Biblical Interpretation*, ed. Craig Bartholomew and Elaine Botha (Grand Rapids: Zondervan, 2004), 144–71.

12. So, for example, Peter Enns, *Inspiration and Incarnation: Evangelicals and the Problem of the Old Testament* (Grand Rapids: Baker Academic, 2005), 40, and, to a lesser extent, Don Pederson, "Biblical Narrative as an Agent for Worldview Change," *International Journal of Frontier Missions* 14:4 (1997): 163–66.

13. George Gaylord Simpson, *The Meaning of Evolution* (New Haven, CT: Yale University Press, 1967), 365.

14. William Shakespeare, *Macbeth*, V.v.26–28.

Told this way it is not simply a local tale, dealing with a limited group of people: it tells the big story of the whole world.

If Genesis 1–11 is to serve as the front end of this big story, we can recognize that, like other claimants to be the true big story, it has historical impulse behind its writing. From its style and its function as prehistory and protohistory, we can also see that to call its focus "ancient science" takes us away from the text—whether we think that science is now discredited (in which case the text has no historical referentiality), or if we think its science is authoritative. Science as such may indeed play a role in constructing a worldview story, though it will need to be rendered into a poetic idiom, and the conclusions go well beyond the power of the sciences into what C. S. Lewis called myth making (as George Gaylord Simpson has done in the quotation above).[15]

As I have indicated, I take the purpose of Genesis to begin with opposing the origin stories of other ancient peoples by telling of one true God who made heaven and earth, and who dignified humankind with a special nobility, namely, the task of ruling the world wisely and well. Further, our discussion of the cohesion of Genesis 1–11 with the rest of Genesis also pointed the way toward appreciating both the meaning of the whole book and the place of Genesis 1–11 in the book: Genesis identifies the people of Israel, who followed Moses out of Egypt, as the heirs of God's promises to Abraham. We find in Genesis 12 that God called Abraham so that his family would be the vehicle of God's "blessing" to "all the families of the earth"—and, since Genesis 10 recounts the various "families" (or "clans") of the earth, this means to all non-Israelite peoples everywhere. Hence the purpose of Genesis 1–11 is to set the stage for Genesis 12–50, and it does this by clarifying that the God who called Abraham is in fact the one true God for whom all humankind yearns.[16]

This narrative plays a role in the entire Pentateuch: God is true to his promises to the patriarchs in raising up Moses, who will lead them out of Egypt and eventually to the promised land, and who also will serve as the spokesman by whom God provides a social system that is designed to foster the flourishing of this people; by the people's faithfulness and flourishing the

---

15. C. S. Lewis, "The Funeral of a Great Myth," in *Christian Reflections*, ed. Walter Hooper (Grand Rapids: Eerdmans, 1967), 82–93.

16. This narratival-historical approach makes better sense of the texts than those that pursue "timeless truths," of which Tsumura gives some samples: "mankind tends to destroy what God has made good" (Clines), or "the human propensity to trespass upon the divine sphere" (Oden). See David T. Tsumura, "Genesis and Ancient Near Eastern Stories of Creation and Flood: An Introduction," in *I Studied Inscriptions from before the Flood: Ancient Near Eastern, Literary, and Linguistic Approaches to Genesis 1–11*, ed. Richard S. Hess and David T. Tsumura (Winona Lake, IN: Eisenbrauns, 1994), 27–57, especially pp. 51–52.

rest of the world will have the chance to receive the knowledge of the one true God (as in Deut 4:6–8). Other parts of the Hebrew Bible echo this purpose. The prophets, for example, denounce the people's unfaithfulness while they also hold forth the hope of the gentiles' eventual blessedness, a hope that calls the members of Israel to piety and obedience (as in Isa 1:2–2:5). Psalm 72:17, in words echoing Genesis 22:18; 26:4, prays that by way of the Davidic dynasty the whole gentile world will one day "be blessed in him" (whoever "he" might be).[17] The laws fit within this overarching narrative; hence we may legitimately find in the Pentateuch an attempt at a worldview story.[18]

Gilbert Rorison captures well why the way that the story begins matters a great deal:

> A law of life for the individual present, a hope for the individual future, must each repose on a doctrine of the collective human past. All creeds must cast anchor on some scheme of beginnings. Cosmogonies may be sober and sound, or they may be frivolous and foolish. But it was always seen, as it is evident still, that to forego a cosmogony is to dispense with a religion.[19]

6.C ANACHRONISM AND HISTORY

Genesis serves an identity-shaping purpose, namely, to enable its audiences to see themselves as the proper heirs of the characters depicted. With what rhetorical features might it achieve this purpose? I have already noted that some kind of historical impulse likely lies behind the stories; and here we will explore whether we should expect its manner of description to aim for *historical verisimilitude*—that is, to seek to capture all the details of life exactly as the characters would have known them, even if the characters' mode of life was quite different from that of the audience. We will look, therefore, for

---

17. The psalm begins with a reflection on Solomon or some other descendant of David, but I read it to look forward to the ultimate goal of the Davidic dynasty and thus to point to a person we may call the Messiah. For this reading, and its connection to the Genesis texts, see T. Desmond Alexander, "Further Observations on the Term 'Seed' in Genesis," *TynBul* 48:2 (1997): 363–67.

18. Linda Stargel, "The Construction of Exodus Identity in the Texts of Ancient Israel: A Social Identity Approach" (PhD thesis, University of Manchester, 2016), helpfully draws on sociological theories to describe the community-shaping function of the Pentateuch stories. However, some shortcomings severely limit the applicability of her work: (1) She does not recognize Moses's prophetic role, which entails his power to declare some beliefs and practices legitimate and others illegitimate; he is not merely a codifier of the community; (2) she does not start with creation as a foundational category, which means she does not account for Gen 1–11; and (3) she properly sees Israel's story as one of enjoying a privilege, but she does not do justice to their calling to be a vehicle of blessing to the whole creation.

19. Gilbert Rorison, "The Creative Week," in *Replies to "Essays and Reviews,"* ed. E. M. Goulburn, et al. (New York: Appleton, 1862), 242–98, quote on p. 259.

ways the text of Genesis invites the audience to see themselves in the events; and we will consider whether Genesis might employ *anachronism*—that is, describing its scenes in terms of things in the audience's world.

Anachronisms and their relationship with history and rhetoric vary. In fact, they force us to define what we mean by the word *history*. For some, being literally minded, a narrative conveys history only when it is straightforward and factual; that is, only when it aims at historical verisimilitude. In terms of our discussions here, that notion assumes that history writing generally has the illocutionary force of conveying information and doing so accurately. This notion therefore expects that the poetic elements are minimal and that the preferred language level is on the range from the ordinary to the scientific. I will call this "antiquarian history."

Other notions of history restrict the name "proper history" to the sorts of things that trained historians write, for example, with critical evaluation of sources. Some have even proposed that genuine history writing must exclude all reference to the activities of God or the gods—though the advocates of this view do not necessarily deny that such beings exist and have acted.[20] These latter two versions of history writing suffer from an intractable confusion—at least in ordinary language—in that they make it possible for the scholar to say, "This narrative is *not* 'historical,' but that does not mean it did not happen." That kind of confusion suggests to me that we could profitably analyze these definitions as infelicitous technical usages, or even in Lewisian fashion, as "tactical definitions" (see ch. 2 above). I will try to use words without these intractable confusions. Richard Averbeck does a better job of defining history writing from within the perspective of those doing the writing:

> Thus, *history* is the general term used for what is happening when a civilization takes account of its own past from its own point of view.[21]

These confusing definitions reflect a preference for a kind of objectivity with suspicion of the storyteller's control of how he or she tells the story, how the characters are portrayed, and what details are included or left out. A moral or ideological motive, by this preference, leads to some kind of deflection from the idealized objectivity. Now, this preference is itself

---

20. For helpful discussion, see V. Philips Long, *The Art of Biblical History* (Grand Rapids: Zondervan, 1994), 58–87, chapter 2.
21. Richard Averbeck, "The Sumerian Historiographic Tradition," in "Story, History, and Theology," in *Faith, Tradition, and History: Old Testament Historiography in its Near Eastern Context*, ed. A. R. Millard, James K. Hoffmeier and David W. Baker (Winona Lake, IN: Eisenbrauns, 1994), 79–102, quote on p. 82 (emphasis original).

an ideological value and therefore lacks the strict objectivity it proclaims. Besides, no historian is genuinely neutral, nor do we wish him or her to be—at least we want him to select what to tell us about. Nevertheless, we do have an intuition of "fairness" in reporting that does not require a nonexistent objectivity.

The biblical writers are clear that they read an ideological program in the narratives. For example, Psalm 78:5–8 offers this take on sacred history:

> He established a testimony in Jacob
>   and appointed a law in Israel,
> which he commanded our fathers
>   to teach to their children,
> that the next generation might know them,
>   the children yet unborn,
> and arise and tell them to their children,
>   so that they should set their hope in God
> and not forget the works of God,
>   but keep his commandments;
> and that they should not be like their fathers,
>   a stubborn and rebellious generation,
> a generation whose heart was not steadfast,
>   whose spirit was not faithful to God.

Indeed, the Pentateuch itself presents a reason for its own writing (Deut 31:8–13):

> It is the LORD who goes before you. He will be with you; he will not leave you or forsake you. Do not fear or be dismayed." Then Moses wrote this law and gave it to the priests, the sons of Levi, who carried the ark of the covenant of the LORD, and to all the elders of Israel. And Moses commanded them, "At the end of every seven years, at the set time in the year of release, at the Feast of Booths, when all Israel comes to appear before the LORD your God at the place that he will choose, you shall read this law before all Israel in their hearing. Assemble the people, men, women, and little ones, and the sojourner within your towns, that they may hear and learn to fear the LORD your God, and be careful to do all the words of this law, and that their children, who have not known it, may hear and learn to fear the LORD your God, as long as you live in the land that you are going over the Jordan to possess."

So the real discussion is between what I have called "antiquarian history" and what we might call "rhetorical history." The texts I have cited (and many others) show that we have every reason to expect rhetorical history in the Bible; but does that mean it is not history in some true sense? We appreciate that in ordinary language to say that something is "historical" is to say that there are actual persons and events for it to refer to and these persons and events really existed. This does not determine the literary form or rhetorical setting in which the referring takes place, however. The notion of true statements we developed in chapter 4 above can help us as well, namely, in saying that cooperation with the illocutionary force is appropriate (which includes morally right). Hence, we must insist that *"history" is not a literary form*; it is rather *a way of referring to persons and events* with a proper moral orientation.[22]

I am not seeking to show in detail whether or not, by these criteria, we can authenticate the material in Genesis 1–11 as true history; at this point I aim only to clarify what the question should (and should not) mean.

In rhetorical history, especially when the subject matter is the distant past—as we have in prehistory and protohistory—we might expect to find anachronisms, possibly even in abundance, depending on the rhetorical purpose. A scholar of comparative literature, Joseph Luzzi, draws on Johann Wolfgang von Goethe (1749–1832) to the effect that "the poet cannot report past events without imparting his own moral world view to his characters."[23] Thus some level of anachronism is inevitable, not only for poets but also for all tellers of rhetorical history. Luzzi comments on a well-known literary anachronism found in Shakespeare's *Julius Caesar* (Act 2, scene 1, lines 205–210), where a clock strikes:

> Shakespeare likely understood that the ancient Romans marked time by sundial and not pendulum; presumably, however, he also realized that his audiences would respond more instinctively to chimes than to an imagined shadow of a sunbeam as a harbinger of imminent tragedy.[24]

That is, a concern for historical verisimilitude would diminish the effect on the audience. Certainly, I am not drawing a strong parallel between Shakespeare's historical plays and the Bible; I suspect that the biblical audiences

---

22. Contrast the position of Kenton Sparks, "Genesis 1–11 as Ancient Historiography," 110–39: "Historical representation maintains a very close relationship between the narrative and actual events" (p. 114).

23. Joseph Luzzi, "The Rhetoric of Anachronism," *Comparative Literature* 61:1 (2009): 69–84, at 71.

24. Ibid., 71 n6.

had a higher expectation for the actuality of the persons and events than Shakespeare's did. Even so, the rhetorical device of anachronism is a helpful one and is misleading (or unhistorical) only if the audience had reason to believe that the narrative offered this kind of antiquarian information.[25] At some point, depending on the text, we may feel that the anachronism crosses a line: were a character in *Julius Caesar*, for example, to have consulted a watch, we would object.[26] A general rule for predicting the exact location of that line a priori remains elusive, and we must take the examples case-by-case.

A particular author can use anachronisms for his or her own purposes. And far from being a barrier to understanding the past, anachronisms actually can promote understanding; as Luzzi put it,

> From an epistemological perspective, the strategies of temporal dislocation typical of anachronism can work to produce knowledge about the past that subverts the more rational and empirical elements traditionally associated with disciplines like history and philosophy.[27]

There is no reason to suppose that ancient Near Eastern writers and audiences required historical verisimilitude in literary compositions dealing with prehistory and protohistory in order for them to be credible.[28] Indeed, as late as 1598, Caravaggio's painting of Judith beheading Holofernes (Jdt. 13:7–8) has the women's clothing, and probably the large knife, portrayed anachronistically;[29] there is no reason to declare such paintings unhistorical *on that basis.*

Looked at this way, we can expect to find anachronisms in Genesis 1–11 in ways that we will not find them in other passages. For example, the book of Ruth describes a transaction in which a sandal was handed over and even explains it as "the custom in former times in Israel" (Ruth 4:7). The antiquarian notice implies that the author expects that his audience is unfamiliar

---

25. We must not confuse this with the largely appropriate concern of Bible translation specialists who wish to keep the translations from being unnecessarily misleading. See, for example, P. J. N. Lawrence, "Oh No, He's Still Wearing His Watch! Avoiding Anachronism in Old Testament Translation," *Bible Translator* 59:1 (2008), 14–17.

26. Ironically, Lawrence's article begins with a time-piece in the same play that Luzzi uses for his discussion.

27. Luzzi, "The Rhetoric of Anachronism," 82.

28. See the thoughtful discussion in Andrew Malone, "Acceptable Anachronism in Biblical Studies," *Bible Translator* 67:3 (2016): 351–64.

29. As do Lucas Cranach's in 1530 and Artemesia Gentileschi's in 1614. In fact, as C. S. Lewis observed about the Middle Ages, "They pictured the whole past in terms of their own age. So indeed did the Elizabethans . . . It is doubtful whether the sense of period is much older than the Waverley novels" (that is, 1814). Lewis, *The Discarded Image*, 183.

with the custom, presumably because it has fallen out of use. Further, the book presents a situation in which the institutions of kinsman redeemer and levirate marriage were joined, which is not how the Torah specifies these institutions.³⁰ Probably the author needed to distinguish the sandal as a mark of transaction from the sandal as a mark of shame (Deut 25:9–10), and part of the purpose of the book is the historical apologetic for the line that produced David, from a marriage that arose in times that were less than ideal. There seem as well to be features of the life-settings of the patriarchs of Genesis 12–15, Abraham, Isaac, Jacob, and Joseph, that reflect their times in the second millennium BC. This, by the way, is one of the arguments in favor of seeing ancient tradition, rather than free composition, behind these patriarchal stories: Their manners and customs reflect accurate recollections of the time in which the events occurred, not simply the time of whoever wrote the stories down.³¹

But even in the case of the patriarchal stories, we can find some expressions that reflect the interests of the audience more than they aim to capture the participants' experiences. For example, in Genesis 26:5 we learn the Lord's verdict on Abraham: He "obeyed my voice and kept my charge, my commandments, my statutes, and my laws." Now these are terms that properly apply to the Mosaic legislation, which did not exist for Abraham.

Samuel Greengus surveys the variety of ways that Jewish ancient and medieval writers explained the situation.³² He finds especially attractive the idea that the charge, commandments, statutes, and judgments refer to the "Noahide" laws, which God laid upon all nations. This is feasible, but we still have Abraham portrayed as an ideal Israelite—whose example his descendants ought to emulate, particularly since this obedience was given as the reason for God's continued blessing.

Similarly, in Genesis 12:10, Abraham "went down to Egypt," and, when Pharaoh misbehaved, "the LORD afflicted Pharaoh and his house with great plagues"—using one of the words for the ten plagues (Exod 11:1). No doubt

---

30. For what to make of this situation, see C. John Collins, "Homonymous Verbs in Biblical Hebrew: An Investigation of the Role of Comparative Philology" (PhD thesis, University of Liverpool, 1988), 65–67 (focusing on the use of the verb גאל [ga'al], "to redeem").

31. On this last point, see A. R. Millard, "Methods of Studying the Patriarchal Narratives as Ancient Texts," in *Essays on the Patriarchal Narratives*, ed. A. R. Millard and Donald J. Wiseman (Leicester: Inter-Varsity Press, 1980), 43–58. Daniel Fleming, "History in Genesis," *WTJ* 65 (2014): 251–62, offers a sensitive discussion that both affirms the air of authenticity in the Patriarchal stories and recognizes that these stories' manner of telling is geared to the later audiences. As a side note, I observe that the Pentateuch's priestly material also shows its antiquity, being suited to life before the exile—though I will have to make that case in another study.

32. Samuel Greengus, "The Anachronism in Abraham's Observance of the Laws," *HUCA* 86 (2015), 1–35.

the point was to allow the audience to identify with Abram, in order for them to see themselves as his proper heirs (the purpose of Genesis).

Genesis 1–11 is different from the patriarchal stories that follow in that I find anachronism to be an essential feature of its style. We can divide these anachronisms into those that are demonstrable, those that are likely, and those that look reasonable (but are hard to prove).

We start with the demonstrable anachronisms. For example, many have noted that Genesis portrays the garden of Eden as if it were a sanctuary: one entered from the east, with cherubim present (Gen 3:24; Exod 27:13; Ezek 11:1); Yahweh "walked about" in it (Gen 3:8; Lev 26:11–12). Perhaps the trees of the garden are like the lampstands, and the gold, precious stones (for onyx and gold together in the priest's garments, see Exod 28:20; 39:6, 13), and rivers also correspond to furnishings in the tabernacle. As the Israeli commentator Yehudah Kiel put it, "The 'garden' was therefore the first place on earth where the Shekinah dwelt."[33] The first audiences would have known the Israelite sanctuary and would have read of Eden in terms of that. That would enable them to interpret their sanctuary as a kind of heir to the garden (a homology).

The promised land is to be a kind of reconstituted garden of Eden, a fruitful garden that displays God's presence to all the world. Identifying Eden's location suffers from difficulties because two of the four rivers are unknown (Gen 2:10–14).[34] This lends an air of mystery to the text, and we might wonder whether the name Gihon for the second river (Gen 2:13)—one of the unknowns—might have been chosen to evoke the Gihon spring in Jerusalem (1 Kgs 1:33), which was a sacred spot even before the temple (1 Kgs 1:45).

As I discussed in the last chapter, the first audiences would have known the six-day work week, followed by a Sabbath (any time after the events of Exod 16:22–30). I have already observed that God's observing of this pattern tells Israel that their calling is to recapture the creation order and that the ideal human life consists of imitating God.

Finally, Adam can be seen as a kind of ideal Israelite. He and Eve speak Hebrew, as their wordplays show (Gen 2:23; 4:1, 25); in fact, seeing the evil of the serpent's temptation depends on a Hebrew grammatical feature (the infinitive absolute, "surely": 2:17; 3:4). It is easier to find this to be an anachronism than to spend time wondering whether Hebrew was the original human language! Adam works the ground, he sets the pattern for Israelite marriage,

---

33. Yehudah Kiel, *Sefer Bere'shit*, vol. 1, chs. 1–17, Da'at Miqra' (Jerusalem: Mossad HaRav Kook, 1997), עו. See also Gordon Wenham, *Genesis 1–15*, WBC (Nashville: Word, 1987), 86.

34. These difficulties are not necessarily insuperable. See C. John Collins, *Genesis 1–4: A Linguistic, Literary, and Theological Commentary* (Phillipsburg, NJ: P&R, 2006), 119–20.

and he has a commandment to obey—and violation can get him exiled from the garden. His relationship to the various kinds of animals is echoed in Hosea 2:18; 4:3 and above all in Psalm 8, where the Israelite sings of himself or herself as the heir of Adam. The first humans are to "subdue" (Heb. כבשׁ, *kabash*) the "earth" (Heb. ארץ, *'erets*) in 1:28, while the Israelites expect to "subdue" the "land" (Num 32:22, 29; see also Josh 18:1). Does Adam simply *personify* Israel, as some have suggested?[35] That is not likely, since genealogies take Genesis from Adam to Abram. Rather, Adam is portrayed in terms that enable the Israelite reader to embrace his role in a people, Israel, that is a fresh start on humankind. That is, the "Adam-as-Israel personified" reading has things exactly backwards.

Next, we have a number of features of Genesis 1–11 that are probably best explained as likely anachronisms. For example, Cain and Abel offer sacrifices: "an offering of the fruit of the ground" and "of the firstborn of the flock and their fat portions" (Gen 4:3–4). Both of these are recognizable in the sacrificial system of Israel: the produce offering (Deut 26:2; Lev 2:1–16) and the firstborn (Deut 15:19–23). Interestingly enough, Cain brought a produce offering, which in Israel feeds only the priests, while Abel brought a peace offering, which feeds the worshipers and their dependents. Did the author want us to suppose that Cain and Abel observed the Israelite system? I doubt it. As I read the narrative, I find that it shows that Abel's heart orientation was right, while Cain's was not.[36] The narrative serves the purposes both of showing the downward trend of humankind after the disobedience of Genesis 3, and of reinforcing the importance of worshiping from the heart.

A second likely anachronism is the way Noah must distinguish between "clean" and "unclean" animals (Gen 7:2, 8). The clean animals are fit for sacrifice, which figures in the story later (Gen 8:20)—an episode that, as I will argue in chapter 7, is crucial to the story's communicative import. Further, the creation account gives no hint that the clean-unclean distinction is inherent in the nature of the animals; in the Bible this distinction served to set Israel apart from the gentiles (see Lev 20:24–26).[37] The very first mention of a clean animal occurs right here; we do not even know what they are unless we already have Leviticus 11. Perhaps we are to think that Noah had some idea of what kinds of animals are right for sacrifice, but we need not suppose that it was identical to the system found in the books of Moses. How could it be,

---

35. This is how Peter Enns sees him in *Evolution of Adam*, 65–70.

36. For literary exposition, see Collins, *Genesis 1–4*, 199–200, 208–15.

37. For a helpful discussion of these laws from a Jewish perspective, see Meir Soloveichik, "Locusts, Giraffes, and the Meaning of *Kashrut*," *Azure* 21 (Winter 5766 / 2006): 62–96. This is why the early Christians had no difficulty in doing away with these laws (see Acts 10:9–29; Mark 7:19).

when Noah was not an Israelite?[38] Perhaps the specific burnt offering is also anachronistic—that is, Noah made a sacrifice but the term "burnt offering" had a very precise sense in Israel that may go beyond what Noah might be supposed to think (much as those in Gen 4:3–4). In sum, Genesis interprets Noah's behavior in line with Israelite practice. Since Noah functions as a new start on humankind, it serves the ordinary Israelite to be able to see his or her own life as having continuity with Noah's.

Finally, in a group of texts it is reasonable—though hard to prove—to find anachronisms. Consider the occupations of Cain and Abel (Gen 4:2), "keeping sheep" (Abel) and "working the ground" (Cain). Now, humans have been keeping stock animals and working the ground for crops for millennia. Does our text insist that humans began this immediately upon their expulsion from the garden and that the practices resembled those in Israel? The best answer is, not necessarily: After all, how else might an Israelite talk about them?[39]

In the same way, Genesis 4:17–22 describes people in the line of Cain who pioneered various crafts that would have been familiar to the Israelite audience: city building, ranching, musical instruments, and metalworking. According to the present state of paleoanthropological thinking, these crafts belong to the Neolithic era (ca. 10,000–ca. 3,000 BC), that is, in the era just before records from ancient Egypt and ancient Mesopotamia survive.[40] It is possible to read these verses as describing the trailblazers of the skills that eventually led to the crafts the audience would be familiar with. In fact, Umberto Cassuto argued that the Hebrew terms "father" and "forger" can be read with these nuances.[41] Again, I will argue in chapter 7 that this description of crafts serves a purpose, especially in contrast to the mystique that derived from the high Mesopotamian culture (which held that their kind of kingship descended from the gods).[42]

---

38. See Ezek 14:14, 20, which mentions Noah, Daniel, and Job as ancient exemplars. "Daniel" in this context is probably the figure known as Dan'il in the Ugaritic poem (although I expect that, in order to commend the man, Ezekiel knew more about him than what we find in that particular story). I give my rationale for taking the figure as Dan'il rather than biblical Daniel in Collins, "Noah, Deucalion, and the New Testament," 403–26, especially p. 409 n15.

39. These practices do go back a long way. For example, there may be some evidence that the earliest stages of what became farming long predate the Neolithic period (which began ca. 10,000 BC). See D. R. Piperno et al., "Processing of Wild Cereal Grains in the Upper Paleolithic Revealed by Starch Grain Analysis," *Nature* 430 (August 2004): 670–73, which reports findings that people were processing wild cereal grains—a predecessor to cultivation—more than 20,000 years ago.

40. See Davis A. Young, "The Antiquity and the Unity of the Human Race Revisited," *Christian Scholars Review* 24:4 (1995): 380–396.

41. Umberto Cassuto, *Genesis, Part I*, 235–37. I provide some philological support for this in Collins, "Homonymous Verbs in Biblical Hebrew," 232–33.

42. Daniel Lowery, *Toward a Poetics of Genesis 1–11: Reading Genesis 4:17–22 in Its Near Eastern Context* (Winona Lake, IN: Eisenbrauns, 2013), 110–14, has offered some valuable literary suggestions about the passage, which support this way of reading it.

A last example is the occasion on which God "formed the man of dust from the ground," at least as rendered in the ESV. It was when no vegetation had sprung up, "for the LORD God had not caused it to rain upon the land," at the time when "a mist was going up from the land" (Gen 2:5–7).[43] This certainly makes sense in light of the Palestinian climate. Near the end of the dry season, the plants would be brown but ready to spring up once the rains began in the fall; observe that the reason the text gives was that it had not yet rained.[44] The land here, in which God forms the man before translating him to the garden, is unnamed; as I suggested, "it is not clear whether this is a strong claim of the historical location or simply a literary device that recounts the event in terms familiar to the audience."[45] The features of the text make the second option reasonable: the land, or the ground from which the man was taken, is the place where man is formed, from which he is removed to Eden, toward which he is sent away, and to which he is eventually to return by his death and dissolution (Gen 2:7, 15; 3:19, 23). The audience of the text are to work their land (Israel), seeing their liturgical life as their way back to the garden, other ways having been barred (Gen 3:24).[46]

6.D LITERARY STYLE AND LANGUAGE LEVEL

What kind of thing, at the literary and linguistic level, is the material of Genesis 1–11? It is entirely possible, of course, that there are *several* kinds of things in the varied material—the narrative style of 1:1–2:3 need not be the same as that of 2:4–11:26. And there might be subsets, for example the genealogies and Table of Nations, that differ as well.

In a 2015 volume on diverging views on how to read Genesis 1–11, the editor asked the contributors to classify the genre of Genesis 1–11.[47] The request suffered from a shortcoming, namely, not having a clear and workable definition of "genre." It comes as no surprise that the authors do not agree. In my discussion in chapter 2, I mentioned some of the difficulties that this term presents, especially as Bible specialists have tended to focus on the literary

---

43. For grammatical and lexical details, see C. John Collins, "Discourse Analysis and the Interpretation of Genesis 2:4–7," *WTJ* 61:2 (1999): 269–276; idem., *Genesis 1–4*, 108–12.
44. In traditional Judaism, Rosh HaShanah, the agricultural new year, is connected to the creation story.
45. Collins, *Genesis 1–4*, 253 n6.
46. See Lowery, *Toward a Poetics of Genesis 1–11*, 70, for support.
47. Charles Halton, ed., *Genesis: History Fiction, or Neither? Three Views on the Bible's Earliest Chapters* (Grand Rapids: Zondervan, 2015), with contributions from James Hoffmeier ("Genesis 1–11 as History and Theology"), Gordon Wenham ("Genesis 1–11 as Protohistory"), and Kenton Sparks ("Genesis 1–11 as Ancient Historiography").

form. If we draw on Carolyn Miller's perspective on "genre as social action" (§2.B.4 above), we can get further: I suggested in chapter 5 that Genesis 1–11 serves as prehistory and protohistory, and this is a *social function*, not a *literary form*. The main literary form (see 6.E below) is prose narrative, and that prose varies in its style and register and thus in its language level.[48]

The current discussion is pointing us in the direction of finding little or even no scientific language in Genesis 1–11 at the same time as a clear historical impulse lies behind the narrative. Two types of readers insist that, if Genesis is historical, we must read it "literally"—by which they mean that we must treat it as if it were an effort at scientific description. First, we have the "young-earth creationists": they are sure that we are to call all of Genesis history and that, therefore, we must read it as "straight" description.[49] Second, we have those who think that Genesis means to be an ancient scientific description but that we ought not believe it as having any bearing on history.[50] Neither of these approaches does justice to the kind of literature we have in Genesis—a kind that has been recognized by Jewish and Christian believers from the earliest stages.

In more than one place C. S. Lewis attributed to the church father Jerome (AD 347–420) the literary judgment that the early chapters of Genesis are told in the form of a folktake or popular narrative, "after the manner of a popular poet."[51] No Jerome scholar has identified a place where Jerome actually issued this kind of sentiment. In fact, the words that Lewis uses in quotation marks appear in a letter written by the Oxford scholar John Colet (1467–1519), a proto-reformer and premier English man of letters in his day. Colet wrote a series of letters in Latin to a certain Radulphus ("Ralph"), whose identity is unsure and who seems to have asked about the story of Lamech in Genesis. Colet took the opportunity to explain much about how to read the creation story in Genesis, and in the course of his explanation said:

---

48. In Halton, ed., *Genesis: History Fiction, or Neither?*, Wenham uses the designation "protohistory," but without this kind of distinction. Sparks, in his response to Wenham, objects that "protohistory" does not correspond to categories known from elsewhere in the ancient world (106–7). My discussion in chapter 5 shows that Sparks's objection fails, especially if we focus on the social action performed.

49. See, for example, Douglas Kelly, *Creation and Change: Genesis 1.1–2.4 in the Light of Changing Scientific Paradigms* (Fearn, Ross-shire: Christian Focus, 1997), especially pp. 41–42; he states clearly, "The text of Genesis is clearly meant to be taken in a literal, historical sense" (51).

50. See, for example, Denis Lamoureux, *Evolutionary Creation: A Christian Approach to Evolution* (Eugene, OR: Wipf & Stock, 2008), 150: "Therefore, since the heavens are not structured in this way [i.e., according to a literalistic reading of Genesis 1], Gen 1 cannot be a historical account of the actual events that created the heavens."

51. See Lewis, *Reflections on the Psalms*, 109. See also *Miracles: A Preliminary Study* (New York: Macmillan, 1960), 33; "Dogma and the Universe," in *God in the Dock: Essays on Theology and Ethics*, ed. Walter Hooper (Grand Rapids: Eerdmans, 1970), 38–47, especially p. 42.

Moses arranged his details in such a way as to give the people a clearer notion, and he does this *after the manner of a popular poet*, in order that he may the more adapt himself to the spirit of simple rusticity.[52]

Although we cannot trace this assessment of Mosaic style to Jerome, we can nevertheless find a distinguished pedigree for it.[53] The earliest named Jewish philosopher, Aristobulus (mid-second century BC), deals with how to read the passages in the Pentateuch that speak of God having hands, arm, face, and feet. He explains the Mosaic style:

> For our lawgiver Moses, when he wishes to express his meaning in various ways, announces certain arrangements of nature and preparations for mighty deeds, by adopting phrases applicable to other things, I mean to things *according to their appearance* [κατὰ τὴν ἐπιφάνειαν].[54]

The church historian Eusebius of Caesarea (AD 260/265–339/340) insists that the account in Genesis is popular, not philosophical (*Praep. Ev.*, 11.7 [522-*d*])—which would be his word for scientific:

> This then is what we have to say of [the Hebrews'] Natural Science of the Universe. But as they divided this subject into two parts, the one which concerns things perceived by the senses *they did not think it necessary to make known accurately to the multitude, nor to teach the common people the causes of the nature of existing things, except only so far as it was necessary for them to know that the universe has not been self-created*, and has not been produced causelessly and by chance from an irrational impetus, but is led on by the Divine Reason as its guide, and governed by a power of ineffable Wisdom.

We find similar judgments in Augustine (*On Genesis by the Letter*):

> 2.6.13: But the scriptural style comes down to the level of the little ones and adjusts itself to their capacity by putting before them each

---

52. From his second letter to Radulphus (1497). English translation from Frederick Seebohm, *The Oxford Reformers* (London: Longmans, Green, 1869), 51 (emphasis original). Another translation, with the Latin original, appears in J. H. Lupton, ed., *Letters to Radulphus on the Mosaic Account of the Creation, Together with Other Treatises, by John Colet, M.A.* (London: George Bell, 1876), 9–10.

53. We can only guess why Lewis attributed the sentiment to Jerome. The wording quoted suggests that Lewis had read the Seebohm edition of the letters (Lupton's rendering is "after the manner of some popular poet," which is also close). In the first letter Colet had mentioned Jerome as a careful scholar familiar with the original Hebrew.

54. Aristobulus (Frag. 2, §3), preserved in Eusebius, *Praep. ev.*, 8.10 (376-*b*).

single kind of creature one by one, and then looking back at the eternal formula of each kind in the word of God.

2.9.20: It must be stated very briefly that our authors knew about the shape of the sky whatever may be the truth of the matter. But the Spirit of God who was speaking through them did not wish to teach people about such things which would contribute nothing to their salvation.

Thomas Aquinas was similar (*Summa Theologica*):

But Moses describes what is obvious to sense, out of condescension to an uneducated populace [*rudi populo*]. (1ª, q. 70 art. 1 ad. 3; 1ª, q. 68 ans. 3 similar)

John Calvin carried along this same tradition (*Commentary on Genesis*, at Gen 1:6; 1:16; 6:14):

At Genesis 1:5: Nothing is here treated of but the visible form of the world.... The waters here meant are such as *the uneducated and unlearned* [*rudes quoque et indocti*] may perceive.

At 1:16: Moses wrote in *a popular style* [*populariter*] things which without instruction, *all ordinary persons* [*omnes idiotae*], endued with common sense, are able to understand.... [Moses] was ordained a teacher as well of the *unlearned and uneducated* [*indoctis et rudibus*] as of the learned.

At 6:14: Moses everywhere spoke *in a homely style*, to suit the capacity of the people.... Certainly, in the first chapter, he did not treat scientifically of the stars, as a philosopher would do; but he called them, *in a popular manner* [*populariter*], according to their appearance to the *uneducated* [*rudium*], rather than *according to the thing itself* [*ex re ipsa*], "two great lights."

Observe how the style came to be connected with a version of what I called audience criticism in the previous chapter.

Colet has the most extensive application of his literary assessment, calling Moses "a good and devout poet."[55] He followed Augustine (and perhaps Philo) in thinking that it suited the Creator to make all things at once and

---

55. Colet, letter 4 to Radulphus; Lupton, *Letters to Radulphus*, 27.

that the six days are a literary device fitted to the understanding of the "rustic" audience. Colet regularly uses Latin words related to *fingo*, "to imagine or portray," and he sets out, in his third and fourth letters, to address what he believes to be the rhetorical purpose of the account:

> It was the design of Moses, (1) to speak worthily of God; (2) *to satisfy the minds of ordinary people*, in respect of matters known to them; (3) to preserve an order in events; (4) above all, to lead the people on to religion, and the worship of God.
>
> Another reason . . . was that, by imitating God, whom poet-like he portrayed as having worked six days and rested on the seventh, the people might be led to rest on every seventh day, and to the contemplation and worship of God.
>
> With consummate ingenuity, as well as devotion, he portrayed God as spending six days on the fabric of the universe, and to have rested on the seventh, that he might, in the first place, commend to the minds of men a religious rest on every seventh day; and *might also convince an ignorant multitude*, by the authority and example of God, that every seventh day was consecrated to divine worship and contemplation.[56]

Colet, in his own way, even anticipates the modern view that the Genesis origin story opposes those of heathen peoples. He explains why the account has the vegetation (Day 3) preceding the light bearers (Day 4):

> It was the design of Moses to mention the earth's fertility and production of vegetation, before he mentioned the stars, to show that the fruitfulness of the earth did not depend on the stars . . . lest the vulgar should suppose, as often happens, that the power of generation lay wholly in the sun and the other stars.[57]

Because Colet considers the six days a literary device, he is free to think this way about the rhetorical intention, without any obligation to suppose—as many creationists have felt required to do—that some alternate light source was in operation before the fourth day.[58] Colet also made some helpful

---

56. Colet, letters 3 and 4 to Radulphus; Lupton, *Letters to Radulphus*, 20, 27 (slightly modified from Lupton's English rendering to bring out the use of *fingo*, emphasis added).
57. The idea is as old as Theophilus, who was Patriarch of Antioch (ca. AD 169–83), *To Autolycus*, 2:15.
58. Israel Baroway, "The Bible as Poetry in the English Renaissance: An Introduction," *Journal of English and Germanic Philology* 32:4 (1933): 447–80, commends the importance of Colet in English letters but misportrays the achievement as something daring. The tradition of audience criticism mentioned

suggestions to his friend Radulphus, and we will take advantage of them in our theological reading in chapter 7.

None of these authors I have mentioned thought that their literary judgment was to the disadvantage of Genesis. Indeed, as Lewis put it,

> But if you compare [the Genesis story] with the creation legends of other peoples—with all those delightful absurdities in which giants to be cut up and floods to be dried up are made to exist *before* creation—the depth and originality of this Hebrew folk tale will soon be apparent. The idea of *creation* in the rigorous sense of the word is there fully grasped.[59]

Further, those making the literary judgments as to the text type and function might not have fully employed that judgment in the way they treated specific texts. Lewis notes this of some medieval scholars:

> Obviously their *auctors* will contradict one another. They will seem to do so even more often if you ignore the distinction of kinds and take your science impartially from the poets and philosophers; and this the medievals very often did in fact though they would have been well able to point out, in theory, that poets feigned.[60]

In this light, not every exegetical move these authors (or others) have made is of equal value.

Applying this assessment, we recognize that in Genesis 1–11 we do not have even an attempt at a scientific account; it is not even what some call "ancient science." Now, authors who refer to science in the ancient Near East are not always clear what they mean, but they generally have in mind statements about the world that are open to investigation, to explain what things are and how they work, with technical terminology—what eventually came to be called "natural philosophy."[61] The endeavor aims at giving a true account and eliminating ambiguity; hence one diagnostic for whether an ancient work is intended to be, or taken to be, scientific, is what people are expected to do

---

here, together with the reading of Augustine, shows that Colet has perceptively combined these strands rather than initiated a departure.

59. Lewis, *Miracles*, 33 (emphasis original).

60. Lewis, *The Discarded Image*, 11. (See further an egregious example on pp. 147–48.)

61. For discussion of the various meanings of "science" and a lively awareness of anachronism and equivocation, see David Lindberg, *The Beginnings of Western Science* (Chicago: University of Chicago Press, 1992), 1–4. Lindberg also makes the distinction between science and technology, which perhaps also sheds light on the difference that science came to make: People could do plenty of sophisticated things, such as make buildings and navigate and breed stock, without an explanatory theory.

with the statements. For example, does the communication itself invite people to affirm any details or to plan a journey based on the geography?

In Genesis, however, we have something different. We allow for things like pictorial description, anachronism, and symbolism. Indeed, I suggested that one goal of the storytelling in Genesis is to provide an alternative story to those told in other cultures of the ancient Near East (especially in Mesopotamia).[62] The Mesopotamian stories include divine action, symbolism, and imaginative elements; the purpose of the stories is to lay the foundation for a worldview, without being taken in a literalistic fashion. At the same time, these stories refer to what their tellers and audiences took to be actual events. Thus, Genesis aims to tell the story of beginnings the "right" way, to counter the other stories; it professes to offer the divinely authorized way for its audience to picture the events (which leaves some leeway in scientific theorizing, as we will see).[63]

6.E LITERARY STYLE AND ARCHITECTURE OF GENESIS 1–11

The literary form, language, and architecture of Genesis 1–11 support the notion of Colet and the rest that the early chapters of Genesis exhibit a style for which a scientific reading is unsuited. In fact, these features point the way to seeing the proper function of the chapters along the lines I have already suggested.

To begin with, the whole of Genesis 1–11 is basically narrative—in the sense that there is a storyline, that there are persons and events, and that the conditions change as the characters act. These chapters also fit into the *toledot* pattern of the whole of Genesis, where sections are introduced with some variation of "these are the *generations* [*toledot*] of so-and-so" (Gen 2:4; 5:1; 6:9; 10:1; 11:10, 27; 25:12, 19; 36:1, 9; 37:2). Desmond Alexander provides a good summary of their literary role:

> First, they are like chapter or section headings in modern books. Some of them introduce major narrative sections, indicating a new stage in the development of the plot. . . . Second, the *toledot* headings function like a

---

62. The notion that Genesis is to be set over against other ancient origins stories is as old as the Jewish writer Josephus (first century AD) and the Christian apologists (notably Eusebius, in his *Preparation for the Gospel*, early fourth century).

63. J. I. Packer captured, in his inimitable and crisp fashion, many of the conclusions reached in this section. See his "Hermeneutics and Genesis 1–11," *SwJT* 44:1 (2001): 4–21.

zoom lens on a camera. They focus the reader's attention on a particular individual and his immediate children.[64]

Hence, we may say that, generally speaking, the *toledot* mark things related to the plot as it moves through the characters and their descendants.

Now, Genesis 1:1–2:3 stands outside of this pattern and thus serves as a kind of preamble to the whole. The fact that, as we have seen, it is well integrated into Genesis will keep us from concluding that it is somehow to be set apart from the whole book. Nevertheless, it has its own narrative style.

Genesis 1–11 is, without question, overall narrative. Generally in Hebrew, prose narrative carries its events along with the *wayyiqtol* verb tense,[65] and we encounter only a few breaks in that pattern. The clearest break from the pattern is in chapter 10, the Table of Nations, which is set off by verses 1 and 32, both beginning with the word "these" (Heb. אלה, *'elleh*). The genealogies, 5:1–32 and 11:10–26, keep the narrative verb syntax, which implies that they serve some function in the narrative. This function is most likely twofold: first, the genealogies establish a line of continuity between the audience (by way of their ancestor Abram) and the earliest humans; and second, they serve as a kind of fast forward to move the story rapidly past the intervening persons. This continuity ensures that readers will comprehend that it is still the same overarching story.

The opening pericope, 1:1–2:3, stands before the first *toledot* notice. It comes as no surprise, then, if we find it both continuous with the rest of the book and discontinuous in some respects. The most noticeable discontinuity is in the narrative style. The linguist Robert Longacre—a pioneer in applying discourse analysis in biblical studies—wrote this about the pericope:

> Nowhere else in the Hebrew Bible do we find an actor repeatedly referred to by a noun phrase which is not reduced to anaphora carried by the third person form of the verb. "And God did/said" occurs no less than thirty-one times in chapter 1 and 2:1–3. In ordinary narrative style we would not, e.g., tell the story with multiple mention of his name: "And Abraham did A. Then Abraham did B. Then Abraham did C. Then Abraham did D." etc. The sonority and dignity thus attained by repeating the name of the Divine Actor have no parallel in any other

---

64. T. Desmond Alexander, *From Paradise to the Promised Land: An Introduction to the Pentateuch* (Grand Rapids: Baker Academic, 2002), 102.

65. It was once common to refer to this "tense" form as "waw-consecutive/conversive + imperfect." Basically this form in narrative translates to "and" + simple past tense.

passage of Biblical Hebrew. Furthermore, the verb "be" *hayah* used in its special narrative form *wayehi* occurs with unusual force, while in most places the verb "be" has a lower status in narrating. Early in the creative process God says, "Let there be light . . . let there be a firmament . . . and let there be lights." The *fiat* is exactly parallel in force to other commands such as "Let the waters be gathered together" and "let dry land appear." Each divine proposal is answered by the corresponding feature springing into being *wayehi* or *wayehi ken*. "And it was (so)." Whether we want to call such diction and discourse structure a poem or not is somewhat arbitrary; it is certainly unusually elevated style and probably sui generis. It is in this context that *yôm* day appears ringing down with a periodicity of its own alongside the divine fiats and their responses in creation.[66]

Based on these observations from Longacre, I conclude that we can call the style of 1:1–2:3 "exalted prose narrative." In addition to the features that Longacre remarked on, we can add the following:

1. The pericope consists of an almost liturgical recounting of God's achievements.[67]
2. We have a highly patterned presentation of the days. Each day begins with "and God said" and ends with "and there was evening, and there was morning, the nth day."
3. The narrative is exceedingly broad in its taxonomies. Thus, in 1:12 we find plant life falling into two categories, "(small) plants" and "trees"; and in 1:24 land animals falling into three categories, "livestock" (domesticable stock animals), "creeping things" (small animals such as mice, lizards, and spiders), and "beasts of the earth" (larger wild animals). No doubt the first users of this text, had they been looking for a useful taxonomy, would have wanted something more specific—unless taxonomic utility was not the purpose or proper use of the text. No single species, other than man, gets its proper Hebrew name,

---

66. Longacre (1922–2014) was a member of the Presbyterian Church in America, and in November of 1998 wrote this in a memo to that body's Creation Study Committee, quoted on pp. 2347–48, n113, of the Committee's report (2000). Emphasis is original. The report is online at http://www.pcahistory.org/creation/report.pdf.

67. Some have even called the passage liturgical in origin. For example, Moshe Weinfeld, "Sabbath, Temple, and the Enthronement of the Lord—the Problem of the *Sitz im Leben* of Genesis 1:1–2:3," in *Mélanges Bibliques et Orientaux en l'honneur de M. Henri Cazelles*, ed. A. Caquot and M. Delcor, AOAT 212 (Neukirchen-Vluyn: Neukirchener, 1981), 501–12. While I do not agree with all that lies behind such a statement, I do judge that it captures something about the passage that is there.

nor do we learn how the earth "brought forth vegetation" or how the animals appeared in their respective environments.

4. The name for the heavens, רקיע [*raqia'*], the "expanse," is unusual and probably rhetorically "high" or poetic (see Pss 19:1; 150:1; Dan 12:3; Ezek 1:22–26; Sir 43:1, 8).
5. The sun and the moon are given very allusive names ("greater light" and "lesser light"), names that are not normal for the Bible.[68]
6. God takes a rest on his Sabbath (but every faithful person knows that God never gets tired).
7. The events are, in the nature of the case (creation), unique, which supplies a good reason for a unique style.

A creationist, Steven Boyd, has contended that our pericope is *plain narrative*:

> My findings in this step were that the probability that Genesis 1:1–2:3 is narrative is between .999942 and .99987 at a 99.5 percent confidence level. I conclude therefore that *it is statistically indefensible to argue that this text is poetry.*[69]

James Barr held a similar view;[70] in fact, both Barr on the one side and Boyd on the other take a basically Jowett-esque stance on what constitutes a "plain reading" of the biblical text.[71] Boyd is quite sure that there are only two options for interpreting the pericope: either it is "extended poetic metaphor" or it is "narrative";[72] and, since it is narrative, therefore its reading should be like that of any other narrative in the Old Testament.[73]

Both of these sides suffer from the problems associated with the term "genre" (see ch. 2 above). Here our distinction between literary form, social function, style, and register, together with Lewis's notion of language types,

---

68. Psalm 136:7–9 clearly echoes our pericope; there the author speaks of the "great lights" (verse 7; אורים גדלים [*'orim gedolim*]), echoing Gen 1:16 (המארת הגדלים [*hamme'orot haggedolim*]), but also explicitly mentions the "sun" and the "moon."

69. Steven Boyd, "The Genre of Genesis 1:1–2:3: What Means This Text?" in *Coming to Grips with Genesis: Biblical Authority and the Age of the Earth*, ed. Terry Mortenson and Thane Ury (Green Forest, AR: Master, 2008), 163–92, quote on p. 176 (emphasis original).

70. See, for example, James Barr, *Fundamentalism* (Philadelphia: Westminster, 1977), 42.

71. Indeed, two of Boyd's co-contributors cite Barr with approval: Todd Beall, "Contemporary Hermeneutical Approaches to Genesis 1–11" and Trevor Craigen, "Can Deep Time Be Embedded in Genesis?" in *Coming to Grips with Genesis*, 131–62, especially p. 161 (Beall); 193–210, especially p. 204 (Craigen).

72. Boyd, "The Genre of Genesis 1:1–2:3," 166.

73. Ibid., 191. See also Beall's conclusion in the same volume, "Contemporary Hermeneutical Approaches to Genesis 1–11," 161–62.

comes to the rescue. The literary form is *narrative*, while the style or register is *exalted prose*.[74] Further, these factors indicate something about the language type that we may expect, namely, that it will lean toward the poetic side of the spectrum from ordinary language. This is no doubt what led Longacre to declare, "Whether we want to call such diction and discourse structure a poem or not is somewhat arbitrary," and Gilbert Rorison to call it "the oldest and sublimest poem in the world."[75] As Alexander Heidel put it, "the whole chapter [of Genesis 1] is written in a solemn tone and in dignified prose, which easily glides over into poetry."[76] This will in turn enable us to see what social function the pericope served, as part of the worldview story—a part that invites public recitation and celebration.[77] We are now ready to begin exposition in the next chapter.

---

74. I have not really disagreed, therefore, with Vern Poythress, "Dealing with the Genre of Genesis and Its Opening Chapters," *WTJ* 78 (2016): 217–30. This pericope has features that allow the classification narrative (and a "non-fiction account") and features that distinguish it from what follows.

75. Longacre, "Memo to the Creation Study Committee" (cited above); Gilbert Rorison, "The Creative Week," 288.

76. Alexander Heidel, *The Babylonian Genesis* (Chicago: University of Chicago Press, 1951), 92–93 n41.

77. Biblical scholars have recognized that the notion "exalted prose" cuts across some of the simplistic poetry-prose dualities in their study of, for example, Phil 2:6–11. The passage is not ordinary prose, but calling it poetry raises other issues. Hence it is labeled "exalted prose" or "rhythmic prose" or some other term aiming to capture nuances. See Adela Yarbro Collins, "Psalms, Philippians 2:6–11, and the Origins of Christology," *BibInt* 11:3–4 (2002): 361–72.

Chapter 7

GENESIS 1–11: A RHETORICAL-THEOLOGICAL READING

Now that I have laid out the tools, it is time to put them into practice by offering an integrated rhetorical-theological reading of this portion of the book of Genesis. In chapter 10 I will take up the question of whether this way of reading gives us a sensible and robust way of talking about God's action, especially in the creation process.

I have already argued that the Pentateuch as a whole (at whatever time we think it came near its final shape) provides a constitution for Israel, depicting them as God's people, specially chosen out of all the peoples of the earth, who have an ultimate mission as the vehicle of God's blessing to the rest of the world. The particular form of government for this people is to be a theocracy, or, in our terms, a church-state nexus.

I have also suggested that the constitution is unusual in that it comes in the guise of an overarching narrative, with even God's giving of the various laws presented as events within the narrative. This narrative serves as the worldview story for Israel, and Genesis 1–11 serves as the front end of that story—the pre-history and proto-history.

The key element of a community's worldview is its big story, by which the members take their place as meaningful players. The story explains the answers to the basic questions:

Where did we come from?
What does the good life look like?
What has gone wrong?
What has been done about it (by gods, or nature, or man, or some combination)?

Where are we now in the whole process?
Where is the whole thing headed?

But a worldview also provides a set of cultural symbols consisting of events and artifacts that reinforce the story. Further, the worldview includes a set of standard practices that embody a way of being in the world.[1]

I therefore seek a rhetorical-theological reading that explores how Genesis 1–11 supports these aspects of the life that were supposed to define Israel—a life from which, according to the prophets, Israel all too frequently demurred.

The kind of rhetorical-theological reading that I am seeking combines the disciplined text-grammatical approach associated with discourse analysis in the Longacre tradition (with its attention to things like pericope delineation, participant reference, foreground and background events, and peak) with literary sensitivity (characterization, causal connection of episodes, repetitions) and awareness of the social function of a text for the community—all the while showing respect to the theological interest of the Bible (the unfolding story).

In the discussion that follows I offer reasons for taking the sections of Genesis 1–11 as pericopes, where each is part of the whole but also has its own internal coherence. The amount of space I devote to the different sections is disproportionate to the amount of text. This disparity stems from the relevance of the pericope to science and faith discussions, the level of disagreement among students of the texts that I must adjudicate, and finally, the relative prominence that the text plays in the whole of the biblical story. Walter Vogels has captured well what I see in Genesis 1–11 and what I am arguing for here:

> One can never stress enough the importance of the first eleven chapters of Genesis in the Bible as a whole. We often think of the Bible as being the history of Israel, but if this were the case, the Bible then would be the only national history which starts with creation. . . . The first eleven chapters of Genesis do not speak of Israel, but of humanity, of all of us, to whatever race or tribe we may belong. . . . The readers are invited to start their reading of the Bible not with the history of Israel nor even with Jesus but with these profound reflections about humankind. The first pages of any book are always important because they set the tone.[2]

---

1. I have adapted these from N. T. Wright, *The New Testament and the People of God* (Minneapolis: Fortress, 1992), 122–26.
2. Walter Vogels, "The Human Person in the Image of God (Gn 1,26)," *Science et Esprit* 46:2 (1994): 189–202, quote on pp. 189–90.

7.A CREATION AND THE FALL (GEN 1–4)

7.A.1 CREATION (GEN 1–2)
7.A.1.a: Genesis 1:1–2:3

Genesis 1–11 opens with a magnificent account of God's work of creating over the course of six days, with a rest on the seventh day (1:1–2:3).

The first pericope ends at 2:3, where 2:4a opens with "these are the generations," a phrase that typically begins a new section in Genesis. Further, the remainder of 2:4 is chiastic in arrangement, which indicates that we ought not divide it; its entirety serves to open the next passage:

These are the generations
  a of the heavens
    b and the earth
      c when they were created,
      c′ in the day that the LORD God made
    b′ the earth
  a′ and the heavens.

No one knows the composition history of Genesis 1 and 2—whether they were originally separate, and if so what role they played. All we really know is that they have been skillfully put together (as argued in ch. 5). I show below why I think that in their current form these two passages are best read as the overall story of the six days, followed by an elaboration of certain events on the sixth day.

In chapter 6 I suggested the style of the first pericope to be exalted prose. The level of description is quite broad. For example, no creature—animal or plant—gets its normal name other than humankind (אדם, *'adam*). At the same time, the literary form is narrative, with the *wayyiqtol* verb tense carrying the storyline. Each of the six working days begins with "and God said" and finishes with "and there was evening, and there was morning, the nth day." The seventh day is different: It does not begin with God's work nor does it have an ending mark.

We have to decide how to take the first verse, "in the beginning God created the heavens and the earth" (1:1). Some have proposed alternative translations, such as "When God began to create the heavens and the earth . . ." (NRSV margin) or "in the beginning when God created the heavens and the earth" (NRSV text); but the simplest rendering of the Hebrew as we have it is the conventional one (which is how the ancient versions in Greek and Latin took it). Some find a difficulty in the lack of a definite article in the opening words: בְּרֵאשִׁית [*bere'shit*] is what we have, while (so the argument goes) the conventional rendering should have בָּרֵאשִׁית [*bare'shit*]. (This argument lies behind the alternative renderings.) Because we have no evidence that any ancient author found this a problem, the conventional reading stands.[3]

We still have the question of whether the verse supplies a summary of the whole account, serving as a kind of title for all of 1:2–2:3, or as the first event of the narrative—an event that is generally taken to refer to the origin of the material world. The strongest argument for the first option, taking it as a title, is that Genesis 1 provides an alternative origin story to those of other nations (whether Egyptians or Mesopotamians), and those other stories start with a watery situation. In addition, "the heavens and the earth" are said by those who prefer the "title" reading to refer to the completed product of creation rather than some unfinished stage along the way. The strongest argument for the second option, the initial event, is that this is the normal usage of the syntax we find here. That is, our pericope is a narrative that uses the *wayyiqtol* tense for its storyline; the *wayyiqtol* sequence begins in 1:3. In 1:1 we have an adverbial ("in the beginning") that opens the verse, and the clause's verb is in the perfect tense form (ברא, *bara'*, "created"). In such cases the clause designates a background action that took place before the main storyline got under way.

Let me add more reasons to the syntactic reasoning for the second option (initial event), which I find compelling. It makes sense of the narrative flow. In what follows, both the heavens and the earth will be worked on but will also receive their names even before completion. For example, the expanse of heaven is named in 1:7, but it is not finished: It later receives the lights (1:14) in the heavens. The earth is even clearer. It goes from being "without form and void" (1:2)—that is, not yet ready for human habitation—to being the dry land on which the plants grow (1:9–12).[4]

The clause-to-clause relations further support this. Verse 1 had ended with "the heavens and the earth," and verse two begins with "and the earth"

---

3. The medieval Jewish scholar Rashi (1040–1105) had provided arguments for construing it as "in the beginning of God's creating the heavens and the earth." See his commentary included in Yehudah Kiel, *Sefer Bere'shit [Genesis]*, Da'at Miqra (Jerusalem: Mossad Harav Kook, 1997). Robert Holmstedt, "The Restrictive Syntax of Genesis i 1," *VT* 58 (2008): 56–67, offers grammatical reasons for interpreting it as "in the initial period in which God created the heavens and the earth." Holmstedt acknowledges that the pericope is "prose (its 'poetic' features notwithstanding)" (p. 58) but takes no account of text-grammatical conventions for narrative prose—conventions that support the traditional readings of the phrase and the clause-to-clause relationships.

4. This corresponds to the semantic ranges of the Hebrew words: "heaven" (שמים, *shamayim*) can be the outer realm of God and his council, and it can be the visible sky. The "earth" (ארץ, *'erets*) can be the whole world, or the dry land, or some particular land, or even the soil on top of the ground.

(וְהָאָרֶץ, *weha'arets*). To begin a sentence in a narrative with the conjunction "and" attached to any other element besides a narrative verb puts that element into focus and signals that the author is commenting on the element. The comment, then, is most readily understood as commenting on the condition of the earth of 1:1 as the first creation day gets under way (1:3). By this analysis (standard for the discourse-grammar approach), the unfinished earth (1:2) is the condition as the first divine speech comes forth (1:3). As David Tsumura put it (showing awareness of the ancient audience), "The phrase [*tohu wabohu*, 'without form and void'] reminds the audience, who lives on an earth, already inhabited with plants and animals, of the situation of the earth as 'not yet' the normal one they know by experience."[5]

Further, this way of reading 1:1 does the best job of explaining the exegetical tradition that led to the notion of creation from nothing (see discussion in ch. 8). I fully recognize that advocates of other readings of the opening verse often also affirm a doctrine of creation from nothing, and they may or may not find a way to get it from Genesis;[6] but (as I show in ch. 8), the interpretive tradition does tend to associate the doctrine with this third way of reading 1:1. Finally, as I will argue here, it provides a clearer alternative to the origin stories of other peoples, insisting that not even water is ultimate, only God is.[7]

The storyline begins in 1:3 with the first narration tense (*wayyiqtol*) verb, "and God said." Each day begins with this expression and ends with the refrain, "and there was evening, and there was morning, the nth day."[8] The

---

5. David Tsumura, "The Doctrine of Creation *ex nihilo* and the Translation of *tōhû wābōhû*," in *Pentateuch Traditions in the Late Second Temple Period: Proceedings of the International Workshop in Tokyo, August 28–31, 2007*, ed. Akio Moriya and Gohei Hata (Leiden: Brill, 2012), 3–21, quote on p. 19. Tsumura criticizes the ESV/RSV rendering (used here), but it lends itself to his interpretation easily enough.

6. For a fine example, see Gilbert Rorison, "The Creative Week," in *Replies to "Essays and Reviews,"* ed. E. M. Goulburn, et al. (New York: Appleton, 1862), 242–98, especially p. 251.

7. For more technical discussion, see Nicolai Winther-Nielsen, "'In the Beginning' of Biblical Hebrew Discourse: Genesis 1:1 and the Fronted Time Expression," in *Language in Context: Essays for Robert E. Longacre*, ed. Shin Ja Hwang and William Merrifield (Dallas: SIL International, 1992), 67–80; Collins, *Genesis 1–4*, 50–55; John Day, *From Creation to Babel: Studies in Genesis 1–11* (London: Bloomsbury, 2014), 6–8; Vern Poythress, "Genesis 1:1 Is the First Event, Not a Summary," *WTJ* 79 (2017): 97–121. In my estimation, Kiel, *Sefer Bere'shit*, ב, offers a good rationale for taking 1:1 as a summary. But, in view of the text-grammatical conventions, which he does not address, his arguments are unsatisfactory.

8. I have shown why this common rendering of the daily refrain does the best job of the data in "The Refrain in Genesis 1: A Critical Review of Its Rendering in the English Bible," *BT* 60:3 (July 2009): 121–31. The article was partly prompted by A. Steinmann, "אחד as an Ordinal Number and the Meaning of Genesis 1:5," *JETS* 45:4 (December 2002): 577–84, who had argued that the refrain was to be understood as "and the evening and the morning were one day," etc. (similar to the AV and Latin Vulgate). Steinmann replied in "Night and Day, Evening and Morning," *BT* 62.3 (2011): 145–50 (84 n35, 86 n41), and I commented briefly in footnotes in my essay, "Reading Genesis 1–2 with the Grain: Analogical Days," in *Reading Genesis 1–2: An Evangelical Conversation*, ed. J. Daryl Charles (Peabody: Hendrickson, 2013). Steinmann has continued to argue in "A Note on the Refrain in Genesis 1: Evening, Morning, and Day as Chronological Summary," *JESOT* 5:2 (2016–17), 125–40. I do not

evening followed by morning, in ancient Israel, denotes the night-time, the daily rest of the laborer. That is, the refrain indicates that we have a divine work week followed by a Sabbath. The Sabbath here (2:1–3) has two features that should drive our interpretation: the first is that it has no ending, which invites the audience to wonder whether it continues—as the interpretive tradition, as early as Aristobulus in the second century BC, has taken it.[9] Second, any attentive Israelite might have reasoned that God does not get tired and therefore would have inferred that the presentation here and elsewhere (such as Exod 31:17) is *analogical*: God's work and rest are *like* human rest and work in some ways and *unlike* it in other ways (for the audience to ascertain). That is, these creation days are God's workdays, and, since the divine Sabbath does not correspond in length and character to a human Sabbath, we need not concern ourselves with the exact relationship of this work week to a human work week.

By my grammatical analysis, then, the six days begin in 1:3 while 1:1–2 stand as background to the narrative, describing conditions as the work week got under way. But this implies further that the divine (analogical) work week need not be the first days of the earth nor of the universe. The text-grammatical features are entirely non-committal as to how long before the work week the whole universe is supposed to have come into being.

Most narratives in the Bible have a peak, which, as Robert Longacre defines it, is the zone of maximum linguistic turbulence—that is, there are textual devices that draw attention to the event. This account rises to its peak at 1:27 with its threefold and repetitive structure:

> So God *created* man in his own image,
> > in the image of God he *created* him;
> > male and female he *created* them.

The first verb carries the *wayyiqtol* sequence of the narrative, while the second and third simply restate the same event, using the same verb in the perfect

---

see that anything substantive has been added to the arguments in the original two articles. Steinman is making heavy weather of a matter that, as far as syntax and semantics (not to mention qualified readers) are concerned, ought to be smooth sailing. The goodness of fit with the literary features of the text—the focus of this discussion here—solidifies that judgment.

9. Aristobulus, as cited in Eusebius, *Praep. ev.*, 13.12 [667*b*]): "But what is clearly stated by the Law, that God rested on the seventh day, means not, as some suppose, that God henceforth ceases to do anything, but it refers to the fact that, after He has brought the arrangement of His works to completion, He has arranged them thus for all time. For it points out that in six days He made the heaven and the earth and all things that are therein, to distinguish the times, and predict the order in which one thing comes before another: for after arranging their order, He keeps them so, and makes no change."

tense form. That is, we do not advance the storyline, and we therefore dwell on the event.

The peak focuses attention on humankind as created in God's image and after his likeness. We have already noted (ch. 6) that the text never defines what the image and likeness are, neither here nor at 5:1–3; 9:6; this has given rise to a variety of proposals for what the image means. I will not canvas the options here but will attend to how the story works and how it involves the audience.

A good reader will note that the image and likeness apply only to humankind in this account and will conclude that it is therefore distinctive of them. That intuitive observation finds decisive confirmation in 9:5–6, which contrasts humans (in God's own image, v. 6) with the other animals. Our text does not explain whether the distinction lies in human activities, or in their capacities, or in their place within a community (or some combination thereof). The literary presentation invites an attentive audience to work out what the "image" and "likeness" might mean. We can assume that an audience of agricultural laborers would be well aware that humans are different from animals; they have experience of ruling over the animals and of managing their environment. Further, we do not have the simple nouns "image" and "likeness" here, but rather the nouns occur in combination with the prepositions "in" and "after" (Hebrew ב [*b*] and כ [*k*]). In Hebrew, "A is *in the image of* B" and "A is *after the likeness of* B" generally mean that A is *like* B in some respect and usually implies that A is a solid embodiment of resemblance.[10] If we couple that with the display of God's character here—he speaks, he plans, he exercises aesthetic and moral approval—we can suspect that the implication is that God made humankind so that they would imitate his attributes and character, especially as they rule his creation. That is, the image of God in Genesis 1 functions as a calling for humankind: to use all their capacities, those they share with the other animals and especially those that set them apart, in establishing a community that exercises dominion over God's world, a dominion that reflects God's faithfulness, wisdom, benevolence, and creativity.

This becomes even clearer when we appreciate the homology presented here.[11] God is presented *as if* he were a craftsman going about his work week. According to Exodus 16:22–26, the implied audience already know what a six-day work week followed by a Sabbath is. That is, our account presents

---

10. See, for example, Ps 58:4, where "venom *like* the venom of a serpent" is literally, "venom *after the likeness of* the venom of a serpent" (see also Dan 10:16.) See discussion in Collins, *Genesis 1–4*, 65–66.

11. On homology as a specialized kind of metaphor, see discussion in chapter 3 above.

God's creative activity, likening it to the kind of work week with which the audience were already familiar; but, once they have grasped the analogy and imaginatively entered into it, they can actually revise their own practices of work and rest to make them more like the way that God has gone about his.

Because of the analogical presentation, questions that we might ask concerning, for example, how long it supposedly took to do the work, fade into the background. Further, as I argue later in chapter 10, the passage is silent about what sorts of processes are said to be involved in this work week (such as how the plants and animals came to be in their distinct "kinds"); it does not say whether there were, or were not, any processes.

Furthermore, the text has a clear sequence: The "march of the days is too majestic a progress to carry no implication of ordered sequence."[12] However, the sequence serves the literary presentation, which, being analogical, may or may not carry implications about what we might call the "referential sequence." The illocutions and social functions of the text, as given below, do not depend on a close correspondence between presentational sequence and referential sequence. At the same time, the logic of the presentational sequence makes good sense, at least from the perspective of informal observation: from the preparation of dry land, to the provision of plants for the (herbivorous) animals to eat, to the aquatic swarms and the fish, to the land animals, and finally to humankind.[13]

In view of this brief discussion of the textlinguistic details we may conclude that the story in the very first pericope is *about* God's work of fashioning the world as the ideal place for human beings to live, to love God and one another, and to rule in wisdom and benevolence.

This pericope also has several aspects of illocution or rhetorical force. First, it shapes for Israel their vision of the good human life, as participating in a community that aspires to imitate God. And the imitation of God is to be done by finite human creatures, here on the earth—these are aspects of what God pronounced "very good." Showing this forth, for the sake of the world, is the fundamental calling of Israel. As Kenneth Seeskin observed, "How can we imitate something whose true nature is utterly mysterious?"[14] The notion of the image of God, which establishes some kind of analogical resemblance between God and humanity, allows for ethical and philosophical exploration of what imitation would look like.

---

12. Derek Kidner, *Genesis*, TOTC (InterVarsity Press, 1967), 54.
13. This logical progression is probably why Plato's *Timaeus*, 31–34, has roughly the same order of events of heavens and earth, heavenly lights, and animals.
14. Kenneth Seeskin, *Thinking about the Torah* (Philadelphia/Lincoln: JPS/University of Nebraska, 2016), 104.

On the literary side, the linguistic peak often has some bearing on the resolution of the central conflict of the narrative. There is no conflict here in Genesis 1, however, which puzzles some writers. But surely that is part of the rhetorical function of this text. The creation is fully obedient to the divine command and offers no resistance, still less any conflict.[15] It was once common to hold that "the deep" (1:2, Heb. תְּהוֹם, *tehom*) corresponds to (or is even derived from) Tiamat of the Babylonian story Enuma Elish, where the god Marduk must defeat Tiamat and use half of her split body to form a roof-like sky.[16] According to this reading, Genesis 1 originated from a story of conflict, and scholars debated how much of that conflict remains in the current form. But philologists have long known that the identification of *tehom* with Tiamat does not work (even though the terms are etymologically related);[17] and there is little reason to find any kind of conflict in Genesis 1, whether it be theomachy (battle amongst the gods) or *Chaoskampf* (battle against Chaos).[18] Instead, in Genesis God issues his command and the creation perfectly complies. There is nothing evil, or even resistant, in the initial "without form and void" condition of the earth (1:2); rather, it is ready to be made suitable for human life (and thus "very good," 1:31) and for humankind to fill it and to rule it with wisdom and benevolence, thus bringing out the full potential of the creation (as a sanctuary filled by God's presence).

And far from humankind being made to relieve God of work he did not like doing, they are dignified with his image (Gen 1:27), and with the task of ruling the creation in a wise and benevolent way (1:26, 28). Human "work" at the beginning was to enjoy caring for Eden and to spread its blessings throughout the world.[19] The painful toil people now experience is not

---

15. G. W. Coats, *Genesis, with an Introduction to Narrative*, FOTL (Grand Rapids: Eerdmans, 1983), 47, calls the passage a "report," his term for narratives that do not have the complications of a plot. Although his classification is unhelpful, he has rightly seen that there is no conflict that has to be resolved.

16. For one example out of many, see Gerhard von Rad, *Genesis*, OTL (Philadelphia: Westminster, 1961), 48: "*Tᵉhôm*, 'primeval flood,' is unquestionably connected with the Babylonian Tiamat, that primeval dragon of chaos."

17. The Assyriologist Alexander Heidel, *The Babylonian Genesis* (Chicago: University of Chicago Press, 1951), 98–101, lays out the philology. See further David Tsumura, *The Earth and the Waters in Genesis 1 and 2: A Linguistic Investigation* (Sheffield: Sheffield Academic Press, 1989), who strengthens the philological case and also refutes the idea that the etymological relationship between the two words means that the one is literarily dependent on the other.

18. I take the Hebrew *tehom* as a poetical name for the open sea, which may be applied rhetorically to other items. Others take it as a term for subterranean waters, the lower parts of the three-tiered universe. See Ellen van Wolde, "'Creation Out of Nothing' and the Hebrew Bible," in *Creation Stories in Dialogue: The Bible, Science, and Folk Traditions*, ed. R. Alan Culpepper and Jan G. van der Watt (Leiden: Brill, 2016), 157–76, especially pp. 160–61. Passages such as Exod 15:5, 8; 51:10; 63:13; Pss 33:7; 77:16; 104:6; 106:9; 148:7; Job 28:14; etc., together with usage in, for example, Ugaritic, support my reading.

19. This idea is the main theme of Gregory Beale's *The Temple and the Church's Mission* (Downers Grove, IL: InterVarsity Press, 2004).

a proper part of the creation; it results from human disobedience, which requires divine redemption. Genesis 5:29 explicitly links later generations' "painful toil" (Heb. עצבון, *'itsabon*) to God's curse that followed the disobedience of Adam and Eve (Gen 3:16, 19).

Second, in recounting God's activity as being like that of a craftsman, it leads the audience to admire the work as an achievement. The world God made is filled with beauty, a beauty that is on display even in the unruly (such as the sea) and unappealing (such as the creeping things). Even items that are forbidden either for sacrifice or for food (such as invertebrates with which the waters swarm) participate in this beauty and bounty.

Third, the account does not deny the existence of any other deities, but it leaves no ambiguity about their relevance. If God is the sole actor, then there is nothing for these other deities to do. Certainly, the sun, moon, and stars—which other ancient peoples would deify[20]—are creatures of the one God, and their purpose is to enable human beings (and especially Israel) to worship the one God.[21] They are to serve humankind and not the other way around. This speaks volumes to an ancient agrarian people, whose livelihood depends on the regularity and predictability of the rains and sunshine and who, as the rest of the Old Testament makes plain, were readily tempted to hedge their bets by including deities of weather and fertility into their religious life. The church father Athanasius applied this aspect in his apologetic works, *Contra Gentes* and *De Incarnatione*, which use the argument that there is one will that governs the universe, not many (polytheism) or none (materialism).

A further point emerges as we employ Longacre's approach to discourse grammar and attend to the main storyline verbs in the passage (using the *wayyiqtol* tense) that begin in 1:3. It leaps out at us that almost all of these verbs have "God" (אלהים, *'elohim*) as their grammatical subject: God says, sees, divides, makes, etc. The exceptions are either the cases where the event is the fulfilling of God's command ("and it was so," 1:3, 7, 9, 11, 15, 24, 30; "and the earth brought forth") or the recurring "and there was evening and there was morning." God is the actor; he has all the initiative, and his speech yields its inevitable results from a compliant world. This further reinforces

---

20. Eusebius's note shows why this would be relevant to ancient Israel (*Praep. ev.*, 17-*b*), "It is reported then that Phoenicians and Egyptians were the first of all mankind to declare the sun and moon and stars to be gods, and to be the sole causes of both the generation and decay of the universe, and that they afterwards introduced into common life the deifications and theogonies which are matters of general notoriety."

21. As Allen Michael Scult put it, "The Pentateuch's account of creation establishes God's 'lordship' by what might be called 'rhetorical reduction.' By the subtle use of this technique, the powers of the world are reduced from the panoply of divine forces in paganism to one." See Scult, "The Rhetoric of the Pentateuch: An Analysis of the Hebrew Concept of God" (PhD diss., University of Wisconsin, 1975), 79.

the points about God's ownership and rule of his world and the irrelevance of any other deities that might exist.

In a number of works John Walton has contended that the interests of the creation story lie with the origins of the *functions* of the things described rather than with their *material origins*.[22] Before addressing the unnecessary antithesis behind this argument, I first affirm that it represents a genuine and important observation. That is, the account in Genesis 1—and elsewhere in the Bible, for that matter—focuses very little if at all on how the things work. Walton's explanation for why this is, however, does not satisfy, as others have noted.[23] The description in Genesis is somewhere on the continuum from ordinary to poetic language and thus will not be concerned with the inner workings of the things it depicts. The audiences, however, will be familiar with the items described—land, waters, plants, animals—as things within their world, things that serve particular functions because they have the properties they have. It is hard to imagine a fruit as food without its material properties. The account in Genesis speaks of the properties that support the functions, making it clear that these all come from God.[24]

7.A.1.b: Genesis 2:4–25

The second pericope is Genesis 2:4–25. Its style is closer to that of normal narrative, that is, the kind found in Genesis 12–50. At the same time the events are remote, and the description of the garden's location (vv. 10–14) adds to that by combining familiar places (Tigris and Euphrates) with unfamiliar (Pishon) and the likely anachronism (Gihon, as mentioned in ch. 6 above).

This pericope is traditionally taken as a complement to the first one rather than as a second creation story (which has become the conventional reading in the modern era), as discussed in chapter 5 above (and see 8.C

---

22. See, for example, John Walton, "Reading Genesis 1 as Ancient Cosmology," in *Reading Genesis 1–2: An Evangelical Conversation*, ed. J. Daryl Charles (Peabody: Hendrickson, 2013), 141–69. See also Ellen van Wolde, "'Creation Out of Nothing' and the Hebrew Bible."

23. Walton has made a special study of the ancient Near Eastern background for the Hebrew Bible, and it is this to which he appeals. However, his fellow specialist in such background material, Richard Averbeck, has shown that material concerns do in fact have a place in other peoples' origins stories. See, for example, Averbeck, "Response to John Walton," *Reading Genesis 1–2*, 170–72. But even if these other cultures actually did lack an interest in material origins (for some reason that must remain mysterious), that does not establish that Genesis would tell a story that also lacked it.

24. Indeed, consider two psalms that reflect on Gen 1. The functions of the various elements in Ps 104 derive from their material properties. Psalm 8 describes the heavenly bodies as the work of God's fingers. This is most naturally understood as a reference to the imparting of material properties to the various components of the heavens—properties that enable them to mark out time for man the worshiper (the force of the time markers of Gen 1:14). These factors undercut any idea that material and function are really separable anywhere in the Bible.

below).²⁵ Certainly the chiastic arrangement of 2:4 supports that by inviting the reader to connect the "heavens and the earth when they were created" (echoing 1:1–2:3) with the activity of "the Lord God" (the deity's name in 2:4–3:24). Further, God "forms" the man under conditions that evoke the seasonal pattern of Palestine: that is, the text explains the lack of vegetation by saying that it had not yet rained. In the absence of a man to work the ground, say by irrigating, this sounds like the end of the dry season, at the time when a mist was going up as the rains were about to begin. That is, the timing of when the plants were *created* plays no part in this description; they were absent not for lack of having been created yet but because of natural factors familiar to the audience. This is the setting in which the formation takes place. We also saw, in chapter 5, that the text of Genesis 5:1–3 also ties the two pericopes together; that is, the man formed in 2:7 is called Adam (2:20; 3:17, 21; 4:25), a proper name based on the word for humankind, who are created "in the likeness of God, male and female" (1:27; 5:1–2).

The simplest way to follow this arrangement is to recognize that the first event in 2:4–25 is the forming (2:7) and that what precedes (2:5–6) is setting, that is, the conditions when the Lord God formed. Somewhat more controversial, though entirely in keeping with the syntax and word meanings, is to take the Hebrew word ארץ [*'erets*] as "land" rather than "earth" in 2:5–6 (as it means in 2:11–13). We are focused on the conditions in a particular place, from which the man will be taken (2:8, 15) and to which he must return after the events of Genesis 3 (3:23).²⁶

The actor who does the creative work in Genesis 1 is God (Heb. אלהים, [*'elohim*]), while in the second pericope he is the Lord God (Heb. יהוה אלהים [*yhwh 'elohim*]).²⁷ One function of the chiasmus in 2:4 is to identify these two referents. The first name, God, denotes the deity as transcending the creation: "God is so called as the summary of all that commands reverence, as absolute majesty and power."²⁸ As I argued:

---

25. For further argument, see David Tsumura, "Genesis and Ancient Near Eastern Stories of Creation and Flood," in *"I Studied Inscriptions from before the Flood": Ancient Near Eastern, Literary, and Linguistic Approaches to Genesis 1–11*, ed. Richard Hess and David Tsumura (Winona Lake, IN: Eisenbrauns, 1994), 27–57, at 27–30.

26. For more detail, see Collins, *Genesis 1–4*, 108–12.

27. A form of source criticism uses the variation in the divine name as one of the criteria for discerning the separate sources from which the account has been put together. The text as we have it, though, exhibits a coherent rhetoric of its own, regardless of whatever processes of composition might lie behind it.

28. Franz Delitzsch, *A New Commentary on Genesis* (Edinburgh: T&T Clark, 1888), 113. See also Umberto Cassuto, *Commentary on the Book of Genesis* (Jerusalem: Magnes, 1961 [Hebrew original, 1944]), 86–88.

The name also stresses his relation to the whole of creation as its sole source and owner. Such a deity is in the perfect position to commit himself to care for everything, and to expect the whole creation to honor and love him. Thus when Israelite faith makes provision for Gentiles to know the true God, it is true to its own foundational understanding of God and man; if at any time Israel as a whole, or any of its members, presume on their ethnic privilege, they are denying something fundamental.[29]

The God whom Genesis presents, then, is starkly different from any of the deities presented in other stories of origins. As C. S. Lewis observed,

> But the difference, though subtle, is momentous, between hearing in the thunder the voice of God or the voice of a god. As we have seen, even in the creation-myths, gods have beginnings. Most of them have fathers and mothers; often we know their birth-places. There is no question of self-existence or the timeless. Being is imposed upon them, as upon us, by preceding causes. They are, like us, creatures or products; though they are luckier than we in being stronger, more beautiful, and exempt from death. They are, like us, actors in the cosmic drama, not its authors.[30]

Now, Lewis wrote from familiarity especially with Greco-Roman and Germanic myths (e.g., Hesiod, *Theogony*, 45),[31] but the basic ideas apply as well to those from the ancient Near East (which is hardly surprising, since Hesiod owes so much to the East).[32] Allen Scult describes the result of this:

> We have said that because the gods live within nature and do not transcend it, their will cannot be, in any sense, absolute. Consequently the will of the gods cannot function as a framework for communication

---

29. Collins, *Genesis 1–4*, 75–76.
30. Lewis, *Reflections on the Psalms*, 82.
31. David Sedley, *Creationism and Its Critics in Antiquity* (Berkeley: University of California Press, 2007), 2–4, discusses features of Hesiod's presentation that influence later stages of Greek philosophy, especially in regard to what he calls "creationism" (which we might call "evident design of the cosmos" to distinguish from the specifically Christian notion).
32. See, for example, the discussion of paganism in Scult, "The Rhetoric of the Pentateuch," 45–69. Certainly, many details of Scult's discussion should be brought up to date, but the basic idea remains. For a careful account of the Near Eastern influence in Hesiod, see Scott Noegel, "Greek Religion and the Ancient Near East," in *The Blackwell Companion to Greek Religion*, ed. Daniel Ogden (London: Blackwell, 2006), 21–37; Carolina López-Ruiz, "Cosmogonies and Theogonies," in *Oxford Classical Dictionary* (March 2016), available from her web page (osu.academia.edu/CarolinaLopezRuiz).

between man and the gods, for the ultimate power in the universe always defines the nature of communication with the gods. . . .

In paganism, however, all gods are subject to the superior power associated with the primordial realm. The rules that govern the operation of that power, while known to the gods, are not expressions of their will. This radical split between the will of the gods and the superior power of the primordial realm defines the nature of communication with the supernatural in paganism. As Kaufmann observes, "The distinctive mark of all pagan rituals is that they are not directed toward the will of the gods alone. They call upon self-operating forces that are independent of the gods, and that the gods themselves need and utilize for their own benefit."[33]

The Genesis ideology paves the way for the constant effort on the part of Israel's prophets to clarify that the rituals do not enable the worshiper to manipulate God, but rather to relate to him. The deity presented here is above his creation and separate from it; he rules over it. Although what we might call philosophical theology is in short supply in the Hebrew Bible (it awaits the Jewish interaction with Hellenism), the groundwork is here laid.

But this transcendent deity is also called "the Lord God," using the covenant name "the Lord" (usually vocalized as "Yahweh"), a name that is explained in Exodus 3:14, "I will be what I will be" (ESV margin). The focus is on God's presence with and care for his people: "I will be with you" (Exod 3:12; see also 6:2–8).[34] The Exodus account portrays the use of this name for the deity as a special privilege for Israel. Identifying the covenant God of Israel with the universal Creator lays the foundation for Israel's calling as God's new start on humankind; it also assures the people that this faithful deity is worthy of their trust and admiration.

The two pericopes together offer difficulties for those who look for chronological consistency. For example, most readers of 1:3, 14–18 have taken the verses to imply that God made light before he made the light bearers. Now, the Hebrew words are not as decisive on this point,[35] but let us for the moment accept the force of this reading. That is, the account narrates the

---

33. Scult, "The Rhetoric of the Pentateuch," 59–60. He cites Yehezqel Kaufmann, *The Religion of Israel* (Chicago: University of Chicago Press, 1960), 13.

34. Agreeing with Cassuto, *A Commentary on the Book of Exodus*, 37–38. Cf. S. R. Driver, *Exodus*, CBSC (Cambridge: Cambridge University Press, 1911), 40: The verb אהיה [*'ehyeh*], "I will be," here "expresses not the abstract, metaphysical idea of being, but the being of Yahweh as revealed and known to Israel."

35. See Collins, *Genesis 1–4*, 56–58.

presence of light before the proper preparation of the light bearers. It would be artificial in the extreme to appeal, as some do, to passages such as Revelation 22:5 ("They will need no light of lamp or sun, for the Lord God will be their light") for the idea that God provided some other light source (or was himself the light source). Rather, the narration order connects with the audience's perception that our narrator is asking us to imagine these events without making a strong connection to physical descriptions in order to make a point, as Colet had long ago suggested:

> It was the design of Moses to mention the earth's fertility and production of vegetation, before he mentioned the stars, to show that the fruitfulness of the earth did not depend on the stars ... lest the vulgar should suppose, as often happens, that the power of generation lay wholly in the sun and the other stars.[36]

Further, once God brings the man to the garden, we read that he "formed" the various kinds of animals (2:19), which does not correspond to the order of events in 1:20–27. Now, we can make a straightforward textlinguistic argument for reading that God *had formed* the animals;[37] but let us leave that aside for the present, since this is not the most striking feature of the passage, and the audience probably knows not to look for strict sequencing in this literary presentation. Rather, we find that all these animals come before the man to receive names, in order to prove that none of them is the "helper fit for him" (2:20). On the face of it, this looks like a long parade, and we might wonder how many hours or days it would have taken! Again, had our narrator focused our attention on chronological issues, we would have expected some kind of help here—and we receive none. We are in the realm of picturing the events, without concern for how they might have looked had we been there.

The second pericope comes to its peak in 2:23–24. The project announced in 2:18, of making a fitting helper, has reached a glorious conclusion, and the results have enduring consequences (for marriages in the audience's day). Further, the man's exultant cry of 2:23 is heightened, or poetic, speech. The complementarity of "male and female" (1:27), where together they are in God's image and after his likeness, finds explanation in a wordplay: "she shall be called Woman [Heb. אשה, *'ishah*], because she was taken out of Man [Heb. איש, *'ish*]." The audience ought not waste time wondering whether

---

36. John Colet, "Letter 3 to Radulphus," in *Letters to Radulphus on the Mosaic Account of the Creation, Together with Other Treatises, by John Colet, M. A.*, ed. J. H. Lupton (London: George Bell, 1876), 19, 21.

37. Collins, *Genesis 1–4*, 134.

Adam really said such a thing in Hebrew, since they know to allow for anachronism. It is enough for them to see the close connection between husband and wife in the ideal conditions of Eden, both for the purpose of feeling the horrifying distance between this and their present experience, and also for the image of beauty toward which the covenant is designed to restore them.

The marriage of this man and this woman will serve as an ideal for human marriage in general, an ideal that is not easy to make a reality. The marriage is not simply for the couple, however. It brings children into the world and thus forms the basis of human communities. Ancient audiences would take for granted sexual complementarity: that is, that to produce a baby requires the union of a man and woman, and other kinds of union were known to be unfruitful.[38] But complementarity would have gone further than that, especially in an agrarian culture. In such a setting, division of labor would naturally follow, for most people, from the obvious differences between men and women. Men's greater average upper body strength would dictate that heavy tasks, whether in farming or in fighting, would fall upon them; biological necessity would require women to be present with their children to nurse them.[39] There is no doubt that in the Old Testament the physical dimorphism leads to complementary roles in the community as well.

In a context like this, it would be easy to reason that distinction of role corresponds to distinction of value. Indeed, the Greek poet Hesiod is ambivalent about women in respect to man. The poet tells us that "Zeus who thunders on high made women to be an evil to mortal men, with a nature to do evil" (*Theogony*, 600–601), and that "the man who trusts womankind trusts deceivers" (*Works and Days*, 375). At the same time, he can celebrate: "for a man wins nothing better than a good wife, and again, nothing worse than a bad one" (*Works and Days*, 702–703). Hesiod is relevant not simply because he came from the ancient Mediterranean world but also since his *Theogony* exhibits clear connections with the Mesopotamian origins stories.[40]

---

38. The Atrahasis story (tablet I) provides a non-Israelite example of this recognition. The gods made fourteen pieces of clay, seven males and seven females. The account is immediately followed by instructions for the perpetual practices after childbirth. For the text, see Stephanie Dalley, *Myths from Mesopotamia* (Oxford: Oxford University Press, 2000), 16–17. The Greek expression "according to nature" for a fruitful union also reflects this perspective. See C. John Collins, "Echoes of Aristotle in Romans 2:14–15: Or, Maybe Abimelech Was Not So Bad After All," *Journal of Markets and Morality* 13:1 (Spring 2010): 123–73, at 146.

39. In this light, it is no mystery why Proverbs should focus on the disaster that befalls a family whose *son* is lazy (Prov 10:1–5). His absence from the harvesting workforce is keenly felt. With the right kind of imagination, a wise audience can by analogy discern the corresponding ways in which a daughter's diligence matters.

40. Straightforward examples of this connection include the initial chaos (unformed matter, not necessarily bad), out of which the deities arose (*Theog.*, 116), and the making of humans from mud (*Works and Days*, 61, 70). Thorkild Jacobsen finds another connection: Hesiod's people of the Silver Race have

The Genesis creation story provides a counter-narrative to such reasoning, with its demarcation of the original creation plan as over against what has happened due to human rebellion. A good audience ought to put together the common participation in the image of God (Gen 1:27) and the mutual need of man and woman (2:18–24) to counteract this easy line of reasoning. That is, for an attentive and competent audience, the proper response to degradation and exploitation is to declare that it is wrong, and thus to dislike it.[41]

In the course of this pericope our narrator does not stop to explain many things. For example, he mentions "the tree of life" that "was in the midst of the garden, and the tree of the knowledge of good and evil" (2:9). What are these trees, what are their effects, and how are we to imagine that they convey their effects? The LORD God solemnly warns Adam, "in the day you eat of it you shall surely die" (2:17). Why did God put the tree in the garden if he intended to prohibit eating its fruit? What kind of "death" did he threaten here—and does the transgression warrant the penalty? And God speaks the warning specifically to Adam, using a masculine singular "you." Does he expect other humans to comply as well? We will have to keep reading before we can propose answers to these questions, and we will have to recall the literary expectation for *showing* over *telling*.

Rhetorically, the passage serves at least two functions. First, it sets up the horror of Genesis 3: The disobedience takes place in a setting overflowing with God's abundant provision. No one should blame God for human waywardness. Second, the passage should foster yearning in those who receive it: the innocence, freshness, and abundance of the garden contrast starkly with everything the audience members know about their own families and livelihoods. Human beings in general crave some kind of happy era to which they wish to be restored; Genesis 2 gives that lost setting a name, and, by its pleasurable description, makes its recipients willing for whatever conditions God might set for the restoration. This yearning plays an additional role in

---

a childhood of 100 years (*Works and Days*, 127–31), much like the entries in the Lagash King List (etcsl.orinst.ox.ac.uk/cgi-bin/etcsl.cgi?text=t.2.1.2#). See Jacobsen, "The Eridu Genesis," *JBL* 100:2 (1981): 513–29. Samuel Noah Kramer, interpreting a Sumerian text, uses terms that evoke Hesiod's Golden Race (*Works and Days*, 109–120): The lines of the text "portrayed those happy golden days of long ago when man, free from fear and want, lived in a world of peace and prosperity." See Kramer, "The 'Babel of Tongues': A Sumerian version," *JAOS* 88:1 (1968): 108–11, quote on p. 109. Ian Rutherford, "Hesiod and the Literary Traditions of the Near East," in *Brill's Companion to Hesiod*, ed. F. Montanri, A. Rengakos, and C. Tsagalis (Leiden: Brill, 2009), 9–35, is much more hesitant about the extent of influence from the Near East on Hesiod. Since native Greeks attribute so much of their thought to the Near East, it is unreasonable to *deny* influence, though proper caution is surely in order.

41. Not every reader received the narrative that way, to be sure. For example, Louis Feldman draws attention to aspects of misogyny in Josephus. See his *Flavius Josephus, Translation and Commentary, vol. 3: Judean Antiquities 1–4*, Flavius Josephus: Translation and Commentary, ed. Steve Mason (Leiden: Brill, 2000), 17–18.

the lives of the faithful, as a pattern toward which they are being shaped as they embrace God's covenantal arrangements and instructions.

7.A.2 THE FALL AND ITS CONSEQUENCES (GEN 3–4)
7.A.2.a: Genesis 3:1–24

The third pericope, Genesis 3:1–24, offers a straightforward sequence of events but, unsurprisingly, requires our full attention in order to read it well. The events flow from a conversation between the serpent and the woman (whom we take to be the same woman of 2:22–25). The conversation leads to the woman eating the fruit of the forbidden tree, after which the narrator abruptly introduces the man (3:6), who also ate when she gave him some. Then the LORD God pronounces sentences on the serpent, the woman, and the man, and expels them from the garden.

Who or what is the serpent? Is it just a snake, and does this story descend from an etiological account of why humans loathe snakes? Does that not explain the mode of travel, on its belly (3:14)? If we recall who the audience was and orient ourselves toward the author's *showing*, we can readily see our way clear through this thicket. First, Israelite peasants would likely know that snakes do not talk, which means that if one does talk, it results from some kind of interference with it (much as Balaam's donkey, Num 22:28). Further, the snake's argument is unspeakably foul: It implies that God is a liar (3:4 "you will not 'surely die,'" echoing 2:17 with flat out denial). The snake further suggests that God has withheld something that the humans deserve to have, and it undermines confidence in God's motives. Further, an ancient Near Eastern author can use a serpent as a figure of deception and thievery. In the Gilgamesh Epic, Utnapishtim (the Noah, Atrahasis, Ziusudra, or Deucalion figure) has told Gilgamesh of an underwater plant that rejuvenates a man's life. Gilgamesh dove down deep for it and brought it with him, but while he was bathing in a cool pond on his way home, a serpent snatched the plant away, and Gilgamesh returned home a mortal still.[42]

We should imagine that Israelites already had a sense of dark powers hostile to humans. Genesis 1 had not denied the existence of such powers, although the passage made it clear that these powers could not outwit or overrule the Creator God. The features of this serpent certainly fit such a dark power. We cannot say when someone first used a name like Satan (adversary or accuser, as in Job 1:6) for the chief of these dark powers; but there is

---

42. Gilgamesh, 11.258–295. For translation, see Dalley, *Myths from Mesopotamia*, 118–19; Alexander Heidel, *The Gilgamesh Epic and Old Testament Parallels* (Chicago: University of Chicago Press, 1949), 91–92.

nothing unsuited to the way the text works to find that powerful and hostile being as the one represented here.[43]

God declared that the serpent, for its deed of deceiving the woman, would "eat dust" (3:14). This expression would probably not have evoked the snake's diet; we have to suppose that at least some Israelites had seen them eating rodents, lizards, or other snakes. The expression conveys, then, not a diet, but humiliation and defeat (Mic 7:17; Isa 49:23; Ps 72:9). Likewise, to "go on the belly" (also in 3:14) may refer to travel in some contexts (Lev 11:42), but in this heightened speech is better suited to describe the cringing of a beaten foe.

The literary and rhetorical question of what is "in" a text comes to the fore when we discuss what to call what Eve and Adam did in Genesis 3 and its consequences. Shall we say that they sinned and that this was how sin came into the world, as most traditional readers, Jewish and Christian, have done? James Barr—whom I have taken as the exemplary determined literalist—goes so far as to say:

> First, it is not without importance that the term "sin" is not used anywhere in the story ... nor do we find any of the terms usually understood as "evil," "rebellion," "transgression" or "guilt." ...
> Secondly, within the Hebrew Bible itself the story of Adam and Eve is nowhere cited as the explanation for sin and evil in the world.[44]

Barr had apparently set out to offer what he viewed as a close reading of the biblical text, but his lack of methodological reflection over what makes for a good close reading is striking. In the first place, for a thing to be present in a text it is not necessary that its customary name be used. Here we have a solemn command (Gen 2:17), followed by a conversation in which one party had implied that God is a liar and not worthy of trust and loyalty; as a result, the human pair do exactly what was prohibited (3:6). It comes as no surprise, then, that God asks, "Have you eaten of the tree of which I commanded you not to eat?" (3:11)—that is, "Have you done what I commanded you not to do?" which is as good a paraphrase for "Have you disobeyed my command?" as we could ask for. This is basic lexical semantics—a topic on which James Barr contributed so much. Further, as I have noted several times, the author's technique expects an audience attuned to showing over telling—and the text

---

43. In the LXX the rendering is "the devil/slanderer" (ὁ διάβολος) in Job 1:6; 1 Chron 21:1, where the Hebrew has *hassatan* ("the adversary, Satan"). In Wisd 2:24 it is also "the devil." In Matt. 4:1, 10, these are equivalent names for the being who tempts Jesus (see also Rev 12:9; 20:2).

44. James Barr, *The Garden of Eden and the Hope of Immortality* (Philadelphia: Fortress, 1992), 6.

shows us plenty. An ideal audience would disapprove, and strongly, of the serpent's suggestions and of the humans' compliance. In other words, they would readily call what they see here "sin."

Further, we can see easily enough, without explicit telling, that this was some kind of "fall." The humans were part of what was "very good" at first (Gen 1:31); when we read of the "curses" that follow their disobedience (3:16–19) and see that the humans are driven from the garden so that neither they nor their descendants can return (3:22–24), and then see how one of their children lies to and then murders another (4:8) and then produces descendants who decline so far from the ideal as to boast of excessive vengeance (4:23–24), we wonder where all that evil came from. We can easily infer that "painful toil" is an intruder from which people need relief (5:29); it was introduced in 3:16–17 ("pain"). Then a little later we read that "every intention of [man's] heart was only evil continually" (6:5), and the great flood did not change that (8:21); surely this is not what the Maker intended. It cannot be part of the "very good" condition, so proper cooperation with the text must include inferring that it came from the disobedience. No biblical author calls the event a "fall," but that is a good descriptor; the term appears in Greek-speaking church fathers by the early fourth century.[45]

But there is something else to say about this disobedience: God gave his command to Adam (in Gen 2:16–17, "you" is masculine singular), and Eve appropriated it for her own (3:2, "we"; in 3:3, "you" is plural). The consequences of the disobedience affect not only Adam and Eve but also their descendants. So, there must be some sense in which Adam represents humankind. As early as Irenaeus (*Haer.*, 3.9.8), a Christian calls the arrangement with Adam a "covenant," which would explain how Adam serves to represent humankind. The Canadian Catholic scholar Walter Vogels understood the force of the Eden narrative (Gen 2) in this way:

> Thus in [the Yahwist's] mind, the divine plan for man was universal, the tie which existed between Yahweh and Israel was nothing else than the bond which existed between God and mankind from the beginnings of the history of the world.... The Yahwist author thus attributes to all of mankind what Israel considered to be her own privilege, without explicitly using the word "covenant."[46]

---

45. E.g., Eusebius (*Praep. ev.*, 7.8 [307-*d*]) and Athanasius (*Against the Pagans*, §3).

46. Walter Vogels, "Covenant and Universalism," *Zeitschrift für Missionswissenschaft und Religionswissenschaft* 57:1 (1973): 25–32, quote on pp. 26–27. See also his "L'universalisme de la préhistoire," *Église et Théologie* 2 (1971): 5–34, and "L'alliance primitive universelle," *Église et Théologie* 3 (1972): 291–322.

This observation fits well with the literary features I have already identified for these chapters of Genesis: the reliance on showing rather than telling, the use of anachronisms based on Israel's experience, the grounding of Israel's calling in the world. (See further the discussion in ch. 8 below.)

Finally, for this section, among the questions that the text does not explicitly answer is what "the knowledge of good and evil" is and how a tree can convey it. We must infer. While we are to take the humans as "good" (1:31), that does not imply that they were what we might call morally fully matured. As a matter of fact, I find the explanation given by the Greek fathers Theophilus of Antioch and Irenaeus (and the modern Semiticists Franz Delitzsch, Alexander Heidel, and Terence Mitchell of the British Museum) quite persuasive. The first humans were morally good but not yet confirmed or matured in their goodness. In prohibiting the fruit of the one tree God intended to give them a chance to exercise their moral muscles and so to advance to maturity.[47] Thus "the tree of the knowledge of good and evil" was "the tree by which they would come to know good and evil," preferably knowledge from above, like God (Gen 3:22), who knows good and evil and always chooses the good—but possibly from below, as those mastered by evil (which is what happened).

This understanding of "the tree of knowledge of good and evil" allows us to grasp the function of "the tree of life." Theologians and exegetes have different perspectives on what kind of access Adam and Eve are portrayed as having had to the tree of life. In Genesis we simply have the planting of the tree (2:9) and then God's concern, after the disobedience, that the man might "reach out his hand and take also of the tree of life and live forever" (3:22), which leads to the expulsion. Those who think that Adam by his obedience was intended to earn a reward will probably prefer to think of access to the tree as part of that reward; by this way of thinking the expulsion is part of the penalty for their disobedience. Others, however, noting that there was no prohibition on this tree, suppose that they already had access, but that, due to their expulsion, will have it no longer. The rhetoric of the passage reminds us that the text gives the people of Israel a way to envision the events so that

---

47. Irenaeus, *Haer.*, 4.38.1, 3; Theophilus, *To Autolycus*, 2.24, 25, 27; Delitzsch, *A New Commentary on Genesis*, 1:138; Heidel, *The Gilgamesh Epic and Old Testament Parallels*, 142; Terence Mitchell, "Eden, Garden of," in *New Bible Dictionary*, ed. I. Howard Marshall et al. (Downers Grove, IL: InterVarsity Press, 1996), 289a-290b, at 289b. An irony results from some who have claimed to offer an "Irenaean" view, which actually contradicts what Irenaeus himself held. See for example, W. Sibley Towner, "Interpretations and Reinterpretations of the Fall," in *Modern Biblical Scholarship: Its Impact on Theology and Proclamation*, ed. Francis A. Eigo (Villanova, PA: Villanova University Press, 1984), 53–85, at p. 60. For a careful study of Irenaeus on this topic, see Anders-Christian Jacobsen, "The Importance of Genesis 1–3 in the Theology of Irenaeus," *Zeitschrift für antikes Christentum* 8.2 (2005): 299–316.

they can see their own connection to the events. Genesis describes the garden as a kind of sanctuary so that Israel can see their tabernacle (and later temple) as the reinstitution of the garden's intimate fellowship with God; and thus the tree-like lampstands evoke the trees of the garden—which means that access to the sanctuary is access to the benefits of the trees. The question of what it was like for Adam and Eve fades into the background. The real question is: *What is God offering to the Israelite worshiper?*

The pictures in later writers of "a tree of life" (Prov 3:18; 11:30; 13:12; 15:4; Pss Sol. 14:3; Rev 2:7; 22:2, 14, 19) suggest that its function is some kind of sustenance, especially for the faithful. In Revelation it takes on a kind of sacramental significance, namely, that it conveys spiritual benefits to those who take it in faith. Some have called it magical, though that word can be pejorative (and might also assume a literalistic or fairy-tale reading of Genesis). If, with Lewis, we define magic as "objective efficacy which cannot be further analysed," we can use the term. The tree is then like the sacraments (and perhaps emblematic of them), "Here is big medicine and strong magic."[48]

7.A.2.b: Genesis 4:1–26

Genesis 4 breaks down into three paragraphs; they all show cohesion and can be taken together. Each of the paragraphs is a little vignette. The first paragraph (4:1–16) covers two famous sons of Adam and Eve. Cain's birth comes with great hope, as his mother's proclamation expresses: "I have gotten a man with the help of the Lord" (4:1). But that hope is dashed when Cain resents the regard shown to his younger brother Abel and ends up murdering him. The peak of this paragraph is 4:10–12, where God pronounces his sentence on the murderous Cain in terms reminiscent of his sentences in 3:14–19. Cain "went away from the presence of the Lord," a fugitive.

The second paragraph (4:17–24) gives an account of Cain's descendants, some of whom made noteworthy achievements: city building, nomadic livestock herding, musical instruments, and metallurgy. But they also include a bigamist, Lamech, who boasts of his vengeful spirit. Neither the narrator nor any of the characters so much as mention the Lord—Cain has indeed gone away from the presence of the Lord.

The third paragraph (4:25–26) explains the origin of Seth, another son of Adam and Eve. According to the genealogy of Genesis 5, Seth is the son through whom the Israelites trace their ancestry back to the first humans.

---

48. C. S. Lewis, *Prayer: Letters to Malcolm* (London: Collins, 1977), letter xix.

The chapter as a whole provides the sequel to the fall story of Genesis 3. We have the first child born to Adam and Eve and also the first account of a murder. We see the origins of what to an Israelite would have been cultural accomplishments, coming from a man who "went away from the presence of the LORD," which, as we will see, is relevant to people who have left a higher culture (Egypt), who believe themselves descended from a man who left a higher culture (Abram, from Ur, whose culture is seen as a gift from the gods), and who will face the temptation to assimilate to peoples with cultures that seem in some ways higher (such as the Canaanites and Philistines). The passage makes it clear that these achievements may be useful, but they are not good in and of themselves—certainly not worth compromising their faithfulness in order to have.

A sensitive audience would grasp that humankind has declined, dramatically, from their pristine "very good" condition. The traditional notion of a first disobedience, which drew into human life all manner of evil and degradation, accounts for this decline.

The account of Seth relieves some of the bleakness: In all of this degradation God retains his merciful intentions, not simply for individuals but for humankind. As Desmond Alexander has argued, the term "offspring" not only evokes the promise of 3:15, it also ties in to the larger offspring theme of Genesis (12:7; 13:15–16; 15:5, 13, 18; 17:7–10, 19; 21:12; 22:17–18; 24:60; and so on)—with Israel as the offspring in view.[49] The people of Israel can see themselves as emblematic of God's interest in all humankind.

Any attentive reader will notice that the rhetorical-theological reading of Genesis 1–4 offered here, employing literary-linguistic-rhetorical tools, comports well with, and helps to explain, the reading offered by Christian authors, especially Paul—and, in fact, by many traditional Jewish writers. I am aware that the influential James Barr has written, "Old Testament scholars have long known that the reading of the story [in Genesis 3] as the 'Fall of Man' in the traditional sense, though hallowed by St Paul's use of it, cannot stand up to examination through a close reading of the Genesis text."[50] Of course that depends on what we mean by close reading. At the very least, this result of mine can allow some insight into what kind of reading strategy Paul apparently promoted—we may call Paul a "Sternbergian" reader in honor

---

49. T. Desmond Alexander, "From Adam to Judah: The Significance of the Family Tree in Genesis," *EvQ* 61.1 (1989): 5–19; idem, "Genealogies, Seed and the Compositional Unity of Genesis," *TynBul* 44.2 (1993): 255–70; idem, "Further Observations on the Term 'Seed' in Genesis," *TynBul* 48.2 (1997): 363–67.

50. James Barr, *The Garden of Eden and the Hope of Immortality*, ix.

of Meir Sternberg's valuable book on reading biblical narrative.[51] For some, seeing this to be Paul's apparent reading strategy will strengthen confidence in the tools I have discussed, while for others it will strengthen confidence in Paul as reader—while there will no doubt be still others who will find in this coherence reason to doubt the validity of the tools.

7.B FROM ADAM TO NOAH (GEN 5)

Genesis 5 is a genealogy depicting the line of Adam through Seth down to Noah and his three sons—the prominent figures of the flood story (Gen 6–9). As I suggested before, the genealogies perform two basic functions: they establish continuity for the audience and they rush the timeline ahead, noting that much is being skipped over. We do not have in Genesis 1–11 what I earlier called antiquarian history.

The Israelite audiences counted themselves as descended from Shem, one of the sons of Noah. Indeed, their picture of the other peoples (the clans or families of the earth) has those peoples too as descended from the sons of Noah. This genealogy in Genesis 5 ignores the descendants of Cain, although some of the names may be chosen so as to heighten the contrast with Cain. In fact, other descendants of Seth are left out of this genealogy as well; no one is in focus except that line of descent that led to Noah. This matters to Israel because Noah, as we will see, is a kind of new start on Adam and thus a predecessor to Abram. Israel must be firmly established in their role in the world.

The pattern for each person is quite fixed:

When A had lived X years, he fathered B.
   A lived after he fathered B Y years and had other sons and daughters.
   Thus the days of A were Z (= X + Y) years, and he died.

The text says nothing about who those siblings of each B were; it does not even say whether B was the firstborn. The form is a linear genealogy, which lists only one member of each generation. The genealogy of 11:10–26 is likewise of this form, in contrast to the segmented genealogies of Genesis 10, which show more of a family tree "branching out into clans and lineages."[52]

---

51. Meir Sternberg, *The Poetics of Biblical Narrative: Ideological Literature and the Drama of Reading* (Bloomington: Indiana University Press, 1985). See also the discussion in ch. 2 above.
52. Yigal Levin, "Understanding Biblical Genealogies," *Currents in Research: Biblical Studies* 9 (2001): 11–46, quote on p. 12.

We may legitimately find a distinction of function between these two kinds of genealogies: The first seems more focused on actual descent, while the second does involve kinship but also possibly extends its reach to include alliances and places of habitation.

The genealogy lists ten fathers: Adam$_1$ to Seth$_2$ to Enosh$_3$ to Kenan$_4$ to Mahalalel$_5$ to Jared$_6$ to Enoch$_7$ to Methuselah$_8$ to Lamech$_9$ to Noah$_{10}$. The aesthetically pleasing number ten invites us not to worry about whether the genealogy intends to cover every generation from Adam to Noah. The author of Matthew's Gospel supplies a good analogy: He uses the Greek equivalent for the Hebrew "fathered" to move the storyline along,[53] and he skips generations as needed in order to finish with three sets of "fourteen generations" (Matt 1:17). Since any reader of Matthew could have checked these names against the Old Testament and Second Temple sources, we can suppose that including an exhaustive list was not the purpose of such genealogies, either in Matthew or in Genesis.[54]

Further, the lifespans are exorbitant, from a high of 969 to a low of 777, with the 365 years of Enoch being an outlier—"God took him" (Gen 5:24) rather than "he died." One might guess that the text presents these as the actual lifespans of the figures; but there is reason to believe that some kind of symbolism is at work—even if we cannot be sure what it is. (See below for a proposed symbolism in the lifespan of Lamech.) This likely presence of symbolism (for all that no one knows for sure its details) tells against every effort to construct a chronology from these genealogies. Many think that the Sumerian King List is suitable background for this genealogy and its companion in 11:10–26 (see §5.B.1 above). Although there are limitations to such comparisons, we can nevertheless find help in this one. For example, the King List has kings before the great flood with absurdly inflated lengths for their reigns of thousands of years (see discussion in ch. 5). After the flood the numbers trend downward, much as those in 11:10–26. We might suppose, then, that the author of Genesis is by this means reinforcing to his audience that he is telling a tale that overlaps with others that they have heard about

---

53. The Hebrew verb in Genesis 5 for "to father" is הוליד [*holid*], which the LXX renders with γεννάω—the verb that Matthew uses.

54. This general line of argumentation is credited to William Henry Green, "Primitive Chronology," *BSac* 47 (April, 1890): 285–303. Recently, Jeremy Sexton has called this into question, specifically for the genealogies of Genesis 5 and 11, in "Who Was Born When Enosh Was 90? A Semantic Reevaluation of William Henry Green's Chronological Gaps," *WTJ* 77 (2015): 193–218. Sexton follows an unnecessarily narrow interpretation of the verb involved and does not take adequate account of the larger literary factors. See the critique of Sexton, from a creationist perspective, in Andrew Steinman, "Gaps in the Genealogies in Genesis 5 and 11?" *BSac* 174 (2017): 141–58.

the far-off times—again, always with the implication that Genesis is telling these tales the right way.

We should consider what effect these numbers would have on an ancient audience. Quite apart from whether there is some kind of symbolism and figure in these numbers, certainly on their face they create a sense of distance between the characters and the audience—for whom "three-score and ten" (Ps 90:10 AV) was a worthy achievement. Gordon Wenham mentions some explanations that have been proffered, which he counts as having some merit (and to be much better than the mathematical operations on the numbers, which entail their own problems). For example:

> Cassuto . . . sees in the ages of the patriarchs, relatively low when contrasted with the enormous reigns of Sumerian kings, another aspect of anti-Mesopotamian polemic. The Hebrew writer was intent on scaling down the alleged ages of man's earliest forbears. Though they lived a long time, none reached a thousand years, which in God's sight is but an evening gone (cf. Ps. 90:4). Gispen suggests that these figures are designed to show that though the narrative is dealing with very distant times, it is a sort of history, and that however long men lived, they were mortal.[55]

These are helpful. We can take this with features of the text:

1. the overall trend downward in total lifespan (which perhaps signals the decline from man's pristine condition);
2. the repetitive refrain "and he died" for each figure (except Enoch);
3. the location in a set of genealogies that lead eventually to Abram and therefore are in some sense intended as historically referential.

Thus, in addition to the literary function of speeding past numerous generations without much comment, the form of the genealogy shapes the story for Israel by strengthening the idea that the call of Abram is in the context of increasingly desperate human need.

The Adam entry gets more space than most of the other entries, probably since he is the headwaters of this line of descent. The detail on Adam connects this genealogy with the creation and fall stories of Genesis 1–4. Of the other figures in the genealogy, only Enoch and Lamech get anything further said

---

55. Gordon Wenham, *Genesis 1–15*, WBC (Dallas: Word, 1987), 134.

about them than the formula. Enoch is singled out for a commendable kind of piety: he "walked with God" (5:22, 24, Heb. התהלך, *hithallek*). This piety anticipates the Pentateuch ideals: see Noah in 6:9; Abram in 17:1; 24:40; 48:15; and the way that God will "walk" among his people (Lev 26:12; Deut 23:14). This piety led to Enoch's earthly sojourn being cut short, "for God took him"; this would be odd if length of earthly life were an absolute good. Apparently, then, there are higher values and rewards than simply length of days, and the text assumes that there lies something worthwhile beyond the grave for the faithful (see also Elijah's end, 2 Kgs 2:9–12) without saying much about it here, leaving us to wonder about those details and to draw inferences.[56]

The details about Lamech make narrative sense, as they introduce Noah, the main human character of what follows. The hopeful note, however, stands in contrast to what happens: Noah is to "bring us relief" (5:29). The name "Noah" (Heb. נֹחַ, *noah*) sounds more like the word "to rest" (Heb. נוּחַ, *nuah*) and only sounds like the first part of "to bring comfort" (Heb. ינחמנו, *yenahamenu*), but even more, what kind of rest or relief does he bring? As it turns out, the relief applies only to a small number of humans—in other words, the "us" in Lamech's speech appears narrowed down in its reference. However, in the perspective of Genesis, this narrowing yields hope for the ultimate end of the human family, which indicates that most of Noah's contemporaries are excluded from participating in that hope (and the flood story will explain why). This notion finds support in the way that the terms "painful toil" and "the ground that the LORD has cursed" (5:29) pick up words from the divine sentence in 3:16. Through Noah, as a fresh start on humankind, relief will come.

The length of Lamech's life, 777 years, leads to a rhetorical conclusion. In chapter 5 above I noted that some find a link between the genealogy descended from Cain (Gen 4:17–22) and that from Seth (5:6–32). Both lists end with a figure named Lamech (Heb. למך, *lemek*), and the contrast between them is stark. The first Lamech had taken God's assurance of sevenfold vengeance on anyone who kills Cain (4:15) and multiplied it by eleven for even a blow—that is, vengeance was no longer in God's hands, and it was fiercer (4:23–24). The Hebrew for "seventy-sevenfold" is שבעים ושבעה [*shib'im weshib'ah*], "seventy

---

56. Heidel, *The Gilgamesh Epic and Old Testament Parallels*, 137–223, offers a comparative study of Mesopotamian and Old Testament views of the afterlife. Commentators sometimes draw a connection with the verb "take, receive" (Heb. לקח, *laqah*) used here with the same verb in Pss 49:15; 73:24. Certainly these psalms cannot be holding out the prospect of translation like that of Enoch or Elijah, and the verb is common enough to make it hard to recognize as a technical term. However, it may be that the psalms do at least hint at these events as indicators of a happy afterlife in God's presence for the faithful.

and seven" (4:24). In 5:31 the second Lamech's lifespan is 111 times seven years; in Hebrew, שבע שבעים שנה ושבע מאות שנה [*sheba' shib'im shanah usheba' me'ot shanah*], "seven and seventy years and seven hundred years." The 77 part comes first, in opposite order to that in 4:24. The first Lamech speaks bluster and threat; the second Lamech speaks hope and faith. The first embraces humans' descent into sin and departure from God; the second bemoans it and looks for the gracious act of God. Rhetorically, the contrast enlists the audience to approve of the second and to side with him so that they can be loyal to God's purpose through Noah—of whom Abram, and thus Israel, are the proper heirs.

The passage ends with the sons of Noah: Shem, Ham, and Japheth. This is the only entry in the genealogy that gives the names of anyone who is not in the direct line of descent that leads to Israel, and the narrative logic is clear. All three of these men will play a role with their father Noah in the next events—in the flood and its aftermath and in re-populating the earth with the families of the earth.

7.C THE GREAT FLOOD (GEN 6–9)

The story of the great and catastrophic flood, so familiar to so many people today—even to those with little other acquaintance with the Bible—proceeds in a straightforward manner in Genesis. Many of the peoples in the ancient Mediterranean world had stories of a ruinous flood: the Mesopotamians, those of Asia Minor, and the Greeks and Romans as well. Early Jewish and Christian apologists had little doubt that these all could refer to the same event, although of course they "corrected" the other stories in light of Genesis. In fact, the generally assumed actuality of the event plays a role in why New Testament authors would allude to the other traditions when speaking of the flood.[57]

This gives us good reason to expect that the biblical version of the flood story addresses crucial points in the other versions—and especially in the Mesopotamian. This hardly means that the Genesis version *derives from* the Mesopotamian; rather, it aims to refer to these events in the "right" way, that is, with a narrative that shapes the audience's stance in accord with the overall plan and purpose of the Pentateuch.

In a pair of valuable studies that employ the tools of his grammatically oriented form of discourse analysis, Robert Longacre has demonstrated the

---

[57]. I have given a discussion of this matter in C. John Collins, "Noah, Deucalion, and the New Testament," *Biblica* 93:3 (2012): 403–26.

overall cohesion of the flood story, labeling each paragraph as setting, episodes, peak, and secondary peak.[58] I find Longacre's analysis persuasive, but I also find it odd that he considers the "sons of God" tale (6:1–4) to be "an incident preposed to the flood story proper"[59] and thus leaves it out of his discussion. In the same way, he ends his analysis with 9:17 and thus leaves out the (discreditable) sequel that explains the curse on Ham (9:18–29).

One might argue that we should omit 6:1–8 from our discussion of the flood story, since "these are the generations" appears in 6:9—which perhaps implies that readers are to expect a new section. Numerous factors, however, lead me to treat all of these passages together as parts of a separate section of the larger tale of Genesis 1–11. The genealogical account of the previous section comes to a tidy close with 5:32, the sons of Noah. Further, if we follow the reading that sees in the sons of God some kind of angelic/demonic interference with humankind (see below), then we have in verses 1–4 an explanation of a contributing factor to how the "wickedness" came to be so "great" (6:5).[60] More finely, the sons of God "saw" (6:1), and the LORD "saw" (6:5). As Ronald Hendel suggests, "These related key-words subtly downgrade the Sons of God in comparison with Yahweh—the former see women's bodies with lust, while the latter sees the human heart with insight."[61] He also notes that the verb "multiply" in 6:1 is cognate to the adjective "great" in 6:5 (Heb. רוב [rob] and רבה [rabbah], both from רבב [rbb]).[62]

There is a clear connection between 6:5 ("every intention of the thoughts of his heart was only evil") and 8:21 ("the intention of man's heart is evil from his youth"), which means that they belong together in the larger section. Finally, 6:7 announces God's plan to blot humankind out, a feat that the flood carries out.

---

58. Robert Longacre, "The Discourse Structure of the Flood Narrative," in *Society of Biblical Literature 1976 Seminar Papers*, ed. G. MacRae (Missoula: Scholars, 1976), 235–62. See also Robert Longacre, "Interpreting Biblical stories," in *Discourse and Literature*, ed. Teun A. van Dijk (Amsterdam/Philadelphia: John Benjamins, 1985), 169–85.

59. Longacre, "Discourse Structure," 236.

60. The time limit of 120 years (6:3) *may* indicate a new span allowed for human life, though it might (and more plausibly in context) give the amount of time during which God is allowing humankind to come to repentance. Delitzsch, *A New Commentary on Genesis*, i:229–31, discusses both options (preferring the second, agreeing with Rashi). See also David Clines, "The Significance of the 'Sons of God' Episode (Genesis 6.1–4) in the Context of the 'Primaeval History' (Genesis 1–11)," *JSOT* 13 (1979): 33–46.

61. Ronald Hendel, "The Nephilim Were on the Earth: Genesis 6:1–4 and its Ancient Near Eastern Context," in *The Fall of the Angels*, ed. Christoph Auffarth and Loren Stuckenbruck (Leiden: Brill, 2004), 11–34, quote on p. 13.

62. One might also wonder whether the mention of human population increasing evokes the Mesopotamian versions of the flood tale, in which the gods attempt to reduce human population (see below). If so, the biblical narrative raises an expectation in order to refute it and thus highlights the difference between the true deity and those involved in the Mesopotamian stories.

These cohesive factors also evoke the creation story of Genesis 1, producing a sad irony. Just as God repeatedly "saw" that things in his creation were "good" (Heb. טוב, *tob*), so the sons of God "saw" that the daughters of man were "good/attractive" (again, Heb. *tob*). The humans were to be fruitful and "multiply" (1:28; Heb. רבה, *rbh*); and the humans who "multiplied" (6:1; Heb. רבב, *rbb*, similar to *rbh*) proved a grief to God. The original commission for humankind was to fill the earth with wise and benevolent rulers (1:28), but instead they filled the earth with violence (6:11). Not only does this lend further support to reading Genesis 3 as the story of humankind's catastrophic fall (where else could this horrifying disconnect come from?), it also prepares us for the un-creation and re-creation themes in the flood story. God will "blot out" his wayward creatures (6:7), but not so as to eliminate the whole creation: He will make a fresh start with Noah, renewing the human commission for him (with changes, because no human is ever innocent like Adam again).

Among the arguments for including 9:18–29 in this larger section we can mention the way that it brings the Noah story to a close before Genesis moves on to the Table of Nations in 10:1. Further, 9:18 (the sons of Noah by name) picks up 5:32 and anticipates 10:1.

With these things in mind, we can augment Longacre's analysis by thinking of the flood story proper as beginning in 6:5, with 9:18–29 as the sequel to the story.

7.C.1 The Setup (Gen 6:1–4)

The flood story opens with a mysterious pericope about "the sons of God" and "the daughters of man" (6:1–4). Identifying these parties, as well as the "Nephilim" and "mighty men who were of old" has occasioned much debate.[63] The simplest way is to ask whether the term "sons of God" has a normal usage in Hebrew and then to consider whether there is any history of identification. As to the first, there are instances in which the "sons of God" designate God's people (Deut 14:1; Hos 1:10; see also Mal 2:11, "the daughter of a foreign god"); however, there are also cases in which the term

---

63. The options and arguments are well laid out in Delitzsch, *A New Commentary on Genesis*, i:222–226. A valuable resource, with whose conclusions I generally align, is Robin Routledge, "The Nephilim: A Tall Story?" *TynBul* 66:1 (2015): 19–40. Jaap Doedens has provided a breathtakingly comprehensive study in "The Sons of God in Genesis 6:1–4" (PhD diss., Theologische Universiteit van de Gereformeerde Kerken in Nederland te Kampen, 2013). He includes literary and speech-act considerations in his discussion of the passage's function (ch. 5), finding it primarily to be opposing idolatry by exposing its source in the unions of heavenly beings and humans. Though I largely agree with most of this work, I differ from him on a few exegetical points and in my emphases of the in-context rhetorical function of the passage.

denotes heavenly beings, although these are normally good (Pss 29:1; 89:6; Job 1:6; 2:1; 38:7).[64]

The tradition of reading comes to our aid. The LXX varies in its rendering of "the sons of God". Some manuscripts use the literal οἱ υἱοὶ τοῦ θεοῦ, while others (particularly Alexandrinus) use οἱ ἄγγελοι τοῦ θεοῦ, "the angels of God." Both the Nephilim and the mighty men come into Greek as οἱ γίγαντες, "the giants"—a term with potential associations in Greek stories. Philo of Alexandria (ca. 25 BC–AD 50) follows the reading "angels" without discussion but denies that giants have anything to do with the beings in Greek stories (Philo, *On the Giants*, 6, 58). Josephus, however, allows for a comparison (*Ant.*, 1, 73):

> For many angels of God, consorting with women, fathered children who were insolent and despisers of every good thing because of the confidence that they had in their power. For, according to tradition, they are said to have committed outrages comparable to those said by the Greeks to have been done by giants.

The simplest way to read the mention of "angels" who sinned in Jude 6 and 2 Peter 2:4 seems to be with reference to Genesis 6:1–4. None of these texts proposes a biological theory about how these sons of God acquired bodies: anything from possession to actual incarnation would suit the overall biblical picture.[65]

The Nephilim are apparently further identified as the "mighty men who were of old" (Gen 6:4); they could also be either the sons of God or the children of these unions. The ESV is representative of English versions in taking the relevant part of verse 4 as,

> The Nephilim were on the earth in those days, and also afterward, when the sons of God came in to the daughters of man and they bore children to them. These were the mighty men who were of old, the men of renown.

---

64. For documentation see Hendel, "The Nephilim Were on the Earth."

65. Some Christian commentators object, appealing to Jesus' saying in Matthew 22:30, which they take to mean that angels *cannot* marry. For example, see Mark Rooker, "The Genesis Flood," *SBJT* 5:3 (2001): 58–74, especially p. 61. Victor Hamilton, *Genesis 1–17*, NICOT (Grand Rapids: Eerdmans, 1990), 262 n5, mentions and rejects this approach. A ready reply to that line of argument would be to note that the Dominical saying asserts that people in the resurrection "neither marry nor are given in marriage, but are *like* the angels in heaven." These are good angels, loyal to God; and further, this refers to angels in their proper nature, not in some kind of (perverse) incarnate condition.

This certainly implies that the Nephilim were the children and identifies them with the "mighty men." Not everyone follows this, however, but this is the simplest way to take the Hebrew.[66]

The backcloth of this short pericope is likely the prevalence of tales about heroic figures in what the ancients would have taken to be the very old days. Gilgamesh, for example, is said in the epic to have been two-thirds divine and one-third human; in the Sumerian King List, perhaps more prosaically, his father was a *lillu*, a term of uncertain meaning but usually taken to have some kind of demonic associations.[67] Other peoples also attributed some kind of divinity to heroic figures from the past.[68]

Some find difficulties in how short this little scenario is and wonder if it has been abbreviated from something larger. But perhaps the brevity of the text derives from its use of common knowledge: These "mighty men who were of old" were also "men of renown," which implies that the audience is to employ their background knowledge of such stories. Further, some want to call this passage an extract from a myth—but that term does not have a well-regulated meaning. For Genesis, the question is not whether such heroes with divine claims actually existed—it takes for granted that they did—but rather whether their claimed power ought to strike fear into the faithful Israelite.

The function of this little pericope is therefore pretty clear. After the disobedience of Adam and Eve, humankind is now susceptible to demonic interference and, apart from divine protection, are helpless. The Israelite audience, however, should grasp that even these figures are subject to God's judgment, and thus the faithful ought not to fear them. This comes to the fore in the incident of the spies when the ten unfaithful ones reported (Num 13:33), "And there we saw the Nephilim!" A good reader of the Numbers text would reason that the Nephilim were probably all killed in the flood, and therefore these spies have exaggerated—or, if any are left, they are still not capable of resisting the true God. That is, the audience would bring to bear

---

66. I am agreeing with, for example, Kiel (*Sefer Bereshit vol. 1*, קנב), Wenham (*Genesis 1–15*, 143), and Delitzsch (*New Commentary*, 1: 231–33). On the other hand, John Day, *From Creation to Babel*, 81–83, reads the Nephilim as already existing. Delitzsch's explanation for the way the sentence begins with "the Nephilim" (not, "*and* the Nephilim") as giving emphatic prominence is satisfactory and allows the pericope to make sense in its present literary context.

67. *Gilgamesh Epic*, I.ii.1; for English text, see Heidel, *Gilgamesh Epic*, 18; Dalley, *Myths from Mesopotamia*, 51. *Sumerian King List*, iii.18. See also Thorkild Jacobsen, *The Sumerian King List* (Chicago: University of Chicago Press, 1939), 90–91 (with discussion at n131). An up-to-date text and English translation is also available at Oxford University's Electronic Text Corpus of Sumerian Literature site, etcsl.orinst.ox.ac.uk, line 113, which renders the word "phantom." See also Dalley, *Myths from Mesopotamia*, 40–41.

68. Compare Hesiod, *Works and Days*, 159–60 ("a god-like race of hero-men who are called demi-gods, the race before our own").

a version of the saying that one of Tolkien's characters says, "He that flies counts every foeman twice," and come to an account for the spies' report.[69] Either way, the ten spies speak with, and encourage, culpable unbelief (Num 14:11).[70] These ancient heroes, adored by other peoples, do not deserve such adoration. Genesis will set others up as worthy of emulation, such as Noah and Abram—but even they have their serious flaws.

7.C.2 THE FLOOD STORY PROPER (GEN 6:5–9:17)

The short introductory pericope (6:1–4) sets the context for the flood story proper (6:5–9:17). An ancient audience would recognize many elements from what they would count as a traditional Mesopotamian tale. But they would recognize many elements of difference as well; and these differences direct attention to the purpose for telling the flood story. For example, in the Mesopotamian stories the gods made humankind to do the work they do not wish to do, but they regret their action and decide to eliminate humanity because people have multiplied and become so noisy that the gods cannot rest (which was their original goal in making man).[71] In Genesis, by contrast, God is moved solely by moral concerns, judging "wickedness," "evil intention," and "violence" (Gen 6:5, 11). Humankind were to "fill the earth" (1:28), presumably with goodness and wisdom, but now the earth is filled with violence (6:11). In fact, 6:12 ("and God saw the earth and behold, it was corrupt") evokes 1:31 (the original goodness of the creation)—and the transformation from very good to corrupt supports the conventional reading of Genesis 3 as a fall.

In Mesopotamia a god defies the divine assembly and secretly has a man build a boat to escape, while in Genesis God chooses to deliver the man Noah. In Mesopotamia, after the flood the man makes a sacrifice, and the gods "smelt the fragrance, gathered like flies over the offering, and when they had eaten the offering" they changed their minds about destroying humankind. In Genesis God indeed "smelt the pleasing aroma" and declared that he will "never again curse the ground because of man" (Gen 8:21)—but he does not depend on the sacrifice for food. The presentation of deity is therefore markedly different.

---

69. J. R. R. Tolkien, *The Two Towers* (New York; Houghton Mifflin, 1965), book 3, chapter 7 ("Helm's Deep").

70. This literary point is lost on some, e.g., Hendel, "The Nephilim Were on the Earth": "The continuance of the Nephilim [in Numbers] contradicts the testimony of the flood story ... The likely solution to this problem is that the writer was heir to traditions about the Nephilim that were not internally consistent" (p. 22).

71. This is clear in *Atrahasis*, Tablet ii.

Some of the differences are of slighter import, as in how many days the rain fell. More interesting is the shape and dimensions of the boat. The Mesopotamian boat is shaped like a cube in some readings or a coracle in others—in other words, not practical at all.[72] The biblical ark has a shape and size that would actually have allowed it to float. This kind of realism is consistent with what we saw in the order by which the birds are released (in 5.A.1 above): The sequence in Genesis seems to correspond well with the natures of the birds.

The flood story ends (9:1–17) with God commissioning Noah in terms that are clearly evocative of his commissioning of Adam: "Be fruitful and multiply and fill the earth" (9:1). But there is adaptation as well: In contrast to the garden and its fruits, Noah will have "every living thing" as food (although meat was consumed before this, see 4:4).[73] This sends a signal to Israel: Their distinction of foods does not arise from nature (that is, the creation order) but from the special restriction that God has a right to set. That system serves as an emblem and enactment of God separating Israel from the other peoples, which ought to govern their social behavior (Lev 20:22–26).[74]

In 9:9 God establishes his covenant with Noah and his family ("you" is plural here), with their offspring, and with the rest of the animal world. These words echo the divine speech in 6:18, perhaps as the fulfillment of it. This covenant goes beyond humankind and embraces the animal kingdom as well. This may look like an advance on the arrangement with Adam, but it is more likely an explication of it. Even though the word "covenant" is not used for God's relationship with Adam, it is a good and accurate word. Adam's task was to exercise dominion over the creatures on God's behalf, and when he disobeyed the rest of the creatures suffered with him for it.

The rainbow will be a "sign of the covenant" (9:12). The sign functions to remind God of his promises (9:15–16), although one imagines that the people of Israel for their own part will also draw conclusions from the rainbow. The other institution of a sign of the covenant comes in 17:11, circumcision.[75] We may suppose that the connection is deliberate and that therefore the passage is

---

72. For the cube shape, see *Gilgamesh*, XI.i.29–30, 57–58. For discussion, see Heidel, *Gilgamesh Epic*, 236. Dalley, *Myths from Mesopotamia*, 111, translates differently, and on 133 n125 makes it sound more like a river-going coracle (of astounding dimensions).

73. An Israelite would recognize the offering of the firstborn by *righteous* Abel as a kind of peace offering (see Deut. 15:19–23), which involves the worshiper and his dependents *eating* the meat.

74. For a helpful discussion, see Meir Soloveichik, "Locusts, Giraffes, and the Meaning of Kashrut," *Azure* 23 (Winter 5766 [2006]): 62–96. Hence the effort in *Letter of Aristeas*, 142–47, to ground the food laws in the natures of the beasts is misguided. Soloveichik rightly grasps why Christians could abolish these laws, since, for Christians, "the distinction between Jew and Gentile no longer exists" (pp. 76–77).

75. The Sabbath is also to be a "sign" *and* a "covenant": Its function is to exhibit God's creation pattern of work and rest (Exod 31:13, 16–17).

inviting Israelites to ponder the similarities; that is, the mark of circumcision assures the people that God will regard its meaning. Later in the Pentateuch it will be necessary to make sure that Israel grasps that the sign is intended to bring with it an internal reality as well (Deut 10:16; 30:6); it is not a kind of magic by which to manipulate God.

Nothing in the text implies that no rainbow had ever appeared before; rather, something already in existence has been given a new purpose. Since there is evidence that other peoples practiced circumcision before it was given to Abram (acknowledged in Jer 9:25–26), we may suppose that to be another similarity between the two signs.

God, in reinstating his covenant with humankind (and thus with the whole creation) through Noah, is reaffirming his commitment to the creation. Indeed, Israel, who are to see themselves as Noah's proper heirs, should also see themselves as a token of God's enduring commitment to his world—a world that he intends ultimately to bless through them (12:2–3). At the same time, the corruption in human nature also survived the flood (6:5; 8:21), which provides a problem that God must solve, by grace.

7.C.3 THE SEQUEL TO THE FLOOD STORY (GEN 9:18–29)

The section about Noah concludes with an episode that brings little credit to Noah but that also introduces a stance toward Canaan, the son of Ham from whom will come the peoples Israel must dispossess (10:15–20). Part of the rhetoric of the Pentateuch, for the sake of its implied audience, is a moral conviction of their right to follow Yahweh's instructions through Moses. Later in Genesis Yahweh will explain that in Abram's day, "the iniquity of the Amorites is not yet complete" (15:16)—implying that in Joshua's day it has come to completion. (Compare the list of nations in 15:18–20 with that in 10:15–20.)

Noah drunkenly displays himself in his tent—which is in private but shameful nonetheless. Leviticus 18:8 forbids anyone in Israel to uncover his father's nakedness ("you" is masculine singular), and thus the audience would evaluate Ham's actions as disrespectful, in comparison with the respectful actions of his brothers (9:22–23). Noah's behavior shows that, for all his goodness (6:9), it is as true for him as it is for all the rest of humankind that the evil inclination of his heart remains. God's project of restoring Adamic innocence will take some more doing, and Israel must see themselves as a further step toward finishing that project.[76]

---

76. Kenton Sparks, "Genesis 1–11 as Ancient Historiography," in *Genesis: History Fiction, or Neither?*, 110–39, especially p. 134, contends that Noah is not portrayed as doing wrong here but as innocently

Readers of Genesis have commonly taken the flood to be worldwide.[77] The language of Genesis need not require this; after all, the expression "all the earth" (Gen 7:3; 8:9) reappears in Genesis (41:57) where it certainly means the eastern end of the Mediterranean world. No doubt the covering of the mountains (7:19) tends in the direction of universality—but only if we are expecting straight description, with no room for either hyperbole or qualification (that is, where "all" = "all of what interests us"). Perhaps, though, it at least is supposed to have destroyed all humankind other than Noah's family? It is hard to be sure that the narrative requires that, or even that the question is important. I expect that the first audiences of the story, peasants with a limited geographical horizon, would have just heard the tale and formed a mental picture of a wide-spread, massively catastrophic flood. To ask what would we have seen had we been in North America at the time, or whether the ark's passengers included polar bears, seems extraneous to the function of the text—and extraneous as well to its truth value in light of its function.

Not every responsible reader has insisted that the flood destroyed all human life. Josephus—who could at times be more literalistic than I think is warranted—seems to have allowed for other escapees besides Noah's family (*Ant.*, 1, 109 [1.4.1]):

> The sons of Nochos, being three, Semas and Iaphthas and Chamas, who were born a hundred years before the Flood, were the first who came down from the mountains into the plains and made their dwelling there. And they persuaded *the others* [τοὺς ἄλλους] who were very much afraid because of the deluge and who were hesitant to descend from the lofty places to take courage and to follow their example.

Louis Feldman suggests that the *others* "seems to imply that there were others who survived the Flood, besides the immediate family of Noah."[78] Feldman elsewhere argued that Josephus has deliberate echoes of passages in Plato's dialogues, and I agree that here he is probably evoking a passage from

---

discovering the power of wine. This underappreciates the way that wine is a blessing in the Pentateuch (Gen 14:18) but also a danger if misused (Gen 19:30–38), which is why priests on duty must forego it (Lev 10:9). Everyone in the audience would have known this full well. Further, Noah exposed himself, which is held to be shameful (Exod 20:26), and this was the occasion for Ham's shameful deed. The narrator invites the ideal audience to apply these values in assessing these events.

77. For a capable presentation of this position, see Richard Davidson, "The Genesis Flood Narrative: Crucial Issues in the Current Debate," *AUSS* 42:1 (2004): 49–77.

78. Louis Feldman, *Flavius Josephus, Translation and Commentary, vol. 3: Judean Antiquities 1–4*, Flavius Josephus: Translation and Commentary, ed. Steve Mason (Leiden: Brill, 2000), ad loc.

Plato's story of the flood in his *Laws*; the point is that Josephus's reading of the Bible allowed the connection.[79]

7.D ALL THE FAMILIES/CLANS OF THE EARTH (GEN 10:1–11:9)

This section opens with the final mention of the three sons of Noah by name: Shem, Ham, and Japheth (5:32; 6:10; 7:13; 9:18).[80] In keeping with the "these are the generations" markers in Genesis, I will take the section to stretch all the way through 11:9; 11:10 begins with "these are the generations."

There is also a kind of notional coherence to the separate portions of the section. In the previous mention of Noah's sons, the narrator had told us that "from these the people of the whole earth were dispersed" (Heb. נפצה, *napetsah*, 9:19).[81] This section now explains how that happened, by tracing the three sons and their descendants into the regions to which they "spread" (Heb. נפרדו, *nipredu*, 10:5) or "dispersed" (10:18, using Heb. פוץ, *puts*, with a likely evocation of *napats*).[82] Further, the Tower of Babel incident has people unwilling to be dispersed, but God "dispersed them from there over the face of all the earth" (11:4, 9, Heb. *puts*).[83]

7.D.1 The Table of Nations (Gen 10:1–32)

Verses 1 and 32 set this section off as an envelope or inclusio, with their mention of the "sons of Noah" and the time setting of "after the flood."

---

79. For my discussion, with bibliography for Feldman, see Collins, "Noah, Deucalion, and the NT," 412.

80. The names always appear in the same order even though Ham is said to be the youngest son (9:24). They appear in this order in 1 Chr 1:4, though the genealogy that follows lists the descendants of Japheth, Ham, and then of Shem, no doubt because of the interest in Abraham's (and Israel's) lineage from Shem, which then takes over the account.

81. The Hebrew is נפצה כל־הארץ [*napetsah kol-ha'arets*], literally "all the earth was dispersed." The usage of the verb suggests that "all the earth" is a metonymy for "all the population of the earth" (so BDB, 659a). The LXX paraphrases as διεσπάρησαν ἐπὶ πᾶσαν τὴν γῆν, "they [= people] were dispersed upon all the earth."

82. Similar to 9:19, this too involves a metonymy: נפרדו איי הגוים [*nipredu 'iyye haggoyim*], "the coastlands of the nations were spread (or divided)," and thus "the [peoples of] the coastlands of the nations."

83. Carol Kaminsky, *From Noah to Israel: Realization of the Primaeval Blessing After the Flood* (London: T&T Clark, 2004), 30–42, argues that the dispersal is a divine judgment—so much so that she prefers the English "scatter" over "disperse." The translation question need not detain us, as it seems unnecessary (as both words can be positive, negative, or neutral). The issue is still the contextual one, of whether this is a judgment. Kaminsky counters those who find the dispersal to be a fulfilling of the creation mandate. It is simpler, as I see it, to leave the term neutral, that is, the passages are concerned to set Israel in the context of the people who will surround them and gives an account of *how* things came to be this way. *Some* of it involves divine judgment but not all of it. I cannot see that the passages are much concerned with *how much* divine judgment is behind the scene that Israel will encounter.

Although the three sons of Noah are always listed in the same order—Shem, Ham, Japheth (Gen 5:32; 6:10; 7:13; 9:18; 10:1; 1 Chron. 1:4)—the details of their clans follow the order Japheth, Ham, and Shem. This order of coverage makes sense: The people of Japheth are not on the immediate horizon for Israel, while those of Ham will be; and Shem is the ancestor whose line is picked up in 11:10 and traced out to Abram.

The key word for Genesis is the term "clans" or "families" (Heb. מִשְׁפְּחוֹת, *mishpehot*) in 10:5, 18, 20, 31, 32. The call of Abram is so that in him "all the families/clans of the earth shall be blessed" (12:3).

The Table of Nations covers the peoples with which the original audience would have been familiar: the descendants of Japheth filled the coastlands around the Mediterranean and perhaps north around Anatolia and the Black Sea (10:2–5). The sons of Ham came to occupy northeastern Africa, the eastern shore of the Mediterranean and the shores of the Red Sea, and thus came to Mesopotamia (10:6–20). The descendants of Shem headed primarily to the Fertile Crescent and Arabia (10:21–31). Since this is a segmented genealogy (including more than one descendant for each generation, with clans and lineages), we can allow for wider principles than simply family connections to govern the entries.[84] The entries themselves make this clear, since we have personal names mixed with ethnic names in the same listings (as in 10:15–18).[85] In an archaeological study, Donald Wiseman concluded that the names suit an ancient context: "It would not be unreasonable to assume that the information in this chapter could therefore be known to Abraham."[86] He also argues that owing to Egyptian knowledge based on trade, international dealings, and warfare, "It is becoming increasingly clear that the geographical information in Genesis 10 could have been available to the Egyptian court when Moses received his education there in the fifteenth or fourteenth century B.C."[87] Wiseman's study appeared in 1955 and has not

---

84. See, for example, Allen Ross, "The Table of Nations in Genesis 10—Its Structure," *BSac* 137 (Oct-Dec 1980), 340–53; idem, "The Table of Nations in Genesis 10—Its Content," *BSac* 138 (Jan-Mar 1981): 22–34; Yigal Levin, "The Family of Man: The Genre and Purpose of Genesis 10," in *Looking at the Ancient Near East and the Bible through the Same Eyes*, ed. K. Abraham and J. Fleishman (Bethesda: CDL Press, 2012), 291–308.

85. Kenton Sparks, "Genesis 1–11 as Ancient Historiography," 115, 122, supposes that the mention of, for example, "Egypt" (v. 6) constitutes a claim that "the nation of Egypt was the progeny of a fellow named Egypt." This misses the way that the segmented genealogy does much more than simply trace ancestry, but it also misses the way elsewhere in the chapter gentilics are clearly marked (as in vv. 16–18). Indeed, the descendants of Egypt are plurals (vv. 13–14): Ludim, Anamim, Lehabim, etc. Sparks's literalistic reading strategy fails to suit the context.

86. D. J. Wiseman, "Genesis 10: Some Archaeological Considerations," *Journal of the Transactions of the Victoria Institute* 87 (1955): 14–24, at 24.

87. . Wiseman, "Genesis 10: Some Archaeological Considerations," 24.

gone unchallenged;[88] but at least we can conclude that it shows that Genesis 10 has the appropriate air of antiquity to achieve its purpose. That purpose, as I have suggested already, has less to do with the details of antiquarian history and more to do with putting the environment encountered by the implied audience and their heirs into context for the people of Israel in the land.

Ham's descendants receive the longest description here. The logic for recounting the Canaanite peoples roughly in the middle of the whole passage is clear (10:15–20). They will be relevant for the Abraham story and also for Israel's occupation of the land, since they inherit the curse of 9:25–27. Later in Genesis these peoples will show various dispositions: some as friends to Abraham (14:13); some as mysterious and possibly transcendent figures (14:18); some as societies of appalling wickedness (18:20); and some as those with whom Abraham's family must not assimilate (24:3–4). That is, they do not appear in Genesis as uniformly depraved—nor do they appear that way in the conquest story of Joshua, which is why there are provisions for sparing some of them and even incorporating them into Israel's life (Josh 6:25; 9:27).

The other descendants of Ham also bear on Israel's life. Egypt gets much less attention than the land of Shinar (Mesopotamia), however, and this calls for an explanation. Perhaps the origin of Abram in Ur of the Chaldeans explains it. He came out of a highly developed culture with a history of distinguished accomplishments—although he was not descended from the founders of that culture (11:10–26). Further, Nimrod was "a mighty hunter" (10:8–9), echoing the "mighty men" (6:4); just as the great flood did not eliminate the "evil intention" of humankind (6:5; 8:21), it did not remove the prospect of powerful rulers, either.[89]

The family line of Shem includes a notice about Peleg (meaning "division"), in whose days "the earth was divided" (10:25). The exact reference is obscure, although the same verb in Psalm 55:9 ("divide their tongues") supports the idea that this was concurrent with the time period of the Tower of Babel (11:1–9; see below).

These families or clans "spread abroad on the earth after the flood" (10:32). For the narrative of Genesis, this serves to establish the setting in which Abram was called, and it stresses for the people of Israel their common humanity with all the varied people groups they will encounter. The laws of the Pentateuch allow the Israelites to make some distinctions between their

---

88. See the discussion in Yigal Levin, "The Family of Man: The Genre and Purpose of Genesis 10," 304–5.

89. Josephus, *Ant.*, 1.113, interprets Nimrod (transliterated Νεβρώδης) as the instigator for the Tower of Babel, though the textual connection for this is tenuous (11:2 could be taken as describing the first people to come to Shinar).

own folk and the gentiles (Deut 23:19–20),[90] but for the most part they insist on one standard for both kinds of people; indeed, gentiles may participate in Israel's worship of the true God if they meet the conditions (Exod 12:48–49; Lev 16:29; Lev 19:34; Josh 8:33).

We note, of course, that the genealogies focus on ethnic and territorial, not linguistic, affiliation. Thus, some of the sons of Ham spoke what we call a Hamitic language, such as Egyptian. On the other hand, those in the line of Ham who settled in the land of Shinar spoke—as far as the Hebrews were concerned—what is called a Semitic language, namely, Akkadian (dialects of which they shared with the Shemites coming from Asshur). And any Israelite would have been able to tell that Hebrew and Canaanite or Phoenician are closely related.

Three of the names in the Ham list recur in the Shem list: Havilah (Heb. חוילה, *hawilah*, vv. 7, 29), Sheba (Heb. שבא, *sheba'*, vv. 7, 28), and Lud (Heb. לוד, *lud*, vv. 13 [as plural, Ludim], 22). These may be intended as separate names with the similarities simply there to remind the audience of the ultimate unity of humankind. It is also possible that various peoples have merged with or replaced earlier populations and thus the resulting people groups belong to both lineages.[91]

A modern reader will of course notice that many people groups—say, east Asians or northern Europeans—get no mention at all. Our discussion of the extent of the great flood applies here: For the purposes of Genesis the author will have listed the people groups likely to be known to an ancient Israelite. That is, "all" means "all who are relevant to this particular conversation"; Genesis does not seem to have aimed to give an exhaustive listing of all peoples in the world. This point finds support in the way that Genesis 10 lists seventy descendant nations (fourteen from Japheth, thirty from Ham, and twenty-six from Shem). As Allen Ross notes (drawing on Cassuto), "the seventy nations correspond to the number of the families of Israel [Exod 1:5], for God arranged their boundaries according to the number of the Israelites (Deut. 32:8)."[92] From the number seventy in Exodus 1:5 Cassuto infers:

---

90. This distinction serves as a legal arrangement. For the commended ideal of conduct (which goes beyond the letter of the laws), Ps 15:5 levels even this distinction. See Derek Kidner, *Psalms 1–72*, TOTC (Downers Grove, IL: InterVarsity Press, 1973), 82.

91. See Kenneth Kitchen, *On the Reliability of the Old Testament* (Grand Rapids: Eerdmans, 2003), 438; T. C. Mitchell, "Nations, Table of," in *New Bible Dictionary*, ed. I. Howard Marshall et al., (Downers Grove, IL: InterVarsity Press, 1996), 803a–807a, especially 805b.

92. Ross, "The Table of Nations in Genesis 10—Its Structure," 342–43. Note that the argument as stated assumes the Masoretic Text of Deut 32:8, whereas many prefer the minority reading represented by a Qumran text and the Septuagint. See ESV text and footnote there.

Just as the nations of the world number seventy, according to Genesis X, so the children of Israel total seventy; they form a small world that parallels the great world, a microcosm corresponding to the macrocosm.[93]

Geographically, the people of Israel will occupy a central place with respect to these other peoples. That is, they will be surrounded by Japhethites, Hamites, and Shemites, with whom they share a common humanity and to whose families or clans they are to be a vehicle of blessing—which even applies to some of the people of Canaan (e.g., Josh 6:25; 9:26–27).

7.D.2 The Tower of Babel (Gen 11:1–9)

The beginning of the brief portion about the Tower of Babel (11:1–9) sets the events in some unknown time when "the whole earth had one language and the same words" (v. 1). Following right after Genesis 10, this assumes that the separate languages mentioned there (10:5, 20, 31) are not yet operative, at least not so as to divide groups from one another. Perhaps the tradition that associates these events with the days of Peleg (10:25) offers a suitable time period.[94] Thus, the story does not present this incident as *sequential* to the ends of the family histories in chapter 10 but rather as happening some time during the development of the separate families.

Since the events take place in Shinar (11:2), perhaps the focus here is on the Hamites who settled there (10:10) more than on the whole world without qualification.

The passage describes the building practices by analogy with how a Palestinian would build: In place of stone and mortar, these people in Shinar used baked bricks and bitumen. The tower is commonly thought to be a kind of ziggurat, the sort of sacred building to be expected here, although archaeological evidence puts ziggurats starting in 2200 BC (the Genesis story probably places its events much earlier than that).[95] Perhaps a ziggurat is in view, though the Hebrew word "tower" (Heb. מגדל, *migdal*) applies to a wider range of structures. It seems to be a temple of some sort, which explains why its top was to be in the heavens, the dwelling place of the divine.[96]

---

93. Umberto Cassuto, *Commentary on the Book of Exodus* (Jerusalem: Magnes, 1983 [1951]), 8.

94. Psalm 55:9, "divide their tongues," uses the verb פלג [*pallag*], related to the name Peleg. Delitzsch, *Psalms*, 2:159, makes the connection, as does Yehudah Kiel, *Sefer Bereshit*, רע, agreeing with Rashi.

95. See Jeremy Black and Anthony Green, *Gods, Demons and Symbols of Ancient Mesopotamia: An Illustrated Dictionary* (London: British Museum, 1992), s.v. "ziggurat."

96. Black and Green, *Gods, Demons and Symbols of Ancient Mesopotamia*, s.v. "Temples and Temple Architecture." Temples were often built on the ruins of their predecessors. Some archaeologists suppose that in a ground-level temple "the deity normally resided and received worship," while the higher ones "are thought to have been used as a portal by a god on his visits to earth" (175a).

The account is generally classified as an etiology, as if its purpose is to explain why the languages of the various peoples differ.[97] If that is so then it would be describing how the dispersion of the peoples was connected to their diverging languages (10:5, etc.). However, we should consider the comment on Genesis 10 on the assumed universality of the tale to be applicable here; that is, what does it mean by *all* people? Further, we should also pursue what role the story plays in the whole of Genesis for the sake of its implied audience. That consideration likely points in another direction.

The people of Babel want to make a name for themselves, and their tower is intended to reach up to heaven. They also want to resist their dispersion. This is the region out of which Abram will be called to leave for another land; and God promises to make great his *name* (12:1–2). The Hebrew name Babel analyzes as "the gate of God" (Heb. בב־אל, *bab-'el*), but the pericope gives a new and probably sarcastic interpretation, connecting it with the verb בלל [*balal*] "to confuse." By repeating the word "name" (11: 4, 9), the account enhances the sarcasm: They did indeed make a name for themselves, and the name was "confusion." The city Babel (Babylon) would likely have had an aura of prestige for the audience; but the wordplay on its name serves to put its superiority into perspective. Greatness comes from adhering to Yahweh and following his call.[98]

7.E FROM SHEM TO ABRAM (GEN 11:10–26)

This section resembles the genealogy of Genesis 5. Both genealogies list ten generations and both end with a man having three named sons. It gives the line of descent from Noah's son Shem to Abram and his brothers Nahor and Haran—all of whom leave Ur with their father Terah to Haran (Harran) in northern Mesopotamia. Each of the three sons will play a role in the rest of Genesis: Haran's son Lot accompanies Abram, while Nahor's family provides wives for Isaac and Jacob. This explains why the final entry in the genealogy departs from the pattern of naming only one son.

---

97. There is a Sumerian fragment that tells how Enki, the Sumerian god of wisdom, confounded the speech of humans from its primeval unity. The story is not complete enough for us to say why Enki was thought to have done so. See Samuel Noah Kramer, Kramer, "The 'Babel of Tongues': A Sumerian version," *JAOS* 88:1 (1968): 108–11.

98. W. G. Lambert, "A New Look at the Babylonian Background of Genesis," *JTS* 16:2 (1965): 287–300, argues that "the description of Nimrod's kingdom and the account of the Tower of Babel [in Genesis] both presume a period when legends were clustering around the city of Babylon" (p. 300), which would post-date the time of Hammurabi (i.e., after ca. 1750 BC). If that is so, then we should see this as an anachronism, using the more current city as a stand-in for its antecedents. In any event, there is no need to date the tale here to as late as Sargon II (722–705 BC) of Assyria, as Kenton Sparks does (in "Genesis 1–11 as Ancient Historiography," 135).

The form of each entry is a little shorter than that in Genesis 5:

When A had lived X years, he fathered B.
And A lived Y years after he fathered B and had other sons and daughters.

Unlike Genesis 5, no totals for the lifespans are given in the text.

From Shem to Abram is, like Genesis 5, ten generations: $Shem_1$ to $Arpachshad_2$ to $Shelah_3$ to $Eber_4$ to $Peleg_5$ to Reu_6 to $Serug_7$ to $Nahor_8$ to $Terah_9$ to $Abram_{10}$. The first five of these are repeated from 10:21–31. If Peleg is to be connected to the Tower of Babel, then the storyline of 11:10 has been backed up to precede the events of 11:1.

As with Genesis 5, the tidiness of ten generations probably suggests that the author has not aimed to name every single member of the lineage. There is no indication, however, of what governed the choice of which names to record; it may be arbitrary. Since the genealogy offers no vignettes along the way, we can infer that its purpose is limited primarily to advancing the storyline and establishing continuity of descent.

Chapter 8

WHAT OTHER READERS HAVE SEEN IN GENESIS 1–11

*I*n this chapter I want to explore how other ancient readers of the Bible have seen some of the issues we are tackling. Have they a unified take on the story? Does it play a crucial role in their own messages?

These ancient readers will come from the writers of the Old Testament, the intertestamental literature (especially the Apocrypha), the New Testament, and the Greek-speaking world shortly after the New Testament (Josephus and the early Christian fathers).

How these authors use our material will help us in a number of ways. First, they can provide testimony to how the material should be read. That is, for them (at least those late enough) the texts were canonical and part of public worship, intended to impart identity and aspirations to the community of God's people—which is the context that makes sense for these texts. As I argued in chapters 1–2, a Jowett-esque search for some kind of original meaning of a biblical text, prior to its incorporation into the canon, assumes a number of things about the canonization process (and the persons involved), which it ought to justify (things that are actually hard to justify).

Further, the Jowett-esque search assumes that a reading that coheres with the whole canon is somehow unworthy of critical scholarship. I judge, however, that such a search takes inadequate critical account of the social setting of ancient Israel that lies behind the canonization process. The biblical materials are attributed to divinely authorized spokespersons whose task is to tell the true story of the people of God.

Some find the notion of an authoritative canon troubling or insupportable. Jowett's heir, James Barr, speaks for many in saying, "'Scripture' is what the Church has decided ought to be normally read in worship."[1] In context, Barr argues that other materials besides the canonical should be included in our study—a point that I quite agree with. However, the idea that the canon results from an arbitrary exercise of authority by religious leaders fails as an explanation, both for the historical process of canonization and for the nature of religious authority we find in the Bible. James Packer has summarized the historical situation more accurately: "The church no more created the canon than Newton created the law of gravity; recognition is not creation."[2]

As to the exercise of religious authority, consider some of the data. I have given reasons for rejecting the idea that the Pentateuch was Israel's own *self*-definition: The assumption flies in the face of the Pentateuch's role as standard and corrective. Further, the Old Testament speaks of those who, while not direct conveyors of divine revelation, nevertheless have the task of teaching that revelation to God's people: That is the job of the priests (Lev 10:10; Deut 33:10).

There is also the responsibility to administer that revelation in governing Israel according to principles of justice and equity; the priests carry out this task as well, joined by the local judges and elders (Deut 17:8–13). Unfortunately, some will claim authority illegitimately (false prophets, as in Deut 13:1–5; 18:20–22; Jer 23:16–22). Those who lead the people of God must be on their guard and ensure that the people do not listen to such prophets. Also, the canonical word is not given to be a tool in the hands of the legitimate authorities but to be their guide and even corrective (see Deut 17:16–20).

Those who collected the canon managed to include within it, then, materials that are not only skeptical of human power as such (in the Pentateuch), but downright critical of those who hold it (in the prophets and some psalms). Perhaps we might suppose that these collectors were driven by madness or short-sightedness to retain as sacred Scripture things that undermined their claims to arbitrary power—or perhaps they were driven by religious loyalty, as the faithful have always believed. It is true that the canon contains texts that foster critique of human power, holds the wielders of power accountable to a standard external to themselves, and even condemns the pursuit of power for the sake of self-enrichment. At the same time, abusive situations have arisen

---

1. James Barr, *Biblical Faith and Natural Theology* (Oxford: Oxford University Press, 1993), 205.
2. James I. Packer, *Truth and Power* (Downers Grove, IL: InterVarsity Press, 1996), 68. For details, see F. F. Bruce, *The New Testament Documents: Are They Reliable?* (Downers Grove, IL: InterVarsity Press, 1991), ch. 3; and R. T. Beckwith, *The Old Testament Canon of the New Testament Church* (London: SPCK, 1985). More recent studies include Tomas Bokedal, *The Formation and Significance of the Christian Biblical Canon: A Study in Text, Ritual, and Interpretation* (London: Bloomsbury, 2014); Michael Kruger, *The Question of Canon: Challenging the Status Quo in the New Testament Debate* (Downers Grove, IL: InterVarsity Press, 2013).

nonetheless—but that shows that the social system of the people of God requires not simply the canon, but also a certain kind of persons exercising leadership and calling leaders to account. And it can be costly to call leaders to account—the cases of Jeremiah and Thomas Becket come to mind.

In the current scene there are different trends for looking at these matters. Barr represents the historical-critical approach, which privileges the scholar's sense of the original meaning of a text. Another prominent approach, which Barr strongly opposed, is the canonical reading, often associated with Brevard Childs (1923–2007), which privileges the canon as a completed product. More recently the theological interpretation approach has grown up, which builds on Childs's canonical reading and also gives a place for the tradition of interpretation among the faithful. I have no intention of offering here a proper assessment of these movements and their offshoots. I will note, however, that the sociolinguistic factors I have discussed in this work show why the Jowett-Barr notion of the original meaning actually makes unsatisfactory assumptions about a text's origins. Historical criticism can provide us with tools for interpretation, but, to the extent it focuses on reconstructing the processes by which the present text came to be, it will disappoint us.[3] It is true, as John Poirier argued, that scholars such as Barr sought to theologize in some fashion—so, in their own way, they were doing "theological reading."[4] However, they failed to produce readings that withstand scrutiny, and they also failed to account for the biblical texts' function within the canon. It does better justice to the state of things to look for the meaning of a biblical passage with an eye to its function in the canon and to pay regard to how others have used the text.[5] That is, the canonical reading and theological interpretation approaches reflect a sound intuition—an intuition that sociolinguistic considerations support.[6]

We may at times conclude that we cannot see the Genesis text in the same way as one of our ancient authors. For example, many disagree with reading Genesis 1:1 as making a home for creation ex nihilo (even when they do affirm

---

3. For trenchant analysis of this point, see C. S. Lewis, "Modern Theology and Biblical Criticism," in *Christian Reflections* (Grand Rapids: Eerdmans, 1967), 152–66.
4. John Poirier, "'Theological Interpretation' and Its Contradistinctions," *TynBul* 60:2 (2009): 105–18. Poirier is defensive of James Barr without appreciating his connection to Jowett. His problem with "theological reading" lies in two places: (1) they should not have a name that implies that others do not seek theological readings; and (2) their approach can be misused. I do not count either of these as arguments against the movement as such (although it may well warn us of possible pitfalls to avoid).
5. Gordon McConville, a specialist in Old Testament exegesis, acknowledges some appropriate critiques of the canonical approach as Childs presents it but ultimately supports a refined version of that approach. McConville, "Biblical Theology: Canon and Plain Sense," *SBET* 19:2 (2001): 134–57.
6. I might fault the canonical approach as (appearing) unduly fideistic in its account of why the canon takes a privileged place, but that is different from the rightness of the privilege itself.

that doctrine). That may mean that we have seen something that the ancient writer did not; it might also mean that we are mistaken—whether that be mistaken about the Genesis text or mistaken about what the later writer was doing with Genesis (since not every use is an interpretation). But, at least with canonical authors, we show better critical judgment if we give them the benefit of the doubt. After all, they were closer to the culture than we are. This, by the way, is why, out of the mass of Second Temple Jewish literature, the Apocrypha and Josephus are good choices. Not only are they readily available (and general intelligible), but they are also more-or-less mainstream. The same will apply to the early, Greek-speaking, Christian fathers.[7] We may think of them as "qualified" readers, deserving of respect.

Of the several ways I could proceed in this chapter, here is what seems most suited to the overall scope of this study. First, I will explore a few texts that seem to confirm the idea that we have a foundational story in Genesis 1–11—what Charles Talbert called a "foundation myth (telling about creation, fall, redemption, and judgment)."[8] Then I will look at a few texts that seem to allude to (or at least depend on) the various episodes of Genesis 1–11. I will keep the discussion focused on selected topics pertinent to my overall purpose and thus not all details will receive the attention they merit.

8.A THE BIG STORY

I begin with Psalm 136, a hymn that calls on the worshiping congregation to give thanks to the Lord, who has shown his steadfast love throughout the history of God's people. The psalm states its theme in verse 1 and repeats it in verse 26 as an envelope:

> Give thanks to the LORD, for he is good,
>   for his steadfast love endures forever.

The creation (vv. 5–9), the exodus (vv. 10–15), the guidance through the wilderness and the conquest of the land (vv. 16–22), and the many deliver-

---

7. For example, in my essay, "The Eucharist as Christian Sacrifice: How Patristic Authors Can Help Us Read the Bible," *WTJ* 66 (2004): 1–23, I considered how early Patristic authors' use of "sacrificial" terminology in reference to the Eucharist was fully compatible with the New Testament presentation of a "peace offering" background for the Christian ceremony. Eventually, some Christian writers added in the factor of an atoning sacrifice to their discussion, wandering from the proper background: in the Latin-speaking west, Cyprian (third century), while in the Greek-speaking east, Cyril of Jerusalem (fourth century). Both traditions diverged on this point, though the Greek-speakers diverged later.

8. Charles Talbert, *Reading Acts: A Literary and Theological Commentary on the Acts of the Apostles* (New York: Crossroad, 1997), 92.

ances under the judges (vv. 23–25) all illustrate how "his steadfast love"—particularly his commitment to his own people—"endures forever." Verses 5–9 recall Genesis 1:

> to him who by understanding made the heavens,
> for his steadfast love endures forever;
> to him who spread out the earth above the waters,
> for his steadfast love endures forever;
> to him who made the great lights,
> for his steadfast love endures forever;
> the sun to rule over the day,
> for his steadfast love endures forever;
> the moon and stars to rule over the night,
> for his steadfast love endures forever.

The wording follows that of Genesis 1 with a few additions and modifications. Verse 5 adds "by understanding" (compare Prov 3:19); verse 6 speaks of "spreading out" the earth (compare Isa 42:5); and verses 8 and 9 name the sun and moon explicitly.

To speak of the LORD's "steadfast love" in the works of creation is to assert that the creation is the arena in which God pursues his relational purposes for man. Some theologians have drawn a line between creation and redemption; but Psalm 136 does no such thing, moving seamlessly from one to the next. Further, the psalm looks beyond Israel to "all flesh" (v. 25), that is, all humankind—"the God of heaven" (v. 26) is the "God of gods" and "Lord of lords" (vv. 2–3), the universal Creator who rules his world for the ultimate benefit of all. Thus, the basic shape of our story lies behind the psalm, with the fall portion being implicit in the way that nations (who serve other gods) have resisted God's purposes for Israel.

The beginning of Chronicles also echoes Genesis 1–11. In 1 Chronicles 1:1–4 we have a summary of the genealogy of Genesis 5. Verses 5–23 summarize the Table of Nations in Genesis 10 and verses 24–27 cover the genealogy of Genesis 11:10–26. Chronicles then moves right into the descendants of Abraham, leading up to the postexilic era of Judah. The purpose of starting the book with nine chapters of these genealogies is to place the postexilic audience in their proper narrative context: They are to see themselves as the true heirs of the ancient people of God, for better and for worse. They are being given a fresh chance to do what their ancestors did not do, to be faithful to the covenant. To do this, it begins not with Israel's election but with the whole human family. As Roger Beckwith put it, Chronicles is placed last in the canon "as a recapitulation of the whole Biblical story, from the Creation to the return."[9] That is, the beginning of Chronicles summarizes Genesis 1–11 in order to establish for the restored community of Judah that they are still participating in this particular story.

I suspect that this universal story lies behind the way that Luke's Gospel traces the descent of Jesus back to Adam (Luke 3:23–38); this would suit the universal thrust of Luke (see 24:47), as well as of its second volume, with its familiar interest in "the end of the earth" (Acts 1:8). It would be a mistake to conclude that Matthew, in tracing Jesus back only as far as Abraham, is thereby ethnocentric. His theme is, after all, that the heir of David will bring his blessing to all the gentiles (Matt 28:18–20).

Several psalms reflect on the creation story, building on the admiration and celebration found in Genesis and making it a part of corporate song. For example, in Psalm 8 the LORD's "majestic name" is "above the heavens" (v. 1), but humankind are nevertheless the objects of his attention:

> When I look at your heavens, the work of your fingers,
>   the moon and the stars, which you have set in place,
> what is man that you are mindful of him,
>   and the son of man that you care for him?
> Yet you have made him a little lower than the heavenly beings
>   and crowned him with glory and honor.
> You have given him dominion over the works of your hands;
>   you have put all things under his feet,
> all sheep and oxen,
>   and also the beasts of the field,
> the birds of the heavens, and the fish of the sea,
>   whatever passes along the paths of the seas.

The wording differs from that of Genesis 1. For example:

1. the "sheep and oxen" (v. 7) are more specific terms than the "livestock" of Genesis 1:24–25;
2. the "beasts of the field" (v. 7) uses the Hebrew word בהמה [behemah], "beast," differently from how it is used in Genesis (where it is "livestock");

---

9. Roger T. Beckwith, *The Old Testament Canon of the New Testament Church* (London: SPCK, 1985), 158.

3. the word for "have dominion" (v. 6) is a synonym of the word used in Genesis 1:26; and
4. the "setting in place" of the moon and stars (v. 3) uses a different word from that in Genesis 1:17.

Nevertheless, most will agree that the psalm evokes the creation story and suppose that humans being "crowned with glory and honor" (Ps 8:5) has something to do with their being "in God's image" and "after his likeness" (Gen 1:26). Note further that the psalm fully accepts the identification of Yahweh ("the LORD"), the covenant God of Israel, with אלהים [*'elohim*, "God"], the universal, transcendent Creator (the force of Gen 2:4, see discussion in chapter 7).

Psalm 104 is a long hymn of praise about how the created order continually reveals God's glory as it provides so abundantly for all living things. As is the case with Psalm 8, it clearly evokes Genesis 1:1–2:3 without repeating its terminology; it also identifies "God" the Creator with "the LORD." The works of the six days are reflected in the psalm, as Kidner has set them out:

Day	Psalm 104	
Day 1	2a:	light
Day 2	2b-4:	the "firmament" divides the waters
Day 3	5–13:	land and water distinct
	14–18:	vegetation and trees
Day 4	19–24:	light-bearers as time-keepers
Day 5	25–26:	creatures of sea
Day 6	21–24:	land animals and man
	27–30:	food for all creatures[10]

The structure should not be pressed, as we can see from the way that the land animals and man (vv. 21–24) precede the sea creatures (vv. 25–26). Even more, this is not simply a reflection of the Genesis account as an event; rather, it celebrates the way that this created order still continues in human experience. This reliability of the creation lies behind the phrase, "he set the earth on its foundations, so that it should never be moved" (v. 5). As I argue

---

10. Kidner, *Psalms 73–150*, 368. John Goldingay, *Psalms*, BCOT (Grand Rapids: Baker Academic, 2008), ad loc., somewhat agrees with this, though he also finds some tensions between Genesis and the psalm. Goldingay's sense of tension could have been alleviated simply by acknowledging the differing social goals of the two compositions—as well as appreciating that the force of Ps 104 is that the creation order of Genesis still pertains due to God's unwavering generosity to humankind.

in chapter 9, the Hebrew words of this text (see also Pss 93:1; 96:10) stress the stability of the created order under God's constant benevolent supervision. This too is worthy of celebration.[11]

The psalm acknowledges the existence of human sin but in only one verse (35), which treats humans who sin as a blot on the otherwise good creation—that is, it presupposes something like the fall story reading of Genesis 2–3 in which human rebellion represents an alien invader to the creation (Ps 104:35):

> Let sinners be consumed from the earth,
>   and let the wicked be no more!
> Bless the LORD, O my soul!
> Praise the LORD!

Singing this psalm shapes the worshipers' hearts in two ways: first, it leads them to delight in the world, recognizing that it is a good place that God made (even now, after Gen 3); and second, it enables them to see that sinners and the wicked—which probably refer not simply to people who sin but to those who dwell in their sin and refuse the LORD's grace—are a stain on God's world. Hence the worshiper will be glad to be faithful to the God who made the world and keeps it working and will be careful not to identify with those who rebel against the covenant.

8.B CREATION OF MATERIAL EX NIHILO?

When it comes to where the stuff of the universe came from, it has long been common for Jews and Christians to say that God made it from nothing. What is the relationship between that affirmation and Genesis? Some say that the idea does not belong to the biblical creation story at all;[12] others say that it might or might not be latent in Genesis, but the notion did not become explicitly formulated until a later stage forced the hand of the orthodox

---

11. Some suppose that passages such as Ps 104:10, "you make springs gush forth in the valleys," deny causal powers to created things. In the discussion of divine action (ch. 10 below), I show how the rhetoric of such passages shapes the worldview of the worshiping congregation (and also affirms the role of created causation).

12. For a sampling see Jon Levenson, *Creation and the Persistence of Evil: The Jewish Drama of Divine Omnipotence* (Princeton: Princeton University Press, 1988), 5; William Brown, "Divine Act and the Art of Persuasion in Genesis 1," in *History and Interpretation: Essays in Honor of John H. Hayes*, ed. M. P. Graham et al. (Sheffield: Sheffield Academic Press, 1993), 19–32; Othmar Keel and Silvia Schroer, *Creation: Biblical Theologies in the Context of the Ancient Near East* (Winona Lake, IN: Eisenbrauns, 2015), 139; Ellen van Wolde, "'Creation Out of Nothing' and the Hebrew Bible," in *Creation Stories in Dialogue: The Bible, Science, and Folk Traditions*, ed. R. Alan Culpepper and Jan G. van der Watt (Leiden: Brill, 2016), 157–76.

(such as the second and third century AD conflict with Gnosticism).[13] Some theologians even consider the doctrine a mistake (or at least one that can be used harmfully).[14]

As I argued in chapter 7, the function of the creation story in ancient Israel was to stress the supremacy of the Creator and to identify him with the covenant God of Israel. No other deities have any claim on Israel's attention, and such attention, if given, is to no avail. Further, the ideal life of a person and a community consists in imitating God; the day-to-day life of an agriculturalist provides the setting in which this is to be lived out. The language and message are not what we would call philosophical—but that hardly implies that they have no philosophical implications, implications that can await further elucidation.

In chapter 7 I mentioned the three general ways of taking the opening sentence of Genesis and briefly gave my contextual reasons for supporting a conventional translation ("in the beginning God created the heavens and the earth") and for treating that as denoting an action that is represented as having taken place before the storyline of Genesis 1 got under way. In this chapter I will take that conclusion for granted and add another reason, namely, that the Jewish and Christian traditions came to articulate a notion of creation from nothing and that one of their bases for that was their reading of Genesis 1:1.

The traditional notion of creation from nothing derives from the conventional way of reading Genesis 1:1 by way of a clear logic. In its original setting, Genesis contrasts with other origin stories in that there is one God who is supreme over all matter. In fact, this God is self-sufficient, such that the world depends on him and not he on it—hence, for example, the purpose of sacrifice cannot be to feed God in any literal sense. Further, the creation expressed God's power: The creation answers to God's wishes, and God was under no restraint or constraint from matter, which cannot resist his will. Finally, God produced a good creation: It suits his purposes, bears his

---

13. This view is generally associated with Gerhard May, *Creatio ex nihilo: The Doctrine of 'Creation Out of Nothing' in Early Christian Thought* (London: T&T Clark, 1994). Paul Copan, "Is *creatio ex nihilo* a Post-Biblical Invention? An Examination of Gerhard May's Proposal," *TJ* 17 (1996): 77–93, counters May's view by arguing that the traditional doctrine is more firmly rooted in the biblical materials than May seems to allow.

14. For discussion among theologians (for and against), see articles in *Modern Theology* 29:2 (2013), especially David Burrell, "*Creatio ex nihilo* Recovered" (6–21); Paul Gavrilyuk, "Creation in Early Christian Polemical Literature" (22–32); Virginia Burrus, "Nothing Is Not One: Revisiting the *ex nihilo*" (33–48); Kathryn Tanner, "Creation *ex nihilo* as Mixed Metaphor" (138–55). Brian Robinette, "The Difference Nothing Makes: *Creatio ex nihilo*, Resurrection, and Divine Gratuity," *Theological Studies* 72 (2011): 525–57, agrees with the historical take of Gerhard May on how the doctrine developed (see below) and considers this development to be of great value (rather than a diversion).

imprint, and deserves admiration as an excellent achievement. Sin is therefore an alien invader into God's good world, and the consummation will entail the complete banishment of all sin and evil. The world God made is thus the right kind of place for human beings to live out their story.

In Genesis 1:1 the verb "create" means to make a new beginning—not of itself implying from nothing.[15] However, "the heavens and the earth" refer to everything in the material universe, and "in the beginning" tells us what time the author had in mind. Hence, if God created everything at the beginning, then before the beginning—whatever that might mean—there was nothing: no heavens, no earth, no matter at all. That is, while the text does not of itself assert creation ex nihilo, that is a reasonable inference from the text.

Genesis of itself says little about how God fashioned the world. In addition to the initial creation event (1:1, taken as an action antecedent to the storyline), it simply has God saying his commands, which are then fulfilled (see fuller discussion in ch. 7 above). By the conventional reading, God displays his power first by calling the universe into existence and then by shaping the earth as a fit place for his human creatures to live. The world did not make itself; rather, God made it without any help and without any resistance. The author of Psalm 33 took this feature and made it into a hymn (vv. 6, 9):

> By the word of the LORD the heavens were made,
>   and by the breath of his mouth all their host. . . .
> For he spoke, and it came to be;
>   he commanded, and it stood firm.

In Genesis 1 we have the repeated phrase "and God said" (Heb. verb אמר, *'amar*), which the psalm paraphrases as "the word of the LORD" (Heb. noun דבר, *dabar*).[16] The psalm uses Genesis to the effect that each time God "spoke" (v. 9, Heb. verb, *'amar*), what he commanded produced its enduring

---

15. I argue for this in C. John Collins, *Genesis 1–4: A Linguistic, Literary, and Theological Commentary* (Phillipsburg, NJ: P & R, 2006), 67–68.

16. For the "word" of the LORD in Ps 33:6, the LXX uses the Greek word λόγος. In Wis 9:1 we have "the word" as the supernatural agency of God (see also 16:12; 18:15): "O God of my fathers and Lord of mercy, who has made all things by your word." But whereas in Ps 33:6 and Wis 9:1 the "word" may be just a personification, in John's Gospel it is a person, who is distinct from God ("with God") and at the same time *is* God (John 1:1): "All things were made through him" (John 1:3). Since "God" in Gen 1 (LXX, ὁ θεός) did the making, we can follow John's thought as saying that "God made the world *through* the Word." Psalm 33:6 uses the dative and Wis 9:1 uses the equivalent instrumental ἐν, "*by means of* the word," in contrast to John's "*through* [διά] him." The distinction does not seem to make any difference. Colossians 1:15–20 echoes Genesis but filters it through the LXX of Proverbs. For discussion, see C. J. Collins, "Colossians 1,17 'Hold Together': A Co-Opted Term," *Biblica* 95:1 (2014): 64–87.

effect. The "breath of his mouth" (v. 6, Heb. רוּחַ, *ruah*) also echoes the presence of "the Spirit of God" (Gen 1:2, Heb. *ruah*). The creation fully complies with God's wishes, without resistance (still less with conflict).

The notion that God "spoke, and it came to be" (Ps 33:9) sets up a pattern whose logical conclusion is the philosophical doctrine of creation from nothing—a doctrine quite distinct from those held by Israel's neighbors and ideological competitors (for whom matter preexists the deities).

Another text from the Hebrew Bible strongly comports with the underlying idea of creation ex nihilo, though without stating it explicitly (Isa 45:5–7, 18):

> I am the Lord, and there is no other,
>> besides me there is no God;
> I equip you, though you do not know me,
> that people may know, from the rising of the sun
>> and from the west, that there is none besides me;
> I am the Lord, and there is no other.
> I form light and create darkness,
>> I make well-being and create calamity,
>> I am the Lord, who does all these things. . . .
> For thus says the Lord,
> who created the heavens
>> (he is God!),
> who formed the earth and made it
>> (he established it;
> he did not create it empty,
>> he formed it to be inhabited!):
> "I am the Lord, and there is no other."

The references to "light" and "darkness," as well as "created the heavens" and "empty" (Heb. תֹהוּ, *tohu*), evoke the Genesis creation story and bring it to bear on the possibility that other deities might have a claim on the Judeans' loyalty and trust. The Lord proclaims not simply his oilness but also his absolute supremacy, which is one of the implications of the creation doctrine. As Robert Grant put it, God "created the heavens, formed the earth and made it, established it and created it (Isaiah 45:18). Could the author tell us more plainly that matter was not preexistent?"[17]

---

17. Robert Grant, *Miracle and Natural Law in Graeco-Roman and Early Christian Thought* (Amsterdam: North Holland Publishing, 1952), 136.

The texts in the Hebrew Bible come from settings in which a non-philosophical articulation is adequate. The Second Temple era, especially in its interaction with Hellenism, faced a new pressure, namely, to address what everyone thought was an intellectually higher culture. To see how these Jewish and then Christian writers took the idea, we begin with the Greek translation of Genesis (mid-third century BC). The first verse is,

In the beginning God made [ἐποίησεν] the heaven and the earth.

As to the syntax of the Greek clause, this agrees with the usual rendering of the verse in Hebrew. The discussion here will show that most readers also took this as the first event. They, along with the LXX, are not so clear about how this relates to the storyline, but it will not matter much here.[18] More interesting is the rendering of Hebrew *bara'* ("he created") with Greek ἐποίησεν ("he made"). Readers of the New Testament might have expected a form from κτίζω, which in the New Testament generally means "I create." Two factors are probably at work here: first, the Greek κτίζω had likely not, by the time of the LXX, acquired the sense "create"—that is a development of its earlier sense, "to found (as a city)."[19] The second factor, which was fruitful in its consequences, is the way that esteemed authors such as Plato use ποιέω and cognates (with the passive forms supplied by γίνομαι and cognates) for the Maker's work. The Greek word ποιέω, like Hebrew *'asah*, has a broad range of possible referents and certainly does not of itself imply "to make from nothing" (nor, as mentioned above, does the more specific Heb. term *bara'*). However, neither does this breadth *exclude* the possibility of using the verb for that notion, and this produces some of the uncertainty in reading the old texts. Some authors clearly use this verb for that notion, while others seem by the term not to have gone so far, or even to be unclear.

The connections between Genesis and the gentiles' highly regarded origin stories and especially Plato's *Timaeus* became important for Greek-speaking

---

18. The Greek rendering of the Hebrew *bere'shit* is ἐν ἀρχῇ, which is easily understood as "in *the* beginning"—that is, the absence of the article causes no trouble at all. A Greek author, Anaxagoras (fifth century BC) can refer to the time of creation (from primordial mingling) with ἦν γὰρ ἐν ἀρχῇ, "for in [the] beginning it was." (Quoted in Eusebius, *Praep. ev.*, 750-b.)

19. Indeed, when a Jewish author such as Philo or Josephus uses κτίζω, one cannot be sure which sense is intended. See, for example, Josephus (end of first century AD), *Ant.*, 1, 27 [I.1.1] (mentioned below). Philo (early first century AD) clearly uses the word in its older sense: *On the Creation*, iv (17), "when a city is founded" (ἐπειδὰν πόλις κτίζεται; p. 19) "to found a mighty state" (μεγαλόπολιν κτίζειν). For God's creative activity, Philo seems to prefer ποιέω—with the LXX—and sometimes συνίστημι—probably appropriated from Plato's *Timaeus*, on which see Collins, "Colossians 1,17 'Hold Together': A Co-Opted Term," 64–87.

Jews and Christians.[20] The connection to Plato in particular gives what I take to be the key to how the Jewish and Christian discussion of creation ex nihilo developed. In contrast to those who think the second-century controversy over Gnosticism pushed Christians to define the doctrine, I think that the evidence suggests an earlier origin because there was, first, a trajectory of theologizing, moving from the ordinary and non-philosophical categories to the philosophical; and second, the pressure to come to grips with Plato— partly as an exercise in intellectual integrity and partly as a response to the (well-grounded) fear of marginalization in the Greco-Roman world.

Let us consider 2 Maccabees 7:28, from perhaps the first century BC. A mother encourages her son to be courageous in the face of his impending martyrdom under Antiochus:

> I urge you, my child, to look at the heaven and the earth and see everything that is in them, and recognize that *not out of things that already existed did God make them* [οὐκ ἐξ ὄντων ἐποίησεν αὐτὰ ὁ θεός], and so too the human race *comes into being* [or, *is made*; γίνεται].[21]

The idea is that even the evil tyrant is a creature of the Almighty, and the God who made us can bring us back by resurrection. One does not have to accept 2 Maccabees as canonical to find this helpful. It represents the way that pious mainstream Jews understood the origin of things as a practical doctrine. To say it is practical is not to say it is of no theological or philosophical import. As J. C. O'Neill pointedly put it, "Of course the style of the mother's words is parenetic and prayerful, but who has decreed that parenesis and prayer cannot contain exact and specific doctrine?"[22] At the same time, we can acknowledge that the practicality of the statement should make us reticent about taking this as a decisive articulation.[23]

---

20. I have mentioned a few in Collins, *Genesis 1–4*, 243 n15. Along these lines Eusebius, *Praep. ev.*, 553-d, notes that both Genesis 1:17 and *Timaeus*, 38-c use τίθημι for God "setting" the heavenly bodies. See below for Athanasius's use of a *Timaeus* passage to argue that the Christian ex nihilo doctrine is more consistent with Plato's theology than Plato was.

21. I find the reading of this passage in J. C. O'Neill, "How Early Is the Doctrine of *creatio ex nihilo*?" *JTS* 53:2 (2002): 449–65, very helpful. O'Neill notes a textual variant: In place of οὐκ ἐξ ὄντων ("not out of things that [already] existed"), read ἐξ οὐκ ὄντων ("out of things that did not [already] exist"). Rahlfs' LXX apparatus (which is brief) does not register the variant. I do not see that it will make much difference in my discussion.

22. O'Neill, "How Early Is the Doctrine of *creatio ex nihilo*?" 449. See also Daniel Schwartz, *2 Maccabees* (Berlin: de Gruyter, 2008), 312–13.

23. Markus Bockmuehl, "*Creatio ex nihilo* in Palestinian Judaism and Early Christianity," *SJT* 65:3 (2012): 253–70, at 257–58, is right to be reluctant, though I think he is overly cautious about this passage, since its Greek terms came to be used unambiguously in this discussion (as we will see).

New Testament texts that seem to display this interpretation include the following:

Revelation 4:11:
> Worthy are you, our Lord and God,
> to receive glory and honor and power,
> *for you created all things* [ὅτι σὺ ἔκτισας τὰ πάντα],
> *and by your will they existed and were created* [καὶ διὰ τὸ θέλημά σου ἦσαν καὶ ἐκτίσθησαν].

Hebrews 11:3:
> By faith we understand that *the universe was created by the word of God* [κατηρτίσθαι τοὺς αἰῶνας ῥήματι θεοῦ], *so that what is seen was not made out of things that are visible* [εἰς τὸ μὴ ἐκ φαινομένων τὸ βλεπόμενον γεγονέναι].

Although the Greek word "create" (κτίζω) need not of itself mean to originate from nothing in Revelation 4:11, the combination "they existed and were created" certainly sets the weight in that direction—again, however, non-philosophically. In Hebrews most take the "seen" thing as the world we experience by our senses, "the universe" of the first part of the verse; it was "not made" out of "visible things," that is, its origin is from non-sensory things, "the word of God" earlier in the verse.[24] Hebrews 11 calls on its readers to "see" beyond what immediately presents itself to their senses (attractions and threats), so the origin and dependence of the material world is pertinent.[25]

Theologians examining this subject rarely address the opening of John's Gospel, but, as Ian McFarland suggests,[26] it should be given more attention:

> *In the beginning* was the Word, and the Word was with God, and the Word was God. He was in the beginning with God. All things *were made* through him, and without him *was* not any thing *made* that *was made*. In him was life, and the life was the light of men. The *light shines* in the *darkness*, and the darkness has not overcome it. (John 1:1–5)

---

24. See Franz Delitzsch, *Commentary on Hebrews* (Edinburgh: T&T Clark, 1876), 2:215–22. Delitzsch connects these with "ideas" in the mind of God, although this perhaps goes beyond the demands of the text.

25. Some will find a difference of emphasis in ῥῆμα (used here) and λόγος for "word," but there does not seem to be much variation between them in the LXX.

26. Ian McFarland, *From Nothing: A Theology of Creation* (Louisville: Westminster John Knox, 2014), especially pp. 85–107.

The expressions "in the beginning" (ἐν ἀρχῇ), "were made" (ἐγένετο, passive of ἐποίησεν), light, and darkness all evoke Genesis 1:1–5 in the LXX, while "shines" (φαίνει) takes us to Genesis 1:15.[27] The terms are not specific enough to make this a full-throated affirmation of creation ex nihilo, though the overall sense tends in that direction. "The Word" that in the beginning already was is responsible for the making of everything that is not God: he is the source of being and life for all, and nothing in creation—not even "darkness"—can "overcome" his light and life.[28]

A text that is just a little later gives what became the standard Jewish view of the subject. The book of 2 Baruch comes to us in Syriac (a dialect of Aramaic) but has a heading that indicates the book has been translated from Greek. The thoughts in the book apparently come from after the fall of Jerusalem in AD 70 and may date from as late as the first couple of decades in the second century. In 21:4 the character Baruch (see Jer 32:12) prays these words:

> O hear me, you who *made* the earth, the one who fixed the *firmament* by the word and made firm the height of heaven by the *spirit*, the one who *from the beginning of the world* called *that which did not yet exist* and they obeyed you.[29]

The echoes of Genesis 1 are quite plain here,[30] and the expression "that which did not yet exist" [*da'dakkeil la' hawa'*][31] corresponds well with similar Greek expressions described here (e.g., οὐκ ἐξ ὄντων, 2 Macc 7:28). In fact, the Syriac sounds similar to Romans 4:17, which describes God as the one "who gives life to the dead and calls into existence the things that do not exist."[32] The book asks the reader to imagine the historical Baruch, the scribe

---

27. It is true that the LXX uses σκότος for "darkness," while John 1:5 uses σκοτία. The terms are interchangeable in John, however (see John 3:19, and compare 1 John 1:5–6), so this makes no difference.

28. This is in general agreement with McFarland's helpful discussion. However, he takes the sense of γίνομαι here as "come into being," which is theoretically possible for the verb but (as I think) contextually unlikely because of the way it is used as the suppletive passive of ποιέω.

29. English translation is based on A. F. J. Klijn, "2 (Apocalypse of) Baruch," in *The Old Testament Pseudepigrapha*, ed. James Charlesworth (New York: Doubleday, 1983), 2:628 (modified to represent the Syriac). I accept the common emendation of original *bml'h*, "in its fullness" to *bmlt'*, "by the word."

30. The Syriac for "made" is the verb *'abad*, which corresponds to Hebrew *'asah* and Greek ποιέω (which likely lies behind this. In the LXX it represents both *bara'* and *'asah* (cf. Gen 1:1; John 1:3). "The firmament" is *raqi'a'*, the Aramaic equivalent to Hebrew *haraqia'*. The "spirit" also corresponds to the term of Genesis 1:2; "from the beginning of the world" is *min reish 'alma'*, surely equivalent to Hebrew *bere'shit* (Gen 1:1).

31. ܗܘܐ ܠܐ ܕܕܟܝܠ (I use the vowel-pointing conventions of the Bible Society in Israel's edition of the Syriac Peshitta, 1986.)

32. This supports the off-hand remark in O'Neill, "How Early Is the Doctrine of *creatio ex nihilo*?": "Rom. 4:17 and 1 Cor. 1:28 seem to be homiletical allusions to an agreed and fixed belief" (p. 462).

of Jeremiah, as the actor; and the terms of the prayer are therefore expected to be recognizably conventional, which means its acceptance should predate the book's composition.

The Midrash Genesis Rabbah attributes to Rabban Gamaliel—probably not Gamaliel I (Acts 5:34; 22:3) but his grandson, Gamaliel II, both Rabban—a conversation in which he pronounced a woe upon a certain philosopher who had suggested that God had used preexisting matter (*tohu, bohu*, darkness, water, wind, and the deep) to create. Gamaliel insisted that God created all these to begin with.[33] That is, the notion of ex nihilo creation is, by this point, commonly held by Christians and Jews. The Jewish mainstream projects this back into the first century AD, while 2 Baruch seems to push it back even further.[34]

The notion likely lies behind at least two other Jewish texts that represent the early period: Joseph and Aseneth comes from somewhere between the first century BC and the second AD. In 12:1–2 Aseneth, an Egyptian lass who converts to Joseph's God, prays to God the Creator in what is surely intended to sound quite traditional and well established:

> Lord God of the ages,
> who created all (things) and gave life (to them),
> who gave breath of life to your whole creation,
> who brought the invisible (things) out into the light,
> who made the (things that) are
> and the (ones that) have an appearance from the non-appearing
>   and non-being.[35]

There are many textual decisions to be made with this piece that will not detain us. We should note, however, that the editor of the standard English translation connects these words to "one of the essentials of Jewish and Christian cosmology."[36] That is, it links most naturally with creation ex nihilo.

---

33. Gen. Rab. 1:9. For text see H. Freedman and M. Simon, eds., *Midrash Rabbah: Genesis* (London: Soncino, 1939), 1:8.

34. Bockmuehl, "*Creatio ex nihilo* in Palestinian Judaism and Early Christianity," 261–68, mentions a number of Second Temple Jewish texts whose force leads in the direction of ex nihilo creation without saying it explicitly. Bockmuehl also notes features of Genesis Rabbah that may locate its present form as a third- or fourth-century composition—but he does not say whether he thinks the reference to a first-century figure is fictitious. Nevertheless, the connection of the view with a traditional figure most likely supports the text's assertion that the view itself is traditional.

35. See C. Burchard, "Joseph and Aseneth," in *The Old Testament Pseudepigrapha*, 2:177–247.

36. Burchard, "Joseph and Aseneth," 220 n. e, which cites, among others, 2 Bar 21:4; Rom 4:17; Heb 11:3; Herm. Vis. 1:1, Mand. 1:1.

The *Letter of Aristeas* is generally dated in the second century BC—though it could be as early as the latter third century BC or as late as the first century AD. It tells the story of how the Pentateuch was rendered into Greek at the request of Ptolemy II Philadelphus (285–247 BC) but also addresses issues of Jewish witness and identity in the face of the wider world, especially the higher culture of Hellenism. In a passage that is probably a sample of the satire on idolatry (a trope popular with Jews and later with Christians), the high priest Eleazar says:

> [134]All mankind except ourselves believe in the existence of many gods, though they themselves are much more powerful than the beings whom they vainly worship. [135]For when they have made statues of stone and wood, they say that they are the images of those who have invented something useful for life and they worship them, though they have clear proof that they possess no feeling. [136]For it would be utterly foolish to suppose that any one became a god in virtue of his inventions. *For the inventors simply took certain objects already created and by combining them together*, showed that they possessed a fresh utility: *they did not themselves create the substance of the thing*, and so it is a vain and foolish thing for people to make gods of men like themselves.[37]

Although it is true that the thought is not here developed and that the text does not make a positive affirmation about the origin of matter, it does seem that O'Neill has captured what the text takes for granted:

> Inventors are contrasted with the true God. Inventors simply take existing objects already created, and combine them together. They do not themselves create the substance of the things (τὴν κατασκευὴν αὐτῶν οὐ ποιήσαντες αὐτοί). . . . The conclusions may not need to have been made explicit because they belonged to the common currency of belief.[38]

In the terms of good-faith communication (ch. 4 above), this would be part of the world of assumptions shared between author and audience, which establishes the validity of the author's point.

Christian authors also confess the notion. The Shepherd of Hermas

---

37. Using the translation of R. H. Charles (1913); for the verse numbers see R. J. H. Shutt, "Letter of Aristeas," in *The Old Testament Pseudepigrapha*, 2:7–34.

38. O'Neill, "How Early Is the Doctrine of *creatio ex nihilo*?" 455.

(which predates Irenaeus, ca. AD 175),[39] speaks of God, "who dwells in the heavens and *created out of nothing the things that are* [ὁ κτίσας ἐκ τοῦ μὴ ὄντος τὰ ὄντα], and increased and multiplied them" (Herm. Vis. 1:1). He later gives a brief minimal confession of faith (Herm. Mand. 1:1):

> First of all, believe that God is One, *who created all things and set them in order, and made out of what did not exist everything that exists* [ὁ τὰ πάντα κτίσας καὶ καταρτίσας καὶ ποιήσας ἐκ τοῦ μὴ ὄντος εἰς τὸ εἶναι τὰ πάντα], who contains all things but is himself alone uncontained.

The verb "set in order" (καταρτίσας) echoes the same term in Hebrews 11:3 (ESV "created") on the same subject. The implication of the words is clear, and they resemble the wording of 2 Maccabees 7:28 (and perhaps 2 Bar 21:4) and become standard in later Christian writing on the subject (as below). The words here function as part of a brief creed, which implies that it was already firmly established by the time the book was written.

The Greek-speaking Christian writers Theophilus of Antioch (later second century) and Athanasius (fourth century) discussed the difference between Plato and Moses on this point. Although it was common (as far back as Aristobulus, second century BC) to claim that Plato learned his wisdom from the books of Moses, Christian authors usually exercised a critical appreciation of Plato.[40] Theophilus and Athanasius both attributed to Plato the notion that matter preexisted the creation, being virtually co-eternal with God. For all their high regard for Plato, they rejected this position, both because they found it inconsistent with Plato's larger views and because they found it inconsistent with the Bible (including Genesis). For example, Athanasius, *De Incarnatione*, §§2–3, reasons (3:13–16):

> For *God is good*—or rather, the source of all goodness—*and the good has no envy for anything.* Thus, because he envies nothing its existence, he made all things out of nothing through his own Word, our Lord Jesus Christ.[41]

---

39. English based on Michael Holmes, *The Apostolic Fathers* (Grand Rapids: Baker, 1999), 328–527.
40. So too Irenaeus, *Haer.*, 2.14.4. Athenagoras (second century), in his *Plea for the Christians*, is not clear whether Plato really held to preexisting matter, but he is clear that "it is not reasonable that matter should be older than God, for the efficient cause must of necessity be older than the things that are made"—a philosophical argument for ex nihilo creation (§19). (Unless otherwise noted, Patristic texts are cited from *ANF*, *NPNF¹*, and *NPNF²* editions.) Likewise, Eusebius (fourth century), *Praep. ev.*, 557-cd, is clear that Moses declared the universe had a beginning. In context he tries as hard as he can to enlist Plato on the side of the same view.
41. English based on Robert Thomson, ed., *Athanasius: Contra Gentes and De Incarnatione* (Oxford: Clarendon Press, 1971), with emphasis added.

The italicized portion comes from Plato's *Timaeus*, 29-*e*,[42] and the discussion follows an appeal to Genesis 1:1, Herm. Mand. 1:1, and Hebrews 11:3. Both Theophilus and Athanasius use the Greek expression ποιεῖν τὰ πάντα [or, ὄντα] ἐξ οὐκ ὄντων "to make all things [or, the things that are] out of things that were not" (Theophilus, *Ad Autolycum*, 2:4, 10; Athanasius, *De Incarnatione*, 3:15).[43]

Two important texts, one pre-Christian Jewish and the other Christian, offer a wrinkle to this discussion. First, the deuterocanonical book Wisdom of Solomon addresses God and describes creation this way (11:17–18):

> For your all-powerful hand,
> which *created the world out of formless matter*
> [κτίσασα τὸν κόσμον ἐξ ἀμόρφου ὕλης]
> did not lack the means to send upon them
> a multitude of bears, or bold lions,
> or newly-created unknown beasts full of rage.

The passage stresses God's infinite resources to bring any judgments he chooses upon those whose "foolish and wicked thoughts" lead them "astray to worship irrational serpents and worthless animals" (v. 15), particularly as it was shown in the plagues in Egypt. Hence a practical application of creation ex nihilo suits the context quite well. However, the author speaks of "formless matter," which is held to allude to works like Plato's *Timaeus* where the primordial stuff is "formless" (50-*d*, 51-*a*).[44] Many read this as an affirmation of Plato's picture and thus an actual disaffirmation of true creation ex nihilo, but there are reasons to be cautious about that. First, the needs of the context do not require that God create these beasts from nothing (nor does Genesis suggest that the first beasts were made from nothing), so this text need not be commenting on the initial creation. It is not impossible to take "formless matter" as an interpretation of the "invisible and unfurnished" (Gen 1:2, LXX, ἀόρατος καὶ ἀκατασκεύαστος) earth,

---

42. Athanasius's fellow Alexandrian Philo had likewise appealed to this passage in Plato. See Philo, *On the Creation of the World*, v (21).

43. See also Athanasius, *De Incarnatione*, 3:4–6: "Through the Word God made the universe to be from non-existence, which previously in no way existed at all," (ἀλλ'ἐξ οὐκ ὄντων καὶ μηδαμῇ μηδαμῶς ὑπάρχοντα τὰ ὅλα εἰς τὸ εἶναι πεποιηκέναι τὸν θεὸν διὰ τοῦ λόγου), which is similar to the text in 2 Baruch. Irenaeus, *Haer.*, 4.38.3, writes similarly of "things not yet existing" (τὰ μηδέπω ὄντα), which also resembles the 2 Baruch text.

44. Plato does not here use ὕλη, "matter," for the primordial stuff. That noun, however, did become a part of the parlance, as evidenced by Theophilus (*Ad Autolycum*, 2:4, 10) and Athanasius (*De Incarnatione*, 2.17, 19, 21, etc.).

implying a two-stage creation of calling the world into existence as raw material and then furnishing and preparing it, as Josephus did (*Ant.*, 1, 27 [I.1.1]), Gamaliel was reported to have done (Gen. Rab., 1:9), and possibly Philo also did (*On the Creation*, vii [29]), and Theophilus of Antioch unambiguously did (*Ad Autolycum*, 2:10).[45]

One difficulty in deciding how to read the stance of Wisdom of Solomon 11:17 on ex nihilo creation is the problem of ascertaining what ideas might have been possible for an educated Jew in Alexandria in the first couple of centuries BC. Harry Wolfson, a highly regarded scholar of ancient philosophy, argued that, rightly understood, Philo actually did affirm ex nihilo creation and this two-stage process.[46] Others of course disagree, and more recently Gerhard May has dismissed this reading.[47] It is not for me to weigh in on Philo in particular, although the factors described here show why it is more credible to read Wisdom of Solomon 11:17 in a way consistent with ex nihilo creation.[48] The author of Wisdom of Solomon does follow biblical ideas closely elsewhere: In 1:14 the writer says that God "created all things that they might exist" (ἔκτισεν εἰς τὸ εἶναι τὰ πάντα), while in 9:1 God is the one "who has made all things by your word" (ὁ ποιήσας τὰ πάντα ἐν λόγῳ σου). Further, he does not say that the "formless matter" is eternal, and we ought, if possible, to prefer a reading of a book like Wisdom of Solomon that coheres with the main stream of thought and also takes into account the book's acceptability among later generations of the faithful.[49]

The case of Justin Martyr is similar. In his *First Apology* he stresses the indebtedness of Plato to Moses, and thus writes (§59):

---

45. See Louis Feldman, *Judean Antiquities 1–4: Translation and Commentary*, Flavius Josephus, Translation and Commentary (Leiden: Brill, 2000), 10 nn. 36–37. Feldman thinks that Josephus' use of ἔκτισεν rather than ἐποίησεν in his version of Gen 1:1 "implies more clearly *creatio ex nihilo*." He also suggests that both Josephus and Philo read Gen 1:2 as indicated here.

46. See Harry Wolfson, *Philo: Foundations of Religious Philosophy in Judaism, Christianity, and Islam* (Cambridge: Harvard University Press, 1962), 2:295–324.

47. Gerhard May, *Creatio ex nihilo: The Doctrine of 'Creation Out of Nothing' in Early Christian Thought* (London: T&T Clark, 1994), 9 n32. See the earlier work of Henri Bois, *Essai sur les Origines de la Philosophie Judéo-Alexandrine* (Paris: Fischbacher, 1890), 268.

48. O'Neill, "How Early Is the Doctrine of *creatio ex nihilo*?," 456–61, rejects May's arguments, and offers a stronger variation of Wolfson's.

49. The discussion of Wisdom of Solomon 11:17 is an old one. Commentators who agree with the general line taken here include Christians and Jews, such as William Deane, *The Book of Wisdom* (Oxford: Clarendon, 1881), 171, who notes that Augustine makes no objection to our passage; J. A. F. Gregg, *The Wisdom of Solomon*, CBSC (Cambridge: Cambridge University Press, 1909), 110–111; Joseph Reider, *The Book of Wisdom* (New York: Harper & Brothers, 1957), 145. Menahem Stein, "*Sefer Hokhmat Šᵉlomoh*," in *HasSefarim HaHitsonim*, ed. Avraham Kahana (Tel-Aviv: Masada, 1959), vol. 1, book 2, תצה. Those opposing include David Winston, "The Book of Wisdom's Theory of Cosmogony," *History of Religions* 11:2 (1971): 185–202, especially pp. 192–93.

And that you may learn that it was from our teachers—we mean the account given through the prophets—that Plato borrowed his statement that *God, having altered matter which was shapeless, made the world* [ὕλην ἄμορφον οὖσαν στρέψαντα τὸν θεὸν κόσμον ποιῆσαι], hear the very words spoken through Moses, who, as above shown, was the first prophet, and of greater antiquity than the Greek writers; and through whom the Spirit of prophecy, signifying how and from what materials God at first formed the world, spoke thus: "In the beginning God created the heaven and the earth. And the earth was invisible and unfurnished, and darkness was upon the face of the deep; and the Spirit of God moved over the waters. And God said, Let there be light; and it was so." So that both Plato and they who agree with him, and we ourselves, have learned, and you also can be convinced, that *by the word of God the whole world was made out of the substance spoken of before by Moses* [λόγῳ θεοῦ ἐκ τῶν ὑποκειμένων καὶ προσδηλωθέντων διὰ Μωϋσέως γεγενῆσθαι τὸν πάντα κόσμον]. And that which the poets call Erebus, we know was spoken of formerly by Moses.

We may, if we wish, infer from this that Justin simply read Genesis as implying that matter preexisted the creation (which is how most take Plato). However, even here caution is needed; one commentator on the Greek text remarks:

> Justin seems in this passage to avoid the belief in the eternity of matter. For he regards οὐρανός and γῆ as the ὑποκείμενα of the κόσμος, and these had been created by God.[50]

Further, as Harry Wolfson observed,

> Now while [Justin] does not explicitly say that the "unformed matter," out of which both he and Plato, following Moses, believe the world to have been created, was created, that certainly was his belief, for elsewhere he says that "God alone is unbegotten" but "all other things after Him are created," almost the same words used by Tatian in his statement that the pre-existent matter was created.[51]

---

50. A. W. F. Blunt, *The Apologies of Justin Martyr*, Cambridge Patristic Texts (Cambridge: Cambridge University Press, 1911), 87 n16.

51. Harry Wolfson, "Plato's Pre-Existent Matter in Patristic Philosophy," in *Religious Philosophy* (Cambridge: Harvard University Press, 1961), 170–81, quote on p. 174. May, *Creatio ex nihilo*, 124 n33, dismisses Wolfson's reading but without really engaging the cross-reference and without considering the apologetic purpose. O'Neill, "How Early Is the Doctrine of *creatio ex nihilo*?," 454–55, insists on this reading.

This is difficult, and, if Wolfson is right we might wish that Justin had been clearer—although Justin may well have interpreted his apologetic purpose as pushing him toward an indecisive expression here.

The result of all this is that we may legitimately see a trajectory from the basic idea of creation in the Hebrew Bible with ex nihilo never formulated as a philosophical doctrine but still present *in nuce*.[52] The idea becomes more clearly formulated as we approach the Christian era, and in the first century AD is expressly stated (though again, non-philosophically).[53] The controversies of the second century may have played a role in forcing further definition, but I suspect that two other factors were more important. First, there was the question of what to do with Plato, who was generally counted as worthy of high respect and whose thought Christians wanted to recruit in support of their beliefs. Second, there were inner driving forces within the biblical worldview itself, as Wolfson noted:[54] If God is the Maker and Father of this All (as Plato affirmed) and if God alone was unoriginated and self-sufficient, it was only a matter of time before the doctrine of creation would be framed the way Theophilus, Irenaeus, and Athanasius framed it.[55]

We have no need to read the later texts back into the earlier ones; rather, we simply recognize that the later texts are acting as if their reading of Genesis is part of the shared picture of the world between the authors and audiences. Besides the fact that some of these authors cite Genesis as part of the rationale, it is hard to find another place besides Genesis 1:1 on which these could be depending, and thus we do well to suppose that they were reading Genesis 1:1 to imply creation from nothing. I have given syntactical reasons that at least show that the conventional interpretation of Genesis 1:1 is feasible (I think they show much more!); in light of what we have seen here, if we were to read it differently we would have to conclude that these readers badly

---

52. Even though Bockmuehl, "*Creatio ex nihilo* in Palestinian Judaism and Early Christianity," assesses some of the particular passages differently than I do, he nevertheless agrees, against May, that the doctrine as it came to be formulated is "firmly rooted in Scripture and pre-Christian Jewish literature" and thus should not be treated as "a second-century afterthought, primarily a backlash against Gnosticism" (p. 270).

53. In fact, Menahem Kister, "*Tohu wa-Bohu*, Primordial Elements and *Creatio ex Nihilo*," *Jewish Studies Quarterly* 14 (2007): 229–56, suggests that Jews and early Christians interacted with each other in developing their basically unified view on this.

54. Wolfson, "Plato's Pre-Existent Matter in Patristic Philosophy," 176–80. Wolfson lists five points, of which I have focused on three.

55. James Noel Hubler, "*Creatio ex nihilo*: Matter, Creation, and the Body in Classical and Christian Philosophy and Aquinas" (PhD diss., University of Pennsylvania, 1995), generally agrees with May on these points—though he does not interact with Wolfson, nor do all of the texts mentioned here figure into his discussion. He notes (p. 110) that Aristotle used the Greek ἐκ τοῦ μὴ ὄντος ("from the non-existent") in a relative sense ("for generation is *from the non-existent* to the existent," *Gen. an.*, 741-*b*, 23–24). It is true that the Greek expression itself does not decide, but the contexts differ enough that the exegesis offered here stands.

misunderstood or misappropriated their constitutional source—a conclusion that, though conceivable, should carry a heavy burden of proof.

Theologians and apologists have been quick to seize the cosmological theory of the big bang as a scientific correlate to the ex nihilo doctrine. This is no surprise, since the scientific theory confronts us with a beginning that cannot be explained as the result of factors inherent in the cosmos itself—after all, the cosmos did not exist until the big bang. Further, the theory traces itself back to a Belgian priest-astrophysicist, Georges Lemaître (who insisted, quite properly, that the theory derived from the equations, not from Genesis).[56]

A good example is the physicist Robert Jastrow (1925–2008), who had a distinguished career at NASA. Labeling himself "an agnostic in religious matters," he found himself drawn by what he saw as the similarities between the contemporary big bang theory and conventional ways of reading Genesis: "All the details differ, but the essential element in the astronomical and biblical accounts of Genesis is the same; the chain of events leading to man commenced suddenly and sharply, at a definite moment in time, in a flash of light and energy."[57]

Indeed, as Ernan McMullin put it,

> If the universe began in time through the act of the creator, from our vantage point it would look something like the big bang cosmologists are now talking about.[58]

While this is encouraging, several factors should give us pause before we identify the big bang with the ex nihilo creation event. To begin with, Genesis does not offer a scientific theory, as I have argued already. Further, the doctrine, among Christians and Jews, was formulated in an era in which science, in at least one of its primary branches (Aristotle's cosmology), held the universe to be eternal. In the nineteenth century when the reigning scientific cosmology for origins was the "nebular hypothesis" (which has been incorporated into modern cosmology), traditional Christians sought to give it an interpretation that led to ex nihilo creation, something they would not do today.[59] I mean no insult to this theory or to any other when I note that such

---

56. See Marcia Bartusiak, "Before the Big Bang," *Technology Review* 112:5 (September/October 2009): MIT News Section, M14–15.

57. Robert Jastrow, *God and the Astronomers*, 2nd ed. (New York: Norton, 1992), 14. This second edition has helpful appendices from Dr. John O'Keefe (a Christian astronomer) and Steven Katz (a Jewish professor of religious studies).

58. Cited in David Kelsey, "The Doctrine of Creation from Nothing," in *Evolution and Creation*, ed. Ernan McMullin (Notre Dame: University of Notre Dame Press, 1985), 176–196, quote on p. 190.

59. For example, Gilbert Rorison, "The Creative Week," in *Replies to "Essays and Reviews,"* E. M. Goulburn, et al. (New York: Appleton, 1862), 242–98, especially pp. 269–75.

theories seem to have the property of being subject to challenge and revision (or even discarding).

In fact, Aquinas (1225–1274), in his effort to co-opt Aristotle's philosophy into the service of Christian doctrine, had to address the way that Aristotle had held that the universe is eternal (analogous to modern steady-state theories). Aquinas argued, therefore, that philosophy cannot prove either that the universe did have a beginning or that it did not—although proper philosophical analysis can undermine some of the conclusions associated with Aristotle (for example, "Nothing except God can be eternal"). The doctrine of a beginning is to be held by faith, namely, by trusting the scriptural revelation.[60]

Christians and Jews, therefore, though they can be happy with the big bang type of theories, do not depend on them for their doctrine of an absolute beginning.

More recently, theologians have questioned whether the beginning is to be taken as an actual event. By this argument, the doctrine of creation ex nihilo is not really about what happened but about how the faithful are to be disposed toward God and the world, namely, (as Ian Barbour put it):

> (1) a sense of dependence, finitude and contingency; (2) a response of wonder, trust, gratitude for life, and affirmation of the world; and (3) a recognition of interdependence, order, and beauty in the world.[61]

Curiously enough, Hellenistic interpreters of Plato also queried whether the story in the *Timaeus* was to be taken as describing real events or was simply a mythical embodiment of certain (timeless) truths; the arguments seem to favor the intended event-ness of the story.[62]

Christians have, however, commonly assumed that creation implies an actual beginning. This is, in fact, built in to the narrative form of the Christian story: a good creation, marred by an actual fall, in which God is busy working redemption, and which he will ultimately bring to full fruition. As Colin Gunton notes,

> It does not follow [from creation ex nihilo] that creation was an arbitrary act upon the part of God. It was, rather, purposive, and in two senses:

---

60. Thomas Aquinas, *Summa Theologica*, I.46.
61. Ian Barbour, *Religion in an Age of Science* (San Francisco: Harper & Row, 1990), 133.
62. See David Sedley, *Creationism and its Critics in Antiquity* (Berkeley: University of California Press, 2007), 98–107.

that it derives from the love of God, not simply his will; and that it exists for a purpose—to go somewhere we might say.⁶³

The dispositions that Barbour outlined are indeed quite crucial; and the faithful have derived them *from the story*.

8.C RELATION OF GENESIS 1 AND 2

Jews have traditionally read the activities of Genesis 2 as an expansion of the creation of humankind on the sixth day of Genesis 1. Many source-critical analyses of Genesis find the two to be in tension with each other, even labeling them separate creation accounts. Another kind of reading supposes that the events of Genesis 2 are presented as *subsequent* to those of Genesis 1 and thus do not necessarily represent the beginnings of humankind.⁶⁴

First, let us be clear that Genesis in its present form supports the traditional reading of the first two pericopes. Several of the links between Genesis 1 and Genesis 2–3 mentioned in chapter 5 above are relevant here as well. For example, the reversal of "blessing" (1:28) to "cursing" (3:17) and the ironic "multiply" (1:28; 3:16). I think that the "not good" of 2:18 has the literary effect of alerting us that we are not yet at the "very good" of 1:31.⁶⁵ Further, the account of Adam's offspring (5:1–5) both continues the characters of Genesis 2–4 and clearly echoes Genesis 1:26–27—for example, the verb "create" and the nouns "likeness" and "image." Indeed, while 5:1 is rightly rendered as "when God created *man*" (because of its echo of 1:27), it could easily be "when God created *Adam*" (because the Hebrew for "man," אדם [*'adam*], lacks the definite article).

A number of texts agree with this traditional reading. For example, Psalm 104:14 describes "plants for man to cultivate" (or, "plants for the work of man"; see also v. 23), using a characteristic term from Genesis 2–3, "work" (Heb. עבד, *'abad*, Gen 2:5, 15; 3:23). That is, a song so dependent on Genesis 1 folds in terms more distinctive of Genesis 2. Similarly, Tobit 8:6 ("you *made* [a verb in the LXX of Gen 1] Adam and made his wife Eve as a *helper* [Gen 2] and support") and Wisdom of Solomon 10:1 ("Wisdom protected the first-*formed* [Gen 2:7, LXX] father of the world, when he alone had been

---

63. Colin Gunton, "The Doctrine of Creation," in *The Cambridge Companion to Christian Doctrine*, ed. Colin E. Gunton (Cambridge: Cambridge University Press, 1997), 141–57.
64. See, for example, John Walton, *The Lost World of Adam and Eve* (Downers Grove, IL: InterVarsity Press, 2015), 63–69.
65. See Collins, *Genesis 1–4*, 75.

created [Gen 1:27]") combine the two passages. Finally, in Matthew's Gospel Jesus himself does the same (Matt 19:4–5):

> [Jesus] answered, "Have you not read that he who created them from the beginning *made them male and female* [Gen 1:27, LXX], and said, *'Therefore a man shall leave his father and his mother and hold fast to his wife, and the two shall become one flesh'* [~Gen 2:24, LXX]?"

C. E. B. Cranfield, in his commentary on the Greek text of Mark's Gospel, sees this as the clear import of the way Jesus uses the Genesis texts and says (at the parallel place in Mark, 10:6–8): "If Gen. i and ii are read as one story, it is natural to take ii.21–3 as filling out the bare statement of i.27b."[66]

In 1 Corinthians 15:45 we have a citation of Genesis 2:7; then in verse 49 Paul says, "Just as we have borne the *image* [Gk. εἰκών] of the man of dust, we shall also bear the image of the man of heaven," which evokes Genesis 1:27; 5:3; that is, in Paul's argument the person of Genesis 2:7 is the same as the first man of Genesis 1:27. Similarly, Paul characterizes Christ as both the new Adam (1 Cor 15:45) and as the ideal "image of God" (2 Cor 4:4; Col 1:15–16), which is probably why Luke traces his ancestry back to Adam and then to God.[67]

We add to that the idea that God makes fresh starts on humankind after the disobedience of Adam and Eve, particularly in Noah and then in Abraham and Israel.[68] They are God's way of retrieving what was lost, not only for themselves but also for the world. Israel, both in its land and especially in its temple, is to be a kind of reconstituted garden of Eden, whose role is to anticipate God's presence restored for all humankind.[69] This theme appears in Isaiah 43:1, 7:

> But now thus says the LORD,
>   he who *created* you, O Jacob,
>   he who *formed* you, O Israel:

---

66. C. E. B. Cranfield, *The Gospel According to Saint Mark*, CGT (Cambridge: Cambridge University Press, 1962), 320. Cranfield adds, "Jesus would be innocent of J and P"; but it is more likely that he would be *indifferent* to the prehistory of the canonical text.

67. I expect that Adam as "son" of God ties in to the idea of the Davidic king as "son" of God; the role of the Davidide is to embody true humanity. I touch on this theme in Collins, *Genesis 1–4*, 24 n42, 29 n47.

68. Besides the brief mention in my essay, see also Collins, "Reading Genesis 1–2 with the Grain: Analogical Days," in *Reading Genesis 1–2*, 73–92, especially pp. 74–75.

69. See Christopher J. H. Wright, *The Mission of God: Unlocking the Bible's Grand Narrative* (Downers Grove, IL: InterVarsity Press, 2006), 334, 340.

> "Fear not, for I have redeemed you;
>   I have called you by name, you are mine. . . .
> everyone who is called by my name,
>   whom I *created* for my glory,
>   whom I *formed* and *made*."

The terms for how God established Israel—*created* (cf. Gen 1:27), *formed* (Gen 2:7), and *made* (Gen 1:26)—bring together the terms of Genesis 1–2 to make it clear that Israel is God's new start on humankind, the proper heirs of the first humans in Genesis 1–2.

Consider further that God's goal for his redeemed creation is "a new heaven and a new earth" (Rev 21:1), using terms from Genesis 1:1; 2:1, 4; in this scene there will be Eden come to its full fruition.

Later Jewish tradition continues this line. For example, in the Talmud (Sanhedrin, 38-*a*), the rabbis, in discussing the creation story of Genesis 1 (with Adam created on the eve of the Sabbath), readily refer to Adam and Eve (the couple in Gen 2). The prominent medieval Rabbi Moshe ben Maimon (twelfth century AD; also called Maimonides or Rambam) declared, "All our Sages agree that this [the formation of Adam and Eve] took place on the sixth day, and that nothing new was created after the close of the six days."[70]

Therefore, it is best to take Genesis 1–2 as complementary accounts that really do aim to record the making of the first humans. This Jewish tradition of reading should push us in the direction of seeing if it can be made to work (which it seems to do, as in the ESV, NIV2011-margin, and CSB).[71]

8.D HUMAN ORIGINS AND THE FALL

In chapter 5 I argued that the commission given to the first humans, "be fruitful and multiply" (Gen 1:22), gives cohesion with the rest of the Pentateuch. The implication is that God has appointed Israel as his fresh start on humankind, heirs of the Adamic role. The prophets Jeremiah and Ezekiel continue this theme. Speaking to the faithless people of Israel (the northern kingdom, long gone), Jeremiah anticipates that after they have turned back

---

70. Moses Maimonides, *The Guide for the Perplexed*, trans. M. Friedländer (London: Routledge & Kegan Paul, 1904 [orig. ca. 1190]), 216. For a Hebrew paraphrase see Yehudah Kiel, *Sefer Bere'shit 1–17*, Da'at Miqra' (Jerusalem: Mossad Harav Kook, 1997), מב, n. 7.

71. A rationale comes from Richard Hess, "Genesis 1–2 in Its Literary Context," *TynBul* 41:1 (1990): 143–53, who argues that the pattern of doublets in Genesis 1–11 is for the second element to focus on some details of the first. I have also explored ways in which the chiastic structure of Genesis 2:4 invites a reading strategy of complementarity. See Collins, *Genesis 1–4*, 108–12.

to the Lord they will multiply and be fruitful in the land (3:16), true to their original calling. Later the prophet holds out the same expectation for the people of Judah after their exile (23:3), as does Ezekiel (36:10–11). The author of Acts portrays the expansion of the early church in the same terms (Acts 6:7; 9:31; 12:24; 19:20).

This depends on reading Genesis 1–5 as giving the origin of all humankind as God's treasured creation and also of humankind as having forfeited their place in the garden by disobedience at the headwaters. This disobedience and its consequences are called the "fall"—a term that does not appear in the Bible but can be found in early Greek-speaking Christian fathers.[72] Now, Augustine (from whom Western Christians typically trace their theological ancestry) and the Greek fathers had different ways of explaining how the descendants of the first humans were made sinners, but we should not miss that they agreed on the basic matter, namely, that this disobedience right at the beginning of humankind made the rest of humanity, their children, into sinners.[73] Indeed, this way of telling the story is common property with conventional Judaism as well—with perhaps the proviso that Christians have made much more of the impact of that disobedience upon humankind in general.[74]

In chapter 5 we considered how the rest of Genesis portrays Abraham as the divinely-chosen means of restoring blessing to all the families of the earth, which implies that the blessing was lost. The Table of Nations (Gen 10, see ch. 7 above) describes the various families as having derived from Adam.

Further, a literarily attentive reading of Genesis 3–4 sees how the text shows the spread of sin and trouble, which seem so incompatible with the initially good creation. Additionally, the descendants of Adam and Eve, who

---

72. These fathers use the verb πίπτω and cognates for the "fall." For example, Eusebius (ca. AD 315), *Praep. ev.*, 7.8 [307-d] ("Adam . . . *fell from* [Gk. ἀποπίπτω] his better lot"); Athanasius (AD 293–373), *Contra Gentes*, 3, 8–9 (humans "fell [πίπτω] into selfish desires"); John Chrysostom (AD 347–407), *Homilies on Romans*, x ("He [Adam] *having fallen* [πίπτω], even those who did not eat from the tree, all of them, became mortal because of him"); and Theodore of Mopsuestia (AD 350–428), *Catechetical Homilies*, 14 ("we *fell* and sin corrupted us").

73. That is, we make a big mistake if we think of a position *in general* on the role of Adam and his sin as a distinctively Western or Augustinian issue (as so many do). The Greek-speaking fathers typically hold some version of the idea above: An example is Irenaeus (later second century AD); see Anders-Christian Jacobsen, "The Importance of Genesis 1–3 in the Theology of Irenaeus," *Zeitschrift für antikes Christentum* 8.2 (2005): 299–316. Also outside the influence of Augustine are the Syriac speaker Ephraem the Syrian (AD 306–73), *Commentary on 1 Corinthians*, 1:30 (speaking of the forgiveness we need as mediated through baptism); the Latin-speaking Tertullian (c. AD 160–220), *On the Soul*, 16, 40–41 ("corruption" that came from the sin of Adam); and Cyprian (d. AD 258), *Letters*, 58.5 (to Fidus: the sin of Adam affects even newly-born infants).

74. For a conventional Jewish perspective see Moshe Greenberg, "Mankind, Israel and the Nations in the Hebraic Heritage," in *No Man Is an Alien: Essays on the Unity of Mankind*, ed. J. Robert Nelson (Leiden: Brill, 1971), 15–40. In support of the Jewish and Christian distinction, see the Jewish philosopher Kenneth Seeskin, *Thinking About the Torah* (Philadelphia/Lincoln: JPS/University of Nebraska, 2016), 150–51: "As I see it, Judaism is much closer to Pelagius than it is to Augustine."

did not disobey as they did, nevertheless find themselves forbidden to reenter the garden. For an Israelite, the reentry comes by way of the sanctuary, with its liturgy providing for forgiveness. Genesis does in fact indicate that all humankind suffer from the painful toil introduced in the curses for the first couple's transgression (5:29; see 3:16–17).

Was that first transgression an event, or should we interpret it in a more timeless fashion—say, as the simple observation that humans are sinful or that all humans recapitulate Adam's sin in their own lives?[75] Genesis certainly portrays the fall as an event (or complex of events) that changed the human condition from its initial blessedness. The Second Temple Jewish book of Wisdom of Solomon draws on this (2:23–24):

> for God created mankind for incorruption,
>   and made him in the image of his own character,
> but through the devil's envy death came into the world,
>   and those who belong to his party experience it.[76]

Interestingly, the Greek of "death came into the world" (θάνατος εἰσῆλθεν εἰς τὸν κόσμον) is quite close to the Pauline "sin came into the world through one man, and death through sin" (Rom 5:12, ἡ ἁμαρτία εἰς τὸν κόσμον εἰσῆλθεν καὶ διὰ τῆς ἁμαρτίας ὁ θάνατος). In the context of Romans 5, of course, the words denote an event, since the argument as a whole is a narrative; that is, someone did something (one man trespassed, v. 15) and as a result something happened (sin, death, and condemnation came into the world of human experience), and then Jesus came to deal with the consequences of it all (by his obedience to make the many righteous). The argument gains its coherence from its sequence of events; it is drastically inadequate to say, as some do, that Paul is merely making a comparison here,[77] nor does it account for the corporate solidarity that underlies the Hebrew Bible.[78]

---

75. A clear example of such reading is S. R. Driver, *The Book of Genesis*, Westminster Commentary (London: Methuen, 1904), lxviii–lxix: "Eve and Cain still stand before us, the immortal types of weakness yielding to temptation, and of an unbridled temper leading its victim he knows not whither." Denis Lamoureux seems to fit this category as well, in "No Historical Adam: Evolutionary Creation View," in *Four Views on the Historical Adam*, ed. Matthew Barrett and Ardel Caneday (Grand Rapids: Zondervan, 2013), 65.

76. In verse 23, it has become common to prefer to read "character" (ἰδιότητος) instead of "eternity" (ἀϊδιότητος).

77. James D. G. Dunn, *Romans*, WBC (Dallas: Word, 1988), 289–90, makes just such a suggestion of a "comparison." Scot McKnight, in *Adam and the Genome: Reading Scripture after Genetic Science*, ed. Dennis Venema and Scot McKnight (Grand Rapids: Baker Academic, 2017), describes Paul's Adam as the "literary Adam" who is an archetypal, moral, and exemplary figure—"each person, like Adam, sins and therefore dies because of that sinning" (p. 185). This is equally unsatisfactory, as it really does not grapple with the narrative framework found not only in Paul but also in Jesus.

78. A solidarity that C. S. Lewis saw clearly (and frankly confessed that he did not quite grasp) in

Another connection between Wisdom of Solomon and Paul comes in the way they both fault the gentiles for failing to perceive in the world the marks of the Creator (Wis 13:1–9; Rom 1:20). In these authors' analyses, something has gone wrong in human beings to distort their perception.[79]

The eventitude of the fall story comes through in a gospel passage I have already mentioned. When Jesus makes his declaration on marriage (tying Gen 1:27 and 2:24 together, see above), his opponents ask him why Moses provided for divorce (Deut 24:1–4). Jesus' reply (Matt 19:8): "Because of your hardness of heart Moses allowed you to divorce your wives, but from the beginning it was not so." In context, Jesus is explaining why the law must make provision for divergences from the creation pattern for marriage. Something has entered in to change the human situation.

Some theologians (especially those called Reformed) have called the arrangement with Adam a covenant. This is highly controversial, and the usual reply begins by noting that the Hebrew of Genesis makes no mention of a covenant until 6:18 (referring to God's arrangement with Noah). Nevertheless, the idea may be helpful for envisioning how Genesis can portray humankind in a unified predicament (with Israel as the remedy). Provided the definition of covenant is suitably framed, the notion works, especially as we consider the preference for showing over telling, which expects audiences to make proper inferences. God sets terms with the man and also specifies the condition for the man, namely, obedience. There is a penalty for disobedience ("surely die" [Gen 2:17]); and although God does not spell out a reward for compliance, we can at least say that the relationship will continue. But what do later texts do on this subject?

Sirach 14:17 (second century BC), an intertestamental work explicitly calls the relationship a "covenant" (Gk. διαθήκη; the extant Heb. has *hoq*). The only place in the Hebrew Bible that has been taken to say the same is the controversial Hosea 6:7:

> But *like Adam* [כְּאָדָם] they transgressed the covenant;
> *there* [שָׁם] they dealt faithlessly with me. [80]

The Problem of Pain (London: Geoffrey Bles, 1940), chapter 5. "Legal fiction, adoption, and transference or imputation of merit and guilt, could never have played the part they did play in theology if they had always been felt to be so artificial as we now feel them to be" (76).

79. In my "Colossians 1,17 'Hold Together': A Co-Opted Term," 64–87, I show that the passage in Romans has important contacts with Pseudo-Aristotle's *De Mundo*. And in my "Echoes of Aristotle in Romans 2:14–15: Or, Maybe Abimelech Was Not So Bad After All," *Journal of Markets and Morality* 13:1 (Spring 2010): 123–73, I show why I think that the argument of Romans 1–2 follows the lines of the Genesis narrative.

80. Brian Habig, "Hosea 6:7 Revisited," *Presbyterion* 42 (2016), 4–20, offers a careful analysis of

Some commentators have supposed that the Hebrew for "like Adam" should instead be read as "like humankind" or "like any other human" (as in LXX, ὡς ἄνθρωπος), since *'adam* can mean "humanity." This reading argues that Adam is not said to have transgressed a covenant and that references to the person Adam are rare outside of Genesis 2–5. Of course, humankind is not said explicitly to have transgressed a covenant, either; and to use an argument based on the supposed rarity of references to Adam to delete one possible reference is inexcusably circular.

Others have contended that the particle in the second line, "there," leads us to expect a place named Adam. Such a place is found at Joshua 3:16, a town on the Jordan River north of where the Israelites crossed. Of course this probably means that the Hebrew preposition כ, "like," must be exchanged for ב, "at"—contrary to the evidence of the LXX.[81] Actually, this whole line of argument is misguided: first, because the text is rhetorically high, and we need an argument to limit the reference of "there" to a specific place;[82] and second, because we can examine the use of "there" in Hosea 2:15; 6:7, 10; 9:15; 10:9; 12:4; 13:8. On the surface, these are locative deictics, but generally more than a concrete location is at work. For example, in "*there* I will devour them like a lion" (13:8), the word most naturally means "there in that situation," which also works for 6:7.

It is always possible, of course, that by "there" the author meant something like "right there in the holy land," that is, in the very land that was supposed to be a kind of reconstituted Eden. The rest of Hosea has echoes of Genesis 1–2: Compare 2:18, "a covenant with the beasts of the field, the birds of the heavens, and the creeping things of the ground" (terms from Gen 1:25; 2:19); and 4:3 "the beasts of the field, the birds of the heavens, the fish of the sea" (as in Gen 1:28, the animals over which humankind is to have dominion). Hence, a reference to a covenant having been made with Adam, of whom Israel was intended to be the reinstatement and whom they imitated in their unfaithfulness in the face of abundant generosity from God (as in Hos 2:8–13; 7:15; 11:1–4; 13:4–6) offers high coherence with the whole

---

the text. My remarks here supplement his study. Yehudah Kiel, "Hosea," in *Terê 'Asar*, Kiel et al., Da'at Miqra' (Jerusalem: Mossad Harav Kook, 1990), מה, prefers the "like any human beings" interpretation but notes that a number of esteemed Jewish interpreters ("our teachers of blessed memory") had taken the "like Adam" reading.

  81. It is just possible to think of the current Hebrew text as providing a short form of the fuller *kibe'adam*, "as at Adam," with the second preposition omitted (see Joüon-Muraoka, §133-*h*).

  82. Compare what C. S. Lewis said of the Psalms: "Most emphatically the Psalms are to be read as poems; as lyrics, with all the licenses and all the formalities, the hyperboles, the emotional rather than logical connections, which are proper to lyric poetry." See *Reflections on the Psalms* (Bles, 1958), 3. Note that while Hosea is *not* the Psalms and the poetry is *not* quite the same, the point remains.

book. Those who have thought that the place name interpretation is certainly correct skate lightly over the lexical, grammatical, and literary difficulties that arise for it.[83]

Paul's construct of "in Adam" and "in Christ" (1 Cor 15:22) also supports a covenantal reading of Genesis. To be "in" someone is to be a member of that people for whom that someone is the covenantal representative (as I explain in ch. 11 below).

Jewish and Christian expositors have generally taken Adam and Eve to be real people, the physical first parents of all humankind—formed directly from the loose soil, with no intermediate steps between the dust and humankind. Certainly that fits most easily with the biblical statements themselves. At the same time, it is only right to acknowledge that the wording of Genesis 2 ("formed") is more open to other takes on the process than we might have first thought, since all humans are ultimately "formed from dust" (Ps 103:14, ESV margin). What is more, the wording of Genesis 4 has raised questions for some, such as: Where did Cain, Abel, and Seth get their wives, and of whom was Cain afraid? These questions have in their turn allowed some to wonder whether Genesis leaves room for a larger population than just two at the beginning of the human race.[84] This has taken on new relevance because it has become common among geneticists to infer not only that humans share common ancestry with the apes but also that the initial human population is much larger than two.

The overall shape of the story can accommodate such possibilities, though with limits (and perhaps some unease). For example, Athanasius's account of the fall, though it without question portrays Adam and Eve in the conventional manner, is actually stated in places in the plural, as for example:

> In this way, then, as has been said, did the Creator fashion *the human race* [τὸ τῶν ἀνθρώπων γένος, the race of human beings], and such did he wish it to remain. But *humankind* [οἱ ἄνθρωποι, "human beings"], contemptuous of the better things and shrinking from the apprehension of them, sought rather what was closer to themselves—and what was closer was the body and its sensations. (*Contra Gentes*, 3.1–5)[85]

---

83. So Peter Enns, *The Evolution of Adam: What the Bible Does and Doesn't Say about Human Origins* (Grand Rapids: Brazos, 2012), 83–84.

84. So, for example, Derek Kidner, *Genesis*, TOTC (Downers Grove, IL: InterVarsity Press, 1967), 26–31 (very tentatively). This can be meshed with the imaginative scenario in C. S. Lewis, *The Problem of Pain* (London: Geoffrey Bles, 1940), ch. 5 (Lewis calls it "a 'myth' in the Socratic sense, a not unlikely tale"), by having an actual Adam and Eve as the proper representatives of this population.

85. English based on Thomson, *Athanasius: Contra Gentes and De Incarnatione*.

One can propose scenarios, that is, ways of imagining the events, without committing oneself to the details of the picture: The goal is to show that a critical reading of the science need not falsify the broad outlines of the story. No doubt a better imagination can propose better scenarios. Those who follow the tradition of Jowett and Barr will find such efforts ad hoc and misguided: The simple biblical tale, they will assure us, cannot be reconciled with modern science, and its religious value must be found somewhere else than in history.[86] However, as I have argued here, the very issue is whether Jowett-esque literalism is actually the right way of reading Genesis on its own terms—and if I am right, then the production of scenarios is in fact responsible.

Finally, Paul presents the universal expectations of the promises to Abraham as being fulfilled in the era in which gentiles are coming in (Gal 3:8); he even tells gentile Christians that they have been made children of Abraham and thus share in Abraham's anticipated worldwide inheritance (Rom 4:12–13). Christian believers, both Jewish and gentile, are those in whom God is renewing his image for proper human functioning in their individual and community lives (e.g., Col 3:9–10; 2 Cor 3:18), where the fractured family is once again united. This assumes, first, that the image needs renewing—which implies something has gone wrong; and second, that the fracturing is likewise a distortion of the original scheme. We might add that Luke uses the Greek of Genesis 1:28 (Heb., "be fruitful and multiply"; Greek "increase and multiply") at several occasions in Acts to describe the advancing Christian message (Acts 6:7; 9:31; 12:24; 19:20), which thus portrays these Christians as heirs of the promises to Abraham. In the same way, 1 Peter 2:9 portrays the Christians (Jewish and gentile) as the proper heirs of the privileges of Israel (drawing on Exod 19:5–6 and other places).

Some have said that the story of Genesis 3 figures very little in the rest of the Hebrew Bible and that theological reflection on it comes much later (some even date it to Paul's letters).[87] Now, this is certainly incorrect for the literary features of Genesis itself, but it is also untrue to the very logic of the biblical story. The crucial components (allowing for the stylistic and rhetorical features we have considered) involve a common origin for humankind and a common predicament.

8.E THE FLOOD STORY

The flood story presents us with an interesting phenomenon, namely, that there is good evidence that New Testament writers knew and used versions

---

86. This is the burden of Enns, *The Evolution of Adam*.
87. Examples abound; one is Peter Enns, *The Evolution of Adam*, 81.

of that story from other peoples. That is, in some New Testament texts, the Greek words used to recount the flood story do not match what we have in the LXX, while they do match the Greek found in gentiles' flood stories.[88]

In the Hebrew Bible itself, the only explicit references to Noah and the flood are Isaiah 54:9 and Ezekiel 14:14, 20. Isaiah 54:9 uses God's promise after the great flood as an image for God's enduring commitment to preserve Zion. Ezekiel 14:14, 20 mentions Noah as a member of a trio of exemplary men (Noah, Daniel/Dan'el, and Job) whose righteousness would not be enough to bring God to deliver Jerusalem. If the theory be correct that the three righteous men here are non-Israelites from ancient times, then this passage from Ezekiel shows why a faithful Jew might willingly find connections between the biblical story of Noah and gentile stories of a flood and its pious survivor.[89]

From the Second Temple Jewish scene, the book of Wisdom of Solomon (10:4; 14:6) mentions the story, and Philo of Alexandria (*De Gigantibus*; *De Abrahamo*, 41–46; *De Praemis et Poenis*, 23) even identifies Noah with Deucalion, the hero of a Greek flood story. Josephus (*Ant.*, 1, 72–108 [1.3.1–9]; *Ag. Ap.*, 1, 130 [1.19]) explicitly compares the biblical account with other versions from the ancient Near East. The *Sibylline Oracles*, book 1, retells the biblical account in ways that seem to invite its audience to see parallels with Hesiod's *Works and Days*. Passing mentions appear in Ben Sira (40:10; 44:17–18), Tobit (4:12), 3 Maccabees (2:4–5), and 4 Maccabees (15:31).

---

88. I here draw on my essay, "Noah, Deucalion, and the New Testament," *Biblica* 93:3 (2012): 403–26.

89. The *ketiv* (written in the Hebrew text) at Ezek 14:14, 20; 28:3 has the consonants *dnyl*, while the *qere* (to be read aloud) has the consonants *dny'l* (to which the vowels correspond: *daniye'l*, the normal spelling of "Daniel"). Many students of Ezekiel suppose that the prophet meant someone named Dan'el, an ancient and non-Israelite figure to go along with Noah and Job. See, for example, J. W. Wevers, *Ezekiel*, NCB (Grand Rapids: Eerdmans, 1969), 115; W. Zimmerli, *Ezekiel, vol. 1*, Hermeneia (Philadelphia: Fortress, 1979 [1969]), 314–15; M. Greenberg, *Ezekiel 1–20*, Anchor Bible (New York: Doubleday, 1983), 257–58; and the very traditional Y. Moskovitz, *Sefer Yehezqel*, Da'at Miqra' (Jerusalem: Mossad Harav Kook, 1985), בפ. The person called Dan'il, found in the Ugaritic story of Aqhat, seems to fit the bill. He is one who "defended the rights of the widow, judged the case of the orphan" (*Aqhat* 17, v, 7–8; cf. Prov 31:9; Isa 1:17; *Keret* 16, vi, 33–34). The strongest argument against that identification is the disbelief that Ezekiel would commend "an idolatrous Baal-devotee," as discussed in Harold H. P. Dressler, "The Identification of the Ugaritic Dnil with the Daniel of Ezekiel," *VT* 29:2 (1979): 152–61; and idem, "Reading and Interpreting the Aqht Text," *VT* 34:1 (1984): 78–82. See also D. Block, *Ezekiel 1–24*, NICOT (Grand Rapids: Eerdmans, 1997), 447–49. Dressler would have us take this Daniel as the hero of the biblical book Daniel, "a wise and righteous contemporary" of Ezekiel. Strong arguments for the other side come from John Day, "The Daniel of Ugarit and Ezekiel and the Hero of the Book of Daniel," *VT* 30:2 (1980): 174–84; and B. Margalit, "Interpreting the Story of Aqht," *VT* 30:3 (1980): 361–65. Dressler's position would require the biblical Daniel to be well known to Ezekiel's audience as an exemplar of righteousness; and even on the traditionalist view of Daniel there is scant evidence for this. Further, the mention of Dan'el in connection with Tyre (Ezek 28:3) seems again to support the gentile interpretation. Further, perhaps Ezekiel knew the Dan'il of the Aqhat story from other sources besides the specific tale found at Ugarit. In addition, there is precedent in Gen 14:22 for the LORD accepting the title of a deity worshiped by pious-but-benighted gentiles; and this is plausible when we realize that the Ugaritic tale of Aqhat does not recount that he practiced any of the deeds a prophet would find abhorrent.

The New Testament texts are usually taken to be Matthew 24:37–39, Luke 17:26–27, Hebrews 11:7, 1 Peter 3:20, and 2 Peter 2:5; 3:6. Below I will show why I think Romans 8:21 should be added to the list.

We have ancient flood stories from Mesopotamia, and I have addressed them in chapter 7 above. Today we have them in their ancient editions and languages, but the Hellenistic world had access to these by way of Greek translations. In addition to these, we also have stories from the Greek and Roman world, and Plato gives us one version of it (to which Josephus may have alluded). Further, there is numismatic evidence that Asia Minor in the first century AD had some species of this story as well (perhaps related to Plato's version).

The wording of 1 Peter 3:20 and 2 Peter 2:4–5; 3:5–6 employs terms, in addition to those from the LXX of Genesis, found in Plato's flood stories (among other sources). Several of the church fathers who refer to the flood story connect Noah with Deucalion, as Philo had done (for example, Justin Martyr, *Second Apology*, 7.2; Theophilus of Antioch, *To Autolycus*, books 2 and 3); the tie with Plato supports this move. Eusebius especially, in several places in his *Preparation for the Gospel*, draws the connection not only with the Mesopotamian tales (as Josephus had done) but also with Plato's tale by name (see 9.11 [414-*abc*]; 10.9–10 [486-*c*, 488-*d*, 489-*b*]; 11.15 [588-*b*]).

These authors vary in their perception of the flood's extent. As I showed in chapter 7, Josephus even allows for the possibility of other survivors (at least, Louis Feldman—a highly regarded figure in Josephus studies—reads him this way). Theophilus, however, reads Genesis as describing a universal flood and therefore understands Plato's more localized flood story as incorrect (*To Autolycus*, 3.18–19). I do not see the date of the flood playing much of a role in any of these texts, and the physical extent is not a major factor (other than in Theophilus).

I suggest that the author(s) of 1–2 Peter makes these connections with other versions of the flood story because that will help the letters' audiences feel more deeply about the actuality of the event. That sense of actuality, of eventitude, enables the audience to strengthen their resolve for future faithfulness.

Romans 8:18–25 is often seen as Paul's version of the curses of Genesis 3, describing a world fallen from its innocence, but a number of problems should keep us from reading Paul as telling us how the world is fallen in its very workings. I will show why it is better to take it as an allusion to the flood narrative. Here is the passage:

> For I consider that the sufferings of this present time are not worth comparing with the glory that is to be revealed to us. For the creation

waits with eager longing for the revealing of the sons of God. For the creation was subjected to futility, not willingly, but because of him who subjected it, in hope that the creation itself will be set free from its bondage to corruption and obtain the freedom of the glory of the children of God. For we know that the whole creation has been groaning together in the pains of childbirth until now. And not only the creation, but we ourselves, who have the firstfruits of the Spirit, groan inwardly as we wait eagerly for adoption as sons, the redemption of our bodies. For in this hope we were saved. Now hope that is seen is not hope. For who hopes for what he sees? But if we hope for what we do not see, we wait for it with patience.

Many take the "corruption" to be a feature of the world itself due to human sin. For example, Thomas Schreiner asserts: "Slavery entails corruption, decay, and death, which pervade the natural world."[90] Denis Lamoureux agrees that this is Paul's position, though he prefers to treat it as "ancient biology" that has no bearing on the modern audience:

> Paul also believed that the natural world had changed with the divine judgment of Adam (this is termed the "Cosmic Fall"). He asserts, "The whole creation has been groaning" because it "was subjected to frustration" and is in "bondage to decay."
> Indeed, these are challenging passages to interpret. However, since Paul accepted an ancient biology of the origin of life, it is only consistent that he also accepted an ancient understanding of the origin of death, suffering, and decay.[91]

I do not agree, however, that this represents a good reading of the curses in Genesis 3, nor does it do proper justice to Paul's wording in Romans 8. Certainly Genesis 3:16–17 speak of pain featuring prominently in human experience, apparently of a kind that was not there before. Nevertheless, the words used in Genesis do not imply that some change has taken place in the way the creation works. Rather, the term "cursed" in Genesis 3:17; 4:11; 5:29 (Hebrew √ארר ['rr']) appears in Deuteronomy 28:17–18, where curses fall upon the basket, kneading bowl, the fruit of the womb, the fruit of the ground, the increase of the herds, and the young of the flock. Then the related noun, "curse" (Heb. מארה, *me'erah*), appears in 28:20:

---

90. Thomas Schreiner, *Romans*, BECNT (Grand Rapids: Baker Academic, 1998), 436.
91. Denis Lamoureux, "No Historical Adam: Evolutionary Creation View," 62.

The LORD will send on you curses, confusion, and frustration in all that you undertake to do, until you are destroyed and perish quickly on account of the evil of your deeds, because you have forsaken me.

Verses 38–46 detail the outworking of this. Nowhere does it imply that somehow human sin has distorted the workings of the natural elements. Rather, agriculture is the arena in which God brings his chastisement upon human beings.

When the man sinned, God banished him from the garden "to work the ground from which he was taken" (Gen 3:23)—a place that naturally produces "thorns and thistles" (3:18). The problem with thorns and thistles is that they cannot feed humans, though other creatures may be glad to feast on them. The account never implies that the ground did not produce thorns and thistles prior to this point; instead it indicates that working the ground is to be the arena of pain—and this is due not to a change in the properties of the ground but to the change in humanity and to God's purposes of chastisement.[92] There is no indication that human dominion over the creation has been rescinded, but there is every indication that humans will exercise it badly—exploiting and damaging the creation and using it to exploit and damage other people.

If Paul had Genesis 3 in mind, his Greek makes no explicit allusion to Genesis 3:16–19 (LXX). The closest we get is "groaning" (vv. 22, 23), which may evoke Genesis 3:16, which in the LXX says, "I will surely multiply your pains and your groaning"—but this is uncertain. The important term "pain" (Gen 3:16, 17; עצבון ['*itsabon*] / λύπη) is missing from this passage in Romans, and the word "groaning" is common enough in the LXX (compare Exod 2:24). We therefore have very little ground for supposing that Genesis 3:16 influenced Paul's word choice here. Nor does Romans 8 make any mention of a "curse." The term "futility" (Rom 8:20), if it has a background in the Hebrew Bible at all, would evoke Ecclesiastes, since that is the Greek term for the refrain-like "vanity of vanities."

On the other hand, the theme of the creation (that is, the non-human material world) looking forward to the time when the children of God are revealed in glory—which will happen in their eternal state, in their glory—certainly runs through Paul's text. Further, the fall of humankind did indeed

---

92. For "thorns and thistles" together, see Hos 10:8, where "thorns and thistles shall grow up on their altars"; there it is because the altars are overthrown and abandoned, which supports the view that it is a picture of the land being unfruitful for man. See further along these lines Matt 7:16; Heb 6:8.

have its impact on the created world, according to Genesis. Man was made to have dominion over the creation and to bring the blessings of Eden through all the earth and has fallen from the task, though not from the dominion. Looked at this way, we should not take "futility" as a reference to Ecclesiastes but "as denoting the ineffectiveness of that which does not attain its goal, . . . so long as man the chief actor in the drama of God's praise fails to contribute his rational part."[93]

Let us come back to that key term, "corruption," in Romans 8:21 (φθορά). Its related verb first appears in the LXX of Genesis 6:11–13:

> Now the earth was corrupt [ἐφθάρη] in God's sight, and the earth was filled with wrong-doing. And God saw the earth, and behold, it was corrupt [κατεφθαρμένη], for all flesh had corrupted [κατέφθειρεν] their way on the earth. And God said to Noah, "The time of all flesh has come before me, for the earth is filled with wrong-doing from them. Behold, I will destroy [καταφθείρω] them with the earth.[94]

Seen this way, the creation is in bondage to corruption not because of changes in the way it works but because of the corruption of humankind; and in response to man's corruption God brings corruption to (or destroys) the earth to chastise man. The creation is subjected to futility because it has sinful mankind in it, and thus it is the arena in which humankind expresses its sin and experiences God's judgments. No wonder it "waits with eager longing for the revealing of the sons of God" (Rom 8:19), for then the sons of God will be perfect in holiness and sin will be no more. Paul here portrays the resurrection of the sons of God as a blessing, not only for themselves but also for the whole creation.

I suggest that the position I offer—of finding an allusion to the flood rather than to the curses of the fall—is more consistent with Paul's focus on human glorification and with the picture of Genesis, which does not view the created world as changed in its workings but as the arena in which God works out his purposes for humankind. In other words, finding an echo of the flood story here illuminates Paul's text.[95]

---

93. C. E. B. Cranfield, *Romans*, ICC (Edinburgh: T&T Clark, 1975), I:413–14.

94. The simple verb φθείρω appears in Gen 6:11 LXX, while verses 12–13 use the compound verb καταφθείρω. The word translated "destroy" in verse 13 is actually the same verb, the LXX reflecting a wordplay in the Hebrew.

95. For the argument that Paul alludes to the Noah story in Rom 1:16–32, see C. John Collins, "Echoes of Aristotle in Romans 2:14–15: Or, maybe Abimelech was not so bad after all," *Journal of Markets and Morality* 13.1 (2010): 123–73, especially pp. 148–51.

8.F GENESIS AND HELLENISTIC SCIENCE

In chapter 9 I argue that it would be a mistake to suppose that the biblical writers laid out a picture of the world, primitive or otherwise. Science as we think of it plays no role in their descriptions of the world. At the same time, we must face, frankly, the fact that it became common for some Second Temple Jews (such as Philo and Josephus) and church fathers to associate the biblical statements with the dominant scientific perspectives of their day, namely, the cosmologies of Plato and Aristotle. Further, when it came to computations of the earth's age, these authors argued for what we would call a very low number (which was different from the number that Archbishop James Ussher famously posited).

Surely these indicate that the literalists are right, after all? I suggest instead that this argument misses the social situation in the Hellenistic world and the pressures that situation put on groups like the Jews and Christians. It also fails to appreciate the way that scientific theorizing developed among Greek speakers.

A reader of the ancient philosophers, of whom Plato and Aristotle were the prime examples, will be struck at how they work their theories out. They begin with an observation, stated in ordinary language, and, taking that as true, proceed to take it further.[96] One can see this at work in Eusebius's record of theories about the sun, moon, and stars (*Preparation for the Gospel*, book 15, chs. 23–31), based entirely on observations from the ground—what else could they do? Does the moon have light of its own? What are these bodies made of? And so forth. Sometimes they rest content with the phenomenal, apparently without being aware that they should distinguish between what something looks like and what it is, as in the back-and-forth over whether the moon has its own light or reflects light from the sun (book 15, ch. 29). They were no fools; when a popular tale conflicted with careful testing, they said so. I note in chapter 9 that Aristotle corrected a popular misconception about how the weasel conceives through its ears and gives birth through its mouth, a misconception that some philosophers (including Anaxagoras) had carried forth: This view was due to "insufficient evidence and inadequate consideration" (Aristotle, *Gen. an.*, 3.6 [756b]).

Alexander the Great's conquest of the Near East brought into being a situation in which the élites were culturally Greek, and thus Greek thought

---

96. For a survey of how Greek philosophers developed their theories of cosmology, see Keimpe Algra, "The Beginnings of Cosmology," in *The Cambridge Companion to Early Greek Philosophy*, ed. A. A. Long (Cambridge: Cambridge University Press, 1999), 45–65.

came to wield the highest cultural prestige. Jews found themselves in between two Hellenistic powers, the Seleucid Empire in Mesopotamia and the Ptolemaic in Egypt, which warred over control of Palestine. The Seleucids in fact persecuted the Jews, if the books of the Maccabees are to be believed. In these contexts, cultural marginalization is always a very real threat. Josephus shows himself aware of this in the Greco-Roman world and thus tells the story (in Book 11 of his *Antiquities*) of Cyrus, the Persian king, reading the passages of Isaiah that, as the Jews told it, foretold Cyrus's success before the temple was even destroyed. Later in the same book Josephus tells of Zerubbabel's intellectual exploits in the court of the Persian king Darius: In a debate among the courtiers about what is strongest, Zerubbabel demonstrates that "truth" is the answer. The Letter of Aristeas presents the Ptolemaic king's regard for the Jews and for their Scriptures and has the Jewish scholars discoursing wisely on the philosophical questions put to them in the Egyptian court. A perusal of Menahem Stern's collection will supply further examples—not only of the calumnies that Josephus cited and replied to but also other sources that portrayed Jews negatively (such as Diodorus Siculus, Cicero, Seneca, Quintilian, Martial, and Plutarch) and a few admirers (such as Varro and Strabo).[97]

It is therefore no wonder that Jewish authors made certain moves in such a setting. For example, Aristobulus, the earliest named Jewish philosopher (probably second century BC), is also the earliest known source for the idea that Plato and Pythagoras got their wisdom from reading Moses. This becomes a commonplace, and Eusebius (who preserved the extant fragments of Aristobulus's writing) endorses it.[98] Plato himself attributed the beginnings of philosophy to the Egyptians (*Timaeus*, 21-*b*—22-*a*), and Herodotus also mentioned the influence of the Near East on Greek culture (*Hist.*, 1.170.3; 2.49.3; 2.58.1; 2.109.3; 5.57.1)—thus the Hellenistic culture itself provided the pegs on which to hang the Jewish idea.

The line of thought obviously shows that Hellenistic philosophy was held in high regard. Therefore, it is no surprise that Josephus might sneak in a connection. In his *Antiquities* (1.30 [1.1.1]) he described the "expanse" with a Greek term, κρύσταλλον, meaning either a "crystalline" or "icy" surface. This, as it turns out, is just the way that the pre-Socratic Greek philosopher Empedocles described the heavens in a couple of fragments preserved in Eusebius's *Preparation for the Gospel* (15.30 [839-*a*]; 15.42 [845-*b*]).[99] Nothing

---

97. Menahem Stern, *Greek and Latin Authors on Jews and Judaism, volume 1: From Herodotus to Plutarch* (Jerusalem: Israel Academy of Sciences and Humanities, 1976).

98. See Eusebius, *Praep. ev.*, 13.12.

99. Ibid., 15.42 [845-*b*], quoting Plutarch. Also see *Diogenes Laertius*, 8.77.

in the Hebrew text or the LXX required Josephus to be this specific, but if his goal was to establish the intellectual respectability of the Hebrew Bible (and thus of Judaism)—a goal that surely played a part in his presentation—then this was a good and subtle way to do it. Moses had anticipated Empedocles by centuries.[100] In view of the origin of philosophical cosmologies, there is no mystery as to how the Jews and Christians could correlate their holy books with that cosmology nor in why they would do so. Further, the philosophers at some point achieved enough prestige that no educated person could imagine the heavens except through the picture the cosmologists had provided. Certainly the Jewish and Christian writers took the biblical statements as referential and true, so their relating of such statements to the theories is understandable.

In this setting one can derive advantage from having the oldest wisdom. As an aged Egyptian priest says in Plato's *Timaeus* (22-*b*), "O Solon, Solon, you Greeks are ever children. . . . You are all young in your souls, for you have not in them . . . any ancient belief." Herodotus records that the Egyptians had once thought themselves the oldest people group, until they ascertained that the Phrygians were (*Hist.*, 2.2); certainly it mattered who could claim the most antiquity. In particular, the Jews had to counter the charge that they were the newcomers and thus unworthy of respect.[101] As Theophilus of Antioch put it (*To Autolycus*, 3.30),

> But the Greeks make no mention of the histories which give the truth first [found in the Hebrew Bible], *because they themselves only recently became partakers of the knowledge of letters*; and they themselves own it, alleging that letters were invented, some say among the Chaldeans, and others with the Egyptians, and others again say that they are derived from the Phoenicians.

Theophilus sought to show "the antiquity of our books" (3.1) and that Christian doctrine is "more ancient and true than all poets and authors who have written with uncertainty" (3.16; see also 3.20, 23, 26). Thus, he adds up the numbers from the genealogies of Genesis 5 and 11 (using the LXX); he also proceeds to use the figures from the rest of Genesis and the Hebrew historical books to calculate the time from creation to the death of Emperor

---

100. Occasionally our ancient authors exhibit literary sensitivity. For example, in the midst of presenting the philosophers' debates over cosmological questions, Eusebius casually comments, "But Moses and the Hebrew oracles waste no labour on any of these matters" (*Praep. ev.*, 15.25 [837-*c*]).

101. As James Barr recognized; see his "Pre-Scientific Chronology: The Bible and the Origin of the World," *Proceedings of the American Philosophical Society* 143:3 (1999), 379–87, especially p. 380.

Aurelius Verus (Marcus Aelius Aurelius Verus, d. AD 180) as "5698 years, and the odd months and days" (3.28).

The chronological calculations in these authors, then, are designed to place the Hebrew Scriptures earlier than anything the Greeks or Romans were aware of. Of course, no one today can repeat this same tack. These authors were aware of Berossus, who translated Mesopotamian lore into Greek. We are now able to say that Berossus's sources are far older than the most conservative dates for Moses. Further, no canonical author makes this kind of argument, so no one among the faithful need feel obligated to defend it.

Chapter 9

GENESIS 1–11: WORLD PICTURE AND WORLDVIEW

*I*n chapter 4 I distinguished between world*view* and world *picture*. This distinction helps us in that the specifics of the big story need not depend heavily on the details of the world picture. No doubt that can be too simple, since a big story may, consciously or not, presuppose a particular shape of the world and the items in it.

I have argued that the purpose of Genesis 1–11 is to provide the beginning of the big story for the people of Israel (and, as Christians say, for them too) and thus to lay a foundation for the biblical worldview. Here we will consider whether the biblical materials, especially Genesis, teach or affirm a world picture as well. If we find that it does, we can go on to consider the degree to which its details are bound up in our taking Genesis 1–11 as good-faith communication.

Using our discussion of how communication works (chs. 2–4), we can see that a world picture can operate on at least three levels for an author:

(a) the rhetorical act of *characterization*, in which the author asks the audience to picture things a certain way;
(b) the cognitive act of *conceptualization*, in which the author actually holds to what he counts as an accurate description of the things portrayed;
(c) the illocutionary event of *commitment*, in which an author not only embraces for himself a particular conceptualization but also invites the audience to embrace that conceptualization.

I have already shown how an author's own conceptualization need not require a commitment on the audience's part for good-faith communication and compliance (witness the example of a potion that will affect one's humors). What is more, in the case of the Old Testament it will be difficult to ascertain with certainty an author's precise and theoretical conceptualization of many things in the world, since ordinary and poetic language do not lend themselves to expressing such things. The text as a social act, and not the whole array of things an author thought, is our access point to authorial intention.

You could not know anyone's theory of the movements of the solar system simply from his or her use of the conventional expressions "sunrise" and "sunset"; you cannot even tell if the person has a theory of any sort. And, should you decide that the speaker has a formal theory of a stationary earth with a circulating sun, you do not need to embrace the theory in most ordinary or poetic communications: "sunrise comes later during the winter" is a clear and even accurate sentence for most purposes, regardless of the world-picture beliefs of the one saying it. Similarly, if a medieval person told us, "The barbarians attacked as the sun rose, and the battle continued until the sun set," we would in almost all cases allow his statement to be true, so long as there was a real attack and the fight lasted throughout the daylight. Even if the reporter were a scholar, whose conceptualization of the cosmos we knew, we could not fault him: The events at either end of the daylight are real, and sunrise and sunset are appropriate ways of referring to them. The fact that the reporter takes the terms as literal physical descriptions has no bearing on his historical truthfulness (except in those rare cases in which he requires his audience to subscribe to his physical picture).

These thoughts will help us to navigate arguments such as those put forward by John Walton, a specialist in ancient Near Eastern backgrounds of the Hebrew Bible: "I acknowledge that most Jews in the first century would have believed that all people descended from Adam; but they also believed the world was flat."[1] Now, Walton supplies no references to back up his claim about first-century Jews, and he fails to distinguish between a scholar (who might well have learned what philosophers thought) and a peasant (who probably had no view on the subject at all); I will comment on the subject below. But no text that I know of asks us to embrace a physical description of the world's flatness, and, in the event that a particular author might have held such a view, it plays no part in one's ability to speak truthfully about the past.

Therefore, for a biblical author to teach or affirm a world picture, we will need to see how the picture is embedded in the communicative act.

---

1. John Walton, "A Historical Adam: Archetypal Creation View," in *Four Views on the Historical Adam and Eve*, ed. Matthew Barrett and Ardel Caneday (Grand Rapids: Zondervan, 2013), 89–118, quote on p. 108.

9.A WHAT IS THE SHAPE OF THE WORLD?

Many writers on the Old Testament, from skeptics to critical believers, and some traditional believers as well, consider it obvious that the Old Testament, taken as a whole, affirms an ancient world picture, such as this one in the United Bible Societies' *Handbook on Genesis*, written by William Reyburn and Euan Fry, which has a picture of an "early concept of the universe."[2]

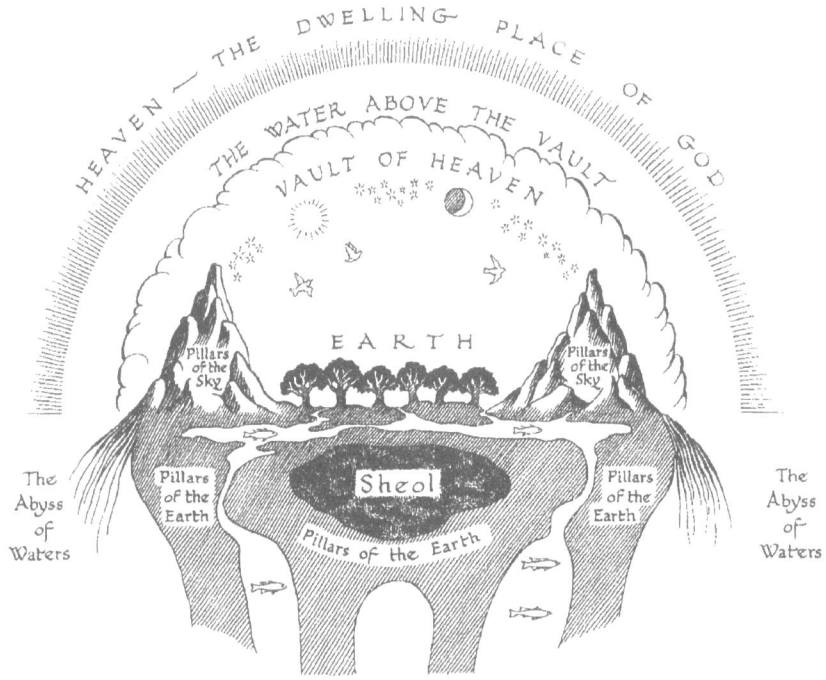

EARLY CONCEPT OF THE UNIVERSE
© United Bible Societies, 1997

In this picture we have a flat earth, with mountainous pillars at either end, and the (solid) vault of heaven under which the sun, moon, and stars travel, with water above it. Below the land lie the pillars of the earth and the subterranean waters (with Sheol at the very center), and the abyss of waters

---

2. William D. Reyburn and Euan McG. Fry, *Handbook on Genesis* (London: United Bible Societies, 1997), 27 (used with permission). Compare a similar picture in Enns, *Inspiration and Incarnation*, 54. See also Robin Parry, *The Biblical Cosmos: A Pilgrim's Guide to the Weird and Wonderful World of the Bible* (Eugene, OR: Cascade, 2014). John Roberts, "Biblical Cosmology: The Implications for Bible Translation," *Journal of Translation* 9:2 (2013), opens his article by saying, "the creation account in Gen 1:1–2:3 depicts a conceptual metaphor of the cosmos that is largely concordant with the cosmologies of ancient Mesopotamia and ancient Egypt" (1), but he does not explore this as a rhetorical possibility, tending to associate the *conceptions* in a physical way.

off to each side. The lists of biblical texts to which these authors, and many others, commonly refer include:

Psalm 104:2–3, 5–9:
> covering yourself with light as with a garment,
>   *stretching out the heavens like a tent.*
> He *lays the beams of his chambers on the waters*;
> he makes the clouds his chariot;
>   he rides on the wings of the wind; . . .
> He *set the earth on its foundations*,
>   so that it should *never be moved.*
> You covered it with the deep as with a garment;
>   *the waters stood above the mountains.*
> At your rebuke they fled;
>   at the sound of your thunder they took to flight.
> The mountains rose, the valleys sank down
>   to the place that you appointed for them.
> You set a boundary that they may not pass,
>   so that they might not again cover the earth.

Psalm 148:4:
> Praise him, you highest heavens,
>   and you *waters above the heavens*!

Job 26:11:
> The *pillars of heaven* tremble
>   and are astounded at his rebuke.

Job 37:18:
> Can you, like him, *spread out the skies,*
>   *hard* as a cast metal mirror?

Job 38:4–11:
> Where were you when I *laid the foundation of the earth*?
>   Tell me, if you have understanding.
> Who determined its measurements—surely you know!
>   Or who *stretched the line* upon it?
> On what were *its bases* sunk,
>   or who laid *its cornerstone,*

> when *the morning stars sang together*
>> and all the sons of God shouted for joy?
> Or who *shut in the sea with doors*
>> when it burst out from the womb,
> when I made clouds its garment
>> and thick darkness its swaddling band,
> and prescribed limits for it
>> and *set bars and doors*,
> and said, "Thus far shall you come, and no farther,
>> and here shall your proud waves be stayed"?

Proverbs 8:28–29:
> when he *made firm the skies* above,
>> when he *established the fountains of the deep*,
> when he assigned to the sea its limit,
>> so that the waters might not transgress his command,
> when he marked out the foundations of the earth,

Amos 9:6:
> who *builds his upper chambers in the heavens*
>> and *founds his vault upon the earth*;
> who calls for the waters of the sea
>> and *pours them out upon the surface of the earth*—
> the Lord is his name.

A "straightforward" reading of these texts supports the picture. In this light, the "expanse" as a solid that will "separate the waters from the waters" makes perfect sense, as do the "lights" set in the expanse (Gen 1:6, 17). Thus, we have Goodwin and Jowett's verdict on Genesis 1.

In fact, we are told, the apostles follow the same world picture. Consider how Paul writes about Jesus in Philippians 2:6–11:

> who, though he was in the form of God, did not count equality with God a thing to be grasped, but emptied himself, by taking the form of a servant, being born in the likeness of men. And being found in human form, he humbled himself by becoming obedient to the point of death, even death on a cross. Therefore God has highly exalted him and bestowed on him the name that is above every name, so that at the name of Jesus every knee should bow, *in heaven and on earth and under*

the earth, and every tongue confess that Jesus Christ is Lord, to the glory of God the Father.

Verse 10 is as clear an affirmation of the ancient three-decker picture of the universe as we could ask for, is it not?[3]

But the prior question of what constitutes a straightforward reading of these texts is never raised. That comes as no surprise for a scholar who subscribes to the Jowett-esque hermeneutic; but I do find it surprising that linguistically oriented writers such as Reyburn and Fry would offer no reflection at all on the poetic nature of these passages or on the proper communicative intent of them.[4] The fact that all of these texts are poetic ought to have given pause.

In addition to the passages already listed, consider the texts about the "pillars of the earth" (1 Sam 2:8; Ps 75:3) or the "four corners of the earth" (Job 37:3; Isa 11:12; 41:9; Rev 7:1; 20:8). All are poetic, and not a single one requires the author or audience to commit themselves to a literal world picture in order to perform a good-faith communication.

Exodus 20:4, which forbids "any likeness of anything that is in heaven above, or that is in the earth beneath, or that is in the water under the earth," is rhetorically high but probably more like ordinary language than poetic. Many take "the water under the earth" to refer to the subterranean waters. It is actually easier to connect it with the parallel in Deuteronomy 4:18 ("the likeness of any fish that is in the water under the earth") and discern that the idea is simply the common-sense observation that the level of the water is below the level of the surrounding land. It is also possible, however, that the usage is a concession *arguendo*: that is, those who use such images fancy that they are representing subterranean deities.[5] Such fancies were indeed a part of Israel's world, but this does not entail an endorsement of a physical world picture.

---

3. Such is the view of Denis Lamoureux, *Evolution? Scripture and Nature say Yes!* (Grand Rapids: Zondervan, 2016), 90–91.

4. An author who publishes in conservative venues and suffers from the same sort of language confusion is Paul H. Seely, as in his "The Firmament and the Water Above, Part I: The Meaning of *raqia'* in Gen 1:6–8," *WTJ* 53 (1991): 227–40; idem, "The Firmament and the Water Above, Part II: The Meaning of 'the Water above the Firmament' in Gen 1:6–8," *WTJ* 54 (1992): 31–46; and idem, "The Geographical Meaning of 'Earth' and 'Seas' in Genesis 1:10," *WTJ* 59 (1997): 231–55. See also Ellen van Wolde, "'Creation Out of Nothing' and the Hebrew Bible," in *Creation Stories in Dialogue: The Bible, Science, and Folk Traditions*, ed. R. Alan Culpepper and Jan G. van der Watt (Leiden: Brill, 2016), 157–76.

5. As Umberto Cassuto, *Commentary on the Book of Exodus* (Jerusalem: Magnes, 1983 [1951]), 242, suggests, "there is a deliberate antithesis here to a practice already existent in the world, particularly in Egypt."

The same factors will apply to whether the biblical texts suggest that the earth has limits of some sort, that is, that the earth cannot be a sphere. After all, the common Hebrew expression for the uttermost reaches of the earth is קְצֵה־אֶרֶץ [*qetseh-'erets*, "the end of the earth"], using a word that might imply a physical end or boundary (as in Exod 16:35, the "border" of the land of Canaan, or Num 33:37, the "edge" of the land of Edom). But as it turns out, the term is widely spread, apparently conventional, and carries no physical assertion with it—as can be seen by the idiomatic and untroubled "ends of the earth" in modern educated English. This seems straightforward, simply from our previous discussion of language types. We can supply some confirmatory evidence as well: We find little to no serious conflict among Jews over whether the earth was spherical—a position well established by the Greek philosophers Plato and Aristotle—nor about other geographical matters as Jews encountered the Hellenistic world. That is, these readers likely did not take the biblical materials as making claims about the shape of the world.[6]

The literary form and language level show us that the passages are imagistic or phenomenal, that is, they do not have the intention of drawing a map. Rather, they manage to refer successfully (everyone can readily identify what they are describing), and they invite the reader to picture the items *as if* they were as described. The presence of anachronism, as discussed in chapter 6, does not defeat the effort to refer successfully and appropriately—because a good audience knows not to seek the wrong sort of information from it.

Consider another alleged feature of the Hebrew world picture, namely, the stationary earth. In chapter 1 I cited the English Egyptologist Charles Goodwin, who insisted:

> The Hebrew records, the basis of religious faith, *manifestly countenanced the opinion of the earth's immobility* and certain other views of the universe very incompatible with those propounded by Copernicus.[7]

Many others have read the biblical materials as portraying a stationary earth, more in line with the Ptolemaic system of cosmology than with the

---

6. To be sure, some important church fathers did speak as if they took the world to be a flat disk—most notably Athanasius, *Contra Gentes*, §§ 29, 36. Now, Athanasius's exact words do not *have to be* read this way, and he does not make a *biblical* argument for this position. Further, he shows an awareness of Plato's cosmology, so it is always possible that *geocentricity* is his point, rather than the shape of the earth.

7. Charles W. Goodwin, "On the Mosaic Cosmogony," in *Essays and Reviews*, Frederick Temple, Rowland Williams, Baden Powell, Henry Bristow Wilson, C. W. Goodwin, Mark Pattison, and Benjamin Jowett (London: John W. Parker and Son, 1860) 207–53, quote on p. 207 (emphasis added).

post-Copernican (which we hold to be truer).[8] The texts come primarily from the Psalms rather than from Genesis, but since the whole picture is held to be pervasive through the Bible, it is worth our attention.

We start with Psalm 93:1:

> The LORD reigns; he is robed in majesty;
>   the LORD is robed; he has put on strength as his belt.
> Yes, the world is established; *it shall never be moved.*

Psalms 96:10 and 104:5 are quite similar. We are told that to call these metaphorical or phenomenal is simply an effort to avoid the obvious meaning in which the psalmists assert physical immobility of the earth. For example, the Christian philosopher Nicholas Wolterstorff finds these texts to reflect "the geocentric cosmology widely shared among the peoples of antiquity. The author expresses this cosmology in his discourse; it's part of what he actually says."[9] Wolterstorff suggests that we can still employ this as divine speech if we look at the function the locution plays in the discourse, which the erroneous idea does not prevent it from performing.[10] No one making this kind of point ever hesitates over whether he or she has read the ancient text correctly.

The fact that these biblical statements occur in *psalms*—that is, in poems composed for public singing or chanting—should lend support to the idea that physical cosmology is unlikely to be the concern of the psalmists or the singing congregations. (I took up the story of how these texts came to be associated with cosmology in ch. 8.)

But there is an even more straightforward way of assessing this insistence, one that is rarely taken. We can look in the Psalms and see what kinds of things are said not to be moved to get an idea of what the verb means in this kind of context.[11] The Hebrew verbal root is מוט [*mwt*]: When used in the *niphal* it is rendered "be moved," "be shaken," or "slip" (of feet or steps). The result is revealing: The other things that do or do not move in Psalms include the *person* (10:6; 13:4; 15:5; 16:8; 21:7; 30:6; 55:22; 62:2, 6; 112:6); a *kingdom*,

---

8. These texts figured in the controversies over Copernicus's proposals for astronomy. See Edward Grant, *In Defense of the Earth's Immobility: Scholastic Reaction to Copernicanism in the Seventeenth Century* (Philadelphia: American Philosophical Society, 1984), 61–63, which provides the theological and exegetical part of that discussion.

9. Nicholas Wolterstorff, *Divine Discourse: Philosophical Reflections on the Claim that God Speaks* (Cambridge: Cambridge University Press, 1995), 209.

10. See Wolterstorff's whole discussion, *Divine Discourse*, 209–16.

11. I have found only one author besides myself who has taken this seemingly obvious tack, namely Alexander McCaul in *Aids to Faith: A Series of Theological Essays by Several Writers, Being a Reply to "Essays and Reviews,"* ed. William Thomson (New York: Appleton, 1862), 253–54 (although not at the same level of detail as here).

such as Zion, the land of Israel, or gentile powers (46:5, compare vv. 2, 6 ["totter"]; 60:2; 82:5; 125:1); and *feet* or *steps* (17:5; 38:16; 66:9; 94:18; 121:3). In other words, the Hebrew term might be rendered "be unstable" with the context pointing to what kind of instability is in view. And, of course, the stability of the world under God's governance—which is deeply relevant to Psalms 93, 96, and 104—is perfectly suited to be the subject of a song in corporate worship. Physical immobility has no bearing in such a context and to find it there is a misreading.

9.B DOES THE SUN "RISE"?

The relative motions of the sun and earth provide a similar topic. Biblical expressions translated "sunrise," we are told, involve a world picture in which the earth is static and the sun physically moves around it.[12] We will not delay ourselves with any discussion of relativistic mechanics, in which stationary is not meaningful; nor will we stop to remind ourselves that what is called Copernican astronomy is no longer considered correct.

We begin by examining the terms that biblical authors used. Hebrew has two common expressions for the sun rising. The noun for "sun" (שמש, *shemesh*) joins with the verb "come forth" (יצא, *yatsa'*: e.g., Gen 19:23; Judg 5:31) or, more often "to shine forth" (זרח, *zarah*: e.g., Gen 32:32; Exod 22:3).[13] Both of these verbs have derived nouns as well. There is one verb for "the sun sets": "go or enter" (בוא, *bo'*) with its derived noun. The usual Greek rendering for sunrise uses the verb ἀνατέλλω (with its cognate noun ἀνατολή), while sunset commonly uses the verb δύνω (and cognate noun δυσμή). The New Testament authors use the LXX terms (as in Matt 5:35; 13:6; Mark 1:32).

The first thing to say is that the degree to which these verbs strongly imply motion is small; "to shine forth" hardly does so at all[14] and "to enter" (*bô'*) is a fairly bland term. These terms are, to be sure, compatible with a number of physical images by which a speaker might portray the scene in his or her mind, but there is no passage in which the portrayal corresponds to an actual physical model. The usage is so widely spread and so consistent that we can only with difficulty avoid the conclusion that it is conventional; and conventionality serves the purpose of ready reference without being concerned

---

12. See, for example, Lamoureux, *Evolution: Scripture and Nature Say Yes!*, 86–87.
13. Lexica may give "rise" as the sense of the verb (so BDB, 280a), but, since it can be used for a "leprous" spot (2 Chron 26:19), "shine forth" represents the sense better.
14. What is treated as its Greek rendering, ἀνατέλλω, appears in 1 Macc 9:23, where the "doers of injustice *appeared*;" perhaps this might be "sprang up," but the element of motion is absent—or at least quite subdued.

with a physical model. One evidence for this is the way that, for example, Greek ἀνατολή ("rising") and δυσμή ("setting, sinking") become words for "east" and "west": Motion plays no part. Suppose, however, we were to persist in our literalism or that we heard someone we knew to hold a Ptolemaic world picture (such as a medieval natural philosopher) use these terms to refer to particular events. Would that person have been successful in his effort to communicate to us about real events? Probably.

We have also seen that many have realized that the audience of the Pentateuch is popular and rustic—that is, an audience like those medieval persons Lewis described: "ditchers and alewives who ... did not know that the earth was spherical; not because they thought it was flat but because they did not think about it at all."[15] In such a case, the way of referring will likely be conventional, combined with poetic portrayal, without an interest in physical details (much like C. S. Lewis's usage of "candlestick," mentioned in ch. 4).

9.C WHERE DOES THE RAIN COME FROM?

For another example, let's consider the separation of the waters described in Genesis 1:6–8:

> And God said, "Let there be an expanse in the midst of the waters, and let it separate the waters from the waters." And God made the expanse and separated the waters that were under the expanse from the waters that were above the expanse. And it was so. And God called the expanse Heaven. And there was evening and there was morning, the second day.

Many find this to imply a picture in which there is an actual body of water above the "expanse" (Heb. רקיע, *raqiaʿ*), which is taken to be a solid (see also Ps 148:4),[16] often on the basis of a literalistic etymological argument. This argument notes the connection of the noun רקיע [*raqiaʿ*] to the verbal root רקע [*rqʿ*], which can refer to stamping out, spreading out, or beating out (to make a metal overlay). Semantically, however, we must distinguish between *sense* and *reference*: The sense of the verb seems to be "to extend something," with a variety of applications (or referents). Further, we should be mindful of Martin Joos's rule of thumb that he called his "Semantic axiom

---

15. Lewis, *The Discarded Image*, 20.
16. See, for example, Paul Seely, "The Firmament and the Water Above, Part I: The Meaning of *raqiaʿ* in Gen 1:6–8," and idem, "The Firmament and the Water Above, Part II: The Meaning of 'the Water above the Firmament' in Gen 1:6–8."

number one": for the sense of a word we seek that which contributes the least to its context (which is another way of minding the distinction between sense, contributed by the word, and reference, contributed by the context).[17] With these in mind we can say that the word *raqia‛* does have the sense of "surface," with the context identifying what kind of surface. Hence the conventional "expanse" suits the word just fine.[18]

The most important piece of evidence is the passage in The Babylonian Epic of Creation that describes what Marduk did to the body of Tiamat after he defeated and slew her (Tablet IV):

> l. 137 He sliced her in half like a fish for drying:
> l. 138 Half of her he put up to roof the sky,
> l. 139 Drew a bolt across and made a guard hold it.
> l. 140 Her waters he arranged so that they could not escape.[19]

No doubt this too portrays waters held back by a firm surface that had been formed from half of Tiamat's body. Now, we have already seen that there are legitimate questions as to whether this Babylonian Epic is a fitting comparison to the Genesis story; and, if it is, in what form its material might have been known to ordinary Hebrews (it did not become a regulative text in Babylon until the first millennium BC). Let us simply allow, *arguendo*, that the story in some form has some bearing in providing a background against which Genesis spoke, assuming that the story predates the written versions we have. The Babylonian text cannot be said to be scientific in any way; it should be clear that drawing a physical picture is not the text's purpose.[20]

In our audience-critical examination (ch. 5), I simply asserted that the Pentateuch texts assume that their ideal audiences have some grasp of the connection between clouds and rain as the means by which water comes from the heavens and postponed demonstration until later. Let us come back to that here.

It comes as no surprise that the Pentateuch assumes that its peasant audience has a clear grasp of certain fundamentals about the weather and the indispensable place of water in supporting crops and livestock. For example, they recollect the climate of Egypt, in which they had to water crops by

---

17. Martin Joos, "Semantic Axiom Number One," *Language* 48:2 (1972): 257–65.
18. For examples of what I take to be unsatisfactory lexical argument, see Ellen van Wolde, "'Creation Out of Nothing' and the Hebrew Bible," 161–62; Lamoureux, *Evolution: Scripture and Nature Say Yes!*, 97–98.
19. Dalley, *Myths from Mesopotamia*, 255. See also Heidel, *The Babylonian Genesis*, 42–43.
20. See Noel Weeks, "Cosmology in Historical Context," *WTJ* 68 (2006): 283–93.

irrigation (Deut 11:10). That climate supplies its water primarily by its rivers and streams, with rain being a small factor. In contrast, the Palestinian climate provides a clear sequence of seasons, with early rains in the fall and later rain in the late winter and early spring, followed by the dry season; the land "drinks water by the rain from heaven" (Deut 11:11–17).[21] The fruitfulness of the land depends on the reliability of this cycle: for rain not to fall is a disaster (see also Lev. 26:4; Deut. 28:24),[22] while for it to fall during the dry season is equally ruinous (1 Sam 12:17—rain falling during wheat harvest in the summer would destroy the crops).[23]

Though they knew that the rain falls from heaven, we might wonder how clearly they might have conceived the water cycle, in which the terrestrial water evaporates, which then returns as rain.[24] Nevertheless, unsurprisingly for agricultural peasants, the texts show that they could assume as common knowledge an awareness of the close connection between clouds, thunder, lightning, hail, and rain (Gen 9:13–16; Exod 9:22–24; 19:16). Other texts outside the Pentateuch show this as well. For example, God tells Elijah that he will "send rain upon the earth" after a severe drought, and Elijah has his servant look for a cloud arising from the far west over the Mediterranean (1 Kgs 18:1, 44).[25] By the way, this last example shows that Israelites were probably aware of what is called phenomenal language: Elijah's servant said that what he saw was "a little cloud like a man's hand rising from the sea" (1 Kgs 18:44). Shortly thereafter "the heavens grew black with clouds and wind" (v. 45). We may suppose that any reasonable person is familiar with the experience of far-off objects *looking* small; and if they describe them as *being* small, the audience can grasp the meaning. This is especially true of this case. Elijah and his servant knew that rain was coming, and they would

---

21. See also 1 Kgs 17:7 a "brook" (a seasonal watercourse; Heb. נחל, *nahal*) had "dried up, because there was no rain." For the climate cycle, see John Bimson et al., *New Bible Atlas* (Downers Grove, IL: InterVarsity Press, 1985), 14–15.

22. From outside the Pentateuch, see Amos 4:7; Isa 30:23; 55:10; Acts 14:17; Heb 6:7; Jas 5:18.

23. From outside the Pentateuch, see Prov 26:1 ("snow in summer or rain in harvest"); Song 2:11 ("the winter is past; the rain is over and gone"); Hos 6:3 ("spring rains that water the earth"); Joel 2:23 and Jer 5:24 ("the early and the latter rain").

24. A modern reads Eccl 1:7 in light of just such a cycle, and this fits the theme of the chapter quite well, in which things endlessly recur; but we should probably resist making it a meteorological assertion. Compare Athanasius (ca. AD 318): "For water is by nature heavy, and tends to flow downwards, while the clouds are light and belong to the class of things which tend to soar and mount upwards. And yet we see water, heavy as it is, borne aloft in the clouds" (*Contra Gentes* 36:4). John of Damascus (d. AD 749), *Exact Exposition of the Orthodox Faith*, 2:9, is even more clear on the water cycle.

25. See also Eccl 11:3 ("If the clouds are full of rain, they empty themselves on the earth"); Zech 10:1 ("Ask rain . . . from the LORD who makes the storm clouds, and he will give them showers of rain"); and Ps 135:7 ("He it is who makes the clouds rise at the end of the earth, who makes lightnings for the rain and brings forth the wind from his storehouses"). Likewise, in Luke 12:54, Jesus takes this connection as common knowledge.

have known that a cloud adequate for the job would be quite large—large enough to blacken the sky.

The poetical author of Job can say that God "binds up the waters in his thick clouds" (Job 26:8), while Deborah's song puts the "heavens" and the "clouds" in what must be synonymous parallelism: "The heavens dropped, yes, the clouds dropped water" (Judg 5:4).[26] Further, "a tumult of waters in the heavens" (Jer 10:13; 51:16) is a wild rainstorm. The wording of Job 36:27–29 is suggestive:

> For he draws up the drops of water;
>   they distill his mist in rain,
> which the skies pour down
>   and drop on mankind abundantly.
> Can anyone understand the spreading of the clouds,
>   the thunderings of his pavilion?

To the extent that any water is stored on high, it is in the clouds.

From outside of Israel, in the Ugaritic story, *Baal and Mot*, Baal is told, "take your clouds, your winds, your thunderbolts (and) your rains" (5, v, 7–8)—that is, this author grasped a connection between rainwater, clouds, and storm.[27]

The Israelites' knowledge is pragmatic rather than theoretical, but true enough for their purposes. These agriculturalists' pragmatic concerns, coupled with a true perception of the causal chain, appear as well in Israel's songs, such as Psalm 147:8:

> He covers the heavens with clouds;
>   he prepares rain for the earth;
>   he makes grass grow on the hills.

In light of this there is no reason to doubt how an Israelite audience would interpret a solemn promise such as Deuteronomy 28:12 ("The LORD will open [Heb. יפתח, *yiptaḥ*] to you his good treasury, the heavens, to give the rain to your land in its season and to bless all the work of your hands"), or a serious fear such as 1 Kings 8:35 ("When heaven is shut up [or restrained, Heb. העצר, *heʿatser*] and there is no rain because they have sinned against you"):

---

26. I use the conventional term for this kind of parallelism, but it is more accurate to say that the two lines are co-referential. See C. John Collins, "Homonymous Verbs in Biblical Hebrew: An Investigation of the Role of Comparative Philology" (PhD thesis, University of Liverpool, 1988), 20–23.

27. See J. C. L. Gibson, *Canaanite Myths and Legends* (Edinburgh: T&T Clark, 1978), 72.

they would have imagined the regular arrival of the clouds and the rains. In the same way "the windows of the heavens," which were "opened" (Gen 7:11; Heb. נִפְתָּחוּ, *niptahu*, as in Deut 28:12) and then "closed" (Gen 8:2), would be taken as a pictorial way of referring to rain from the clouds. This is especially clear, both from the rain's connection to clouds in the context (Gen 9:14–15) and from the colorful use of the "windows of heaven" through which a wider array of abundant things come (2 Kgs 7:2, 19; Mal 3:10; Isa 24:18). Indeed, in the Ugaritic story called *The Palace of Baal*, the lattice-window in the mansion is in poetic parallel to a rift in the clouds for rain and thunder.[28]

So, we could suggest that Genesis means that the waters above the expanse are those contained in the clouds.[29] One difficulty is that the skies are clear for much of the year in Palestine, which might tell against this for Genesis. It is probably better to say that ancient Israelites, or some of them, showed an adequate grasp of the relationship between rain and clouds and that therefore they might be counted on to realize that the description in Genesis is a poetic portrayal. That is, based both on their literary experience and on their preexisting knowledge of the physical world, an ideal audience would have realized that Genesis is less about a physical depiction of the world and more about the kind of depiction that the pagan stories tell about (with a view toward rejecting those other stories). It seems highly unlikely that any of this ideal audience would have taken Genesis as offering a physical description to compete with their already existing utilitarian perception of the rain and sky. In such a setting, then, when the writer of Genesis asks his audience to imagine the world's components as if they were configured this way, he gives us an entirely appropriate way of portraying these components, for that purpose. At the very least, no one had to read Genesis as requiring a commitment to the physical shape of things. Further, the role of the "waters above" in Genesis 1 is to supply the rain that is let loose in the flood account (7:11–12; 8:2); any physical particulars beyond that are extraneous to the story.

9.D A THREE-DECKER UNIVERSE?

Let us now come back to the Philippians 2 passage. To begin with, verses 6–11 make up a distinct section of the book, as New Testament specialists

---

28. The Palace of Baal, 4 vi, 19–31 (*CML*, 64–65). In fact, the Ugaritic word for lattice-window is *'urbt*, cognate to the Hebrew *'arubbah*, "window," in Genesis 7:11; 8:2; and both languages use the verb *pth* for "open."

29. See, for example, Vern Poythress, "Rain Water Versus a Heavenly Sea in Genesis 1:6–8," *WTJ* 77 (2015): 181–91, with an excellent selection of texts from the Old Testament and from some Babylonian and Ugaritic sources.

have noted. There is no agreement on whether it is a preexisting hymn or creed, or something else, or on whether it is poetry or elevated prose; nor on whether it comes from Paul or from another source. But at least the specialists agree that the section's language is higher register than ordinary prose. That in itself points us toward some purpose other than geographical description as its communicative intention.

And that suggestion about intention becomes even clearer when we look at the terms for the realms. The three groups are "those in heaven, those on earth, and those under the earth" (ἐπουρανίων καὶ ἐπιγείων καὶ καταχθονίων): They are three adjectives in the genitive plural, which could be masculine or neuter in gender—a matter to which we will return. The first two adjectives, ἐπουράνιος and ἐπίγειος, appear elsewhere in the New Testament as "heavenly" and "earthly" (John 3:12; 1 Cor 15:40),[30] where the contrast is not spatial but spiritual. That is, the "heavenly" pertains to transcendent things, while "earthly" pertains to unaided human experience. In Ephesians, "the heavenly places" are either the realm of God's acknowledged rule (1:3, 20; 2:6) or else the realm in which other forces contest God's rule (3:10; 6:12). To examine each of these possibilities and to adjudicate between them goes beyond my present scope; it is enough for now simply to repeat, the concern is not with geography or topography but with groups of personal beings.

This applies as well to the third element, "those under the earth" (καταχθονίων). This word does not appear elsewhere in the Greek Bible, in the Old or New Testaments. The closest wording to it occurs in Revelation 5:3, 13, which in English sounds very much like our passage, though the Greek is a bit different: "no one in heaven or on earth or under the earth" (οὐδεὶς ἐν τῷ οὐρανῷ οὐδὲ ἐπὶ τῆς γῆς οὐδὲ ὑποκάτω τῆς γῆς); and "every creature in heaven and on earth and under the earth and in the sea, and all that is in them" (πᾶν κτίσμα ὃ ἐν τῷ οὐρανῷ καὶ ἐπὶ τῆς γῆς καὶ ὑποκάτω τῆς γῆς καὶ ἐπὶ τῆς θαλάσσης καὶ τὰ ἐν αὐτοῖς πάντα). The context shows that the goal is to convey the idea of everything everywhere. From the perspective of one's eyesight, these three regions are an excellent, intuitive way of referring to the various parties, and a good reader can identify them without worrying whether they are geographical statements (especially in a book like Revelation).

We have two references by the apostolic fathers that might help: Ignatius (AD 35–108) writes in his letter to the Trallians (§9:1) about Jesus, who was truly crucified and died "while those in heaven and on earth and under the earth looked on" (βλεπόντων τῶν ἐπουρανίων καὶ ἐπιγείων καὶ

---

30. See also 2 Cor 5:1 "earthly home"; verse 2, "our heavenly dwelling," is literally, "our dwelling that is of heaven" (τὸ οἰκητήριον ἡμῶν τὸ ἐξ οὐρανοῦ), which is closely related.

ὑποχθονίων)—which is a reference to three groups of beings that witnessed the crucifixion, however they may be identified. And Polycarp (perhaps AD 69–155) wrote to the Philippian Christians (§2.1) that to Christ "all things in heaven and on earth are subject" (ὑπετάγη τὰ πάντα ἐπουράνια καὶ ἐπίγεια), which here focuses on the various things in all the creation that are subject.

The background for the specific adjective καταχθόνιος, "that which is under the earth," comes from the wider Greek usage outside the Greek Bible, although the adjective ὑποχθόνιος in Ignatius' *Trallians* seems synonymous. In Greek, prior to the New Testament, καταχθόνιος has to do with "the underworld," the realm of the dead, either as "the god of the underworld" or as "gods of the underworld" (sometimes as deified spirits of the departed).[31]

The usage in Philippians seems almost to be underdetermined, which probably supports the idea that it is a quotation of something known to both Paul and his audience—regardless of whether Paul himself originally wrote it. In any case, these are three groups of beings, above whose names God has bestowed a name on Jesus (v. 9). That is, *location*—if it was ever part of the picture—has faded out of it by Paul's time, surviving as a kind of spatial imagery. In fact, the very word "above" in v. 9 is a topographical metaphor. Specialists debate which three groups of beings are in view here; I suspect that the Greek usage, together with the likely parallel in Ignatius, supports the reading that the three groups are the good angels, human beings, and demons; at least this is how I judge the usage, though others differ.[32] But to find in this passage evidence of a cosmic geography in any sense other than a naming convention looks to be non-cooperation with the text and therefore a faulty reading.

9.E HASN'T EXPLAINING BECOME EXPLAINING AWAY?

It is, in sum, an unacceptable literary confusion to treat the descriptions of the world in the Bible, and particularly in Genesis, as a kind of ancient science. It is true, as I observed in chapter 8, that philosophers often began with the ordinary observation and treated the terminology as if it were scientific. But this was what the learned did; the general audience had no need for it and there is no reason to read Genesis (or any other biblical text) as aiming to supply it.

---

31. See, for example, Homer, *Iliad*, 9,457; Dionysius of Halicarnassus, *Roman Antiquities*, 2,10(3); Strabo, *Geography*, 6,2,1.

32. I agree with the view found in Peter O'Brien, *Philippians*, NIGTC (Grand Rapids: Eerdmans, 1991), 243–45, which includes the departed in the third group as well. John Reumann, on the other hand, would group them as spirits above, humans on earth, and the dead in Hades. See Reumann, *Philippians*, AB (New Haven: Yale University Press, 2008), 356–57. J. B. Lightfoot, *Philippians* (London: Macmillan, 1888), however, argues for a connection to Polycarp, in which case the adjectives would be neuter, and the idea is "everything there is" (see also Rev 5:3, 13).

Ancient writers knew how to speak technically as they needed to. For example, Herodotus aimed to give geographical surveys of the foreign lands he described—and he is detailed enough for us to decide whether he is accurate or not. (I mention Aristotle's scientific argument on the fixity of the kinds in ch. 10.) Babylonian scholars had developed mathematical tools, such as a version of Pythagoras' Theorem, to suit their needs.[33] On the other hand, their maps served a different purpose than straightforward topographical description, namely, to display the relation of foreign places to the world of the Babylonians. (Recall what we saw about the map of the London Underground in § 4.D). The biblical material contains very little that resembles the technical and mathematical works of the Babylonians or the geographical depictions of Herodotus.

Leviticus is famous for its catalogue of unclean animals; it never really gives a general rationale for why some are clean and others unclean. The "weasel" (Lev 11:29 RV; the ESV has "mole rat"; the Heb. is *holed*; the Gk. has γαλῆ, "weasel") was unclean and thus ineligible for sacrifice and eating. Although Leviticus gives no rationale, the Letter of Aristeas explains that it "conceives through the ears and brings forth through the mouth" (Letter of Aristeas, 165–66; see also Barn. 10:8). That this was taken to be authentic natural history becomes obvious when we find that Aristotle refuted it, saying that "Anaxagoras and some of the other physiologers" had alleged precisely this; Aristotle dismissed their work as based on "insufficient evidence and inadequate consideration" (Aristotle, *Gen. an.*, 3.6 [756b]). The technicality of Leviticus with respect to discerning which animals are clean does not bring with it a bent toward scientific explanation oriented toward any kind of natural history.

And yet someone will surely object: The peoples surrounding Israel had their pictures of the world and of course the material in Genesis matches that. There are several lines of reply to that objection. To begin with, we face the same issues in textual interpretation for the other peoples' cosmologies as we do for Genesis, namely, whether the kinds of texts that we possess actually have physical description as part of their illocution.[34]

---

33. For a brief summary, see A. R. Millard, "Cartography in the Ancient Near East," in *The History of Cartography, Volume 1: Cartography in Prehistoric, Ancient, and Medieval Europe and the Mediterranean*, ed. J. B. Hartley and David Woodward (Chicago: University of Chicago Press, 1987), 107–116, especially p. 109. For more detail, see O. Neugebauer, *The Exact Sciences in Antiquity* (New York: Dover, 1969), ch. 2.

34. See, for example, Wayne Horowitz, *Mesopotamian Cosmic Geography* (Winona Lake, IN: Eisenbrauns, 1998), xiii–xiv. Othmar Keel and Silvia Schroer, *Creation: Biblical Theologies in the Context of the Ancient Near East* (Winona Lake, IN: Eisenbrauns, 2015), go even further: "People in the ancient Near East did not conceive of the earth as a disk floating on water with the firmament inverted over it like a bell jar, with the stars hanging from it . . . The textbook images that keep being reprinted of

It may be true that, read literalistically, the texts do say these things; the prior question, of whether we *should* read them that way, hardly gets considered.³⁵ Indeed, it is entirely likely that the Atrahasis Epic and Eridu Genesis are similarly non-scientific and supply no information about ancient Near Eastern conceptions of the world. More to the point, we must take the Hebrew passages on their own terms (which comparative studies often fail to do); that is, the Hebrew texts are written in Hebrew, the Hebrew words mean what they mean in Hebrew (and thus not in Akkadian or Egyptian), and the words are part of a larger, and presumably coherent, literary and social context.³⁶

I am not saying that none of the Bible writers themselves had any such primitive pictures as we have been considering. I am saying that we cannot take their statements as any kind of affirmation of the pictures, that is, the references to physical things are either conventional (much as "four corners of the earth" would be for us) or poetic. And when they are poetic, they are an invitation to the audience to picture the referent *as if* it were such and such. In each case, we can successfully identify the referents and form the suitable picture in order to cooperate (or not) with the communication.

On the other hand, some have tried to vindicate the Bible by showing how its statements anticipate modern scientific findings. Generally speaking, these vindications rest upon the same mistake about language as the dismissal-as-primitive positions do. A simple example is the appeal to Isaiah 40:22, which speaks of God as "he who sits above the circle of the earth": Does that not affirm that the earth is a globe and not a flat sheet? It is more likely that the words refer to the land as far as one can see from any high vantage point as

---

the 'ancient Near Eastern world picture' are based on typical modern misunderstandings that fail to take into account the religious components of ancient Near Eastern conceptions and representations" (p. 78). At least the burden of proof is on those who claim that physical description is crucial. An analogy would be the way moderns might read a medieval bestiary and mistake it for a work of natural history, concluding that the ancients did not know very much (forgetting that hunters had to know plenty). See the discussion in David Lindberg, *The Beginnings of Western Science* (Chicago: University of Chicago Press, 1992), 348–53.

35. An excellent example of hermeneutical naïveté is J. M. Plumley, "The Cosmology of Ancient Egypt," in *Ancient Cosmologies*, ed. Carmen Blacker and Michael Lowe (London: Allen & Unwin, 1975), 17–41. For example, Plumley asserts, "The Ancient Egyptian, in common with other ancient peoples, could not conceive of anything that was not alive in some degree. Having no neuter gender in his language it was necessary for him to classify this or that thing as masculine or feminine" (p. 24).

36. On this point I find Mark Brett's observation telling: "Although ṣelem and dᵉmût are never used in P (and, indeed, never in the Hebrew Bible) with reference to a king, Schmidt has no hesitation in claiming that the motif of the image of God is firmly 'anchored' in this royal tradition." This is not necessarily *fatal* to the line of reasoning that bases its argument on the equivalent terms in other ancient Near Eastern languages, but certainly it shows that more argument is needed. See Brett, "Motives and Intentions in Genesis 1," *JTS* 42 (1991): 1–16, quote on p. 11.

if one marked out the horizon with a compass.[37] The physical shape of the entire earth is not in view here.

In the same way, many have argued that the biblical language about God "stretching out the heavens"[38] (Ps 104:2) can be wondrously correlated to the contemporary idea of cosmic expansion after the big bang. (Examples come readily to hand from popular apologetics web sites, from both young-earth and old-earth creationists.)

As I indicated in chapter 8, I have no quarrel with the idea of the big bang. I agree with those who suggest that it can serve as a physical description of what creation from nothing would have looked like. The continued expansion of the whole universe from that event, which seems to be what the astronomers are measuring, supports the big bang theory. Even if the big bang does not prove that creation from nothing took place as inferred from Genesis 1:1, it is highly compatible with that theological conviction. As a beginning of the universe as we know it, it cannot be the result of physical causes within the universe and thus it puts a sharp point on questions of purpose and ultimate causation.

People who make these moves may have the purest of intentions, but I must nevertheless explain why the texts they use do not achieve the goals set for them. To say it again, the texts that use this language are generally poetic (or rhetorically high), and physical cosmology is simply outside their communicative intent. Instead they portray God "stretching out the heavens" as a man would stretch out the cloth of a tent in order to pitch it. This comes to us both from the explicit "stretching out the heavens like a tent" (Ps 104:2; compare Isa 40:22, "stretches out the heavens like a curtain") and from the literal uses of the same verb for "pitching [or stretching out] a tent" (as in Gen 12:8; 26:25; 33:19; 35:21; Exod 33:7; Judg 4:11; 2 Sam 6:17; 16:22). The biblical texts use this image to stress that it is the LORD alone who fashioned the whole earth and heavens and prepared them as a place for habitation.

Skeptics and "Bible-science defenders" share an assumption in common, namely, that scientific language is the most accurate and therefore the most truthful kind of discourse; and then it follows that for the Bible to be true, it must address these scientific questions. I count this assumption inadequate for real life.

---

37. The word for "circle" is *hug* (חוג), related to the word for "compass" found in Isa 44:13, *mehuggah* (מחוגה).

38. See Job 9:8; Ps 104:2; Isa 40:22; 42:5; 44:24; 45:12; 51:13; Jer 10:12; 51:15; and Zech 12:1, all using the verb *natah* (נטה).

The assumption also leads to hermeneutical problems, as C. S. Lewis identified in Chalcidius, a medieval scholar who translated Plato into Latin:

> His admitted principle of interpretation was one which makes an author more liable to be misrepresented the more he is revered. In hard places, he holds, we must always attribute to Plato whatever sense appears "worthiest the wisdom of so great an authority"; which inevitably means that all the dominant ideas of the commentator's own age will be read into him.[39]

The defenders of the Bible will have to guard themselves from this temptation.

At the same time, it is only honest to acknowledge that many faithful Bible readers have formed a world picture from their readings of the Bible. One factor, which we examined in chapter 8, was the felt need to position the Jewish and Christian Scriptures as worthy of intellectual respect. But this was primarily the work of apologists and philosophers. What of the peasants (whom I have argued are the proper addressees of the biblical material)? C. S. Lewis dealt with similar objections when faced with the critique that the early Christians envisioned the ascension of Jesus and his sitting at God's right hand in physical and spatial terms:

> Remembering, as I do, from within, the attitude of the impatient sceptic, I realize very well how he is fore-armed against anything I might say for the rest of this chapter. "I know exactly what this man is going to do," he murmurs. "He is going to start explaining all these mythological statements away." . . . I freely admit that "modernist" Christianity has constantly played just the game of which the impatient sceptic accuses it. But I also think there is a kind of explaining which is not explaining away. . . . I am going to distinguish what I regard as the "core" or "real meaning" of the doctrines from that in their expression which I regard as inessential and possibly even changed without damage.[40]

Lewis draws a distinction between the core of a Christian doctrine and the particular form by which some people might picture the relevant events, and he reminds us, "Christianity is not to be judged from the fancies of

---

39. Lewis, *The Discarded Image*, 52.
40. C. S. Lewis, *Miracles: A Preliminary Study* (New York: Macmillan, 1960), 69–70 (ch. 10). A very similar discussion appears in Lewis, *The Weight of Glory and Other Addresses*, Walter Hooper, ed. (New York: Simon & Schuster, 1996), 100–101 ("Is Theology Poetry," 1944); see also *God in the Dock*, Walter Hooper, ed. (Grand Rapids: Eerdmans, 1970), 45–46 ("Dogma and the Universe," 1943).

children any more than medicine from the ideas of the little girl who believed in horrid red things."[41]

He then asks us to imagine a scenario:

> We can suppose a Galilean peasant who thought that Christ had literally and physically "sat down at the right hand of the Father." If such a man had then gone to Alexandria and had a philosophical education he would have discovered that the Father had no right hand and did not sit on a throne....
>
> Even if it could be shown, then, that the early Christians accepted their imagery literally, this would not mean that we are justified in relegating their doctrines as a whole to the lumber room. Whether they actually did, is another matter. The difficulty here is that they were not writing as philosophers to satisfy speculative curiosity about the nature of God and of the universe....
>
> Hence the sort of question we are now considering is never raised by the New Testament writers. When once it is raised, Christianity decides quite clearly that the naïf images are false.... We do not find similar statements in the New Testament, because the issue has not yet been made explicit: but we do find statements which make it certain how that issue will be decided when once it becomes explicit.[42]

Or, as he puts it in another place,

> The answer is that the alternative we are offering [the early Christians] was probably never present to their minds at all. As soon as it was present, we know quite well which side of the fence they came down on....
>
> The earliest Christians were not so much like a man who mistakes the shell for the kernel as like a man carrying a nut which he hasn't yet cracked. The moment it is cracked, he knows which part to throw away. Till then he holds on to the nut, not because he is a fool but because he isn't.[43]

Besides Alexandrian analysis, what sorts of principles do the faithful have that can guide them, ensuring that they keep the kernel? One factor in Lewis, which some have overlooked, is his notion of the overarching storyline of the

---

41. Lewis, *Miracles*, 74 (ch. 10).
42. Lewis, *Miracles*, 75–76 (ch. 10).
43. Lewis, *Weight of Glory*, 100–101.

Bible. The story begins with a transcendent God who made a good world, with its human inhabitants morally innocent. By some sort of disobedience they pulled themselves and their offspring astray from God's good plan, and God's activity is thereafter redemptive—that is, he is constantly aiming to provide "forgiveness for having broken, and supernatural help towards keeping, that law," that universal law embedded in the good creation.[44] The rhetorical features of the texts leave some room for discussion over just what kinds of scenarios will be found intellectually satisfying, but the shape of the story puts a limit on our speculations if we want to be sure that we are still telling the same story. This, by the way, is why we should not take Lewis's image of the kernel and shell too strictly, that is, the biblical way of describing things retains its value as the proper way to envision the events and scenery because that imagery shapes the attitudes of the faithful. Thus, the faithful are not free to throw it away in every sense, and Lewis himself did not.

---

44. Lewis, in *Christian Reflections*, 46–47 ("On Ethics," ca. 1943).

Chapter 10

THE PLACE FOR CONFLICT: DIVINE ACTION IN GENESIS 1–11

Part of what makes these chapters of Genesis work is that they regularly present God as *doing* things. He creates the world and fills it with plants and animals; he forms a man and a woman and leads them together; he visits the garden of Eden and pronounces sentence on his disobedient creatures; he speaks to various people, and he provides offspring; he brings a great flood as a judgment and commissions the family of Noah to resume their human calling; he confuses the languages of pretentious humans.

But what did it mean in Genesis for God to be an actor in the story? Is that too philosophical a question for the sacred tale? We could easily multiply remarks, especially from members of the biblical theology movement, saying just that. John Walton speaks for many:

> People in the ancient world had no category for what we call *natural laws*. When they thought in terms of cause and effect, even though they could make all the observations that we make . . . , they were more inclined to see the world's operation in terms of divine cause.[1]

Similarly, N. T. Wright tells us about the Jewish audiences of Jesus, expressing a view that we might consider applying to the earlier audiences of Genesis:

> The very word "miracle" itself, and for that matter the words "natural" and "supernatural," are in fact symptomatic of a very different range of

---

1. John Walton, *The Lost World of Adam and Eve: Genesis 2–3 and the Human Origins Debate* (Downers Grove, IL: InterVarsity Press, 2015), 18 (emphasis original).

possible worldviews from those which were open to Galilean villagers in the first century.[2]

The argument rides on the claim that we cannot find a biblical definition of words such as "nature" and "miracle." Here is how H. Wheeler Robinson, a biblical theology scholar, put the problem:

> The Hebrew vocabulary includes no word equivalent to our term "Nature." This is not surprising, if by "Nature" we mean "The creative and regulative physical power which is conceived of as operating in the physical world and as the immediate cause of all its phenomena." The only way to render this idea into Hebrew would be to say simply "God."[3]

So different, in fact, was the ancient worldview felt to be that the biblical texts are virtually inaccessible to a modern audience and must be recast. Therefore, Rudolph Bultmann asserted:

> It is impossible to use the electric light and the wireless and to avail ourselves of modern medical and surgical discoveries, and at the same time to believe in the New Testament world of spirits and miracles. We may think we can manage it in our own lives, but to expect others to do so is to make the Christian faith unintelligible and unacceptable to the modern world.[4]

10.A HOW SHOULD WE READ GOD'S ACTION IN CREATION?

10.A.1 SETTING OUT THE BIBLICAL METAPHYSIC

I intend to apply my appropriation of Lewis on types of language (ch. 3 above) to this topic. In that chapter I argued that we do not find much in the way of technical language in the Bible, and that will certainly apply here. Nevertheless, we may legitimately address technical and philosophical questions to the biblical materials so long as we respect these texts' communicative intentions. When it comes to matters such as "nature," "cause and effect," and "miracle," the answers to many of those questions will be in the set of

---

2. N. T. Wright, *Jesus and the Victory of God* (Minneapolis: Fortress, 1996), 187–88.
3. H. Wheeler Robinson, *Inspiration and Revelation in the Old Testament* (Oxford: Oxford University Press, 1946), 1.
4. Rudolph Bultmann, *Kerygma and Myth: A Theological Debate* (New York: Harper & Row, 1961), 5.

assumptions that underlie the biblical statements themselves—that is, not only in the picture of the world that the author assumes between himself and his audience but also in the basic worldview stance the biblical authors inculcate.[5]

Many of the relevant underlying assumptions are fairly easy to tease out. For example, the biblical authors, like humans in general, take it for granted that the world and the things in it have properties that make it possible to use things: people make knives out of stone and then learn how to work various metals. A sharpened stick will do for a spear. They would not try to make a knife out of mud or a spear out of running water. People eat some things (such as fish and grains) and avoid others (such as sand), whatever theory of nourishment they might hold. Some animals are good for stock while others are unruly and some downright dangerous. Human cultures in general are aware that a man and a woman are crucial for making babies (even if they differ on what else must be added to the process). This is what we may call an intuitive-level notion of properties and causation.

We find such intuitions plainly taken for granted in the Proverbs, in which wood is necessary for a fire (26:20–21), just as whispering is necessary to a quarrel; milk is the sort of thing that, if you "press" it, you get curds, and a nose is the sort of thing that when "pressed" yields blood (30:33)—just as "pressing" anger yields strife. Honey is good, but if you eat too much, it will cause you to vomit (25:16). Wine and strong drink may lead one astray by properties that they do not share with, for example, water (20:1).

There are many more examples, but these will suffice to show that Israelites had normal intuitions about causation (just as they knew that rain comes from clouds). That is, to put it more philosophically, they had an awareness of "natures" as the kind of causal contribution things make to events—even though they did not use that terminology.[6] This, by the way, shows why Wheeler Robinson's attempt to stop the discussion by way of a definition is so misleading: We are under no obligation to accept his definition, and we may offer one more suitable (as I do below).

At the same time as the biblical writers affirm the causal role of properties (or natures), they also affirm God's intimate involvement in every event. For example, in words addressed to God (Ps 104:10, 14):

---

5. I have offered my exegetical and philosophical analyses in more detail in my book, *The God of Miracles* (Wheaton, IL: Crossway, 2000), with many more examples than I give in this chapter. Here I want to focus on the Lewisian questions of language type and rhetoric. Some material in the section is adapted from my essay, "How to Think about God's Action in the World," chapter 22 in *Theistic Evolution*, ed. J. P. Moreland, Stephen Meyer, Christopher Shaw, Ann Gauger, and Wayne Grudem (Wheaton, IL: Crossway, 2017) and is used with permission from the publisher. Of course in such a volume, the other contributors need not endorse everything that I argue for, and vice versa.

6. They did sometimes speak in terms of "powers" for this idea. See, for example, Wis 16:23.

> You *make* springs gush forth in the valleys . . .
> You *cause* the grass to grow for the livestock . . .

The springs and grass give water and food to the beasts, that is, they causally contribute to their continued well-being. The poetic song does not present divine supervision or causation as an alternative explanation for the natural; rather, it supplements what the eye can see, for rhetorical purposes that we will see shortly. In other words, divine causation and creaturely causation are not competing in a zero-sum game.

At the same time, of course, the biblical writers would not allow that created factors are alone the causes of *everything* that happens. There is always the possibility that God can add something new to the processes he has made—such as the death of the Egyptian firstborn (Exod 12:29), untimely for the Egyptians and right on time for the Hebrews; likewise the parting of the Red Sea at just the right time, regardless of the means God employed (Exod 14:21).

Traditional Christian metaphysics put all these things together by describing God's initial creation—which produced all things—followed by his providential maintaining and ruling what he had made.[7] God's providence *preserves*, *concurs with*, and *governs* every aspect of his creation. I draw on the Lutheran theologian Heinrich Schmid (1811–1885) for a representative description:[8]

---

7. My focus here is on metaphysics in the Western (Latin-based) Christian tradition. I do not mean to exclude the Eastern (Greek-based) tradition from consideration. In fact, so far as I can tell, the notions there are not appreciably different (though the emphases may be). This comes as no surprise, since both traditions developed in conversation with Hellenistic philosophers (indeed, the term *providence* is an appropriation of the Greek noun πρόνοια and cognate verb προνοέω from the philosophers. See their appearance in, e.g., Wis 14:3; 17:2; 3 Macc 4:21; 5:30; 4 Macc 9:24; 13:19; 17:22). The Jewish philosopher Aristobulus (second century BC; his work is preserved in the Greek father Eusebius, *Praep. ev.*, 13.12 [667-*b*]) wrote of the divine Sabbath in Gen 2:1–3: "But what is clearly stated by the Law, that God rested on the seventh day, means not, as some suppose, that God henceforth ceases to do anything, but it refers to the fact that, after He has brought the arrangement of His works to completion, He has arranged them thus for all time. For it points out that in six days He made the heaven and the earth and all things that are therein, to distinguish the times, and predict the order in which one thing comes before another: *for after arranging their order, He keeps them so, and makes no change.*"

8. Heinrich Schmid, *Doctrinal Theology of the Evangelical Lutheran Church*, trans. Charles Hay and Henry Jacobs, (Minneapolis: Augsburg, 1961 [1875]), 170–94 (emphasis original). For the same position from other branches of Western Christianity, see Heinrich Heppe (1820–1879), *Reformed Dogmatics*, trans. G. T. Thomson (Grand Rapids: Baker, 1978 [1950]), 251–80; and Alfred Freddoso (contemporary Roman Catholic), "God's General Concurrence with Secondary Causes: Why Conservation Is Not Enough," *Philosophical Perspectives* 5 (1991): 553–85. Some theologians dispute whether *concurrence* should be included, but Freddoso's essay is, I believe, proof that it must. The Presbyterian theologian William G. T. Shedd, *Dogmatic Theology* (Nashville: Nelson, 1980 [1888–1894]), i:527–30, speaks only of preservation and government, but from his exposition it is clear that his definition of preservation *includes* concurrence.

I. *Preservation* is the act of Divine Providence whereby God sustains all things created by Him, so that they continue in being with the properties implanted in their nature and the powers received in creation. . . . Created things have no power of subsistence in themselves. . . . Therefore *preservation* is also designated as *continued creation*.[9]

II. *Concurrence*. . . . Concurrence, or the co-operation of God, is the act of Divine Providence whereby God, by a general and immediate influence, proportioned to the need and capacity of every creature, graciously takes part with second causes in their actions and effects.[10]

III. *Government* is the act of Divine Providence by which God most excellently orders, regulates, and directs the affairs and actions of creatures according to His own wisdom, justice, and goodness, for the glory of His name and the welfare of men.

The Providence of God ordinarily employs second causes, and thus accomplishes its designs; but God is by no means restricted to the use of those second causes, for He often exercises His Providence without regard to them, and operates thus contrary to what we call the course of nature, and hence arises the difference between *ordinary* and *extraordinary* providence.[11]

In order to keep the focus on the intuitive perception of natural properties, we can recast the relevant part of the definitions this way:

God made the universe from nothing and endowed the things that exist with natural properties; he preserves those properties, and he also confirms their interactions in a web of cause-and-effect relations.

The government rubric, as traditionally understood, allows God to infuse special operations into the unfolding web of cause and effect, according to his

---

9. The term "continued creation" can cause some confusion, since different writers may mean different things by it. Heppe's Reformed compendium uses similar language about "continued creation" but adds a clarification: "*Conservatio* is to be conceived as a *continuata creatio*, resting upon the same command of God as creation . . . At the same time preservation must not be conceived as a continued creation, as though by preservation the essential identity of the once created world were abolished" (pp. 257–58).

10. The expression "graciously takes part" is somewhat vague; it refers to God's confirming the interactions of their causal properties. Heppe (*Reformed Dogmatics*, 258) cites the Swiss theologian J. H. Heidegger (ca. 1700) for a definition: "Concurrence or co-operation is the operation of God by which he co-operates directly with the second causes as depending upon him alike in their essence as in their operation, so as to urge or move them to action and to operate along with them in a manner suitable to a first cause and adjusted to the nature of the second causes."

11. "The form of divine *gubernatio* in which God is active without second causes or uses them in a manner deviating from their orderly appointment and activity is God's performance of miracle." See Heppe, *Reformed Dogmatics*, 263.

purposes—that is, to supply "miracles." Some have mistakenly supposed that this means that a miracle is "a suspension or violation of the laws of nature," "God acting directly or without means," "intervention," or "something we cannot understand 'scientifically'." None of these descriptions captures the biblical portrayal; rather, the idea is that with such an infusion the result goes beyond what the causal properties of the created things would have produced. In terms of the intuitive stance the biblical authors worked with, we can put it this way:

> God is also free to "infuse" special operations of his power into this web at any time, e.g. by adding objects, directly causing events, enabling an agent to do what its own natural properties would never have made it capable of, and by imposing organization, according to his purposes.

This yields a metaphysic in which God is active in every event, every bit as directly in the natural as in the supernatural. Hence, in the Bible, an ordinary pregnancy is God's action (see Ps 139:13–15; Jer 1:5), as is Elizabeth's pregnancy with John and Mary's with Jesus (Luke 1:35–37), though Mary's is presented to us as *super*natural.

This adaptation of the traditional metaphysic handles the biblical materials well and is superior to some of the alternatives that have been on offer. Some of the main alternative metaphysics offered within traditional theism include occasionalism and what I have called "providentialism":

> *Occasionalism*: Created things have no actual causal power, and every event is "supernatural," and thus everything is God's direct action.[12]
>
> *Providentialism*: Every event is in principle the product of created natural forces that God providentially sustains; since everything "natural" is God's direct action, in principle everything is "natural."[13]

Some have even demurred from traditional theism with the idea that human freedom limits God's absolute rule. To examine all the texts appealed

---

12. The occasionalist G. C. Berkouwer, *The Providence of God* (Grand Rapids: Eerdmans, 1952), 196, asserted that a miracle "means nothing more than that God at a given moment wills a certain thing to occur differently than it had up to that moment been willed by Him to occur."

13. E.g., R. J. Berry, a providentialist: "Probably all miracles are susceptible to an explanation other than the supernatural." See *SCB* 9:1 (1997): 77 (a response to P. Addinall's reply to Berry's previous article on "The Virgin Birth of Christ," *SCB* 8:2 [1996]: 101–10); idem., "Divine Action: Expected and Unexpected," *Zygon* 37:3 (2002): 717–27. The term "providentialism" is my own coinage. See Collins, *The God of Miracles*, 26–29. Robert Larmer, "Miracles, Divine Agency, and the Laws of Nature," *Toronto Journal of Theology* 27:2 (2011): 267–90, uses "theistic complementarianism" with the same meaning.

to by each of these schools of thought would take us too far afield; I simply defer to my previous discussion in *The God of Miracles*.[14]

It is inherent in the traditional Christian metaphysic that "miracles"—or better, "supernatural events"—are possible. Under what conditions they may be expected is another question; Christian theologians commonly add provisos about them not being capricious but related to God's pursuit of relationship with human beings.[15] That is to say, they mark key phases in the unfolding story of God's development of his people, and this is particularly the case with the miracles in the Bible.[16] They take place against a backcloth of a regular and reliable world—which is the very thing that makes the departure discernible—a world in which persons make meaningful choices.

These provisos are quite appropriate; at the same time, Christian theism resists the notion that supernatural events are in some way unworthy of God. It is quite true that the doctrine of creation posits a created world that has all its necessary capacities built into it, needing no tinkering. But those capacities are the ones necessary for the world's assigned purpose, namely, of being the background for the lives and choices of rational agents with whom God intends to interact.[17]

The category of agency will help us here because we find people concerned that the possibility of supernatural events endangers the predictability of the world. I would ask people with such concerns to imagine themselves in a room full of energetic toddlers: They will find that the agents act upon their environment, and the items in the environment (skin, tables, drinking cups, toys, animals) will be true to their natures as they are acted upon. Unless we are prepared to insist that all human agency is itself an in-principle-predictable product of physical properties, this concern fails to account for the world as we know it. No doubt if we are being technically theological, we will insist that God among human beings in the world is much more than the adult in a room full of toddlers. But the picture shows that agents employ

---

14. Collins, *The God of Miracles*.
15. The complaint of "caprice" comes up frequently in discussion of miracles when the objectors do not recognize the provisos traditional theologians have laid down. See, for just one example, David Lindberg, *The Beginnings of Western Science: The European Scientific Tradition in Philosophical, Religious, and Institutional Context, 600 B.C. to A.D. 1450* (Chicago: University of Chicago Press, 1992), 242–44, recording such objections (without endorsing them).
16. The role of miracles *outside* of the Bible is controversial, and I am not entering into that discussion here.
17. The objection that miracles are unworthy of a fully fitted creation seems to rely on a metaphor for the world as a machine or artifact: It would be a reproach on the Craftsman if it needed "tinkering." But suppose we change the metaphor and picture the world as a musical instrument and its history as the tune (as Athanasius did, in *Contra Gentes* §38). It is no shame to the Craftsman if his instrument does not have the tune within itself.

the reliable properties of the world, an employment that hardly diminishes the reliability of those properties.

While these special events often address crises of human need, they play two main roles: first, they authenticate divinely approved messengers (prophets and apostles: e.g., Deut 18:21–22; Acts 2:22; 2 Cor 12:12); and second, they make God's interest in the corporate well-being of his people (Israel and the church) especially clear (e.g., Exod 14:30–31). An additional role is that of testifying about God's interest to those outside his own people with a view toward leading them to faith (e.g., Exod 15:14–16).

To claim to have discerned a miracle renders one liable to the charge of committing the "God-of-the-gaps" fallacy. That is to say, suppose we come upon some object or event for which we do not have a naturalistic explanation and then say, "See, God must have done that," and thus proceed to base either our own belief or our apologetic for belief on such an instance. This involves us in a risk. Suppose the sciences eventually provide a natural-process based explanation. Then where does that leave God's involvement in the matter? Are what were once grounds for believing in God thereby made an argument for disbelief?[18]

A serious theological problem is also involved (at least within traditional theism) if we think that it is possible to say of some events or objects, "God made this," and of the natural ones, "God did *not* make this."[19] The doctrine of providence cited above affirms that the products of second causes are every bit as much direct divine action as the miraculous events.

What, then, does it mean to declare that a supernatural event has taken place? How is it discernable, and to whom may we legitimately argue that we have discerned such an event—that is, is the explanation "supernatural" credible only to those who already believe, or is it more publicly accessible?

We begin by recognizing that normally we consider an event "special" when it is more than simply unusual—after all, lots of things are unusual. Rather, we have some notion that the result was both contingent and against our expectations and that it served some important need. Sometimes that

---

18. Fundamentalists are not the only ones to commit this blunder. I have heard religious speakers on the BBC, who would best be described as left-wing Anglican, celebrate ignorance on the causes, for example, of lightning strikes or the 1987 hurricane in the south of England, because that leaves room for God's mysterious action in his world.

19. For example, the subtitle of Douglas Geivett and Gary Habermas, *In Defense of Miracles* (Downers Grove, IL: InterVarsity Press, 1997), is "A Comprehensive Case for God's Action in History." Although some of the authors in the collection try to provide a more careful nuancing to this, it nevertheless shows the problem in popular parlance. A Scripture text such as Ps 119:126, "It is time for the LORD to act," must be taken as *analogical*—that is, it speaks *as if* God were doing nothing about the wicked rather than asserting that he actually is doing nothing.

notion of ours is intuitive, in which case we do not assess our expectations of the outcome too strictly for their reasonableness. In other cases we may apply more rigorous assessment of our expectations, and if they were reasonable, we feel a kind of wonder.

In a few cases we go even further: We conclude that the result should have been otherwise, and we base this on our knowledge of the factors involved. For us to declare an event "supernatural," it must meet this most stringent requirement. But this leads to our difficulty: Are we not simply appealing to gaps in our understanding of the natural course of things? Further, if our sense of its specialness depended on the event being miraculous, then a scientific (or natural) explanation diminishes the specialness.

It will help us to recall the two domains of scientific explanation, the *nomothetic* and the *historical*.[20] In nomothetic explanations we consider what normally happens and explain its causation. We are looking for regularities or laws, hence the name. This domain predominates in most common definitions of science. In historical explanations we are asking what specific chain of cause-and-effect produced the item we are studying. Obviously the two are related, but they are also distinguishable: for example, how animals interact in an ecosystem (nomothetic) versus why a particular species went extinct (historical). No doubt our historical explanations make use of our nomothetic ones.

Now the biblical theist ought not appeal to special divine action in a nomothetic context because in these situations, the ordinary function of God's creation, we recognize that God's activity is that of maintaining the order of what he made. In a context like that, to invoke supernatural causation would involve the God-of-the-gaps fallacy. Further, many historical events, such as the 1980 Mount St. Helens eruption, may in fact be explicable by appeal to natural factors. To attribute these to supernatural action would also be improper (at least, without plenty of further research). On the other hand, there can be unique events that do involve special divine activity (e.g., creation, exodus, virgin birth, resurrection of Jesus). In such cases it would be incorrect and misleading to insist that only natural factors are valid for describing what happened in those events; it would also be empirically inadequate.

In other words, there are gaps and then there are gaps. First, there are *gaps due to ignorance* (Latin: *lacunae ignorantiae causā*), which are simply gaps in our knowledge, which may eventually be filled. But there are also *gaps due to the nature* (Latin: *lacunae naturae causā*) of the things involved: The result goes beyond what these natural properties would have brought about.[21]

---

20. Ian Barbour, *Religion in an Age of Science* (New York: HarperSanFrancisco, 1990), 66–71.
21. John Polkinghorne employs a similar dichotomy of gaps in *Quarks, Chaos, and Christianity*

A wise person would exercise caution in claiming to have discovered a *lacuna naturae causā*, since we do not know everything there is to know about the relevant natural properties. For example, we might speak of a medical miracle when someone recovers from cancer, when all we really have a right to say is that we do not understand the process. (Again, however, the faithful will acknowledge that it is still God's work of healing: see Sir 38:1–15.)

On the other hand, we know enough about some things that we can have confidence when speaking of them. As C. S. Lewis pointed out: "No doubt a modern gynaecologist knows several things about birth and begetting which St. Joseph did not know. But those things do not concern the main point—that a virgin birth is contrary to the course of nature. And St. Joseph obviously knew *that*."[22]

These definitions and qualifications are an abstraction in technical or scientific language; their goal is to help us think clearly. At the same time, the biblical presentation comes to us in ordinary and poetic language. Such presentations will therefore rarely if ever be concerned to spell out the physics and metaphysics of the events they describe; that is something they will typically leave the audience to infer.

Why, for example, does Psalm 104 systematically present God as the cause of all the good things it records? In order to answer that, we first note that the psalm does not deny a proper causal contribution on the part of created things: The springs do what they do in order to supply water for "every beast of the field" (v. 11), and the grass grows in order to feed the livestock (v. 14).

And for the psalm's attribution of divine action, we come back to our points about rhetoric and characterization, as over against conception. John Rogerson captures this perfectly when he says:

> These passages [that express pervasive divine activity] do not represent what the average Israelite felt; they are religious texts, containing a religious interpretation of the natural world, a religious interpretation that was certainly not "given" along with ordinary perception of the world, and which was by no means self-evident to anyone who reflected on the processes of the natural world. . . . The attempt of the Old Testament writers to claim the sovereignty of God over nature and its workings was

---

(New York: Crossroad, 1994), 71–72. He describes gaps that are "patches of contemporary ignorance" and "*intrinsic* gaps in the bottom-up description alone in order to leave room for top-down action" (71, emphasis original). This is especially interesting because Polkinghorne does not favor the scholastic metaphysic given above.

22. Lewis, *Miracles*, 46–47 (chapter 7; emphasis original).

not something easily attained with the help of thought processes or an "outlook" that readily saw the divine in everything. It was rather a courageous act of faith, persisted in when there was often much in personal experience and competing religions and outlooks, that suggested that such a conviction was false.[23]

In other words, we should be seeking to discover what these texts *do*. This explains why, for example, biblical passages would speak of God giving (or withholding) children—not to deny the appropriate pace of the biological process but to shape how parents lean in to the presence (or absence) of their children. After all, in Genesis 30:1–24 we find the characters attributing the children to God's "giving," and this is never set over against the normal human activity by which a man and woman make a baby. (For God's giving and withholding, see verses 2, 6, 18, 19, 23; for the human activity, see verses 3–5, 9–10, 16–17.)[24] This union and its causal properties are part of the creation order (Gen 1:28; 2:24), and even sordid acts do not dissolve the causal nexus (Gen 19:30–38). By the same kind of complementarity, there is no real contradiction between saying *the Lord* incited David to take the census (2 Sam 24:1) and *Satan* incited David to take the census (1 Chron. 21:1).

This combination of metaphysic and rhetorical awareness allows us to analyze the deliverance of Jerusalem from the forces of Sennacherib (2 Kgs 19:35 // Isa 37:36; 2 Chron 32:21), which some have set over against what seems to be a naturalistic telling of the same event by the Greek historian Herodotus.[25] The biblical texts say that an angel of the Lord slew a large number of Assyrian soldiers, which caused the surviving army to flee. Herodotus (*Hist.*, 2.141.5) records an incident in which, during the night, "an army of field mice swarmed through [the Assyrian] camp and chewed up their quivers, bowstrings, and even the handles of their shields." As a result, the army woke up, and defenseless, "many fell as they tried to flee."[26] Let us suppose, *for the sake of this discussion alone*, that these two accounts deal with the same events: Are they competing alternatives?[27] Certainly not. A "supernatural"

---

23. John Rogerson, "The Old Testament View of Nature: Some Preliminary Questions," in *Instruction and Interpretation*, ed. H. A. Brongers et al., Oudtestamentische Studiën 20 (Leiden: Brill, 1977), 67–84, at 79, 84.
24. For discussion of what stance the passage takes toward the mandrakes (vv. 14–18), see ch. 4 above.
25. See further A. R. Millard, "The Old Testament and History: Some Considerations," *Faith & Thought* 110 (1983): 34–53; idem., "Sennacherib's Attack on Hezekiah," *TynBul* 36 (1985): 61–77.
26. English is from Robert Strassler, ed., *The Landmark Herodotus: The Histories* (New York: Anchor, 2007).
27. There are difficulties in this identification, as Richard Briggs, *The Virtuous Reader: Old Testament Narratives and Interpretive Virtue* (Grand Rapids: Baker Academic, 2010), 118, notes.

event can use means (the mice), and, if the mice were a "natural" occurrence, it is still, to the eye of faith, God's act. Indeed, it remains conceivable that Herodotus's telling missed out on the possible function of the mice as symbolic of pestilence, in which case the event had more complexity than Herodotus suggested.[28]

10.A.2 Evaluating Objections

Now we can go back to evaluate the statements that began this discussion. First, John Walton's notion that "People in the ancient world had no category for what we call *natural laws*" and "were more inclined to see the world's operation in terms of divine cause" fails to account for the rhetorical work of passages like Psalm 104. That text decidedly does *not* articulate the ordinary, or default, view; rather, it aims to inculcate the perspective of faith (which includes natural causality, as we saw), which actually *corrects* the default views.

Second, N. T. Wright's characterization of the popular alternative to Hume's anti-miracle argument misses the point. No one worth interacting with ever thought that God was normally absent and that he intervened in a haphazard or arbitrary fashion. Further, the notion of "natural" and "supernatural" is a legitimate abstraction from the biblical materials and gives us a good sense of what a sensible Galilean villager—such as Joseph, the fiancé of Mary—would have understood: Why else would he have thought of divorcing Mary quietly? In other words, the scholastic tradition, though at times it may have treated the biblical passages clumsily, deserves more respect than Wright accorded it.

As for the Bultmann quotation, we can see the combination of *both* a faulty reading of the biblical materials *and* the imposition of a worldview preference (naturalism: the universe as closed system), which is not itself inherent in the scientific outlook (though Bultmann treats it as if it were).[29] I will simply note some things that touch on our topic. Of course, within the biblical worldview we can use the electric lights and the wireless, not to mention modern medicine. These are all technologies that exploit the natural properties of the things God made; they are part of exercising dominion (see Sir 38:1–15). And the spirits and miracles in the Bible do not come willy-nilly, nor capriciously; nor do they undermine the functioning of the natural properties. Some people mistakenly suppose that because we have so many occasions of miracles, therefore the Bible leads us to expect them all the time.

---

28. See Strassler, ed., *The Landmark Herodotus: The Histories*, 184 n2.141.5a.
29. On this point, see Alvin Plantinga, *Where the Conflict Really Lies: Science, Religion, and Naturalism* (Oxford: Oxford University Press, 2011), especially ch. 3. As Plantinga observed, the idea of a closed system of inexorable laws was already out of date in physics when Bultmann wrote.

But, as a matter of fact, the speech act theory idea of "tellability" helps us here:[30] The authors select what events to record precisely because they are worth telling about—probably because they so rarely occur.

10.A.3 Divine Action in the Creation Story

We are now in a position to assess the kind of divine action involved in the creation story. Consider the two most obvious texts in Genesis 1 (vv. 12, 25):

> The earth brought forth vegetation [in compliance with God's wish], plants yielding seed according to their own kinds, and trees bearing fruit in which is their seed, each according to its kind. . . .
>
> And God made the beasts of the earth according to their kinds and the livestock according to their kinds, and everything that creeps on the ground according to its kind. And God saw that it was good.

Several authors are sure they know what sort of divine action is in view here. For example, Denis Lamoureux insists:

> The notion of the immutability of living organisms is clearly present in Genesis 1. That chapter states ten times that plants and animals reproduce "according to its/their kind/s."[31]

Lamoureux's aim is to disentangle the Bible from science altogether: His argument is along the lines of, since we know that this text of Genesis is scientifically wrong, we should go to Genesis for timeless moral and spiritual principles and not for anything like science. Others, however, think that the Genesis sayings on kinds put limits on how much evolution we may legitimately expect to find; these would include young-earth creationists and many progressive creationists (for whom the earth's age is not a theological issue).[32]

This reading that finds Genesis to have fixed the "kinds" immutably ignores a number of literary and rhetorical features of the creation story itself. I have already argued that its style is best categorized as exalted prose. Its language use, then, will vary along the line from ordinary to poetic.

---

30. See Mary Louise Pratt, *Toward a Speech Act Theory of Literary Discourse* (Bloomington: Indiana University Press, 1977), 136–47.

31. Denis Lamoureux, in *Four Views of Historical Adam* (Grand Rapids: Zondervan, 2014), 55.

32. For an exemplary progressive creationist, see Gilbert Rorison, "The Creative Week," in *Replies to "Essays and Reviews,"* ed. E. M. Goulburn (New York: Appleton, 1862), 242–98: "The strata of the earth are the register of divine acts strictly creative and supernatural; each marking a step in an ordered progress culminating at last in a man" (p. 279).

Further, Genesis 1 says nothing about any processes by which God shaped the earth and fashioned the animals. The author does not say there were any, nor does he say there were none. Rather, talking about them is not the purpose of the text. At the same time, the story does mention the "Spirit of God," and it has God repeatedly "saying" things; this makes clear to the audience that the universe did not organize itself and holds open the possibility that God might have added something to whatever mix is involved. (This says nothing against the natural processes.)

Now, the word "kind" is not the same as "species." The Hebrew word (מִין, *min*) means something like "category" or "variety," and its basis for classification is the appearance to the naked eye.[33] Neither does Genesis deal with the question of whether one kind can turn into another: It simply notes that, according to God's plan, the different plants produce their seeds, each according to its kind, and that God made the animals, each by its kind.

I argued earlier (regarding audience criticism in ch. 5) that the original audience consisted primarily of farmers and shepherds. Such people already knew how to get more sheep: You breed them from your sheep and not from camels. If you want to grow barley, you plant barley seeds and not oats. That is, the fact that plants and animals reproduce according to their kinds is not news to the audience, and we should probably look for another function of the text than simply that of supplying information that they already had.

As it turns out, we do have an ancient scientific text about the fixity of the kinds, but it comes from *Aristotle*, not *Moses*. The LXX for the Genesis phrase "according to (its) kind" is κατὰ γένος. Aristotle, in his work *Generation of Animals* (1.1 [715-*b*]), uses the cognate phrase κατὰ τὴν συγγενείαν. He tells us that animals reproduce "according to their kinds," and he then adds an explanation why it must always be so, which is what makes his passage scientific or philosophical: "If the products were dissimilar from their parents, and yet able to copulate, we should then get arising from them yet another different manner of creature, and out of their progeny yet another, and so it would go on *ad infinitum*. Nature, however, avoids what is infinite." We might or might not agree with his reasoning, and it may or may not be possible to employ his overall philosophy even in an evolutionary context,[34] but we can

---

33. See Mark Futato, "מִין [*mîn*]" 4786 in *NIDOTTE*, 2:934–935; Paul Seely, "The Basic Meaning of *mîn*, 'Kind'," *SCB* 9:1 (1997): 47–56.

34. See, for example, James G. Lennox, "Are Aristotelian Species Eternal?" reprinted in Lennox, *Aristotle's Philosophy of Biology: Studies in the Origins of Life Science* (Cambridge: Cambridge University Press, 2000); Christopher Austin, "Aristotelian Essentialism: Essence in an Age of Evolution," *Synthese* 193 (2016): doi:10.1007/s11229–016–1066–4; Mariusz Tabaczek, "An Aristotelian Account of Evolution and the Contemporary Philosophy of Biology," *Dialogo: Proceedings of the Conferences on the Dialogue Between Science and Theology* (November 6–11, 2014): 57–69.

at least recognize how different his scientific-philosophical presentation is from the simple and evocative one we find in Genesis. We can, and should, call Aristotle "ancient science," and I think he deserves respect for what he accomplished.[35] On the other hand, to call Genesis "science," whether ancient or modern, is an enormous literary confusion. Its purpose is, rather, to enable its audiences to celebrate God's work of creation as a magnificent achievement.

Therefore, if it should be the case that there is a natural process that produces something like evolution, the faithful audience of Genesis will still affirm that it is God's process, and therefore designed, reflecting his purposes. To be sure, from a Lewisian perspective, a wholly natural process is not enough to account for everything we see; as Lewis noted,

> Again, for the scientist Evolution is a purely biological theorem. It takes over organic life on this planet as a going concern and tries to explain certain changes within that field. It makes no cosmic statements, no metaphysical statements, no eschatological statements. . . . It does not in itself explain the origin of organic life, nor of the variations, nor does it discuss the origin and validity of reason. It may well tell you how the brain, through which reason now operates, arose, but that is a different matter. Still less does it even attempt to tell you how the universe as a whole arose, or what it is, or whither it is tending.[36]

If there is a designed process of evolution, we may legitimately find places in which the process does not of itself have the capacity to produce the desired results. G. K. Chesterton put it this way:

> No philosopher denies that a mystery still attaches to the two great transitions: the origin of the universe itself and the origin of the principle of life itself. Most philosophers have the enlightenment to add that a third mystery attaches to the origin of man himself. In other words, a third bridge was built across a third abyss of the unthinkable when there came into the world what we call reason and what we call will.[37]

To speak of a "bridge" across an "abyss of the unthinkable" is to say that these three transitions transcend the (divinely designed) processes. This

---

35. For a description of Aristotle's natural philosophy with a sympathetic assessment, see Lindberg, *The Beginnings of Western Science*, 46–68.
36. C. S. Lewis, "The Funeral of a Great Myth," in *Christian Reflections*, ed. Walter Hooper (Grand Rapids: Eerdmans, 1967), 82–93, quote on p. 86.
37. G. K. Chesterton, *The Everlasting Man* (Garden City, NY: Doubleday, 1955 [1925]), 27.

is a philosophical observation not liable to the changing tides of scientific theories. The origin of the universe confronts us with why there is something rather than nothing, and we do not think that the properties of the universe explain its existence. The origin of life from non-life involves instituting an information processing system, which uses the properties of the components but is not fully determined by them.[38] The origin of the human mind leads to a capacity that participates in transcendence.[39] These are not likely to be *lacunae ignorantiae causā*, since there is a principle that shows why the natures of the things involved are not enough. This means that the arguments for finding *lacunae naturae causā* in these places are worthy of discussion: If they are mistaken, the mistake is not self-evident, and the arguments deserve more than the brush-off they often receive.

In the second pericope in Genesis, a description complementary to the sixth day of Genesis 1 tells us that "the LORD God formed the man of dust from the ground and breathed into his nostrils the breath of life, and the man became a living creature" (2:7). As I mentioned in chapter 8 above, most readers have taken this to depict a straight-from-dirt-to-first-human scenario. Many today suppose that for the depiction to be true, it requires such a scenario as a scientific theory. Interestingly enough, some prominent advocates of the traditional metaphysic I have described here did not insist on such a scenario—people such as Chesterton, Lewis, and Benjamin Warfield found no difficulty with a picture that involved ancestry for the first humans, so long as the process also included both divine governance and divine additions.

How might we assess this in light of the kind of study I am offering? First, we must be careful about interpreting the words. For example, how shall we read the words "formed . . . of dust" (Gen 2:7)? The very conservative J. Oliver Buswell said (rightly, I judge) that the wording of Genesis 2:7

---

[38]. This is a major theme of Stephen Meyer in many places, e.g., *Signature in the Cell: DNA and the Evidence for Intelligent Design* (New York: HarperCollins, 2009). Dennis Venema, a biologist, criticizes Meyer on this point in Dennis Venema and Scot McKnight, *Adam and the Genome: Reading Scripture after Genetic Science* (Grand Rapids: Baker Academic, 2017), 89. There is evidence, he says, "that the genetic code has a chemical basis." However, the question is not whether there are chemical biases but rather whether the chemical biases are enough *to explain the whole system*—but if they do, then we may no longer call it an *information* processing system, and this does not seem to be a judgment that biologists are likely to be making.

[39]. C. S. Lewis argued this in many places. See my exploration in "A Peculiar Clarity: How C. S. Lewis Can Help Us Think About Faith and Science," in *The Magician's Twin: C. S. Lewis on Science, Scientism, and Society*, ed. John G. West (Seattle: Discovery Institute Press, 2012), 69–106. Lewis drew on Arthur James Balfour, *Theism and Humanism* (New York: Hodder & Stoughton, 1915). Important figures who agree with Lewis include Plantinga, *Where the Conflict Really Lies*, especially ch. 10; Thomas Nagel, *Mind and Cosmos: Why the Materialist Neo-Darwinian Conception of Nature is Almost Certainly False* (New York: Oxford University Press, 2012); and concisely and trenchantly, Robert Larmer, "Theistic Complementarianism and Ockham's Razor," *Philosophia Christi* 7:2 (2005): 503–14.

gives no specifications as to the process by which the forming was accomplished. The result is all that is specified. Moses is here referring to the simple, obvious fact that the human body is made of the common elements of the soil.[40]

This fact would indeed have been simple and obvious to the audience of Genesis, familiar as they were with what happens when people die: not only would Adam "return to dust" (3:19), all people do. Humans and other creatures are made from dust and return to it (see Ps 104:29; Eccl 3:20; 12:7; Job 10:8–9; Ps 90:3). Hence Psalm 103:14 would observe that God "knows how we are formed, he remembers that we are dust" (using ESV margin)—and the congregation singing these words knows full well that the "forming" involves intermediate steps.

But interpretation has to account for the words as they function within the whole communication. The issue of what processes led to the first humans does not lie on the surface of Genesis, nor was it likely to have been a concern of its first audiences: Rather, the people of God need a name for their common-knowledge perception of human distinctiveness, "the image of God" (Gen 1:27); and they need an affirmation that their ultimate origin lies with the intentions of the Creator. From the way that this text interacts with their preexisting knowledge, a good audience can infer that their human distinctiveness required special divine action to bring it about, and they would find the use of the word "create" (Gen 1:27) quite suited to that.

This does not offer a scientific theory as such, in that it does not involve a theory of how and when and over what stretch of time Chesterton's "bridges over the abysses" were built. It does, on the other hand, support the common-sense challenge to purely naturalistic theories of life's history, a challenge that has long standing in human intellectual history.[41]

Further, this possibility of extra additions along the way is no insult to the Creator's omnipotence. As Lewis also noted,

> Omnipotence means power to do all that is intrinsically possible, not to do the intrinsically impossible. . . . Meaningless combinations of words do not suddenly acquire meaning simply because we prefix to them the

---

40. J. Oliver Buswell, *A Systematic Theology of the Christian Religion* (Grand Rapids: Zondervan, 1962–63), I:159. Buswell himself offered arguments against any idea of a genetic process being involved, which shows his honesty in what he said.

41. I have found it at least as early as Dionysius of Alexandria (d. AD 264), in a fragment preserved by Eusebius (*Praep. ev.*, 780-cd).

two other words "God can." It remains true that all *things* are possible with God: the intrinsic impossibilities are not things but nonentities.[42]

10.B WHERE THE CONFLICT REALLY LIES

The kind of rhetorical and literary rigor I am advocating in this study may seem to some as a way of avoiding the possibility of any conflict whatsoever between the conclusions the scientists might make and those we derive from our reading of the Bible (be it ever so careful). But such conflicts are possible—or else the scientific theories and the biblical assertions cannot be falsified. The discussion in the previous section will enable us, then, to ascertain where actual conflicts can arise and of what sort they will be. Of course, difficulties will come up when either the scientific theory or the biblical reading have overstepped the boundaries established by the kinds of evidence on which they depend. For example, a neuroscientist whose study of the brain leads him to reduce thought simply to the movements of molecules in the brain has not adequately faced the problem he has created by that reduction, namely, that he has denied the validity of the thoughts behind his own reductive thinking.[43] By the same token, the Bible reader who concludes from Mark 5:26 and Luke 8:43 (about the woman with a discharge of blood, whom physicians had not been able to help) that physicians are *always* useless, runs afoul of common experiences (not to mention biblical texts) that endorse the human use of causal properties in relieving distress.

In this section, however, I want to offer some tools for discerning whether there is a real conflict. The philosopher Alvin Plantinga has argued in his book, *Where the Conflict Really Lies: Science, Religion, and Naturalism*, the central thesis: "There is superficial conflict but deep concord between science and theistic religion, but superficial concord and deep conflict between science and naturalism."[44] Now, Plantinga has written about "theistic religion," but his main interest is of course in Christianity and Judaism. These faiths in turn rely on their readings of the biblical passages, which readings may or may not bring in more of the "superficial conflict" that Plantinga writes about. The approach to reading I have developed in this work generally supports Plantinga's point.

I contend in the following several paragraphs that the model of divine action that I described in the previous section makes it clear that this is where

---

42. C. S. Lewis, *The Problem of Pain* (New York: Macmillan, 1962), 16 (ch. 2); emphasis original.
43. This is not a straw man: Anthony Cashmore made just this assertion in the *Proceedings of the National Academy of Sciences* in 2010. For "Lewisian" discussion see Collins, "A Peculiar Clarity: How C. S. Lewis Can Help Us Think About Faith and Science," 69–106.
44. Plantinga states this expressly in *Where the Conflict Really Lies*, ix.

the potential for conflict really lies: someone might deny, a priori, the possibility of divine governance; or, on the other hand, someone might look for a supernatural event when it is "natural." In other words, other issues, such as the age of the earth and the degree of biological descent with modification do not produce such conflicts (at least as I read Genesis). In order to do that, however, I need to introduce some tools for critical thinking that are often overlooked.

In many endeavors we find a range of competing views: in politics, for example, we speak of views as *conservative* (or rightist), over against *progressive* (or leftist). In Bible translation theory, we describe translations as *literal* (or formally equivalent) or *free* (or functionally equivalent). Most people recognize that these polarities are not enough. Any particular person's political views will lie along a spectrum from more conservative to more progressive—and the same applies to Bible translations. But here I want to point out the obvious problem, namely, things are not even that simple. For example, a person might believe in protecting all vulnerable lives from conception to natural death and at the same time also believe in protecting the environment—views that, at least in the United States, are counted as conservative and progressive, respectively. That is, the subjects "sanctity of life" and "environment" are separate variables.

When it comes to creation and science, we have the same kind of spectrum proposed. The variation from strict young-earth creationist to full-blooded evolutionist might look like this:

Deistic/ Naturalistic evolutionist	Theistic evolutionist	Evolutionary creationist	Progressive creationist	YEC

This picture has important strengths, which is why people use it. It recognizes that views lie along a continuum and the categories are not discreet, airtight boxes. On the other hand, this kind of picture does not actually capture the nuances of different positions. For example, what exactly is an old-earth creationist? Where does intelligent design fit in here? That project as articulated by the Discovery Institute crosses over these categories. Speaking for myself, I cannot find my own spot on this spectrum.

And what about Aristotle? As discussed in the previous section, he is both basically naturalistic or Deistic, and non-evolutionary—something for which this spectrum does not account. This difficulty leads to the insight that the classification system combines different dimensions, which ought not be combined: Naturalism in contemporary Western culture tends to be evolutionary, but the example of Aristotle shows that this correlation is not necessary—it is not embedded in the very nature of things.

Perhaps a brief word about naturalism will be in order here, since the word can be used in more than one sense (and I am leaving out its relation to art). *Ontological naturalism* is the claim that natural processes are the only ones relevant to any event. By this view science is the search for the true explanations of each and every thing and event in the cosmos. *Methodological naturalism* aims to bracket the philosophical question of whether, as Hamlet put it, "There are more things in heaven and earth, Horatio, than are dreamt of in your philosophy" (Shakespeare's *Hamlet*, 1.5.167–68), and simply to agree, as a matter of method, only to address the natural causes of things and events. Depending on the person using the term, methodological naturalism can be the modest claim that the scientific study takes the natural processes as far as they can go and does not use the word "miracle" for something that is simply a matter of ignorance. By this understanding, it is legitimate to say that we do not have a credible natural explanation for this, and we probably cannot find one that does not involve an agent, even though that is not our subject of study. The more ambitious claim is that, in principle, science aims to offer a natural explanation in all cases; when coupled with the view that science aims to tell the truth about everything, this harder form of methodological naturalism ends up making a strong ontological claim, and doing so a priori.[45] Obviously the only way it can be right is if we already know beforehand that natural factors are all there is for everything; or else we can give up on the view that science aims to tell the truth and reduce it to a game with arbitrary rules. If we are to retain any kind of connection between science and truth, then scientific reasoning must employ good principles of critical thinking—which lays the a priori assumptions open to critical review.

As I mentioned in the first chapter, my first education focused on science and engineering. The idea of different dimensions leads me to a useful metaphor that reconceives the possibility space.

Consider how we locate items in our experience. Suppose, for example, a friend invited me to join him for a meal at the restaurant of the Four Seasons Hotel in downtown Chicago. If I thought that simply finding the street address (120 East Delaware Place) were enough to get me there, I would go

---

[45]. The (American) National Association of Biology Teachers makes the stronger form of methodological naturalism a part of science, a priori: "Evolutionary biology rests on the same scientific methodologies the rest of science uses, *appealing only to natural events and processes to describe and explain phenomena in the natural world.*" See "NABT Position Statement on Teaching Evolution," adopted in 1995 and modified in 1997, 2000, 2004, 2008, and 2011, accessed January 2016, http://www.nabt.org/websites/institution/?p=92.

hungry: The restaurant is on the seventh floor, while the hotel rooms occupy the thirtieth through forty-sixth floors of the skyscraper. That is, I need more than just the coordinates, which are two dimensions (longitude and latitude); I need a third dimension, namely, height. This picture gives a standard way of representing three-dimensional space:

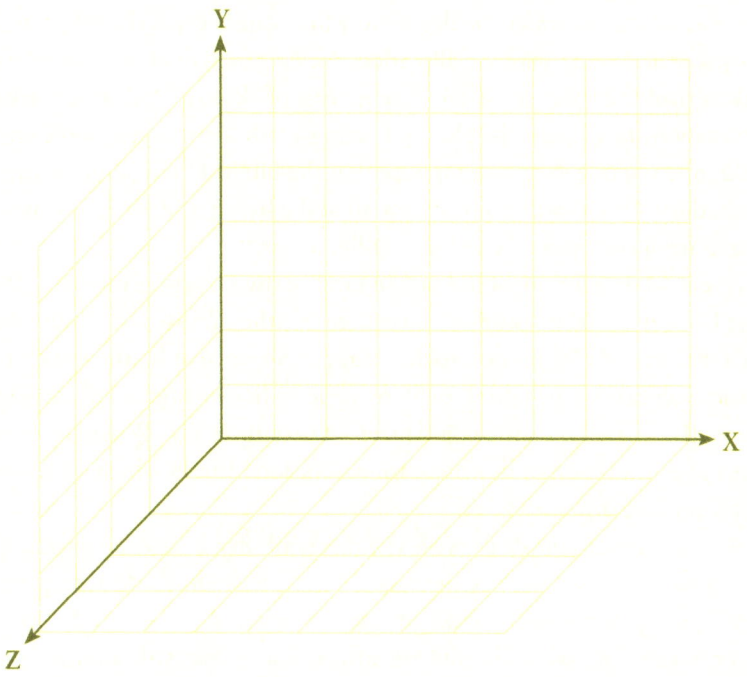

The dimensions, or axes (labelled x, y, and z), allow variation along more than one line; and one can hold one dimension stable while varying the other two.

This three-dimensional representation provides a metaphor for these other subjects we are considering (politics, translation, creation views). The common spectrum picture assumes that we are adequately describing the differing views in terms of variation along only one dimension; but this one-dimensional approach collapses too many ideas into one axis—which means that it is inadequate. In my discussion of genre in chapter 2, I suggested that the term has been used in such a way as to collapse various distinct dimensions (such as literary form, style and register, language level, and social function) so that the term's flexibility actually gets in the way of sound analysis.

The controversies that arise from discussing politics and Bible translation philosophy are as intractable as those that swirl around creation views, so I will confine my treatment here to just the one subject. What dimensions should we use in order to do full justice to the different kinds of perspectives on creation and science?

In order to focus on the question of evolution, we will leave aside for the time being the question of how old the earth is. (After all, even many ardent young-earth creationists accept some development of species from a smaller number of original kinds—say, from those that Noah brought on the ark.)

First, we can consider the degree to which one accepts the origin of species by way of descent with modification. An Aristotelian of the strongest sort would affirm the fixity of "species," or at least of "kinds."[46] Many contemporary creationists, of both the old- and young-earth sorts, accept some level of development, while they also suppose that the biblical "kinds" are some sort of boundary. Others will suppose that all of the living things we currently see descend from the original one (or few) life forms.[47]

A second dimension would be the kind of divine action involved. It can range from none (the naturalistic version), to the almost indistinguishable hands-off (strong Deism), to providential concurrence only (the strong-form theistic evolutionary position), to allowing for what we might call extra infusions of divine guidance and adjustment (of varying levels). Perhaps we might make the extreme end of this dimension occasionalism in which there are no natural causal properties at all.

A third dimension deals with the discernibility of divine action. That is, a person might allow that the Deity (or deities) could add things to the process but leave no clear marks of such addition. Another might suppose that only some of the additions are discernible, while still another might argue that many of them are. Of course, these apply only to those who hold a model of divine action that allows for additions. Those who do not so allow might nevertheless consider some overall purposiveness in the process, discernible to humans (which seems to be the burden of Aquinas's version of the argument from design),[48] or not. And, of course, down at the Deist or naturalist end of this line, they will declare all such acts of discerning to be false positives. Christians who hold some form of intelligent design will vary from those who affirm only large-scale discernibility to those who also affirm the discernibility of smaller-scale extras.[49]

---

46. Aristotle's usage of "kind" seems to be narrower than taxonomic family, though it may be wider than what we now call biological species (see discussion in §10.A above).

47. Using the words of Darwin's closing paragraph in *On the Origin of Species by Means of Natural Selection, or the Preservation of Favoured Races in the Struggle for Life* (6th edition, 1872); Darwin actually spoke of the Creator having breathed life into these original forms.

48. At least as Frank Beckwith reads it. See Beckwith, "How to Be an Anti-Intelligent Design Advocate," *University of St. Thomas Journal of Law and Public Policy* 4, no. 1 (2010): 35–65.

49. The movement called Intelligent Design (ID) tends to shy away from referring to *divine* action

There are more diagnostic dimensions as well. For example, we may also consider the degree to which one's approach to the other dimensions is a priori (say, based on philosophical or exegetical factors), as opposed to a posteriori (a conclusion inferred from one's empirical study). For example, Christians often read Genesis as requiring them to affirm that the kinds set some sort of limit—and this is something they bring to their studies: How does the confirmation they think they are finding in their studies combine the empirics and the expectations? On the other hand, some people insist that the very nature of science requires a commitment to naturalism (even beyond the methodological sort) and will therefore not allow any possibility that anything might have been added to the process. Those who adhere to methodological naturalism for the sake of science must ask whether this limits their ability to tell the truth (as I suspect that it does). If after study one concludes that the process was largely—or even entirely—natural, that is a different matter.

A further factor might be something analogous to what Thomas Kuhn called "commensurability," namely, the degree to which people can be argued into changing their perspective on some of these questions.[50] No doubt there are other dimensions as well.

By this sort of analysis, consider some who have been called "theistic evolutionists," namely, Benjamin Warfield, C. S. Lewis, and G. K. Chesterton. The label "theistic evolution" does not quite capture what they held to—unless we restrict the word "evolution" merely to the biological process of descent with modification, leaving open the question of how God was active and how the modifications were introduced. In the previous section I showed that Lewis and Chesterton would count special divine action to have been indispensable in whatever process was involved in order to arrive at human personhood. Warfield was similar. In fact, they apparently thought the special divine action was discernible, since they argued for it. (As mentioned below, Lewis was much more reluctant to affirm a discernible purpose in the overall process.)

The analogy of several dimensions illuminates what was otherwise dark to me. The present study shows why we need not see Genesis as denying, limiting, or affirming descent with modification, so long as by that we mean a scientific theory, open to examination and critique. The kind and discernibility

and focuses more on "scientific detectability" of features that require more than an undirected natural process, while I have preferred the more intuitive, and perhaps philosophical, term "discernment." Note that I am also distinguishing between *I*ntelligent *D*esign as a *movement*, and *i*ntelligent *d*esign as an *intellectual endeavor*.

50. Thomas Kuhn, *The Structure of Scientific Revolutions* (Chicago: University of Chicago Press, 1970).

of divine action are much more important and a place in which conflict may really lie, as I have suggested: for example, when people wish to define both science and evolution in terms that import a form of naturalism into the definition; or when a reading of the Bible requires one to look for supernatural causation when the events are actually natural (as a good reading of the Bible would have confirmed).

The stress on the overall biblical storyline as a worldview narrative, which gives the big story of the world, comes to bear here. Biblical faith takes assurance that the big story is a purposeful one—that is, it reflects the overall design that Aquinas argued for. Finding design in the universe's properties, commonly called the appeal to fine-tuning, is helpful, though it is hard to know just how contingent the physical properties of the universe are.[51] To appeal to the design of orchestrated events in the world's history is very indecisive. As C. S. Lewis observed, we know far too little to offer anything remotely resembling a reliable reading of these events.[52] Hence the sprinkling of "special" events, which can authenticate the divine spokespersons and make God's interest more visible, can also serve to reassure the faithful of the prophets' interpretation of events and of God's involvement in the world's story.

There may be reasons, scientific and philosophical (and even theological), to subject the various kinds of evolutionary theory to critical review. After all, there are several versions of the theories out there, and the idea of an impersonal and pointless process does not suit the data, either of biology or of the Bible. But my attention here is on what the faithful are supposed to be getting from Genesis; that is, on the perspective of faith, that all this comes from God and reflects his purposes for humankind. What kind of stance, then, should a good reader take in exercising dominion over God's world? One of trust, and confidence, and stewardship, and bold embrace.

---

51. As Simon Conway Morris said of fine-tuning, "All this smacks of design: physicists are rightly wary and the invisible host of multiverses is ever popular." See Conway Morris, "The Boyle Lecture 2005: Darwin's Compass: How Evolution Discovers the Song of Creation," *SCB* 18 (2006): 5–22, quote on p. 8.

52. C. S. Lewis, "Historicism," in *Christian Reflections*, ed. Walter Hooper (Grand Rapids: Eerdmans, 1967), 100–13, while noting that Christianity sees history as "a story with a well-defined plot" (p. 103), shows how unreasonable it is to suppose that one who is not a prophet can interpret how any individual event fits into that story.

Chapter 11

GENESIS 1–11: A HUMANE MORAL VISION FOR ISRAEL AND THE WORLD

I began by suggesting that, even though literalism has now come to be seen as the genuinely honest way of reading the Bible, it has not always been that way. At the same time, the resort to such explanations as phenomenal or poetic language has had the feel of being arbitrary. Even so, the ideas themselves seem valid, at least at the intuitive level; perhaps what we need is methodological rigor? Observations from C. S. Lewis point us to tools and ways of thinking that have been developed by specialists in linguistics, rhetoric, and literary theory. In this work I have laid hold of those tools in order to offer what I hold to be a more rigorous approach to reading Genesis 1–11 (and the rest of the Bible as well)—an approach that retains the intuitions that lie behind Lewis's observations and sets them on a firm footing.

The modern sciences present the faithful with a range of issues that seem to challenge their faith—issues such as how to think about God's action in the world, about human origins and their place in the world, and about the problem of evil.[1] The methods that I have considered here should provide resources for thinking well about these matters. None of these considerations undermines the possibility that Bible writers can refer to real persons and real events (however hard we might find it to confirm or disconfirm that

---

1. I thank the philosopher J. B. Stump for his thoughts in framing this list. He offers his own list in his blog post for Biologos, "4 Theological Objections to Evolution," biologos.org/blogs/jim-stump-faith-and-science-seeking-understanding/4-theological-objections-to-evolution.

reference). Literary and rhetorical analyses cannot of themselves decide whether the telling actually *is* true and to what extent; their task is to clarify what kinds of claims we are deciding about.

I will draw this work to a close with a few thoughts on what it means to appropriate these chapters of Genesis responsibly. I have shown why I think they should not be pressed into a scientific theory, whether of the young-earth or old-earth or evolutionary kind; at the same time, I do see them as providing grounds for a proper critique—or at least pushback—for certain kinds of scientific theories, particularly those that overstep their empirical bounds and begin to make worldview assertions. The places where potential conflict is most acute are those in which the kinds of divine action are in play. This is especially so in the a priori expectations that researchers bring to their studies: By this I mean both the philosophical imposition of methodological naturalism and the troubles that arise from faulty exegesis.

Here I will outline, briefly, how the story ought to function, both for ancient Israel and for the modern Christian. I will also expand a bit on what I said in chapter 6 about the Pentateuch as constitution.

11.A REDEMPTIVE HISTORY AS WORLDVIEW STORY

In chapter 6 I suggested that Genesis 1–11 serves as the front end of the worldview story for ancient Israel. I want here to set that in the larger picture of the history of redemption.

Unfortunately, there is no regulatory agency for what an author should mean by "the history of redemption," so I will offer the definition by which I am working. I start by noting that, in several places, writers in the Hebrew Bible say that God has "redeemed" or "saved" his "people" (such as Exod 15:13; Pss 77:15; 106:4; compare Luke 1:68). The "people" (Heb. עַם [*'am*]; Gk. λαός) is a corporate entity of which the particular persons are its members. That is, the "people" is more than a collection of persons; it has an existence of its own. The person finds his or her identity by way of membership in the people.

Biblical covenants are made with a people, by way of a representative. For example, in Genesis 9:9–17 God makes his covenant with Noah's descendants as well as with all the animal world, through Noah. God's covenant with Abram (Gen 12:1–3) works the same way: The people of Israel participate in the covenant by virtue of their connection to Abram. In fact, the call of Abram holds out the possibility that "in" Abram "all the families of the earth shall be blessed,"[2] an expectation that functions as the eschatology of the Hebrew Bible.[3]

The expression "in Abram" makes sense in this corporate picture; a similar expression appears in 2 Samuel 20:1, where Sheba leads a rebellion against David and disavows any obligation to David and his house (see also 2 Sam 19:43; 1 Kgs 12:16 // 2 Chron 10:16):

> We have no portion *in David*,
> and we have no inheritance *in the son of Jesse*;
> every man to his tents, O Israel!

To "be in X" or to "have a portion in X," then, means to "be a member of that people for whom X is the representative." This provides, I think, the backcloth for the apostolic terms "in Christ" and "in Adam."[4] I have elsewhere analyzed the use of the Hebrew noun זרע [*zeraʿ*], "offspring," proposing ways to discern whether it speaks of one offspring or many and concluding that some texts in Genesis (22:17b–18; 24:60) have a single offspring in view: in this light, "in your offspring shall all the nations of the earth be blessed" (Gen 22:18) clarifies that the gentiles will receive the "blessing" in the particular offspring (whom later ages would call the Messiah; see Ps 72:17)—or at least, so Paul read it.[5]

When the corporate entity, the "people," is the object, verbs like "redeem" and "save" have reference to God's efforts to protect this entity from threats to its existence and to further the conditions under which the lives of the members can flourish (sometimes with the eventual blessing of the gentiles in view as a result). At those times when the corporate life of the people is dominated by unfaithful members, the redemption or salvation includes divine judgments, by which the unfaithful leaders are purged from the people. Thus, for example, God "redeemed" his people (Exod 15:13) by bringing them safely

---

2. The rendering of the *niphal*, ונברכו [*wenibreku*], is controversial. Some prefer a more "reflexive" rendering, "will bless themselves." This sentiment is repeated several times in Genesis, using the *niphal* and *hitpael* indifferently. I suggest that a middle voice rendering, "will get themselves blessed," captures the sense; and the LXX use of the passive ἐνευλογηθήσονται does just fine.

3. Here I agree, e.g., with Christopher J. H. Wright, *The Mission of God: Unlocking the Bible's Grand Narrative* (Downers Grove, IL: InterVarsity Press, 2006), 194–221. In my discussion in 5.A.2 above, I examine and reject R. W. L. Moberly's critique of this approach, in his *The Theology of the Book of Genesis*, Old Testament Theology (Cambridge: Cambridge University Press, 2009), 141–61.

4. See, for example, N. T. Wright, *Paul and the Faithfulness of God, Parts III & IV* (Minneapolis: Fortress, 2013), 825–30. C. S. Lewis, in *The Problem of Pain* (London: Geoffrey Bles, 1940), chapter 5, rightly connects this idea with the mysterious corporate solidarity that underlies the Hebrew Bible.

5. See T. D. Alexander, "Further Observations on the Term 'Seed' in Genesis," *TynBul* 48:2 (1997): 363–67; C. John Collins, "Galatians 3:16: What Kind of Exegete was Paul?" *TynBul* 54:1 (2003): 75–86.

out of Egypt and through the Red Sea with the prospect of a future in which they will dwell in the promised land, and the other peoples hear and tremble. For God to "make his might known among the peoples" (Ps 77:14) may lead to their submission to the true God. Israel is called to be a kingdom of priests (Exod 19:5–6), which I take to be the vehicle by which the gentiles have holy things ministered to them;[6] by Israel's faithful corporate life in the land the gentiles are to come to admire God (Deut 4:5–8).

11.B "HEIRS" OF THE STORY

N. T. Wright describes what worldviews characteristically do for the communities that they define.[7] They provide—

- "the stories through which human beings view reality," and these stories offer answers to the basic questions (who are we, where are we, what is wrong, what is the solution);
- cultural symbols, both artifacts and events such as festivals;
- "a praxis, a way-of-being-in-the-world."

In his exposition of how communities embrace and foster a worldview among their members, Wright stresses the crucial role of the overarching big story as a context for the other stories, for the symbols, and for the praxis. In the Bible, the worldview serves to define a community, that is, the self-identifying question "Who am I?" can only be answered by reference to such questions as "Who are we?" along with "Where are we? How are we? When are we? and Why are we?"

When the Psalms recount God's "wonders" and "mighty deeds" or similar acts (for example, 136:4; 145:4–7), they are having the assembled worshippers call to mind these great deeds of redemption that God has been working. This record should instill a sense of confidence in the community: This people exists for God's purpose of blessing the world, and he will not fail in it, and therefore he will preserve us his people (purifying it as necessary). But it should also foster gratitude: We are here assembled today, in the presence of the Maker of heaven and earth, as a gift. It should also foster a kind of sobriety: Sometimes our ancestors rejected God's good gifts, and it went poorly for them; let us take warning and not repeat their mistakes. Psalm 78

---

6. Agreeing with, for example, Umberto Cassuto, *Exodus* (Jerusalem: Magnes, 1983 [1951]), 227; Wright, *The Mission of God*, 224–25.

7. N. T. Wright, *The New Testament and the People of God* (Minneapolis: Fortress, 1992), 122–25.

makes some of these illocutions explicit (Ps 78:5–8), but other times they are more implicit, available for the sympathetic audience. The corporate focus does not leave the particular person out: Each member of the people is enabled to join his or her own life to the whole, contributing by their faithfulness to the well-being of the body.

Sacred history selects from the total mass of events in order to pursue these purposes. The story envisions a continuous line from creation through redemption (see, for example, Ps 136). Presumably, to be reliable and in good faith, actual referents should lie behind the ways in which the persons and events are reported. At the same time, the process of selection and telling allows for various rhetorical devices, such as idealization, or the treating of the parts of a complex event as if they were a single one; but the use of rhetoric does not of itself destroy historical truthfulness.

The members, then, can see themselves as heirs of the story, as caretakers of it for the next generation, and as participants, whose life choices play some role in the outworking of the story as it proceeds.

11.B.1 For Israel

I have stressed throughout this work how the features of Genesis 1–11 serve as the front end of the basic story for ancient Israel. In the Pentateuch we also find symbols, such as the sanctuary, the sacrifices, the washing ceremonies, the liturgical calendar, and so forth. The story grounds these various symbols in both the creation order and Israel's special calling in the world.

For example, the creation narrative portrays the sun, moon, and stars as markers for the (liturgical) seasons. They are servants to help humankind worship the Maker, not masters themselves worthy of human worship. The decorations of the sanctuary tapestries evoke elements in the creation, such as the stars. These ceremonies and symbols reaffirm Israel's place as God's "treasured possession among all peoples" (Exod 19:5), whose existence is for the eventual blessing of all peoples.

The Pentateuch also contains laws that establish the workings of a social system. Now the question of how these instructions were to work is certainly controversial, and I will only briefly give my judgment (which largely agrees with that of Gordon Wenham and Christopher Wright).[8] I do not think the term "law code" adequately captures the function of the torah laws. For one

---

8. Gordon Wenham, *Story as Torah: Reading Old Testament Narratives Ethically* (Grand Rapids: Baker Academic, 2004); Christopher J. H. Wright, *Old Testament Ethics for the People of God* (Downers Grove, IL: InterVarsity Press, 2004).

thing, the torah statutes, if compiled together, would be too short. I take them to be a set of exemplary rulings that guide the local elders in assessing damages and adjudicating disputes by providing paradigms of justice. The function of the laws is to protect a minimum level of civility within the theocracy (or church-state nexus) that God constituted Israel to be—and this reflects the view that the community's health is a good to be preserved, because the health of the particular person is tied to it. This concern for the community's health provides an orientation for personal ethics. The ethics themselves are only sketched out in the Pentateuch, largely in terms of imitating God and living out the creation ideal, while books such as Proverbs exhibit and exemplify the day-to-day wisdom by which the faithful can put their calling into practice.[9] From this perspective we can see how the Pentateuch offers a set of aspirations for a faithful life within a safe and healthy community, and makes provision for addressing threats to that safety and health.

But the stories, symbols, and practices also define Israel with respect to the other nations. One aspect of this definition is distinction, even separation: Israel is called to be a holy people (consecrated to God and eligible to be in his presence), with institutions not shared by the nations (Lev 20:22–26). At the same time, there is an affirmation of the other peoples: Not only do some of Israel's practices overlap with those of other peoples (even to the point of co-opting),[10] the laws also make room for the sojourner, protecting his civil rights and allowing him to join in Israel's worship of the true God.[11] With this affirmation comes some amount of purification (say, by eliminating class distinctions in how laws apply). These lead us to the prophetic expectation that all peoples one day will adhere to the God of Israel (as in Amos 9:11–12;[12] Isa 2:1–5; Zeph 3:9–10), as well as to the prophetic warning to Israel that their greater privileges bring greater accountability (as in Amos 3:1–2).

---

9. I have explored some of these questions in "Proverbs and the Levitical System," *Presbyterion* 35:1 (Spring 2009): 9–34 and "Psalms 111–112: Big Story, Little Story," *Religions* 7(9) (2016): 115; doi:10.3390/rel7090115 (open access at www.mdpi.com/2077-1444/7/9/115).

10. It is widely agreed, for example, that many of the laws are similar to those found in gentile law codes. Further, the sacrifices in Israel are presented as something more generally human (as in our examination of the sacrifices made by Cain and Abel, and Noah). Readers of Herodotus, for example, would have seen that other peoples have a clean-unclean food distinction (Herodotus, *Hist.*, 2.37.4–5; 2.47.1) and ceremonial cleansing after marital relations (*Hist.* 1.98.1). The best explanation for Proverbs 31:1–9 is that it has been appropriated from a gentile source. Other peoples knew about protecting widows and orphans (see the Ugaritic tale, *Aqhat*, 17.v.7–8).

11. See, for example, Moshe Greenberg, "Mankind, Israel and the Nations in the Hebraic Heritage," in *No Man Is an Alien: Essays on the Unity of Mankind*, ed. J. Robert Nelson (Leiden: Brill, 1971), 15–40.

12. The fact that the LXX of this text (cited in Acts 15:16–17) reads differently does not obscure the main point, that other nations will be "called by my name."

11.B.2 For Christians

Christians, whether Jewish or gentile by descent, are to hold themselves to be the proper heirs of Abraham and the promises made to him (Rom 4:11–12). This means that they also inherit the privileges and calling given to Israel (1 Pet 2:9–10, echoing Exod 19:5–6).

Christians, like the Israelites before them, have been incorporated into a sacred community of "saints" or "holy people" (Rom 1:7). They have community norms and the aspiration of fostering a safe and healthy community. They have symbols, too, in their sacraments (which derive so much meaning from those of the Pentateuch). And, as Abraham's heirs, they are oriented to their place in the world: to be the means by which God brings his blessing to the rest of the creation (Matt 5:14–16; 1 Pet 2:11–12).

In addition to the affirmation of all kinds of persons as potential members of God's people, there is also the affirmation that many of them have seen some things quite truly. Paul expects (rightly) that "even among pagans" a certain kind of sexual malpractice would not be tolerated (1 Cor 5:1).[13] The image of the people of God as a body has roots in the Hebrew Bible (Isa 1:5–6), but its specific form in the New Testament derives ultimately from Aristotle.[14] In chapter 8 I considered ways in which Jews and Christians responded to Plato's creation story, that is, the affirmation was combined with purification when needed.

Thus, Christians are to take Genesis 1–11 as the front end of the big story that defines them. The choice of Abram was always intended to come back to the rest of humankind, and now the day of blessing has arrived. This story has different stages: the arrangement with Israel was for a time, in service of a later stage of the story. That later stage has arrived with the resurrection of Jesus (see Rom 1:1–6). This narrative shape means that there is nothing arbitrary or unseemly in Christians' stance toward many of the practices in the law, such as the prohibition of certain foods—these served their purpose for their stage of the unfolding story. In other cases, laws functioned within the church-state nexus that was Israel, a nexus that no longer defines God's people. But certainly these laws were informed by a broader idea of justice; and certainly some of the requirements are built in to the creation order. (Many literalists, such as James Barr, make unnecessarily heavy weather over this "failure in literality," as they see it.)[15]

---

13. I discuss this in "Echoes of Aristotle in Romans 2:14–15: Or, Maybe Abimelech Was Not So Bad After All," *Journal of Markets and Morality* 13:1 (Spring 2010): 123–73.

14. Aristotle, in his *Nicomachean Ethics*, 1.7.11, and *Politics*, 1.1.11, speaks of the differing members of the *polis*: the eye, the hand, and the foot (see 1 Cor 12:15–16); he also speaks of the differing "functions" (πράξεις, see Rom 12:4).

15. See James Barr, "Literality," *Faith and Philosophy* 6:4 (1989): 412–28, especially pp. 418–19.

11.C CONCLUSION: READING GENESIS 1–11 WELL

All of this supports what Pope Pius XII said in his 1950 encyclical, *Humani Generis*, §38:

> The first eleven chapters of Genesis, although properly speaking not conforming to the historical method used by the best Greek and Latin writers or by competent authors of our time, do nevertheless pertain to history in a true sense.

Or, as I might put it, the faithful are invited to affirm that the way Genesis 1–11 tells the story gives them the divinely approved way of picturing the events and that there are actual events that the pictures refer to. This treats fairly both the common tradition of Christian thinking and the kind of literary material we have in this part of Genesis. And this insight into the storytelling in Genesis will give us both flexibility and clear guidance in thinking about relating the story to the questions raised by the sciences.

Near the end of J. R. R. Tolkien's trilogy, *The Lord of the Rings*, as Frodo is about to leave Middle Earth altogether, he entrusts the Red Book to his loyal companion Sam. Sam will have major responsibilities among the Hobbits; he must give them wise leadership and set a good example as "the most famous gardener in history." Frodo envisions Sam in a public role:

> You will read things out of the Red Book, and keep alive the memory of the age that is gone, so that people will remember the Great Danger and so love their beloved land all the more.[16]

Scripture, especially used in public worship, enables the people of God to remember the dangers from which God has delivered the corporate entity, that they might love their God, their beloved body, and their calling in the world all the more—and devote themselves to these.

Tolkien wrote a letter to his son Christopher as the Second World War's European campaign neared its end. In this letter he captured well both the human predicament and the way in which the biblical story meets that predicament:

Actually, a Rabbi understands the matter of New Testament altering of the food restrictions perfectly well in this light. See Meir Soloveichik, "Locusts, Giraffes, and the Meaning of *Kashrut*," *Azure* 21 (Winter 5766 / 2006): 62–96.

16. J. R. R. Tolkien, *The Return of the King* (Boston: Houghton-Mifflin, 1965), 309.

I do not now feel either ashamed or dubious on the Eden "myth." It has not, of course, historicity of the same kind as the NT, which are virtually contemporary documents, while Genesis is separated by we do not know how many sad exiled generations from the Fall, but certainly there was an Eden on this very unhappy earth. We all long for it, and we are constantly glimpsing it: our whole nature at its best and least corrupted, its gentlest and most humane, is still soaked with the sense of "exile."[17]

---

17. Letter to Christopher Tolkien, 30 January 1945; in J. R. R. Tolkien, *Letters of J. R. R. Tolkien*, ed. Humphrey Carpenter (New York: Houghton Mifflin, 1981), 109–10 (letter 96).

BIBLIOGRAPHY

Alexander, T. D. "From Adam to Judah: The Significance of the Family Tree in Genesis." *EvQ* 61.1 (1989): 5–19.
———. "Genealogies, Seed and the Compositional Unity of Genesis." *TynB* 44.2 (1993): 255–70.
———. "Further Observations on the Term 'Seed' in Genesis." *TynB* 48:2 (1997): 363–67.
———. *From Paradise to the Promised Land: An Introduction to the Pentateuch.* Grand Rapids: Baker Academic, 2002.
Algra, Keimpe. "The Beginnings of Cosmology." Pages 45–65 in *The Cambridge Companion to Early Greek Philosophy.* Edited by A. A. Long. Cambridge: Cambridge University Press, 1999.
Alter, Robert. *The Art of Biblical Narrative.* New York: Basic Books, 1981.
Altholz, Josef. "The Mind of Victorian Orthodoxy: Anglican Responses to 'Essays and Reviews.' 1860–1864." *Church History* 51:2 (1982): 186–97.
Austin, Christopher. "Aristotelian Essentialism: Essence in an Age of Evolution." *Synthese* 193 (2016): doi:10.1007/s11229–016–1066–4.
Averbeck, Richard. "The Sumerian Historiographic Tradition and its Implications for Genesis 1–11." Pages 79–102 in *Faith, Tradition, and History: Old Testament Historiography in its Near Eastern Context.* Edited by A. R. Millard, James K. Hoffmeier and David W. Baker. Winona Lake, IN: Eisenbrauns, 1994.
———. "A literary Day, Inter-Textual, and Contextual Reading of Genesis 1–2." Pages 7–34 in *Reading Genesis 1–2: An Evangelical Conversation.* Edited by J. Daryl Charles. Peabody: Hendrickson, 2013.
Balfour, Arthur James. *Theism and Humanism.* New York: Hodder & Stoughton, 1915.
Bauks, Michaela. "Sacred Trees in the Garden of Eden and Their Ancient Near Eastern Precursors." *Journal of Ancient Judaism* 3 (2012): 267–301.
Barbour, Ian. *Religion in an Age of Science.* New York: HarperCollins, 1990.
Baroway, Israel. "The Bible as Poetry in the English Renaissance: An Introduction." *Journal of English and Germanic Philology* 32:4 (1933): 447–80.

Barr, James. *The Semantics of Biblical Language*. Oxford: Oxford University Press, 1961.
———. *Biblical Words for Time*. London: SCM, 1962.
———. *Comparative Philology and the Text of the Old Testament*. Oxford: Oxford University Press, 1968.
———. *Fundamentalism*. Philadelphia: Westminster, 1978.
———. *Beyond Fundamentalism*. Philadelphia: Westminster, 1984.
———. "Jowett and the Reading of the Bible 'Like Any Other Book'." *Horizons in Biblical Theology* 4 (1985): 1–44.
———. "Literality." *Faith and Philosophy* 6:4 (1989): 412–28.
———. "The Literal, the Allegorical, and Modern Biblical Scholarship." *JSOT* 44 (1989): 3–17.
———. *The Garden of Eden and the Hope of Immortality*. Philadelphia: Fortress, 1992.
———. *Biblical Faith and Natural Theology*. Oxford: Oxford University Press, 1993.
———. "Pre-Scientific Chronology: The Bible and the Origin of the World." *Proceedings of the American Philosophical Society* 143:3 (1999): 379–87.
Bartholomew, Craig and Michael Goheen. "Story and Biblical Theology." Pages 144–71 in *Out of Egypt: Biblical Theology and Biblical Interpretation*. Edited by Craig Bartholomew and Elaine Botha. Grand Rapids: Zondervan, 2004.
Bartusiak, Marcia. "Before the Big Bang." *Technology Review* 112:5 (September/October 2009): MIT News Section: M14–15.
Basson, Alec. "'You Are My Rock and Fortress': Refuge Metaphors in Psalm 31, A Perspective from Cognitive Metaphor Theory." *Acta Theologica* 25:2 (2005): 1–17.
Bawarshi, Anis S. and Mary Jo Reiff. *Genre: An Introduction to History, Theory, Research, and Pedagogy*. West Lafayette, IN: Parlor Press, 2010.
Bayer, Hans F. *Das Evangelium des Markus*. Giessen: SCM R. Brockhaus, 2008.
Beale, Gregory. *The Temple and the Church's Mission*. Downers Grove, IL: InterVarsity Press, 2004.
Beale, Walter. "Rhetorical Performative Discourse: A New Theory of Epideictic." *Philosophy and Rhetoric* 11:4 (1978): 221–46.
Beckwith, Frank. "How to Be an Anti-Intelligent Design Advocate." *University of St. Thomas Journal of Law and Public Policy* 4:1 (2010): 35–65.
Beckwith, Roger. *The Old Testament Canon of the New Testament Church*. London: SPCK, 1985.
———. "Essays and Reviews (1860): The Advance of Liberalism." *Churchman* 108:1 (1994): 48–58.
———. "The Early History of the Psalter." *TynB* 46:1 (1995): 1–27.
Bendor, S. *The Social Structure of Ancient Israel: The Institution of the Family (*beit 'ab*) From the Settlement to the End of the Monarchy*. Jerusalem: Simor, 1996.
Benjamin, James. "Performatives as a Rhetorical Construct." *Philosophy and Rhetoric* 9:2 (1976): 84–95.
Berkouwer, G. C. *The Providence of God*. Grand Rapids: Eerdmans, 1952.
Berry, R. J. "The Virgin Birth of Christ." *SCB* 8:2 (1996): 101–10.

———. Response to P. Addinall's reply to Berry's previous article. *SCB* 9:1 (1997): 77.
———. "Divine Action: Expected and Unexpected." *Zygon* 37:3 (2002): 717–27.
Bilynskyj, Stephen. "God, Nature, and the Concept of Miracle". PhD diss., University of Notre Dame, 1982.
Bimson, John et al. *New Bible Atlas*. Downers Grove, IL: InterVarsity Press, 1985.
Bitzer, Lloyd. "The Rhetorical Situation." *Philosophy and Rhetoric* 1:1 (1968): 1–14.
Black, Jeremy and Anthony Green. *Gods, Demons and Symbols of Ancient Mesopotamia: An Illustrated Dictionary*. London: British Museum, 1992.
Blenkinsopp, Joseph. *Creation, Un-creation, Re-creation*. London: T&T Clark, 2011.
Blunt, A. W. F. *The Apologies of Justin Martyr*. Cambridge Patristic Texts. Cambridge: Cambridge University Press, 1911.
Bockmuehl, Markus. "*Creatio ex nihilo* in Palestinian Judaism and Early Christianity." *SJT* 65:3 (2012): 253–70.
Bois, Henri. *Essai sur les Origines de la Philosophie Judéo-Alexandrine*. Paris: Fischbacher, 1890.
Bokedal, Tomas. *The Formation and Significance of the Christian Biblical Canon: A Study in Text, Ritual, and Interpretation*. London: Bloomsbury, 2014.
Bolhuis, Johan J., Ian Tattersall, Noam Chomsky, Robert C. Berwick. "How Could Language Have Evolved?" *PLOS Biology* 12:8 (August 2014): e1001934.
Borowski, Oded. *Every Living Thing: Daily Use of Animals in Ancient Israel*. Walnut Creek: AltaMira, 1998.
Bowra, C. M. *Heroic Poetry*. London: Macmillan, 1952.
Brett, Mark G. "Motives and Intentions in Genesis 1." *JTS* 42:1 (1991): 1–16.
Briggs, Richard. *The Virtuous Reader: Old Testament Narratives and Interpretive Virtue*. Grand Rapids: Baker Academic, 2010.
Brône, Geert and Jeroen Vandaele, eds. *Cognitive Poetics: Goals, Gains, and Gaps*. Berlin: de Gruyter, 2009.
Brown, Gillian and George Yule. *Discourse Analysis*. Cambridge: Cambridge University Press, 1983.
Brown, William. "Divine Act and the Art of Persuasion in Genesis 1." Pages 19–32 in *History and Interpretation: Essays in Honor of John H. Hayes*. Edited by M. P. Graham et al. Sheffield: Sheffield Academic Press, 1993.
Bruce, F. F. *The Epistles of John*. Grand Rapids: Eerdmans, 1970.
———. *The New Testament Documents: Are They reliable?* Downers Grove, IL: InterVarsity Press, 1991.
Bultmann, Rudolph. *Kerugma and Myth: A Theological Debate*. New York: Harper & Row, 1961.
Burchard, C. "Joseph and Aseneth." in *The Old Testament Pseudepigrapha*. Edited by James Charlesworth. New York: Doubleday, 1983.
Burgers, Christian, Britta Brugman, Kiki Renardel de Lavalette, and Gerard Steen. "HIP: A Method for Linguistic Hyperbole Identification in Discourse." *Metaphor and Symbol* 31:3 (2016): 163–78.
Burgess, Theodore. "Epideictic Literature." *University of Chicago Studies in Classical Philology* 3 (1902): 95–261.

Burnside, Jonathan. "At Wisdom's Table: How Narrative Shapes the Biblical Food Laws and Their Social Function." *JBL* 135:2 (2016): 223–45.

Burrell, David. "*Creatio ex nihilo* Recovered." *Modern Theology* 29:2 (2013): 6–21.

Burrus, Virginia. "Nothing Is Not One: Revisiting the *ex nihilo*." *Modern Theology* 29:2 (2013): 33–48.

Buswell, J. Oliver. *A Systematic Theology of the Christian Religion*. Grand Rapids: Zondervan, 1962–63.

Calvin, John. *Genesis*. Calvin Translation Society. Grand Rapids: Baker, 1979.

Campbell, Paul Newell. "A Rhetorical View of Locutionary, Illocutionary, and Perlocutionary Acts." *QJournSp* 59 (1973): 284–96.

Cansdale, George. *Animals of Bible Lands*. Exeter: Paternoster, 1970.

Carpenter, Humphrey. *Tolkien: A Biography*. Boston: Houghton Mifflin, 1977.

Cashmore, Anthony. "The Lucretian Swerve: The Biological Basis of Human Behavior and the Criminal Justice System." *Proceedings of the National Academy of Sciences*. 12 January 2010 (PNAS Early Edition).

Cassuto, Umberto. *Commentary on the Book of Genesis (Part I)*. Jerusalem: Magnes, 1961 [Hebrew original, 1944].

———. *A Commentary on the Book of Exodus*. Jerusalem: Magnes, 1983 [1951].

Charles, R. H. *Letter of Aristeas*. Oxford: The Clarendon Press, 1913.

Chesterton, G. K. *The Everlasting Man*. Garden City, NY: Doubleday, 1955 [1925].

Childs, Brevard. "The *sensus literalis* of Scripture: An Ancient and Modern Problem." Pages 80–93 in *Beiträge zur Alttestamentlichen Theologie*. Edited by H. Donner et al. Vandenhoeck & Ruprecht, 1977.

Chou, Hsiu-Chin. "The Problem of Faith and the Self: The Interplay between Literary Art, Apologetics and Hermeneutics in C. S. Lewis' Religious Narratives." PhD thesis, Glasgow University, 2008.

Clines, David. "The Significance of the 'Sons of God' Episode (Genesis 6.1–4) in the Context of the 'Primaeval History' (Genesis 1–11)." *JSOT* 13 (1979): 33–46.

Coats, G. W. *Genesis, with an Introduction to Narrative*. FOTL. Grand Rapids: Eerdmans, 1983.

Collins, Adela Yarbro. "Psalms, Philippians 2:6–11, and the Origins of Christology." *BibInt* 11:3–4 (2002): 361–72.

Collins, C. John. "Homonymous Verbs in Biblical Hebrew: An investigation of the role of comparative philology." PhD thesis, University of Liverpool, 1988.

———. "Coherence in James 1:19–27." *JOTT* 10 (1998): 80–88.

———. "Discourse Analysis and the Interpretation of Genesis 2:4–7." *WTJ* 61:2 (1999): 269–276.

———. *The God of Miracles: An Exegetical Examination of God's Action in the World*. Wheaton, IL: Crossway, 2000.

———. "Galatians 3:16: What kind of exegete was Paul?" *TynB* 54:1 (2003): 75–86.

———. *Science and Faith: Friends or Foes?*. Wheaton, IL: Crossway, 2003.

———. "The Eucharist as Christian Sacrifice: How Patristic Authors Can Help Us Read the Bible." *WTJ* 66 (2004): 1–23.

———. *Genesis 1–4: A Linguistic, Literary, and Theological Commentary.* Phillipsburg, NJ: P&R, 2006.

———. "Proverbs and the Levitical System." *Presbyterion* 35:1 (Spring 2009): 9–34.

———. "The Refrain in Genesis 1: A Critical Review of Its Rendering in the English Bible." *BT* 60:3 (July 2009): 121–31.

———. "Echoes of Aristotle in Romans 2:14–15: Or, Maybe Abimelech Was Not so Bad After All." *Journal of Markets and Morality* 13:1 (Spring 2010): 123–73.

———. *Did Adam and Eve Really Exist?* Wheaton, IL: Crossway, 2011.

———. "A Peculiar Clarity: How C. S. Lewis Can Help Us Think About Faith and Science." Pages 69–106 in *The Magician's Twin: C. S. Lewis on Science, Scientism, and Society.* Edited by John G. West. Seattle: Discovery Institute Press, 2012.

———. "Noah, Deucalion, and the New Testament." *Biblica* 93:3 (2012): 403–26.

———. "Reading Genesis 1–2 with the Grain: Analogical Days." Pages 73–92 in *Reading Genesis 1–2: An Evangelical Conversation.* Edited by J. Daryl Charles. Peabody: Hendrickson, 2013.

———. "Colossians 1,17 'Hold Together': A Co-Opted Term." *Biblica* 95:1 (2014): 64–87.

———. "Psalms 111–112: Big Story, Little Story." *Religions* (2016): 7(9), 115; doi:10.3390/rel7090115 (open access at www.mdpi.com/2077-1444/7/9/115).

———. "How to Think about God's Action in the World." Chapter 22 in *Theistic Evolution.* Edited by J. P. Moreland, Stephen Meyer, Christopher Shaw, Ann Gauger, and Wayne Grudem. Wheaton, IL: Crossway, 2017.

———. "1 Corinthians 8:6 and Romans 11:36: A Pauline Confession with a Hellenistic Setting." *Presbyterion* 43:2 (Fall, 2017): 55–68.

———. "The New Covenant and Redemptive History" (forthcoming).

Coogan, Michael David. "A Structural and Literary Analysis of the Song of Deborah." *CBQ* 40 (1978): 143–66.

Cooke, G. A. *The Book of Judges.* CBSC. Cambridge: Cambridge University Press, 1913.

Copan, Paul. "Is *creatio ex nihilo* a Post-Biblical Invention? An Examination of Gerhard May's Proposal." *TJ* 17 (1996): 77–93.

Cranfield, C. E. B. *The Gospel According to Saint Mark.* CGT. Cambridge: Cambridge University Press, 1962.

———. *Romans.* ICC. Edinburgh: T&T Clark, 1975.

Culpeper, Jonathan. "Towards an Anatomy of Impoliteness." *Journal of Pragmatics* 25 (1996): 349–67.

Cutting, Joan. *Pragmatics and Discourse: A Resource Book for Students.* London: Routledge, 2002.

Dalley, Stephanie. *Myths from Mesopotamia.* Oxford: Oxford University Press, 2000.

Darwin, Charles. *The Origin of Species.* Harvard Classics, vol. 11; New York: Collier, 1909 [6th edition of 1872; first edition, 1859].

Davidson, Richard. "The Genesis Flood Narrative: Crucial Issues in the Current Debate." *AUSS* 42:1 (2004): 49–77.

Day, John. *From Creation to Babel: Studies in Genesis 1–11*. London: Bloomsbury T & T Clark, 2014.
Deane, William. *The Book of Wisdom*. Oxford: Clarendon, 1881.
Delitzsch, Franz. *Psalms*. Keil & Delitzsch Commentary. Edinburgh: T&T Clark, 1871 [1867].
———. *Commentary on Hebrews*. Edinburgh: T&T Clark, 1876.
———. *A New Commentary on Genesis*. Edinburgh: T&T Clark, 1888.
Devitt, Amy. "Integrating Rhetorical and Literary Theories of Genre." *College English* 62:6 (2000): 696–718.
Dijk, Teun A. van. *Text and Context*. London: Longman, 1977.
Doedens, Jaap. "The Sons of God in Genesis 6:1–4". PhD diss., Theologische Universiteit van de Gereformeerde Kerken in Nederland te Kampen, 2013.
Dooley, Robert A. and Stephen H. Levinsohn. *Analyzing Discourse: A Manual of Basic Concepts*. Dallas: SIL International, 2000.
Driver, G. R. *Problems of the Hebrew Verbal System*. Edinburgh: T&T Clark, 1936.
Driver, S. R. *The Book of Genesis*. Westminster Commentary. London: Methuen, 1904.
———. *Exodus*. CBSC. Cambridge: Cambridge University Press, 1911.
Dumbrell, William. *Covenant and Creation: A Theology of the Old Testament Covenants*. Carlisle: Paternoster, 1997.
Dunn, James D. G. *Romans*. WBC. Dallas: Word, 1988.
Eisenhart, Christopher and Barbara Johnstone. "Discourse analysis and rhetorical studies." Pages 3–21 in *Rhetoric in Detail: Discourse Analysis of Rhetorical Talk and Text*. Edited by Johnstone and Eisenhart. Amsterdam: Benjamins, 2008.
Emerton, John A. "An Examination of Some Attempts to Defend the Unity of the Flood Narrative in Genesis: Parts 1 and 2." *VT* 37 (1987): 401–420; *VT* 38 (1988): 1–21.
Enns, Peter. *Inspiration and Incarnation*. Grand Rapids: Baker Academic, 2005.
———. *The Evolution of Adam: What the Bible Does and Doesn't Say about Human Origins*. Grand Rapids: Brazos, 2012.
Epstein, Isidore, ed. *The Soncino Talmud*. London: Soncino Press.
Eslinger, Lyle. "The Enigmatic Plurals like 'One of Us' (Genesis i 26, iii 22, and xi 7) in Hyperchronic Perspective." *VT* 56.2 (2006): 171–84.
Fairbairn, Patrick. *Prophecy viewed in its Distinctive Nature, its Special Functions, and Proper Interpretation*. Edinburgh: T&T Clark, 1865; republished as *The Interpretation of Prophecy*. Edinburgh: Banner of Truth, 1964.
Farrer, Austin. "The Christian apologist." Pages 23–43 in *Light on C. S. Lewis*. Edited by Joceyln Gibb. London: Geoffrey Bles, 1965.
Feldman, Louis. *Flavius Josephus, Translation and Commentary, vol. 3: Judean Antiquities 1–4*. Flavius Josephus: Translation and Commentary. Edited by Steve Mason. Leiden: Brill, 2000.
Fleming, Daniel. "History in Genesis." *WTJ* 65 (2014): 251–62.
Fokkelman, Jan. *Reading Biblical Narrative: An Introductory Guide*. Louisville: Westminster John Knox, 1999.
Ford, William. "What about the Gibeonites?" *TynB* 66:2 (2015): 197–216.

Foreman, Benjamin. "'Who Teaches Us More Than the Beasts of the Earth?' Animal Metaphors and the People of Israel in the Book of Jeremiah." PhD thesis, University of Aberdeen, 2009.
Forsyth, Mark. *The Elements of Eloquence: Secrets of the Perfect Turn of Phrase*. New York: Berkley Publishing, 2013.
Frankfurter, David. "Narratives that do things." Pages 95–106 in *Religion: Narrative Religion*. Edited by Sarah Iles Johnson. Farmington Hills, MI: Macmillan Reference USA, 2017.
Freddoso, Alfred. "God's General Concurrence with Secondary Causes: Why Conservation Is Not Enough." *Philosophical Perspectives* 5 (1991): 553–85.
Freedman, H. and M. Simon, eds. *Midrash Rabbah: Genesis*. London: Soncino, 1939.
Friedman, Richard Elliott. *The Bible with Sources Revealed: A New View into the Five Books of Moses*. New York: HarperCollins, 2003.
Frymer-Kensky, Tikva. "The Atrahasis Epic and Its Significance for Our Understanding of Genesis 1–9." *BA* 40.4 (1977): 147–55.
Fueter, Paul. "The Therapeutic Language of the Bible." *International Review of Mission* 75 (1986): 211–21 (also published in *BT* 37: 3 [1986]: 309–19).
Futato, Mark. "מַיִן." 4786 in *NIDOTTE*, 2:934–935.
Gaffin, Richard. *Resurrection and Redemption*. Phillipsburg, NJ: Presbyterian and Reformed, 1987.
Gavrilyuk, Paul. "Creation in Early Christian Polemical Literature." *Modern Theology* 29:2 (2013): 22–32.
Geivett, Douglas and Gary Habermas. *In Defense of Miracles: A Comprehensive Case for God's Action in History*. Downers Grove, IL: InterVarsity Press, 1997.
Getz, Jan Christian. "The Formation of the Primeval History." Pages 107–35 in *The Book of Genesis: Composition, Reception, and Interpretation*. Edited by Craig A. Evans, Joel N. Lohr, and David L. Petersen. Leiden: Brill, 2012.
Gibson, J. C. L. *Canaanite Myths and Legends*. Edinburgh: T&T Clark, 1978.
Gilkey, Langdon. "Cosmology, Ontology, and the Travail of Biblical Language." *Concordia Theological Monthly* 33:3 (1962): 143–54.
Gill, Jerry. "J. L. Austin and the Religious Use of Language." *Sophia* 8 (1969): 29–37.
Goldingay, John. *Psalms*. BCOT. Grand Rapids: Baker Academic, 2008.
Goulburn, E. M., H. J. Rose, C. A. Heurtley, W. J. Irons, G. Rorison, A. W. Haddan, and Christopher Wordsworth. *Replies to "Essays and Reviews"*. New York: Appleton, 1862.
Grant, Edward. *In Defense of the Earth's Immobility: Scholastic Reaction to Copernicanism in the Seventeenth Century*. Philadelphia: American Philosophical Society, 1984.
Grant, Robert. *Miracle and Natural Law in Graeco-Roman and Early Christian Thought*. Amsterdam: North Holland Publishing, 1952.
Green, William Henry. "Primitive Chronology." *BibSac* 47 (April, 1890): 285–303.
Greenberg, Moshe. "Mankind. Israel and the Nations in the Hebraic Heritage," Pages 15–40 in *No Man Is an Alien: Essays on the Unity of Mankind*. Edited by J. Robert Nelson. Leiden: Brill, 1971.

Greengus, Samuel. "The Anachronism in Abraham's Observance of the Laws." *HUCA* 86 (2015), 1–35.

Gregg, J. A. F. *The Wisdom of Solomon*. CBSC. Cambridge: Cambridge University Press, 1909.

Grudem, Wayne. *The Gift of Prophecy in the New Testament and Today*. Wheaton, IL: Crossway, 2000.

Gunton, Colin. "The Doctrine of Creation." Pages 141–57 in *The Cambridge Companion to Christian Doctrine*. Edited by Colin Gunton. Cambridge: Cambridge University Press, 1997.

Habig, Brian. "Hosea 6:7 Revisited." *Presbyterion* 42 (2016): 4–20.

Hakham, Amos. *Sefer Tehillim*. Da'at Miqra'. Jerusalem: Mossad Harav Kook, 1979.

Hallberg, Calinda. "Storyline and Theme in a Biblical Narrative: 1 Samuel 3." *Occasional Papers in Translation and Textlinguistics* 3:1 (1989): 1–35.

Hallo, William W. "Part 1: Mesopotamia and the Asiatic Near East." Pages 3–181 in *The Ancient Near East: A History*. William W. Hallo and William K. Simpson. Fort Worth, TX: Harcourt Brace College Publishers, 1998.

Halton, Charles, ed. *Genesis: History Fiction, or Neither? Three views on the Bible's earliest chapters*. Grand Rapids: Zondervan, 2015), with contributions from James Hoffmeier ("Genesis 1–11 as History and Theology"), Gordon Wenham ("Genesis 1–11 as Protohistory"), and Kenton Sparks ("Genesis 1–11 as Ancient Historiography".

Hamilton, Victor. *Genesis 1–17*. NICOT. Grand Rapids: Eerdmans, 1990.

Harlow, Daniel. "Creation According to Genesis: Literary Genre, Cultural Context, Theological Truth." *Christian Scholars Review* 37.2 (2008): 163–98.

———. Daniel Harlow. "After Adam: Reading Genesis in an Age of Evolutionary Science." *Perspectives on Science and Christian Faith* 62.3 (2010): 179–95.

Häuser, Marc D., Noam Chomsky, W. Tecumseh Fitch. "The Faculty of Language: What Is It, Who Has It, and How Did It Evolve?" *Science* 298 (22 November 2002): 1569–79.

Heidel, Alexander. *The Gilgamesh Epic and Old Testament Parallels*. Chicago; University of Chicago Press, 1949.

———. *The Babylonian Genesis*. Chicago: University of Chicago Press, 1951.

Hendel, Ronald. "The Nephilim Were on the Earth: Genesis 6:1–4 and its Ancient Near Eastern Context." Pages 11–34 in *The Fall of the Angels*. Edited by Christoph Auffarth and Loren Stuckenbruck. Leiden: Brill, 2004.

Heppe, Heinrich. *Reformed Dogmatics*. Grand Rapids: Baker, 1978.

Hepper, F. Nigel. *Illustrated Encyclopedia of Bible Plants*. Grand Rapids: Baker Academic, 1992.

Herrick, James. *The History and Theory of Rhetoric*. Boston: Allyn and Bacon, 2001.

Hess, Richard S. "The Genealogies of Genesis 1–11 and Comparative Literature." *Biblica* 70 (1989): 241–54.

———. "Genesis 1–2 in Its Literary Context." *TynB* 41:1 (1990): 143–53.

Heuboeck, Alois. "Some Aspects of Coherence, Genre and Rhetorical Structure—and Their Integration into a Generic Model of Text." *University of Reading Language Studies Working Papers* 1 (2009): 35–45.

Hoare, F. R. *Eight Decisive Books of Antiquity*. London: Sheed & Ward, 1952.

Hodge, Charles. *Systematic Theology*. Grand Rapids: Eerdmans, 1981 (1871–73).

Hollenbach, Bruce and Jim Watters. "Study Guide on Pragmatics and Discourse." *Notes on Translation* 12:1 (1998): 13–35.

Holmes, Arthur. "Three Levels of Meaning in God-Language." *JETS* 16:2 (1973): 83–94.

Holmes, Michael. *The Apostolic Fathers*. Grand Rapids: Baker, 1999.

Holmstedt, Robert. "The Restrictive Syntax of Genesis i 1." *VT* 58 (2008): 56–67.

Horowitz, Wayne. *Mesopotamian Cosmic Geography*. Winona Lake, IN: Eisenbrauns, 1998.

Howard, David. "Rhetorical Criticism in Old Testament Studies." *BBR* 4 (1994): 87–104.

Hubler, James Noel. "*Creatio ex nihilo*: Matter, Creation, and the Body in Classical and Christian Philosophy and Aquinas". PhD diss., University of Pennsylvania, 1995.

Huenergard, John. *An Introduction to Ugaritic*. Peabody: Hendrickson, 2012.

Humann, Joel R. "The Ceremony of the Red Heifer: Its purpose and function in narrative context." PhD thesis, Durham University, 2011.

Hwang, Shin Ja and William Merrifield, eds. *Language in Context: Essays for Robert E. Longacre*. Dallas: SIL International, 1992.

Jacobsen, Anders-Christian. "The Importance of Genesis 1–3 in the Theology of Irenaeus." *Zeitschrift für antikes Christentum* 8.2 (2005): 299–316.

Jacobsen, Thorkild. *The Sumerian King List*. Chicago: University of Chicago Press, 1939.

———. "Mesopotamia." Pages 125–219 in *The Intellectual Adventure of Ancient Man*. Edited by H. and H. A. Frankfort, John Wilson, Thorkild Jacobsen, and William Irwin. Chicago: University of Chicago, 1977.

———. "The Eridu Genesis." *JBL* 100:2 (1981), 513–29.

Jaeger, Lydia. *What the Heavens Declare: Science in the Light of Creation*. Eugene, OR: Cascade, 2012.

Jastrow, Robert. *God and the Astronomers*. New York: Norton, 1992.

Johnston, Gordon H. "Genesis 1 and Ancient Egyptian Creation Myths." *BibSac* 165.658 (2008): 178–94.

Johnstone, Barbara. *Discourse Analysis*. Oxford: Blackwell, 2008.

Joos, Martin. "Semantic Axiom Number One." *Language* 48:2 (1972): 257–65.

Joseph, H. W. B. *An Introduction to Logic*. Oxford: Clarendon, 1916.

Kaminsky, Carol. *From Noah to Israel: Realization of the Primaeval Blessing after the Flood*. London: T&T Clark, 2004.

Kaufmann, Yehezqel. *The Religion of Israel*. Chicago: University of Chicago Press, 1960.

Keas, Michael. "Systematizing the Theoretical Virtues." *Synthese* (2017), doi:10.1007/s11229–017–1355–6.

Keel, Othmar and Silvia Schroer. *Creation: Biblical Theologies in the Context of the Ancient Near East*. Winona Lake, IN: Eisenbrauns, 2015.

Kelly, Douglas. *Creation and Change: Genesis 1.1–2.4 in the Light of Changing Scientific Paradigms.* Fearn, Ross-shire: Christian Focus, 1997.

Kelsey, David. "The Doctrine of Creation from Nothing." Pages 176–196 in *Evolution and Creation.* Edited by Ernan McMullin. Notre Dame: University of Notre Dame Press, 1985.

Kidner, Derek. *Genesis.* TOTC. Downers Grove, IL: InterVarsity Press, 1967.

———. *Psalms 1–72.* TOTC. Downers Grove, IL: InterVarsity Press, 1973.

Kiel, Yehudah. "Hosea." in *Terê 'Asar.* Yehudah Kiel et al. DM. Jerusalem: Mossad Harav Kook, 1990.

———. *Sefer Bere'shît,* vol. 1, chs. 1–17. DM. Jerusalem: Mossad HaRav Kook, 1997.

Kilmer, Anne Drafkorn. "The Mesopotamian Counterparts of the Biblical Nephilim." Pages 39–43 in *Perspectives on Language and Text.* Edited by Edgar W. Conrad. Winona Lake, IN: Eisenbrauns, 1987.

Kister, Menahem. "*Tohu wa-Bohu,* Primordial Elements and *Creatio ex Nihilo.*" *Jewish Studies Quarterly* 14 (2007): 229–56.

Kitchen, Kenneth A. *On the Reliability of the Old Testament.* Grand Rapids: Eerdmans, 2003.

Klijn, A. F. J. "2 (Apocalypse of) Baruch." in *The Old Testament Pseudepigrapha.* Edited by James Charlesworth. New York: Doubleday, 1983.

Koorevaar, Hendrik. "The Torah as One, Three or Five Books: An Introduction to the Macro-Structural Problem of the Pentateuch." *Hiphil* 3 (2006): http://www.see-j.net/hiphil.

———. "The Books of Exodus, Leviticus and Numbers, and the Macro-Structural Problem of the Pentateuch." Pages 423–53 in *The Books of Leviticus and Numbers.* Edited by Thomas Römer. Bibliotheca Ephemeridum Theologicarum Lovaniensium 215. Leuven: Peeters, 2008.

Kramer, S. N. "Review of Alexander Heidel, The Babylonian Genesis: The Story of Creation." *JAOS* 63:1 (1943): 69–73.

———. "The 'Babel of Tongues': A Sumerian Version." *JAOS* 88:1 (1968): 108–11.

Kruger, Michael. *The Question of Canon: Challenging the Status Quo in the New Testament Debate.* Downers Grove, IL: InterVarsity Press, 2013.

Kuhn, Thomas. *The Structure of Scientific Revolutions.* Chicago: University of Chicago Press, 1970.

Ladrière, Jean. "The Performativity of Liturgical Language." Pages 50–62 in *Liturgical Experience of Faith.* Edited by Herman Schmidt and David Power. New York: Herder & Herder, 1973.

Lambert, W. G. "A New Look at the Babylonian Background of Genesis." *JTS* 16:2 (1965): 287–300.

Lambert, W. G. and A. R. Millard. *Atra-hasis: The Babylonian Story of the Flood.* Winona Lake, IN: Eisenbrauns, 1999 [1969].

Lamoureux, Denis. "No Historical Adam: Evolutionary Creation View." Pages 37–65 in *Four Views on the Historical Adam.* Edited by Matthew Barrett and Ardel Caneday. Grand Rapids: Zondervan, 2013.

———. *Evolution: Scripture and Nature Say Yes!*. Grand Rapids: Zondervan, 2016.
Larmer, Robert. "Theistic Complementarianism and Ockham's Razor." *Philosophia Christi* 7:2 (2005): 503–14.
———. "Miracles, Divine Agency, and the Laws of Nature." *Toronto Journal of Theology* 27:2 (2011): 267–90.
Lawrence, P. J. N. "Oh No, He's Still Wearing His Watch! Avoiding Anachronism in Old Testament Translation." *BT* 59:1 (2008): 14–17.
Lennox, James G. "Are Aristotelian Species Eternal?" reprinted in Lennox, *Aristotle's Philosophy of Biology: Studies in the Origins of Life Science*. Cambridge: Cambridge University Press, 2000.
Lentini, Giuseppe. "The Pragmatics of Verbal Abuse in Homer." in *The Rhetoric of Abuse in Greek Literature*. Edited by H. Tell. Issue 11 [2013] of the open access journal *Classics@* (Center for Hellenic Studies, Harvard.
Lepojärvi, Jason. "God is Love but Love is not God: Studies on C. S. Lewis's Theology of Love." PhD thesis, Helsinki University, 2015.
Levenson, Jon D. *Creation and the Persistence of Evil: The Jewish Drama of Divine Omnipotence*. Princeton: Princeton University Press, 1988.
———. "The Bible: Unexamined Commitments of Criticism." *First Things* 30 (Feb 1993): 24–33.
Levin, Yigal. "Understanding Biblical Genealogies." *Currents in Research: Biblical Studies* 9 (2001): 11–46.
———. "The Family of Man: The Genre and Purpose of Genesis 10." Pages 291–308 in *Looking at the Ancient Near East and the Bible through the Same Eyes*. Edited by K. Abraham and J. Fleishman. Bethesda: CDL Press, 2012.
Levinson, Stephen. *Pragmatics*. Cambridge: Cambridge University Press, 1983.
Lewis, C. S. *The Personal Heresy: A Controversy*. Oxford: Oxford University Press, 1939.
———. *The Problem of Pain*. London: Geoffrey Bles, 1940.
———. *A Preface to Paradise Lost*. Oxford: Oxford University Press, 1942.
———. *Screwtape Letters*. London: Geoffrey Bles, 1942.
———. *Reflections on the Psalms*. London: Geoffrey Bles, 1958.
———. *Miracles: A Preliminary Study*. New York: Macmillan, 1960.
———. *The Discarded Image*. Cambridge: Cambridge University Press, 1964.
———. *Prayer: Letters to Malcolm*. London: Collins, 1966.
———. *Studies in Medieval and Renaissance Literature*. Edited by Walter Hooper. Cambridge: Cambridge University Press, 1966.
———. *Christian Reflections*. Edited by Walter Hooper. Grand Rapids: Eerdmans, 1967.
———. *Studies in Words*. Cambridge: Cambridge University Press, 1967.
———. *God in the Dock*. Edited by Walter Hooper. Grand Rapids: Eerdmans, 1970.
———. *The Weight of Glory and Other Addresses*. Edited by Walter Hooper. New York: Simon & Schuster, 1996.
Lightfoot, J. B. *Philippians*. London: Macmillan, 1888.

Lindberg, David. *The Beginnings of Western Science*. Chicago: University of Chicago Press, 1992.
Loeb Classical Library. Cambridge: Harvard University Press.
Long, V. Philips. *The Reign and Rejection of King Saul*. Atlanta: Scholars Press, 1989.
———. *The Art of Biblical History*. Grand Rapids: Zondervan, 1994.
Longacre, Robert. "The Discourse Structure of the Flood Narrative." Pages 235–62 in *Society of Biblical Literature 1976 Seminar Papers*. Edited by G. MacRae. Missoula, MT: Scholars Press, 1976.
———. "Interpreting Biblical Stories." Pages 169–85 in *Discourse and Literature*. Edited by Teun A. van Dijk. Amsterdam/Philadelphia: John Benjamins, 1985.
———. Memo to the Creation Study Committee of the Presbyterian Church in America (November 1998); quoted on pages 2347–48, n113, of the Committee's report (2000). Online at www.pcahistory.org/creation/report.pdf.
Longman III, Tremper. *How to Read the Psalms*. Downers Grove, IL: InterVarsity Press, 1988.
———. *How to Read Genesis*. Downers Grove, IL: InterVarsity Press, 2005.
López-Ruiz, Carolina. "Cosmogonies and Theogonies." in *Oxford Classical Dictionary* (March 2016), available online osu.academia.edu/CarolinaLopezRuiz.
Lovell, Steven. "Philosophical Themes from C. S. Lewis." PhD thesis, Sheffield University, 2003.
Lowery, Daniel. *Toward a Poetics of Genesis 1–11: Reading Genesis 4:17–22 in Its Near Eastern Context*. Winona Lake, IN: Eisenbrauns, 2013.
Lupton, J. H., ed. *Letters to Radulphus on the Mosaic Account of the Creation, Together with Other Treatises, by John Colet, M.A.* London: George Bell, 1876.
Luzzi, Joseph. "The Rhetoric of Anachronism." *Comparative Literature* 61:1 (2009): 69–84.
Maclean, Norman. *A River Runs through It*. Chicago: University of Chicago, 1976.
———. *Young Men and Fire*. Chicago: University of Chicago Press, 1992.
Maimonides, Moses. *The Guide for the Perplexed*. Translated by M. Friedländer. London: Routledge & Kegan Paul, 1904 [orig. ca. 1190].
Malone, Andrew. "Acceptable Anachronism in Biblical Studies." *BT* 67:3 (2016): 351–64.
Marlowe, W. Creighton. "'Spirit of Your Holiness' in Psalm 51:13." *TJ* 19:1 (1998): 29–49.
May, Gerhard. *Creatio ex nihilo: The Doctrine of 'Creation Out of Nothing' in Early Christian Thought*. London: T&T Clark, 1994.
McCloskey, Donald. "How to Do a Rhetorical Analysis, and Why." Pages 319–42 in *Economic Methodology*. Edited by Roger Backhouse. London: Routledge, 1994.
McConville, Gordon. "Biblical Theology: Canon and Plain Sense." *SBET* 19:2 (2001): 134–57.
McFall, Leslie. *The Enigma of the Hebrew Verbal System*. Sheffield: Almond Press, 1982.
McFarland, Ian. *From Nothing: A Theology of Creation*. Louisville: Westminster John Knox, 2014.

Merrick, James and Stephen Garrett, eds. *Five Views on Biblical Inerrancy*. Grand Rapids: Zondervan, 2013.

Mesthrie, Rajend, ed. *The Cambridge Handbook of Sociolinguistics*. Cambridge: Cambridge University Press, 2011.

Meyer, Stephen. *Signature in the Cell: DNA and the Evidence for Intelligent Design*. New York: HarperCollins, 2009.

Millard, A. R. "A New Babylonian 'Genesis' story." *TynB* 18 (1967): 3–18.

———. "The Canaanites." in *Peoples of Old Testament Times*. Edited by D. J. Wiseman. Oxford: Oxford University Press, 1973.

———. "Methods of Studying the Patriarchal Narratives as Ancient Texts." Pages 43–58 in *Essays on the Patriarchal Narratives*. Edited by A. R. Millard and Donald J. Wiseman. Leicester: Inter-Varsity Press, 1980.

———. "The Old Testament and History: Some Considerations." *Faith & Thought* 110 (1983): 34–53.

———. "Sennacherib's Attack on Hezekiah." *TynB* 36 (1985): 61–77.

———. "Cartography in the Ancient Near East." Pages 107–116 in *The History of Cartography, Volume 1: Cartography in Prehistoric, Ancient, and Medieval Europe and the Mediterranean*. Edited by J. B. Harley and David Woodward. Chicago: University of Chicago Press, 1987.

———. "Story, History, and Theology." Pages 37–64 in *Faith, Tradition, and History: Old Testament Historiography in its Near Eastern Context*. Edited by A. R. Millard, James K. Hoffmeier and David W. Baker. Winona Lake, IN: Eisenbrauns, 1994.

———. "King Lists." Pages 169a–170a in *Dictionary of the Ancient Near East*. Edited by Piotr Bienkowski and A. R. Millard. Philadelphia: University of Pennsylvania Press, 2000.

———. "From Woe to Weal: Completing a Pattern in the Bible and the Ancient Near East." Pages 193–201 in *Let Us Go Up to Zion: Essays in Honour of H.G.M. Williamson*. Edited by I. Provan and M. Boda. Leiden: Brill, 2012.

Miller, Carolyn. "Genre as Social Action." *Q JournSp* 70 (1984): 151–67.

———. "Rhetorical community: The cultural basis of genre." Pages 67–78 in *Genre and the New Rhetoric*. Edited by Aviva Freedman and Peter Medway. London: Taylor & Francis, 1994.

———. "Genre as Social Action (1984), Revisited 30 Years Later (2014)." *Letras & Letras* 31:3 (2015): 56–72.

Miller, Geoffrey David. "Attitudes Toward Dogs in Ancient Israel: A Reassessment." *JSOT* 32:4 (2008): 487–500.

Minton, Bernard. "What Not to Do with Words: Uses of Speech Act Theory in Biblical Hermeneutics." PhD thesis, University of Sheffield, 2014.

Mitchell, Terence. "Eden, Garden of." Pages 289a-290b in *New Bible Dictionary*. Edited by I. Howard Marshall et al. Downers Grove, IL: InterVarsity Press, 1996.

———. "Nations, Table of." Pages 803a–807a in *New Bible Dictionary*. Edited by I. Howard Marshall et al. Downers Grove, IL: InterVarsity Press, 1996.

Moberly, R. W. L. *The Theology of the Book of Genesis*. Old Testament Theology. Cambridge: Cambridge University Press, 2009.
Moore, George F. *Judges*. ICC. Edinburgh: T&T Clark, 1895.
Morris, Simon Conway. "The Boyle Lecture 2005: Darwin's Compass: How Evolution Discovers the Song of Creation." *SCB* 18 (2006): 5–22.
Mortenson, Terry and Thane Ury, eds. *Coming to Grips with Genesis: Biblical Authority and the Age of the Earth*. Green Forest, AR: Master, 2008.
Musselman, Lytton John. *A Dictionary of Biblical Plants*. Cambridge: Cambridge University Press, 2012.
Nagel, Thomas. *Mind and Cosmos: Why the Materialist Neo-Darwinian Conception of Nature is Almost Certainly False*. New York: Oxford University Press, 2012.
Neugebauer, O. *The Exact Sciences in Antiquity*. New York: Dover, 1969.
Noble, Paul. "The *sensus literalis*: Jowett, Childs, and Barr." *JTS* 44:1 (1993): 1–23.
Noegel, Scott. "Greek Religion and the Ancient Near East." Pages 21–37 in *The Blackwell Companion to Greek Religion*. Edited by Daniel Ogden. London: Blackwell, 2006.
O'Brien, Peter. *Philippians*. NIGTC. Grand Rapids: Eerdmans, 1991.
Ogden, C. K. and I. A Richards. *The Meaning of Meaning*. New York: Harcourt, Brace & World, 1946.
O'Neill, J. C. "How Early Is the Doctrine of Creation *ex nihilo*?" *JTS* 53:2 (2002): 449–65.
Ortlund, Eric Nels. *Theophany and Chaoskampf: The Interpretation of Theophanic Imagery in the Baal Epic, Isaiah, and the Twelve*. Piscataway, NJ: Gorgias, 2010.
Oswalt, J. N. "The Myth of the Dragon and Old Testament Faith." *EvQ* 49:3 (1977): 163–72.
Packer, J. I. "Hermeneutics and Genesis 1–11." *SwJT* 44:1 (2001): 4–21.
———. *Truth and Power*. Downers Grove, IL: InterVarsity Press, 1996.
Parry, Robin. *The Biblical Cosmos: A Pilgrim's Guide to the Weird and Wonderful World of the Bible*. Eugene, OR: Cascade, 2014.
Pederson, Don. "Biblical Narrative as an Agent for Worldview Change." *International Journal of Frontier Missions* 14:4 (1997): 163–66.
Percy, Walker. *The Message in the Bottle*. New York: Farrar, Straus and Giroux, 2000.
Piperno, D. R. et al. "Processing of Wild Cereal Grains in the Upper Paleolithic Revealed by Starch Grain Analysis." *Nature* 430 (August 2004): 670–73.
Plantinga, Alvin. *Warranted Christian Belief*. Oxford: Oxford University Press, 2000.
———. *Where the Conflict Really Lies: Science, Religion, and Naturalism*. Oxford: Oxford University Press, 2011.
Plumley, J. M. "The Cosmology of Ancient Egypt." Pages 17–41 in *Ancient Cosmologies*. Edited by Carmen Blacker and Michael Lowe. London: Allen & Unwin, 1975.
Poirier, John. "'Theological Interpretation' and Its Contradistinctions." *TynB* 60:2 (2009): 105–18.
Polkinghorne, John. *Quarks, Chaos, and Christianity*. New York: Crossroad, 1994.
Poythress, Vern. *Symphonic Theology*. Grand Rapids: Zondervan, 1987.

———. "Rain Water Versus a Heavenly Sea in Genesis 1:6–8." *WTJ* 77 (2015): 181–91.
———. "Dealing with the Genre of Genesis and Its Opening Chapters." *WTJ* 78 (2016): 217–30.
———. "Genesis 1:1 Is the First Event, Not a Summary." *WTJ* 79 (2017): 97–121.
Pratt, Mary Louise. *Toward a Speech Act Theory of Literary Discourse.* Bloomington: Indiana University Press, 1977.
Provan, Iain. *Discovering Genesis.* Grand Rapids: Eerdmans, 2016.
Rabin, Chaim. "Discourse Analysis and the Dating of Deuteronomy." Pages 171–177 in *Interpreting the Hebrew Bible: Essays in Honour of E. I. J. Rosenthal.* Edited by J. A. Emerton and Stefan C. Reif. Cambridge: Cambridge University Press, 1982.
Rad, Gerhard von. *Genesis.* Philadelphia: Westminster, 1956.
Rafer, Daniel. "Mythic Structures in the Works of C. S. Lewis." PhD thesis, De Montfort University, 2002.
Rainey, A. F. "A Canaanite at Ugarit." *IEJ* 13 (1963): 43–45.
Reider, Joseph. *The Book of Wisdom.* New York: Harper & Brothers, 1957.
Reumann, John. *Philippians.* AB. New Haven: Yale University Press, 2008.
Reventlow, H. G. *The Authority of the Bible and the Rise of the Modern World.* English Translation, London: SCM, 1984.
Reyburn, William D. and Euan McG. Fry. *Handbook on Genesis.* London: United Bible Societies, 1997.
Richards, Jay Wesley. *The Untamed God: A Philosophical Exploration of Divine Perfection, Simplicity, and Immutability.* Downers Grove, IL: InterVarsity Press, 2003.
Roberts, Alexander, and James Donaldson, eds. *The Ante-Nicene Fathers: Translations of the Writings of the Fathers Down to A.D. 325.* Grand Rapids: Eerdmans, 1953.
Roberts, John. "Biblical Cosmology: The Implications for Bible Translation." *Journal of Translation* 9:2 (2013).
Roberts, Michael. "Geology and Genesis Unearthed." *Churchman* 112:3 (1998): 225–255.
Robichaux, Kerry. "Text-Knowledge Relationships." Pages 363–89 in *Language in Context: Essays for Robert E. Longacre.* Edited by Shin Ja Hwang and William Merrifield. Dallas: SIL International, 1992.
Robinette, Brian. "The Difference Nothing Makes: *Creatio ex nihilo*, Resurrection, and Divine Gratuity." *Theological Studies* 72 (2011): 525–57.
Robinson, H. Wheeler. *Inspiration and Revelation in the Old Testament.* Oxford: Oxford University Press, 1946.
Rogerson, John. "The Old Testament View of Nature: Some Preliminary Questions." Pages 67–84 in *Instruction and Interpretation.* Edited by H. A. Brongers et al. Oudtestamentische Studiën 20. Leiden: Brill, 1977.
Rooker, Mark. "The Genesis Flood." *SBJT* 5:3 (2001): 58–74.
Ross, Allen. "The Table of Nations in Genesis 10—Its Structure." *BibSac* 137 (Oct-Dec 1980): 340–53.

———. "The Table of Nations in Genesis 10—Its Content." *BibSac* 138 (Jan-Mar 1981): 22–34.

Routledge, Robin. "The Nephilim: A Tall Story?" *TynB* 66:1 (2015): 19–40.

Rutherford, Ian. "Hesiod and the Literary Traditions of the Near East." Pages 9–35 in *Brill's Companion to Hesiod*. Edited by F. Montanri, A. Rengakos, and C. Tsagalis. Leiden: Brill, 2009.

Schaff, Philip, ed. (in connection with a number of Patristic scholars of Europe and America). *A Select Library of the Nicene and Post-Nicene Fathers of the Christian Church, First Series*. Grand Rapids: Eerdmans, 1979–1988.

Schaff, Philip and Henry Wace (in connection with a number of Patristic scholars of Europe and America). *A Select Library of the Nicene and Post-Nicene Fathers of the Christian Church, Second Series*. Grand Rapids: Eerdmans, 1983–1988.

Schaff, Philip and David. *The Creeds of Christendom*. Grand Rapids: Baker, 1998.

Schiffrin, Deborah, Deborah Tannen, and Heidi E. Hamilton, eds. *The Handbook of Discourse Analysis*. Oxford: Blackwell, 2001.

Schmid, Heinrich. *Doctrinal Theology of the Evangelical Lutheran Church*. Translated by Charles Hay and Henry Jacobs. Minneapolis: Augsburg, 1961 [1875].

Schreiner, Thomas. *Romans*. BECNT. Grand Rapids: Baker Academic, 1998.

Schwartz, Daniel. *2 Maccabees*. Berlin: de Gruyter, 2008.

Scult, Allen Michael. "The Rhetoric of the Pentateuch: An Analysis of the Argument for the Hebrew Concept of God". PhD diss., University of Wisconsin, 1975.

Sedly, David. *Creationism and its Critics in Antiquity*. Berkeley: University of California Press, 2007.

Seebohm, Frederick. *The Oxford Reformers*. London: Longmans, Green, 1869.

Seely, Paul H. "The Basic Meaning of *mîn*, 'kind'." *SCB* 9:1 (1997): 47–56.

———. "The Firmament and the Water Above, Part I: The Meaning of *raqia'* in Gen 1:6–8." *WTJ* 53 (1991): 227–40.

———. "The Firmament and the Water Above, Part II: The Meaning of 'the water above the firmament' in Gen 1:6–8." *WTJ* 54 (1992): 31–46.

———. "The Geographical Meaning of 'earth' and 'seas' in Genesis 1:10." *WTJ* 59 (1997): 231–55.

Seeskin, Kenneth. *Thinking About the Torah*. Philadelphia/Lincoln: JPS/University of Nebraska, 2016.

Sexton, Jeremy. "Who Was Born When Enosh Was 90? A Semantic Reevaluation of William Henry Green's Chronological Gaps." *WTJ* 77 (2015): 193–218.

Shedd, William G. T. *Dogmatic Theology*. Nashville: Nelson, 1980 [1888–1894].

Shutt, R. J. H. "Letter of Aristeas." in *The Old Testament Pseudepigrapha*. Edited by James Charlesworth. New York: Doubleday, 1983.

Silva, Moisés. *Biblical Words and Their Meaning: An Introduction to Lexical Semantics*. Grand Rapids: Zondervan, 1983.

Simpson, E. K. *The Pastoral Epistles: The Greek Text with Introduction and Commentary*. London: Tyndale Press, 1954.

Simpson, George Gaylord. *The Meaning of Evolution*. New Haven, CT: Yale University Press, 1967.

Ska, Jean-Louis. *Our Fathers Have Told Us: Introduction to the Analysis of Hebrew Narratives*. Rome: Pontifical Biblical Institute, 1990.
Slobin, Dan. *Psycholinguistics*. Glenview, IL: Scott, Foresman and Company, 1974.
Soloveichik, Meir. "Locusts, Giraffes, and the Meaning of Kashrut." *Azure* 21 (Winter 5766 / 2006): 62–96.
Sparks, Kenton. *Sacred Word, Broken Word: Biblical Authority and the Dark Side of Scripture*. Grand Rapids: Eerdmans, 2012.
———. "Genesis 1–11 as Ancient Historiography." Pages 110–39 in *Genesis: History Fiction, or Neither? Three Views on the Bible's Earliest Chapters*. Edited by Charles Halton. Grand Rapids: Zondervan, 2015.
Sperber, Dan and Deirdre Wilson. "Pragmatics." in *The Oxford Handbook of Contemporary Philosophy*. Edited by Frank Jackson and Michael Smith. Oxford: Oxford University Press, 2007), online edition.
Stargel, Linda. "The Construction of Exodus Identity in the Texts of Ancient Israel: A Social Identity Approach." PhD thesis, University of Manchester, 2016.
Stein, Menahem. "Sefer Hokhmat Šelomoh." in *HaSefarim HaHitsonim*. Edited by Avraham Kahana. Tel-Aviv: Masada, 1959), vol. 1, book 2.
Steinmann, A. "אחד as an Ordinal Number and the Meaning of Genesis 1:5." *JETS* 45:4 (December 2002): 577–84.
———. "A Note on the Refrain in Genesis 1: Evening, Morning, and Day as Chronological Summary." *JESOT* 5:2 (2016–17): 125–40.
———. "Gaps in the Genealogies in Genesis 5 and 11?" *BibSac* 174 (2017): 141–58.
Stern, Menahem. *Greek and Latin Authors on Jews and Judaism. Volume 1: From Herodotus to Plutarch*. Jerusalem: Israel Academy of Sciences and Humanities, 1976.
Sternberg, Meir. *The Poetics of Biblical Narrative: Ideological Literature and the Drama of Reading*. Bloomington, IN: Indiana University Press, 1985.
Stockwell, Peter. *Cognitive Poetics: An Introduction*. London: Routledge, 2002.
Stott, John R. W. *The Epistles of John*. Tyndale New Testament Commentaries. Grand Rapids: Eerdmans, 1964.
———. *Christian Counter-culture: The Message of the Sermon on the Mount*. BST. Downers Grove, IL: InterVarsity Press, 1978.
———. *The Message of Acts*. BST. Downers Grove, IL: InterVarsity Press, 1990),
———. *The Message of Romans*. BST. Grand Rapids: InterVarsity Press, 1994.
———. *The Message of 1 Timothy and Titus*. BST. Downers Grove, IL: InterVarsity Press, 1996.
Strassler, Robert, ed. *The Landmark Herodotus: The Histories*. New York: Anchor, 2007.
Stump, J. B. "4 Theological Objections to Evolution." blog post on biologos.org, December 15, 2015 (biologos.org/blogs/jim-stump-faith-and-science-seeking-understanding/4-theological-objections-to-evolution).
Tabaczek, Mariusz. "An Aristotelian Account of Evolution and the Contemporary Philosophy of Biology." *Dialogo: Proceedings of the Conferences on the Dialogue Between Science and Theology* (November 6–11, 2014): 57–69.

Talbert, Charles. *Reading Acts: A Literary and Theological Commentary on the Acts of the Apostles*. New York: Crossroad, 1997.

Tanner, Kathryn. "Creation *ex nihilo* as Mixed Metaphor." *Modern Theology* 29:2 (2013): 138–55.

Temple, Frederick, Rowland Williams, Baden Powell, Henry Bristow Wilson, C. W. Goodwin, Mark Pattison, and Benjamin Jowett. *Essays and Reviews*. London: John W. Parker and Son, 1860.

Thiselton, Anthony. *Language, Liturgy, and Meaning*. Bramcote, Notts: Grove Books, 1986.

Thomson, Greg. "What Sort of Meaning is Preserved in Translation? Part Two: Sense." *Notes on Translation* 3:1 (1989): 26–49.

Thomson, Robert, ed. *Athanasius:* Contra Gentes *and* De Incarnatione. Oxford: Clarendon Press, 1971.

Thomson, William, ed. *Aids to Faith: A Series of Theological Essays by Several Writers, Being a Reply to "Essays and Reviews."* New York: Appleton, 1862.

Tolkien, J. R. R. *The Fellowship of the Ring: Being the First Part of the Lord of the Rings*. Boston: Houghton Mifflin, 1965); Modern Hebrew version, Tel Aviv: Zmora, Bitan, Modan, 1976.

———. *The Two Towers: Being the Second Part of the Lord of the Rings*. Boston: Houghton Mifflin, 1965.

———. *The Return of the King: Being the Third Part of the Lord of the Rings*. Boston: Houghton-Mifflin, 1965.

———. *Letters of J. R. R. Tolkien*. Edited by Humphrey Carpenter. New York: Houghton Mifflin, 1981.

Towner, W. Sibley. "Interpretations and Reinterpretations of the Fall." Pages 53–85 in *Modern Biblical Scholarship: Its Impact on Theology and Proclamation*. Edited by Francis A. Eigo. Villanova, PA: Villanova University Press, 1984.

Trosburg, Anna. "Text Typology: Register, Genre and Text Type." Pages 3–23 in *Text Typology and Translation*. Edited by Anna Trosburg. Amsterdam: Benjamins, 1997.

Tsumura, David T. *The Earth and the Waters in Genesis 1 and 2: A Linguistic Investigation*. Sheffield: Sheffield Academic Press, 1989.

———. "Genesis and Ancient Near Eastern Stories of Creation and Flood: An Introduction." Pages 27–57 in *I Studied Inscriptions from before the Flood: Ancient Near Eastern, Literary, and Linguistic Approaches to Genesis 1–11*. Edited by Richard S. Hess and David T. Tsumura. Winona Lake, IN: Eisenbrauns, 1994.

———. "The Doctrine of Creation ex nihilo and the Translation of *tōhû wābōhû*." Pages 3–21 in *Pentateuch Traditions in the Late Second Temple Period: Proceedings of the International Workshop in Tokyo, August 28–31, 2007*. Edited by Akio Moriya and Gohei Hata. Leiden: Brill, 2012.

United Societies, Bible. *Fauna and Flora of the Bible*. London: United Bible Societies, 1980.

Venema, Dennis and Scot McKnight. *Adam and the Genome: Reading Scripture after Genetic Science*. Grand Rapids: Baker Academic, 2017.

Vogels, Walter. "L'universalisme de la préhistoire." *Église et Théologie* 2 (1971): 5–34.
———. "L'alliance primitive universelle." *Église et Théologie* 3 (1972): 291–322.
———. "Covenant and Universalism." *Zeitschrift für Missionswissenschaft und Religionswissenschaft* 57:1 (1973): 25–32.
———. "The Human Person in the Image of God (Gn 1,26)." *Science et Esprit* 46:2 (1994): 189–202.
Walker, Jeffrey. *Rhetoric and Poetics in Antiquity*. Oxford: Oxford University Press, 2000.
Waltke, Bruce and Cathy J. Fredericks. *Genesis*. Grand Rapids: Zondervan, 2001.
Walton, John H. "The Antediluvian Section of the Sumerian King List and Genesis 5." *BA* 44:9 (1981): 207–8.
———. "Creation in Genesis 1:1–2:3 and the Ancient Near East: Order Out of Disorder After Chaoskampf." *CTJ* 43.1 (2008): 48–63.
———. *The Lost World of Genesis One: Ancient Cosmology and the Origins Debate*. Downers Grove, IL: InterVarsity Press, 2009.
———. *Genesis 1 as Ancient Cosmology*. Winona Lake, IN: Eisenbrauns, 2011.
———. "Reading Genesis 1 as Ancient Cosmology." Pages 141–69 in *Reading Genesis 1–2: An Evangelical Conversation*. Edited by J. Daryl Charles. Peabody: Hendrickson, 2013.
———. "A Historical Adam: Archetypal Creation View." Pages 89–118 in *Four Views on the Historical Adam and Eve*. Edited by Matthew Barrett and Ardel Caneday. Grand Rapids: Zondervan, 2013.
———. *The Lost World of Adam and Eve*. Downers Grove, IL: InterVarsity Press, 2015.
Ward, Michael. "The Son and the Other Stars: Christology and Cosmology in the Imagination of C. S. Lewis." PhD thesis, St Andrews University, 2005.
Weeks, Noel. "Cosmology in Historical Context." *WTJ* 68 (2006): 283–93.
Weinfeld, Moshe. "Sabbath, Temple, and the Enthronement of the Lord—the Problem of the Sitz im Leben of Genesis 1:1–2:3." Pages 501–12 in *Mélanges Bibliques et Orientaux en l'honneur de M. Henri Cazelles*. Edited by A. Caquot and M. Delcor. AOAT 212. Neukirchen-Vluyn: Neukirchener, 1981.
Wendland, Ernst. *Language, Society, and Bible Translation: With Special Reference to the Style and Structure of Segments of Direct Speech in the Scriptures*. Cape Town: Bible Society of South Africa, 1985.
Wenham, Gordon. "The Coherence of the Flood Narrative." *VT* 28 (1978): 336–48.
———. *Genesis 1–15*. WBC. Nashville: Word, 1987.
———. *Numbers*. OTG. Sheffield: Sheffield Academic Press, 1997.
———. *Story as Torah: Reading Old Testament Narratives Ethically*. Grand Rapids: Baker, 2004.
Wilberforce, Samuel. Anonymous review of *Essays and Reviews*. *The Quarterly Review* 109 (1861): 248–301.
Williams, Joseph. *Style: Toward Clarity and Grace*. Chicago: University of Chicago Press, 1995.

Wimsatt, William and Monroe Beardsley. "The Intentional Fallacy." *Sewanee Review* 54 (1946): 468–88; republished in Wimsatt and Beardsley. *The Verbal Icon: Studies in the Meaning of Poetry*. Lexington, KY: University of Kentucky Press, 1954.

Winston, David. "The Book of Wisdom's Theory of Cosmogony." *History of Religions* 11:2 (1971): 185–202.

Winther-Nielsen, Nicolai. "'In the beginning' of Biblical Hebrew Discourse: Genesis 1:1 and the Fronted Time Expression." Pages 67–80 in *Language in Context: Essays for Robert E. Longacre*. Edited by Shin Ja Hwang and William Merrifield. Dallas: SIL International, 1992.

Wiseman, D. J. "Genesis 10: Some Archaeological Considerations." *Journal of the Transactions of the Victoria Institute* 87 (1955): 14–24.

Wolde, Ellen van. "'Creation Out of Nothing' and the Hebrew Bible." Pages 157–76 in *Creation Stories in Dialogue: The Bible, science, and folk traditions*. Edited by R. Alan Culpepper and Jan G. van der Watt. Leiden: Brill, 2016.

Wolfson, Harry. "Plato's Pre-Existent Matter in Patristic Philosophy." Pages 170–81 in *Religious Philosophy*. Cambridge: Harvard University Press, 1961.

———. *Philo: Foundations of Religious Philosophy in Judaism, Christianity, and Islam*. Cambridge: Harvard University Press, 1962.

Wolterstorff, Nicholas. *Divine Discourse: Philosophical Reflections on the Claim that God Speaks*. Cambridge: Cambridge University Press, 1995.

Wooffitt, Robin. *Conversation Analysis and Discourse Analysis: A Comparative and Critical Introduction*. London: Sage, 2005.

Wright, Christopher J. H. *Old Testament Ethics for the People of God*. Downers Grove, IL: InterVarsity Press, 2004.

———. *The Mission of God: Unlocking the Bible's Grand Narrative*. Downers Grove, IL: InterVarsity Press, 2006.

Wright, N. T. *The New Testament and the People of God*. Minneapolis: Fortress, 1992.

———. *Jesus and the Victory of God*. Minneapolis: Fortress, 1996.

———. *The Resurrection of the Son of God*. Philadelphia: Fortress, 2003.

Young, Davis A. "The Antiquity and the Unity of the Human Race Revisited." *Christian Scholars Review* 24:4 (1995): 380–396.

Young, Davis A. and Ralph F. Stearley. *The Bible, Rocks and Time*. Downers Grove, IL: InterVarsity Press, 2008.

Young, Dwight. "The Influence of Babylonian Algebra on Longevity Among the Antediluvians." *ZAW* 102 (1990): 321–35.

Yule, George. *The Study of Language*. Cambridge: Cambridge University Press, 2006.

Zogbo, Lynell Marchese. "Advances in Discourse Study and Their Application to the Field of Translation." Pages 1–29 in *UBS Monograph: Issues in Translation*. Edited by P. C. Stine. United Bible Societies, 1988.

Zohary, Michael. *Plants of the Bible*. Cambridge: Cambridge University Press, 1982.

ANCIENT TEXTS INDEX

OLD TESTAMENT

Genesis
1... 19, 32, 37, 76, 87, 109, 111–12, 115–16, 121, 127, 146, 148, 154, 157, 160–62, 164, 166, 168–69, 187, 205–06, 209–10, 225–27, 247, 256, 260, 277–78
1–2.... 108, 116, 160, 162, 168, 226, 227, 231
1–3......... 24, 178, 228
1–4 ..... 89, 109, 111–12, 144–55, 147, 162, 164, 169, 170–72, 180, 183, 210, 213, 225–27
1–5................ 228
1–9.................115
1–11. 17–19, 24, 27–28, 32, 38–39, 84, 107–17, 119, 123, 125–26, 128, 131, 133–35, 137, 141–43, 144–49, 152–54, 156, 158–60, 162, 169, 181, 186, 192, 195, 199, 204–06, 227, 243, 289–90, 293, 295–96
1–15........144, 183, 189
1–17............... 188
1:1 ..160–62, 203, 209–10, 215, 219–20, 222, 227, 261
1:1–2 163
1:1–5 215
1:1–2:3.. 108, 112, 115,147, 154–56, 160–61, 169, 207, 245
1:1–2:4.............. 148
1:1–4:26............ 114
1:1–11:26........... 112
1:2 ..... 161–62, 166, 211, 215, 219–20
1:3 ...... 161–63, 167, 171
1:5 ....150, 162
1:6 .... 150, 247
1:6–8 ...... 248, 252, 256
1:7 ....161, 167
1:9 167
1:9–12 161
1:10 248
1:11 167
1:12 .... 155, 277
1:14 .... 128, 168
1:14–18 171
1:15 ....167, 215
1:16 ....150, 156
1:17 ....207, 213, 247
1:20 127
1:20–21 127
1:20–27 172
1:22 227
1:23 225
1:24 167
1:24–25 127
1:25 .... 231, 277
1:26 ....111, 166, 207, 227
1:26–27 .... 109, 225
1:27 ... 163, 166, 172, 174, 225–27, 230, 281
1:27b 226
1:28 .... 109, 111–12, 166, 187, 190, 225, 231, 233, 275
1:30 167
1:31 .166, 177–78, 190, 225
2...... 111, 129, 160, 166, 174, 177, 225–27, 232
2–3 ... 121, 208, 225, 265
2–4 ....111, 112
2–5 231
2:1 227
2:1–3 ...... 154, 163, 268
2:3 160
2:4 .... 112, 153, 160, 169, 207, 227
2:4–25 .. 108, 111, 168–69
2:4–3:24 169
2:4–4:26 112
2:4–11:26............ 147
2:4a 160
2:5 225
2:5–6 169
2:5–7 147
2:7 .....111, 122, 147, 169, 225–27, 280
2:8 169
2:9 178
2:10–14 .... 144, 168
2:11–13 169
2:13 144
2:15 ....147, 169, 225
2:16–17 177
2:17 .. 24, 144, 174–76, 230
2:18 225
2:19 .... 172, 231
2:20 ....169, 172

319

2:21–23 226
2:22 111
2:22–25 175
2:23 . . . . 144, 172
2:24 . . . . 226, 230, 275
2:23–24 . . . . 172, 229,
3 . . . . .24, 71, 111, 116, 145,
    169, 174, 176, 180, 187,
    190, 208, 233, 235–37
3–4 228
3:1–24 175
3:2 177
3:3 177
3:4 . . . . 144, 175
3:6 175–76
3:8 144
3:9 . . . . 52, 87
3:11 176
3:14 175–76
3:14–19 179
3:15 180
3:16 . . . .167, 225, 228, 237
3:16–17 . 111, 177, 229, 236
3:16–19 237
3:17 . . . . 169, 225, 236–37
3:18 237
3:19 . . . . 147, 167, 281
3:21 169
3:22 . . . . 111, 178,
3:22–24 177
3:23 . . . . 147, 169, 225,
3:24 . . . . 144, 147
4 . . . . .109, 179, 232
4–5 116
4:1 . . . . 144, 179
4:1–16 179
4:1–26 179
4:2 146
4:3 231
4:3–4 145–46
4:4 191
4:8 177
4:9 . . . . 52, 87
4:10–12 179
4:11 236
4:15 184
4:17–22 . . . . 109, 146, 184
4:18 109
4:23–24 . . . . .177, 184
4:24 185
4:25 . . . . 144, 169
4:25–26 . . . . 109, 179

5 . . . . 109, 111, 117, 179,
    181–82, 199–200,
    205, 241
5:1 . . . . .112, 153, 225
5:1–2 169
5:1–3 . . . . 164, 169
5:1–5 . . . . 109, 225
5:1–32 154
5:3 226
5:3–11 109
5:6–32 . . . . 109, 184
5:18 109
5:21 109
5:22 184
5:24 . . . . 182, 184
5:25 109
5:29 . . . . .111, 167, 177,
    184, 229, 236
5:31 185
5:32 . . . . 186, 194–95
6–9 . . . . 109, 116, 181, 185
6:1 186–87
6:1–4 . . . 110, 186–88, 190
6:1–8 186
6:1–11:9 114
6:3 186
6:4 . . . . 188, 196
6:5 . . . . . 177, 186–87, 190,
    192, 196
6:5–9:17 190
6:7 186–87
6:9 . . . . 112, 153, 184,
    186, 192,
6:10 194–95
6:11 . . . . .187, 190, 238
6:11–13 238
6:12 190
6:12–13 238
6:14 150
6:18 . . . . 191, 230
7:2 145
7:3 193
7:8 145
7:11 256
7:11–12 256
7:13 194–95
7:19 193
8:1 87
8:2 256
8:7 110
8:8 110
8:9 193

8:20 145
8:21 . . . . 177, 186, 190,
    192, 196
9:1 . . . . .109, 112, 191
9:1–17 191
9:5–6 164
9:6 164
9:9 191
9:9–17 290
9:12 191
9:13–16 254
9:14–15 256
9:15–16 . . . . .87, 191
9:17 186
9:18 194–95
9:18–29 . . . . . 186–87, 192
9:19 194
9:22–23 192
9:24 194
9:25–27 196
10 . . . . . . 113–14, 137, 181,
    195–99, 205, 228
10–11 111
10:1 . . . . . 111–12, 153–54,
    194–95
10:1–32 194
10:1–11:9 . . . . .114, 194
10:2–5 195
10:5 . . . . . 194–95, 198–99
10:6–20 195
10:7 197
10:10 198
10:13 197
10:15–18 195
10:15–20 . . . . . 192, 196
10:18 194–95
10:20 . . . . .195, 198
10:21–25 111
10:21–31 . . . . 195, 200
10:22 197
10:25 . . . . 196, 198
10:28 197
10:29 197
10:31 . . . . .195, 198
10:32 . . . 112, 154, 194–96
11 241
11:1 . . . . 198, 200
11:1–9 . . . . . . .114, 196, 198
11:2 198
11:4 . . . . 194, 199
11:7 111
11:9 . . . . 194, 199

11:10 . . . . 111–12, 153, 194, 200	30:1–24 275	39:6 144
11:10–19 111	30:14–18 105	39:13 144
11:10–26 . . . . 111, 154, 181–82, 196, 199, 205	32:32 251	51:10 166
	33:19 261	63:13 166
11:20–26 111	35:21 261	
11:27 . . . . 112, 114, 153	36:1 . . . . 112, 153	**Leviticus**
11:27–12:3 116	36:9 . . . . 112, 153	1:1 131
12 . . . . 112–14, 131, 137	37:2 . . . . 112, 153	2:1–16 145
12:1–2 199	41:57 . . . . 70, 193	4 78
12:1–3 . . . . 113, 290	48:3–4 112	7:33 133
12:2–3 . . . . . 112, 126, 192	48:15 184	10:9 193
12:3 . . . . 113, 195		10:10 202
12:7 180	**Exodus**	11 145
12:8 261	1:5 197	11:3 127
12:10 143	1:7 112	11:13 127
12–15 143	2:24 237	11:29 259
12–50 . . . . 137, 168	3–4 132	11:42 176
13:15–16 180	3:12 171	11:44–45 78
14:13 196	3:14 171	13 77
14:18 . . . . 193, 196	6:2–8 171	16:29 197
14:22 234	9:22–24 254	18:5 102
15:5 180	11:1 143	18:18 192
15:6 81	12:29 268	19:34 197
15:13 180	12:48–49 197	20:22–26 . . . . 191, 294
15:16 192	13:10 128	20:24–26 145
15:18 180	14:21 268	20:26 78
15:18–20 192	14:30–31 272	21:6–8 78
17:1 184	15:5 166	25:23 132
17:7–10 180	15:8 166	26:4 254
17:11 191	15:13 290–91	26:9 112
17:19 180	15:14–16 272	26:12 184
17:20 112	16:22–26 164	26:11–12 144
18:20 196	16:22–30 144	39:6 44
19:23 251	16:23 128	39:13 144
19:30–38 . . . . 193, 275	16:26 128	
21:12 180	16:35 249	**Numbers**
22 126	19:1–9 131	6:8 78
22:12 81	19:5 293	13:33 189
22:17–18 180	19:5–6 . . . . . 233, 292, 295	14:11 190
22:17b–18 291	19:6 78	21:6–9 104
22:18 . . . . 113, 138, 291	19:16 254	22:28 175
24 126	20:4 248	23:9 132
24:3–4 196	20:26 193	32:22 145
24:40 184	22:3 251	32:29 145
24:60 180	22:31 128	33:37 249
25:12 . . . . 112, 153	27:13 144	
25:19 . . . . 112, 153	28:20 144	**Deuteronomy**
26:3–4 112	29:31 78	1:1–5 133
26:4 138	31:13 191	4:1 102
26:5 143	31:16–17 191	4:5–8 292
26:25 261	31:17 163	4:6–8 138
28:3 112	33:7 261	4:18 248

7:1–5 56
7:13 112
8:1 102
10:16 192
11:10 254
11:11–17 254
13:1–5 202
14:1 187
15:19–23 . . . . 145, 191
17:8–13 202
17:16–20 202
18:20–22 202
18:21–22 272
20:16 56
20:16–18 56
23:14 184
23:19–20 197
24:1–4 230
25:9–10 143
25:11 129
26:2 145
28:12 255–56
28:17–18 236
28:20 236
28:24 254
30:6 192
30:16 112
31:1–13 131
31:8–13 140
31:11–13 41
31:24–26 131
32:8 197
33:10 202

Joshua
1:7–8 131
3:16 231
6:22–25 56
6:25 . . . . 196, 198
8:33 197
9:17–21 56
9:26–27 198
9:27 . . . . 56, 196
18:1 145
24:19 56

Judges
2:12 56
4:11 261
4:17–24 102
5:4 255
5:26–27 102

5:30 103
5:31 251

Ruth
4:7 142

1 Samuel
2:8 248
3 42
12:17 254
16:13–14 82
19:24 129
20:30 129

2 Samuel
6:17 261
10:4–5 129
16:22 261
19:43 291
20:1 291
24:1 . . . . 71, 275

1 Kings
1:33 144
1:45 144
8:35 255
10:27 57
12:16 291
14:11 128
17:7 254
18:1 254
18:44 254

2 Kings
2:9–12 184
7:2 256
7:19 256
19:35 275
23:1–25 133
24:14 127

1 Chronicles
1:1–4 205
1:4 195
1:5–23 205
1:24–27 205
21:1 . . . . 71, 176, 275

2 Chronicles
10:16 291
26:19 251
32:21 275

Ezra
3:2 . . . . 125, 131
7:6 . . . . 125, 131
7:10 125

Nehemiah
8:1 131
8:1–8 125
8:14 131
8:14–18 133
9:14 131
9:16 133
9:26 133
9:29 102
9:33–35 133
12:44 133
13:1–3 133

Job
1:6 . . . . 175–76, 188
2:1 188
9:8 261
10:8–9 281
20:16 104
26:8 255
26:11 246
28:14 166
30:1 128
36:27–29 255
37:3 248
37:18 246
38:4–11 246
38:7 188
42:7 104

Psalms
8 . . . . 145, 168, 206–07
8:1 206
8:3 207
8:5 207
8:6 207
8:7 206
10:6 250
13:4 250
15:5 . . . . 197, 250
16:8 250
17:5 251
18:16 76
19:1 156
21:7 250
23:1 76
27:5 76

29:1 188	104:2–3 246	3:19 205
30:6 250	104:2–4 207	5:15–20 65
31 76	104:2a 207	8:28–29 247
31:2 75–76	104:2b–4 207	10:1–5 173
31:2–3 76	104:5 . . . . 19, 207, 250	11:30 179
31: 4 76	104:5–9 246	13:12 179
33 210	104:5–13 207	15:4 179
33:6 210	104:6 166	20:1 267
33:7 166	104:10 . . . . 208, 267	25:16 267
33:9 210–11	104:11 274	26:1 254
38:16 251	104:14 . . . . . 225, 267, 274	26:20–21 267
39:12 132	104:14–18 207	30:33 267
46:2 251	104:19–24 207	31:9 234
46:5 251	104:21–24 207	
46:6 251	104:23 225	**Ecclesiastes**
49:15 184	104:25–26 207	1:7 254
51 82	104:27–30 207	3:20 281
51:5 93	104:29 281	11:3 254
51:11 81	104:35 208	12:7 281
51:13 81	106:4 290	
55:9 . . . . 196, 198	106:9 166	**Song of Songs**
55:22 250	111–112 . . . . 37, 294	2:11 254
58:4 164	112:6 250	
60:2 251	119:126 272	**Isaiah**
61:5 76	121:3 251	1:2–2:5 138
62:2 250	125:1 251	1:5–6 295
62:6 250	135:7 254	1:17 234
66:9 251	136 . . . . 204–05, 293	2:1–5 294
72:9 176	136:2–3 205	8:1 55
72:17 . . . . . . 113, 138, 291	136:4 292	8:1–6 54–55
73:24 184	136:5 205	8:2–3 55
75:3 248	136:5–9 204–05	8:4–6 55
77:14 292	136:6 205	11:12 248
77:15 290	136:7–9 156	20:2–4 129
77:16 . . . . 52, 166	136:8–9 205	24:18 256
78 292	136:10–15 204	30:23 254
78:5–8 . . . . 140, 293	136:16–22 204	37:36 275
82:5 251	136:23–25 205	38:1 55
89:6 188	136:25 205	38:1–6 54–55
90:3 281	136:26 204–05	38:2–3 55
90:4 183	139:13–15 270	38:4–6 55
90:10 183	139:13–16 93	40:22 260–61
93 251	140:3 104	41:9 248
93:1 . . . . 19, 208, 250	145:4–7 292	42:5 . . . . 205, 261
94:18 251	147:8 255	43:1 226
96 251	148:4 . . . . 246, 252	43:7 226
96:10 . . . . 19, 208, 250	148:7 166	44:13 261
103:13 76	150:1 156	44:24 261
103:14 . . . . 232, 281		45:5–7 211
104 . . . . 168, 207, 251,	**Proverbs**	45:12 261
274, 276	3:12 76	45:18 211
104:2 . . . . 207, 261	3:18 179	49:23 176

51:13 261
54:9 234
55:10 254
56:10–11 128
63:10–11 81
72:9 176

Jeremiah
1:5 .... 93, 270
1:16–19 93
3:16 .... 112, 228
5:24 254
8:17 104
9:25–26 192
10:12 261
10:13 255
23:3 .... 21, 228
23:16–22 202
26:17–19 55
32:12 215
51:15 261
51:16 255

Ezekiel
1–20 234
1–24 234
1:22–26 156
11:1 144
14:14 .... 146, 234
14:20 .... 146, 234
16:3 52
16:4–7 53
17:23 101
20:11 102
20:13 102
20:21 102
28:3 234
31:6 101
36:10–11 228
36:11 112
36:27 82
47:10 127

Daniel
4:12 101
4:21 101
10:16 164
12:3 156

Hosea
1:10 187
2:3 129
2:8–13 231

2:15 231
2:18 .... 145, 231
4:3 .... 145, 231
6:3 254
6:7 230–31
6:10 231
7:15 231
9:15 231
10:8 237
10:9 231
11:1–4 231
12:4 231
13:4–6 231
13:8 231

Joel
2:23 254

Amos
3:1–2 294
4:7 254
5:19 104
9:3 104
9:6 247
9:11–12 294

Micah
1:11 129
3:12 .... 55, 129
7:17 176

Zephaniah
3:9–10 294

Zechariah
10:1 24
12:1 261

Malachi
1:8 52
2:11 187
3:10 256

ANCIENT NEAR EASTERN TEXTS

Baal's Palace
4 vi, 19–31 ...... 256n28

Baal and Mot
5, v, 7–8 255

Aqhat Legend
17, v, 7–8 .. 234n89, 294n10

DEUTEROCANONICAL BOOKS

Judith
13:7–8 142

1 Maccabees
9:23 251

2 Maccabees
7:28 .... 213, 215, 218

3 Maccabees
2:4–5 234
4:21 268
5:30 268

4 Maccabees
9:24 268
13:19 268
15:31 234
17:22 268

Sirach
14:17 230
38:1–15 .... 274, 276
43:1 156
43:8 156

Tobit
4:12 234
5:16 128
8:6 225
11:4 128

Wisdom of Solomon
2:23–24 .... 71, 229
2:24 .... 71, 176
9:1 210
9:17 81
10:1 225
10:4 234
11:17 220
11:17–18 219
13:1–9 230
14:3 268
14:6 234
16:23 267
17:2 268

Ancient Texts Index

Pseudepigrapha

Aristobulus
Frag. 2, §3 (in Eusebius, *Praep. ev.*, 8.10 [376-b]) 149n54
(in Eusebius, *Praep. ev.*, 13.12 [667b]) .. 163n9, 268n7
(see Eusebius, *Praep. ev.*, 13.12) 240n98

2 Baruch
21:4 ...... 215–16, 218–19

1 Enoch
(1.9) 94

Joseph and Aseneth
12:1–2 216

Letter of Aristeas
134–37 (134–36) 217
142–47 191
165–66 259

Psalms of Solomon
14:3 179

Sibylline Oracles
1 234

Ancient Jewish Writers

Philo
On the Giants
(De gigantibus)
6 188
58 188

De Abrahamo
41–46 234

On the Creation
iv (17) 212n19
v (21) 219n42
vii (29) 220

De praemis et poenis
23 234

Josephus
Against Apion
1, 130 [1.19] 234
2, 165 [2.17] 133n3

Jewish Antiquities
1, 10 [Preface §3] ... 133n3
1, 27 [1.1.1] .. 212n19, 220
1, 50 [1.1.4] 104
1, 72–108 [1.3.1–9] ... 234
1, 73 188
1, 93–95 [1.3.6] 120
1, 109 [1.4.1] 193
1.113 .... 196n89
1.30 [1.1.1] 240
11 240

New Testament

Matthew
1:5 56
1:17 182
4:1 176
4:10 176
5:4 58
5:14–16 295
5:32 70
5:34 22
5:35 251
5:39 70
5:46 52
6:3 58
7:3–5 52
7:14 58
7:16 237
11:30 58
13 101
13:1–9 78
13:6 251
13:18–23 78
13:21 78
13:24–30 128
13:31–32 100
13:32 101
13:44 74
19:1–12 91
19:4–5 226
19:8 230
19:19 70
19:24 52
20:16 52
22:30 188
24:37–39 235
28:18–20 206

Mark
1:32 251
4:1–9 78
4:13 78
4:13–20 78
4:15 78
4:17 78
4:31 100
5:26 282
7:19 145
10:6–8 226
10:11–12 70

Luke
1:3 124
1:15 93
1:35–37 270
1:44 93
1:68 290
3:23–38 206
8:4–15 78
8:13 78
8:15 78
8:43 282
10:25 102
10:26–27 102
10:28 102
10:29 102
12:54 254
13:19 101
16:18 70
17:26–27 235
20:27–40 91
24:4 82
24:47 206

John
1:1 210
1:3 .... 210, 215
1:5 215
1:1–5 214
3:12 257
3:19 215
12:24 101
15:10 102

Acts
1:8 206

1:10 82
2:5 69
2:22 272
5:29 56
5:34 216
6:7 . . . . 228, 233
9:31 . . . . 228, 233
10:3 82
10:9–29 145
10:30 82
12:24 . . . . 228, 233
14:17 254
15:16–17 294
16:10 102
17:22–31 83
17:28 53
19:20 . . . . 228, 233
19:21 55
20:24 56
21:4 55
21:11 56
21:12 55
21:13 56
21:14 56
22:3 216
28:17 56

Romans
1–2 230
1:1 135
1:1–6 . . . . 135, 295
1:4 81
1:7 . . . . 61, 295
1:8 70
1:16–32 238
1:20 230
2:14–15 . . . . 135, 173, 230,
 238, 295
3:4 81
3:28 80
4:11–12 295
4:12 131
4:12–13 233
4:17 215–16
5 229
5:12 . . . . 71, 229
5:12–14 71
5:15 229
5:18 70
8 236–37
8:18–25 235
8:19 238

8:20 237
8:21 . . . . 235, 238
8:22 237
8:23 237
8:28–39 80
10:5 102
11:26 70
11:36 83
12:4 295
12:13 78

1 Corinthians
1:18–31 83
1:28 215
5:1 295
5:9–11 . . . . 39, 68
5:12 69
7:34 78
8:6 83
12:15–16 295
15:3–8 135
15:22 232
15:36 101
15:40 257
15:45 226

2 Corinthians
3:18 233
4:4 226
5:1 257
12:12 272

Galatians
3:8 233
3:12 102
3:16 . . . . 113, 291

Ephesians
1:1 78
1:3 257
1:4 78
1:20 257
2:6 257
3:10 257
5:27 78
6:12 257

Philippians
2 256
2:6–11 . . . . . 157, 247, 256
2:9 258

Colossians
1:15–16 226
1:15–20 210
1:17 . . . . 83, 210, 212, 230
2:8 83
3:9–10 233
4:14 . . . . 102, 125

1 Thessalonians
1:6 79
3:13 78

1 Timothy
3:16 . . . . 81, 135
4:7 92
5:9–10 92

2 Timothy
1:5 92
2:4–7 60
4:11 102

Titus
1:12 53
2:3 92

Philemon
24 102

Hebrews
6:4–6 79
6:7 254
6:8 237
11 214
11:3 . . . . 214, 216, 218, 219
11:7 235

James
1:19–27 79
2:18–26 81
2:19 81
2:22 81
2:23 81
2:24 80
2:26 81
5:18 254

1 Peter
1:15 78
1:16 78
2:9 233
2:9–10 295

Ancient Texts Index • 327

2:11–12 295
3:5 78
3:20 235

2 Peter
2:4 188
2:5 235
2:4–5 235
3:5–6 235
3:6 235

1 John
1:3 215
1:5–6 215
1:8 59
1:9 58
1:10 59
2:1f. 58
2:18–19 120
2:20 59
3:6 58–59
4:20 71

Jude
6 188
14 94

Revelation
2:7 179
4:11 214
5:3 257–58
5:13 257–58
7:1 248
7:14 52
12:9 176
20:2 176
20:8 248
21:1 227
22:2 179
22:5 172
22:14 179
22:19 179

RABBINIC WORKS

Berakot
31–a 100

Sanhedrin
38–a 227

Genesis Rabbah
1:9 .. 216, 216n33, 34, 220

EARLY CHRISTIAN WRITINGS

Barnabas
10:8 259

Shepherd of Hermas
Mandate
1.1 .... 216n36, 218

Vision
1.1 ...... 216n36, 218–19

Ignatius
To the Trallians
9:1 .... 85n90, 257–58

Polycarp
To the Philippians
2:1 .... 258, 258n32

Athanasius
Against the Pagans
(Contra gentes)
3 .... 177n45
3:1–5 232
3:8–9 .... 228n72
29 .... 249n6
36 .... 249n6
36:4 .... 254n24
38 .... 271n17

De incarnatione
2–3 218
2:17 .... 219n44
2:19 .... 219n44
2:21 .... 219n44
3:4–6 .... 219n43
3:13–16 218
3:15 219

Augustine
On Genesis by the Letter
2.6.13 149
2.9.20 150

Cyprian
Letters
58.5 .... 228n73

Eusebius
Preparation for the Gospel
(Praeparatio evangelica)
.... 120, 153n62

17-b 167n20
553-d 213n20
557-cd 218n40
662-c 56n12
750-b 212n18
780-cd 281n41
7.8 [307-d]..177n45, 228n72
8.10 (376-b) 149n54
9.11 [414-abc] 235
10.9–10 [486-c] 235
10.9–10 [488-d] 235
10.9–10 [489-b] 235
11.7 [522-d] 149
11.15 [588-b] 235
13.12 .... 240n98
13.12 [667b] 163n9,
                    268n7
15.23–31 239
15.25 [837-c] 241n100
15.29 239
15.30 [839-a] 240
15.42 [845-b]..240, 240n99

Irenaeus
Against Heresies
(Adversus haereses)
1:10.1 .... 85n90
2.14.4 .... 218n40
3.9.8 177
4.38.1 .... 178n47
4.38.3 ....178n47, 219n43

John Chrysostom
Homilies on Titus
3 .... 53n5

Homilies on Romans
10 .... 228n72

Justin Martyr
First Apology
59 220–21

Second Apology
7.2 235

Tertullian
On the Soul
16,40–41 .... 228n73

Theophilus
To Autolycus
(Ad Autolycum)
2–3 235

2.4 . . . . .219, 219n44
2.10 . . . . 219n44, 220
2.15 . . . . .151n57
2.24 . . . . 178n47
2.25 . . . . 178n47
2.27 . . . . 178n47
3.1 241
3.16 241
3.18–19 235
3.20 241
3.23 241
3.26 241
3.30 241

GRECO-ROMAN LITERATURE

Aristotle
Generation of Animals
741-b, 23–24 . . . . . 222n55
1.1 [715-b] 278
3.6 [756b] 239, 259

Nicomachean Ethics
1.7.11 . . . . 295n14
2.3.2 [1104-b] 36n7
3.1.1 (1109-b–1110-a)
 . . . . .78n72
6.2.5 [1139-ab]. 36n7

Politics
1.1.11 . . . . 295n14
I.1.9ff [1253a] 27
2.9.9 [1274-b, 26] . . 133n3

Rhetoric
1.3.3–6 43

Diogenes Laertius
8.77 . . . . 240n99

Dionysius of Halicarnassus
Roman Antiquities
2,10(3) 258n31

Herodotus
Histories
1.170.3 240
2.109.3 240
2.141.5 275
2.2 241
2.141.5 275
2.37.4–5 . . . . 294n10
2.47.1 . . . . 294n10
2.49.3 240
2.58.1 240
3.80–82 . . . . 133n3
5.57.1 240
7.141.4 39
7.141–143 39
7.143.1–2 39
7.6.4 . . . . 40n16

Hesiod
Works and Days
61, 70 . . . . 173n40
109–120 . . . . 174n40
127–31 . . . . 174n40
159–60 . . . . 189n68
375 173
702–703 173

Theogony
45 170
116 . . . . 173n40

600–601 173

Homer
Iliad
9,457 . . . . 258n31

Plato
Apology
29d 56n12

Laws 194

Phaedo 130n66
116e–117a 56n12

Republic
8 . . . . 133n3

Theaetetus
176b 92n2

Timaeus . . . 212–13, 224
21-b—22-a 240
22-b 241
29-e 219
31–34 . . . . 165n13
38-c 213n20
50-d 219
51-a 219

Pseudo-Aristotle
De Mundo 230n79

Strabo
Geography
1.2.3 . . . . 92n2
6.2.1 . . . . 258n31

SUBJECT INDEX

Abram/Abraham, 81, 111, 112, 113, 114, 113n22, 124, 127, 131, 132, 137, 143–45, 154, 180, 81, 183, 184, 185, 190, 192, 194n80, 195, 196, 199, 200, 205, 206, 226, 228, 233, 290–91, 295
Adam, 24n26, 71, 71n53, 85, 108n3, 109, 112–13, 113n22, 114n25, 115n27, 116n30, 117n35, 127n61, 144–45, 145n35, 167, 169, 173, 174, 176–83, 180n49, 187, 189, 191–92, 206, 225–26, 225n64, 226n67, 227–32, 228 nn. 72–73, 229n75 and 77, 231 nn. 80–81, 232 nn. 83–84, 233 nn. 86–87, 236, 244, 265n1, 277n31, 280n38, 281, 291
adynaton, 52, 58,
anachronism, 138–39, 141–42, 142 nn. 25 and 28, 143n32, 144–46, 152n61, 153, 168, 173, 178, 199n98, 249
apologetics, 21–22, 25, 25n29, 31–32, 57, 67, 119, 143, 153n62, 167, 185, 221 nn. 50–51, 222–23, 261–62, 272
audience, 17, 28, 32, 35–36, 41–42, 42n18, 47, 50, 52, 58, 60–62, 64, 68–73, 78–79, 83–84, 89–90–91, 94, 96–101, 103, 105–08, 117, 119–21, 123–26, 128–29, 134, 138–39, 141–44, 143n31, 146–47, 150–51, 151n58, 153–54, 162–65, 168–69, 172–77, 173n39, 180–83, 185, 189–90, 192–93, 193n76, 195–97, 199, 205, 217, 222, 230, 234–36, 234n89, 243–44, 248–49, 252–56, 258, 260, 265–67, 274, 278–79, 281, 293
audience criticism. See criticism, audience
audience, implied 125–30, 164, 192, 196, 199

author/speaker intention, 36–40, 36 nn. 8–9, 37 nn. 10 and 12, 40n16, 44–47, 45n30, 46n33, 60–61, 60n24, 65, 71–72, 84–85, 100, 119, 121n45, 151, 183, 244, 248–49, 260n36. See also communicative intention/purpose and illocution

biblical criticism. See criticism, biblical

canon, 20, 23, 28, 37n12, 38–39, 69, 94, 107–08, 126, 131, 133, 201–04, 202n2, 203n6, 206, 213, 226n66, 242
canonical criticism. See criticism, canonical
characterization/characters, 45–47, 92, 97, 99, 124, 138–39, 141–42, 153–54, 159, 179, 183–84, 190, 215–16, 225, 243, 274–75
coherence, 26n32, 44, 79n74, 85, 108–09, 108n1, 109n7, 110, 159, 181, 194, 229, 231
cohesion, 42n18, 44, 108–12, 137, 179, 186, 227. See also coherence
communication, 26, 27n36, 28, 30, 34, 51–52, 60, 63, 76, 89–99, 105–06, 125, 132, 153, 170–71, 217, 243–45, 260, 281
communicative intention/purpose, 28, 37n10, 48, 61, 64–65, 71, 80, 85–86 97, 100, 106, 109, 128, 145, 151, 244, 248, 257, 216, 266. See also author/speaker intention and illocution
community identity, 52, 59, 123, 133, 136n10, 138, 138n18, 201, 217, 290
complementarity, 22, 71n54, 81, 81n80, 172–73, 227, 275

329

constitution, 126, 131–33, 133n3, 158, 223, 290
conversation analysis, 41, 41n18, 56
cooperation, 53, 59–60, 71, 96, 106, 141, 177, 258
cosmos, 83, 170n31, 223, 244, 245n2, 280n39, 284
cosmogony, 19, 19n6, 138, 220n49, 249n7
cosmology, 21, 25n29, 72n56, 95, 115n27, 168n22, 216, 223, 239, 239n96, 241, 241n100, 245n2, 249, 249n6, 250, 253n20, 259, 260n35, 261
creation
    story, 20, 108, 111, 113, 115–16, 116n29, 118–22, 121n45, 122n49, 125–26, 128, 134–37, 138n18, 144, 145, 147n44, 148–61, 148 nn. 49–50, 151–52, 157n74, 160–75, 168n23, 169n27, 173n38, 187, 206–09, 211, 225–27, 245n2, 264, 277–78, 288
    from nothing/ex nihilo, 28, 162, 162n5, 166n18, 168n22, 203, 208–25, 208n12, 209 nn. 13–14, 213 nn. 20–23, 214n26, 215n32, 216n34, 217n38, 218n40, 220 nn. 45, 47 and 48, 221n51, 222n52–53, and 55, 223n58, 248n4, 253n18, 261, 269, 293, 295
Creation Science, 20, 21, 22, 24n28
critically intuitive approach, 26–27, 42, 59, 77n70
criticism
    audience, 124, 150, 151n58, 278
    biblical, 30n41, 33n46, 38, 38n13, 203n3
    canonical, 23, 203–04, 203 nn. 5–6
    historical, 23, 203
    literary, 25–26, 28, 36, 41, 44–48, 50
    rhetorical, 25–26, 26n32, 28, 44, 44n28
    source, 24, 32–33, 109–11, 169n27, 225
    textual, 30n41, 213n21

discourse analysis, 26n32, 33, 41, 41n18, 42 nn. 21–22, 43, 50n46, 110, 147n43, 154, 159, 185. See also textlinguistics

exegesis, 27, 28–29, 33, 39, 49, 55n9, 77, 87, 101n20, 112n18, 113n22, 115n26, 130n66, 152, 162, 178, 187n63, 203n5, 222n55, 250n8, 267n5, 287, 290, 291n5

exile, 38, 125, 127, 143n31, 228
evangelical, 21, 24, 136n12, 162n8, 168n22
event, narrative 45, 46, 71, 74, 94, 99, 103, 116, 117, 119, 123–124, 126, 133n4, 134–36, 139, 141–42, 141n22, 147, 153–54, 156, 158–60, 161, 162n7, 163–64, 165n13, 167–69, 172, 175, 177–79, 185, 193n76, 198, 200, 210, 212, 223, 225, 229, 293, 296

fall, 24, 113, 113n23, 121n44, 134, 135, 136, 160, 175, 177, 178n47, 180, 183, 187, 190, 204, 205, 208, 224, 227–30, 228n72, 232, 235–38, 297
flood/flood stories, 21, 109–11, 109n7, 110 nn. 8 and 14, 114, 114n25, 115n26, 116–18, 118n39, 128–29, 137n16, 152, 166n16, 169n25, 175–79, 181–82, 184–94, 186 nn. 58 and 62, 188n65, 190n70, 193n77, 194n83, 196–97, 233–38, 256, 265
fundamentalism, 23, 23n18, 24, 30–33, 30n41, 43, 68n42, 156n70, 272n18. See also reading, plain

genre, 26n32, 35, 48–50, 48 nn. 38–39, 49n41, 108n3, 123, 134n6, 147–48, 156, 156 nn. 69 and 72, 157n74, 195n84, 196n88, 285

hermeneutics, 19, 23, 24, 25n29, 27, 36n8, 47, 133, 153n63, 156n71, 248, 260n35, 262
hyperbole, 52, 57–58, 57n14, 68, 193, 231n82

illocution, 36n8, 43n25, 51–52, 55–56, 59–61, 67–69, 71–74, 71n52, 79, 90, 97, 100, 106, 139, 141, 165, 243, 259, 293. See also author/speaker intention, communicative intention/purpose and speech act theory

Jesus, 22, 38, 47–48, 58, 72, 79, 81n79, 82, 85, 91, 100–02, 135, 135 nn. 9–10, 159, 176n43, 188n65, 206, 218, 226, 226n66, 229, 229n77, 230, 247–48, 254n25, 257–58, 262, 270, 273, 295

language
    analytical/scientific, 63–64, 66–67, 70, 74n60, 77–78, 83, 88, 92, 148, 261–62, 274,

figurative, 21, 66, 97, 175, 183
imagistic, 64, 77, 83, 249
phenomenal/phenomenological, 21, 63, 63n30, 65, 77–78, 83, 97, 128, 239, 249–50, 254, 289
poetic, 21, 36n9, 46, 46n33, 55n9, 62–66, 62n27, 62n29, 72–74, 72n55, 77, 83, 95, 100, 103–04, 121, 136, 139, 156–157, 161, 166, 168, 172, 244, 248, 252, 255–56, 260–61, 268, 274, 277, 289
lexical semantics, 23n17, 25, 25n31, 30, 41, 43, 60, 60n24, 176
lexicography, 23n17, 25n31, 29
literalism, 18, 20, 22–24, 23, 23 nn. 18–21, 29, 33, 53–54, 57–59, 61, 63–64, 68–71, 71n53, 72, 80n78, 85, 87, 96–97, 97n9, 117, 119, 123, 139, 148, 148 nn. 49–50, 153, 164n10, 176, 179, 193, 195, 209, 233, 239, 244, 248, 252, 260, 263, 289, 295, 295n15. See also plain sense
literary form, 35, 48–50, 72–74, 141, 148, 153, 156–57, 160, 249, 285
literary conventions, 37, 48
linguistics
  in general, 41–43
  Chomskian, 26–27, 26n36, 27 nn. 36–37
  pragmatics, 25–26, 28, 41–43, 41n18, 48, 50–51, 51n1, 53n3, 56, 61, 61n25, 94n4, 107, 108n1
  psycho-, 42, 42n20
  socio-, 25, 27n37, 28, 33, 42–43, 42 nn. 19 and 21, 48, 49–50, 65, 67, 107, 134, 138n18, 203
  text-, 42n18, 42n21, 44, 107, 109, 165, 172
locution, 43n25, 51–53, 55–56, 59–62, 67, 69, 72–73, 90, 97–98, 100–01, 250. See also speech act theory

metaphor, 57n14, 64, 64n32, 74–76, 74n60, 76n67, 77n70, 156, 164n11, 209n14, 245n2, 250, 258, 271n17, 284–85
metaphysic, 83, 121, 171n34, 266–76, 268n7, 274n21, 279–80
metonymy, 52, 194 nn. 81 and 82
morphology, 41, 49
miracles, 18, 30, 70n50, 89n1, 148n51, 152n59, 211n17, 262n40, 265–66,

267n5, 269n11, 270–73, 270 nn. 12 and 13, 271 n.n. 14–17, 272n19, 274, 276, 284

narrative, 44–48, 45 nn. 30–31, 46n34, 55, 72–73, 77n71, 99, 124, 131–132, 132n1, 133, 133n4, 153–64, 154n65, 157n74, 161n3, 166, 166n5, 288
narrator, 45, 45n32, 46, 46n34, 47, 69, 82, 99, 172, 174, 175, 179, 193n76, 194
naturalism, 33n46, 71n50, 276, 276n29, 282–84, 284n45, 287–88, 290
Noah, 109–113, 114n25, 129, 143, 145–46, 146n38, 175, 181, 182, 184–87, 185n57, 190–95, 192n76, 194 nn. 79 and 83, 199, 226, 230, 234–35, 234 nn. 88–89, 238, 238n95, 265, 286, 290, 294n10

paradox, 52, 57–58
personification, 52, 94, 210n16
Paul, 24, 39, 47–48, 53–56, 55n10, 56n12, 61, 68–69, 71, 80–81, 81n79, 83n85, 92, 92n3, 102n21, 113n22, 125, 135, 135n9, 180–81, 226, 229, 229n77, 230, 232–33, 235–38, 238n95, 247, 257–58, 291, 291 nn. 4–5, 295
perlocution, 36n8, 51–52, 55–56, 67
phonology, 41
plain sense, 19–22, 61, 68, 72, 97n9, 156. See also literalism
plot, 45, 134, 153–54, 166, 288n52. See also event
poetry, 34–36, 40–41, 43, 44n27, 46 nn. 33–34, 48–49, 62, 72–74, 82, 102–03, 103n22, 151n58, 157n77, 231n82, See also language, poetic
poetics, 42n20, 44, 44n27, 45n30, 146n42
prophets/prophecy, 39, 45n32, 52–55, 55n9, 120, 132, 138, 138n18, 171, 202, 271–72, 288
psalms, 37, 37n12, 48, 81, 132n1, 202, 231n82

rhetorical-theological reading, 28, 107, 158–59, 180
referent, 57, 60–61, 61n25, 63, 64, 72, 74, 91, 96, 98–99, 105–08, 117, 121, 128, 137, 165, 241, 260, 293
redemptive history 85, 127n57, 290–92
register, 35, 48–50, 49n43, 50n46, 62, 72, 285

relevance theory, 41
rhetoric, 17, 26n32, 28, 33, 35–36, 43–44, 43 nn. 25–26, 49–51, 57, 59–61, 61n25, 95, 134n6, 167n21, 169n27, 178–79, 192, 208n11, 267n5, 274, 293
rhetorical intention/purpose See author/speaker intention and illocution

science
　and faith, 22, 24 nn. 26–28, 25, 32–33, 62n27, 66–67, 77, 83, 148, 152–53, 159, 223–24, 261–64, 270–73
　philosophy of, 29, 47
showing versus telling, 46, 47, 174–78, 230
speech act theory, 25, 36n8, 41, 51–61, 51n1, 72n55, 187n63, 277, 277n30. See also locution, illocution and perlocution

style, literary, 35, 48–50, 49 nn. 42–43, 62, 72–74, 144, 147–57, 277
syntax, 27–29, 30, 41, 42n21, 49

Table of Nations, 147, 154, 187, 194–98, 195n84, 197n92, 205, 228
text grammar, 30, 41
text linguistics, 42 nn. 18 and 21, 44, 107, 109, 165, 172. See also discourse analysis
Tower of Babel, 194, 196, 196n89, 198–99, 199n98, 200
traditionalism, 19, 20–22, 24–25, 30–31, 84, 86, 93, 123, 125, 134, 136, 176, 223, 245, 268, 271, 271n15

young-earth creationism, 21n13, 24, 148, 261, 277, 283, 286, 290

AUTHOR INDEX

Alexander, T. Desmond, 113, 138, 153–54, 180, 291
Algra, Keimpe, 239
Alter, Robert, 45
Altholz, Josef, 18–19
Aquinas, Thomas, 31, 150, 222, 224, 288
Austin, Christopher, 278
Averbeck, Richard, 13, 115, 139, 168
Balfour, Arthur James, 280
Bauks, Michaela, 121
Barbour, Ian, 47, 64, 224–25, 273
Baroway, Israel, 151
Barr, James, 23–24, 30, 33, 61, 68, 72, 80, 97, 156, 176, 180, 201–03, 233, 241, 295
Bartholomew, Craig, 136
Bartusiak, Marcia, 223
Basson, Alec, 76
Bawarshi, Anis S., 48
Bayer, Hans F., 13, 101
Beale, Gregory, 166
Beale, Walter, 43
Beardsley, Monroe, 36–37
Beckwith, Frank, 286
Beckwith, Roger T., 18, 132, 202, 206
Bendor, S., 127
Benjamin, James, 43
Berkouwer, G. C., 270
Berry, R. J., 270
Berwick, Robert C., 270

Bilynskyj, Stephen, 70
Bimson, John, 254
Bitzer, Lloyd, 123–24, 129
Black, Jeremy, 198
Blenkinsopp, Joseph, 113
Blunt, A. W. F., 221
Bockmuehl, Markus, 213, 216, 222
Bois, Henri, 220
Bokedal, Tomas, 202
Bolhuis, Johan J., 26
Borowski, Oded, 128
Bowra, C. M., 46, 103
Brett, Mark G., 32, 37, 121, 260
Briggs, Richard, 275
Brône, Geert, 42
Brown, Gillian, 41,
Brown, William, 208
Bruce, F. F., 58–59, 202
Brugman, Britta, 57
Bultmann, Rudolph, 266, 276
Burchard, C., 216
Burgers, Christian, 57
Burgess, Theodore, 44
Burnside, Jonathan, 77
Burrell, David, 209
Burrus, Virginia, 209
Buswell, J. Oliver, 280–81
Calvin, John, 31, 95, 150
Campbell, Paul Newell, 43
Cansdale, George, 110, 127,
Carpenter, Humphrey, 62, 297
Cashmore, Anthony, 282

Cassuto, Umberto, 109, 146, 169, 171, 183, 197–98, 248, 292
Charles, R. H., 217
Chesterton, G. K., 279–81, 287
Childs, Brevard, 23, 203
Chomsky, Noam, 26–27
Chou, Hsiu-Chin, 25
Clines, David, 137, 186
Coats, G. W., 134, 166
Collins, Adela Yarbro, 157
Collins, C. John, 24, 37, 64, 79, 83, 109, 111–13, 116, 127, 135, 143–47, 162, 164, 169–73, 185, 194, 204, 210, 212–13, 225–27, 230, 234, 238, 255, 267, 270–71, 282, 291, 294–95
Coogan, Michael David, 103
Cooke, G. A., 103
Copan, Paul, 209
Cranfield, C. E. B., 226, 238
Culpeper, Jonathan, 53
Cutting, Joan, 41, 51, 108
Dalley, Stephanie, 110, 118, 173, 175, 189, 191, 253
Darwin, Charles, 66, 286
Davidson, Richard, 193
Day, John, 162, 189, 234
Deane, William, 220
Delitzsch, Franz, 82, 169, 178, 186–87, 189, 198, 214
Devitt, Amy, 48

Dijk, Teun A. van, 41, 110, 186
Doedens, Jaap, 187,
Dooley, Robert A, 108
Driver, G. R., 53
Driver, S. R., 111, 171, 229
Dumbrell, William, 109
Dunn, James D. G., 229
Eisenhart, Christopher, 26
Emerton, John A., 50, 109–10
Enns, Peter, 24, 71, 94, 108, 113–15, 136, 145, 232–33, 245
Eslinger, Lyle, 111
Fairbairn, Patrick, 55
Farrer, Austin, 32
Feldman, Louis, 174, 193–94, 220, 235
Fleming, Daniel, 143,
Fitch, W. Tecumseh, 27
Fokkelman, Jan, 114
Ford, William, 56
Foreman, Benjamin, 77
Forsyth, Mark, 52
Frankfurter, David, 135
Freddoso, Alfred, 268
Freedman, H., 216
Fredericks, Cathy J., 109, 115
Friedman, Richard Elliott, 109–11
Fry, Euan McG., 245, 248
Frymer-Kensky, Tikva, 115
Fueter, Paul, 62
Futato, Mark, 278
Gaffin, Richard, 81
Garrett, Stephen, 95
Gavrilyuk, Paul, 209
Geivett, Douglas, 272,
Getz, Jan Christian, 108
Gibson, J. C. L., 255
Gilkey, Langdon, 72
Gill, Jerry, 72
Goheen, Michael, 13, 136
Goldingay, John, 207
Goodwin, Charles W., 18–20, 22–23, 61, 247, 249
Goulburn, E. M., 19
Grant, Edward, 250
Grant, Robert, 211

Green, Anthony, 198
Green, William Henry, 182
Greenberg, Moshe, 228, 234, 294
Greengus, Samuel, 143
Gregg, J. A. F., 220
Grudem, Wayne, 54, 267
Gunton, Colin, 224–25
Habermas, Gary, 272
Habig, Brian, 230
Haddan, A. W., 19
Hakham, Amos, 81–82
Hallberg, Calinda, 42
Hallo, William W., 116, 123
Halton, Charles, 32, 133, 147–48
Hamilton, Heidi E., 41
Hamilton, Victor, 188
Harlow, Daniel, 108, 117
Häuser, Marc D., 27
Heidel, Alexander, 110, 121–22, 157, 166, 175, 178, 184, 189, 191, 253
Hendel, Ronald, 186, 188, 190
Heppe, Heinrich, 86, 268–69
Hepper, F. Nigel, 101
Herrick, James, 43
Hess, Richard S., 115, 137, 169, 227
Heuboeck, Alois, 26
Heurtley, C. A., 19
Hoare, F. R., 133
Hodge, Charles, 21
Hoffmeier, James K., 57, 115, 139, 147
Hollenbach, Bruce, 42
Holmes, Arthur, 72
Holmes, Michael, 218
Holmstedt, Robert, 161
Horowitz, Wayne, 130, 259
Howard, David, 44
Hubler, James Noel, 222
Huenergard, John, 115
Humann, Joel R., 133
Hwang, Shin Ja, 42, 89, 162
Irons, W. J., 19
Jacobsen, Anders-Christian, 178, 228
Jacobsen, Thorkild, 118–19, 122–23, 173–74, 189

Jaeger, Lydia, 14, 70
Jastrow, Robert, 223
Johnston, Gordon H., 115
Johnstone, Barbara, 26, 41
Joos, Martin, 253
Joseph, H. W. B., 68
Jowett, Benjamin, 18–20, 22–23, 29, 38, 47, 60–61, 72, 97, 107, 156, 201, 203, 233, 248–49
Kaminsky, Carol, 194
Kaufmann, Yehezqel, 171
Keas, Michael, 14, 47
Keel, Othmar, 208, 259
Kelly, Douglas, 148
Kelsey, David, 223
Kidner, Derek, 82, 165, 197, 207, 232
Kiel, Yehudah, 144, 161–62, 189, 198, 227, 231
Kilmer, Anne Drafkorn, 115
Kister, Menahem, 222
Kitchen, Kenneth A., 115–16, 119, 197
Klijn, A. F. J., 215
Koorevaar, Hendrik, 132
Kramer, Samuel Noah, 122, 174, 199
Kruger, Michael, 202
Kuhn, Thomas, 287
Ladrière, Jean, 72
Lambert, W. G, 115, 118, 122, 199
Lamoureux, Denis, 24, 127, 148, 229, 236, 248, 251, 253, 277
Larmer, Robert, 270, 280
Lawrence, P. J. N., 142
Levinsohn, Stephen H., 108
Lennox, James G., 14, 278
Lentini, Giuseppe, 53
Lepojärvi, Jason, 25
Levenson, Jon D., 28, 208
Levin, Yigal, 181, 195–96
Levinson, Stephen, 41
Lewis, C. S., 18, 25–26, 28–38, 41, 43–45, 47–51, 59–60, 62–67, 70, 72–73, 75, 77, 86–87, 94, 96, 99–100, 106, 120–21, 127, 130–31, 134, 137, 142,

Author Index • 335

148–49, 152, 170, 179, 203, 229, 231–32, 252, 262–64, 266, 274, 279–82, 287–89, 291
Lightfoot, J. B., 258
Lindberg, David, 152, 260, 271, 279
Long, V. Philips, 14, 45, 47, 139
Longacre, Robert, 41–42, 109–10, 154–55, 157, 159, 163, 185–86
Longman III, Tremper, 14, 76, 109
López-Ruiz, Carolina, 170
Lovell, Steven, 25
Lowery, Daniel, 146–47
Lupton, J. H., 149–51
Luzzi, Joseph, 141–42
Maclean, Norman, 97
Maimonides, Moses, 227
Malone, Andrew, 142
Marlowe, W. Creighton, 81
May, Gerhard, 209, 220–22
McCloskey, Donald, 66
McConville, Gordon, 203
McFall, Leslie, 53
McFarland, Ian, 214
McKnight, Scot, 229, 280
Merrick, James, 95
Merrifield, William, 42
Mesthrie, Rajend, 27, 42
Meyer, Stephen, 14, 267, 280
Millard, Alan R., 30, 57, 115, 117–19, 122, 143, 259, 275
Miller, Carolyn, 48
Miller, Geoffrey David, 128
Minton, Bernard, 36,
Mitchell, Terence C., 178, 197
Moberly, R. W. L., 112–13
Moore, George Foot, 103
Morris, Simon Conway, 288
Mortenson, Terry, 24, 68
Musselman, Lytton John, 101
Nagel, Thomas, 280
Neugebauer, O., 259
Noble, Paul, 23,
Noegel, Scott, 170
O'Brien, Peter, 258

Ogden, C. K., 74,
O'Neill, J. C., 213, 217
Ortlund, Eric Nels, 77
Oswalt, J. N., 94,
Packer, J. I., 14, 153, 202
Parry, Robin, 245
Pattison, Mark, 18, 249
Pederson, Don, 136
Percy, Walker, 26, 74–75
Piperno, D. R., 146
Plantinga, Alvin, 31, 71, 276, 280, 282
Plumley, J. M., 260
Poirier, John, 203
Polkinghorne, John, 273–74
Powell, Baden, 18, 249
Poythress, Vern, 14, 48–49, 80, 157, 162, 256
Pratt, Mary Louise, 72, 277
Provan, Iain, 124
Rabin, Chaim, 50
Rad, Gerhard von, 132, 166
Rafer, Daniel, 25
Rainey, A. F., 115
Reider, Joseph, 220
Reiff, Mary Jo, 48,
Renardel de Lavalette, Kiki, 57
Reumann, John, 258
Reventlow, H. G., 18
Reyburn, William D., 245, 248
Richards, I. A., 74
Richards, Jay Wesley, 14, 84–85
Roberts, John, 245
Roberts, Michael, 21
Robichaux, Kerry, 89
Robinette, Brian, 209
Robinson, H. Wheeler, 266
Rogerson, John, 274–75
Rooker, Mark, 188
Rorison, Gilbert, 19, 21, 76, 138, 157, 162, 223, 277
Rose, H. J., 19
Ross, Allen, 195, 197
Routledge, Robin, 187
Schaff, David, 135
Schaff, Philip, 85, 135
Schiffrin, Deborah, 41
Schmid, Heinrich, 268
Schreiner, Thomas, 236

Schroer, Silvia, 208, 259
Schwartz, Daniel, 213
Scult, Allen Michael, 129, 167, 170–71
Sedly, David, 130
Seebohm, Frederick, 149
Seely, Paul H., 248, 252, 278
Seeskin, Kenneth, 84, 165, 228
Sexton, Jeremy, 182
Shedd, William G. T., 268
Shutt, R. J. H., 217
Silva, Moisés, 23
Simon, M., 216
Simpson, E. K., 54,
Simpson, George Gaylord, 136–37
Ska, Jean-Louis, 45
Slobin, Dan, 42
Soloveichik, Meir, 145, 191, 296
Sparks, Kenton, 24, 32, 54, 133, 141, 147–48, 192, 195, 199
Stearley, Ralph F., 21
Sperber, Dan, 41
Stargel, Linda, 138
Steen, Gerard, 57
Stein, Menahem, 220
Steinmann, A., 162
Stern, Menahem, 240
Sternberg, Meir, 45, 47, 181
Stockwell, Peter, 42
Stott, John R. W., 33, 54, 57–59, 61, 69–71, 79, 83
Strassler, Robert, 39, 275–76
Stump, J. B., 289
Tabaczek, Mariusz, 278
Talbert, Charles, 56, 204
Tannen, Deborah, 41,
Tanner, Kathryn, 209
Tattersall, Ian, 26
Temple, Frederick, 18, 249
Thiselton, Anthony, 72
Thomson, Greg, 61,
Thomson, Robert, 218, 232
Thomson, William, 19, 21
Tolkien, J. R. R., 62–63, 98, 124, 190, 296–97
Towner, W. Sibley, 178
Trosburg, Anna, 49

Tsumura, David T., 115–16, 137, 162, 166, 169
Ury, Thane, 24, 68,
Vandaele, Jeroen, 42
Venema, Dennis, 280
Vogels, Walter, 159, 177
Walker, Jeffrey, 44, 74–75
Walker, Percy, 26,
Waltke, Bruce, 109, 115,
Walton, John H., 14, 115, 117, 168, 225, 244, 265
Ward, Michael, 25
Watters, Jim, 42
Weeks, Noel, 253
Weinfeld, Moshe, 155
Wendland, Ernst, 42
Wenham, Gordon, 46–47, 109, 125–26, 132–33, 144, 147–48, 183, 189, 293
Wilberforce, Samuel, 19
Williams, Joseph, 67,
Williams, Rowland, 18, 249
Wilson, Deirdre, 41
Wilson, Henry Bristow, 18, 249
Wimsatt, William, 36–37
Winston, David, 220
Winther-Nielsen, Nicolai, 162
Wiseman, Donald J., 115, 195
Wolde, Ellen van, 166, 168, 208, 248, 253
Wolfson, Harry, 220–22
Wolterstorff, Nicholas, 250
Wooffitt, Robin, 41
Wordsworth, Christopher, 19
Wright, Christopher J. H., 113, 126, 226, 291–93
Wright, N. T., 81, 135, 159, 265–66, 276, 291–92, 292
Young, Davis A, 21, 146
Young, Dwight, 117
Yule, George, 41
Zogbo, Lynell Marchese, 42
Zohary, Michael, 101

www.ingramcontent.com/pod-product-compliance
Lightning Source LLC
Chambersburg PA
CBHW011748220426
43668CB00018B/2410